11088

C000177052

The
L|C|P
Foundation
Stage
Resource File

Sue Fryer & Carole Share

with an introduction by Sue Day,
St. Martin's College, Lancaster
Words and music by Sanchia Sewell

© *LCP* Ltd. 2002
LCP • Hampton House • Longfield Road
Leamington Spa • Warwickshire CV31 1XB
Tel: 01926 886914
Fax: 01926 887136
Isdn: 01926 316600
E-mail: mail@lcpuk.co.uk
Website: www.lcpuk.co.uk

ISBN 1 904178 02 2

The authors would like to thank Georgina Howells, NNEB, for her valuable contribution to this publication.

Design
Simon Dainty • Narinder Sandhu • Simon Walmesley
Illustrator
Simon Walmesley
Project Manager
Halina Boniszewska
Editor Anne Furze
Editorial Assistant Nicky Barrett
Proofreader
Lynne Sykes

Contents

Early Learning Goals

Songs

Introduction

What is The *LCP* Foundation Stage Resource File?

The *LCP* **Foundation Stage Resource File** is a complete set of short-term themed activity units, covering the whole framework of the six Early Learning Goals: personal, social and emotional development; communication, language and literacy; mathematical development; knowledge and understanding of the world; physical development; and creative development. **The *LCP* Foundation Stage Resource File** upholds the philosophy of the foundation stage and is underpinned by the principles of the *Curriculum guidance for the foundation stage* (QCA, 2000). The plans reflect how children learn best by promoting active, exploratory and practical experiences. The planned activities involve sensory and relevant life experiences, which engage young children in the fun and joy of learning. The activities are all based on the experiences of the authors - Sue Fryer, a Deputy Head with special responsibility for the Foundation Stage and Carole Share, Senior Lecturer in Early years at the University of Central England. The songs have been composed by Sanchia Sewell, who is an experienced music teacher.

How is The *LCP* Foundation Stage Resource File different from other materials?

The *LCP* **Foundation Stage Resource File** not only provides ideas for activities relating to the Early Learning Goals, it also reflects the real world of the early years setting. It relates to the daily routines, essential partnership relationships with parents, and special events in the lives of 3–4 year-olds, which all contribute to children's learning.

A key feature of **The *LCP* Foundation Stage Resource File** is the excellent interpretation of the 'stepping stones' stages of development in the context of the planned activity. You may have wondered exactly what the stepping stones mean in relation to a particular play activity. You may also have asked yourself how the stepping stones fit alongside planning, practice and assessment. This file will clarify such questions for you because it describes the three stepping stone stages and the Early Learning Goal in terms of the children's play in each unit. This will make it easy for you to assess the stage of development of individual children and plot their progress towards the Early Learning Goals.

How to use The *LCP* Foundation Stage Resource File

You may use the themes flexibly to meet the needs of the children or the nature of the setting within which you work. They are not 'time-related'. You can use them as weekly plans or let them run for longer to follow the children's interest and involvement. If you do this, your curriculum planning will connect with the children's interests and encourage independent and confident learners. The units will save you a lot of time that you would normally have spent on planning, and so you will be able to focus more of your time and energy on interacting with the children to make the themes 'come alive' and inspire children's learning within their setting.

What does each themed activity unit in The *LCP* Foundation Stage Resource File contain?

Each unit focuses on one of the Early Learning Goals. A unit addresses preparation and starting points for the children, related activities in the other areas of learning, supplementary activities, the role of the adult during spontaneous play sessions and a completed planning format. The planning format incorporates all the elements of good practice in planning by including carefully thought out learning objectives and activities, related stepping stone stages of development, key questions and vocabulary and sections for targeted children and evaluations. These are all features of early learning practice that managers and inspectors expect you to address on a daily basis. **The *LCP* Foundation Stage Resource File** provides you with planned activities, shows you how to put these into practice and gives you guidance on how to observe and assess the children in your setting.

Sue Day
Lecturer in Early Years and Teaching Studies
Faculty of Education
St Martin's College
Lancaster

How to use this file

The _LCP_ Foundation Stage Resource File is designed to support the delivery of _Curriculum guidance for the foundation stage_. It addresses each of the Early Learning Goals with themed activity units, giving a balance of opportunity across the range of Early Learning Goals.

There are 35 themes in **The _LCP_ Foundation Stage Resource File**. Each theme is introduced in the same order in which the Early Learning Goals appear in _Curriculum guidance for the foundation stage_:

> Personal, social and emotional development
>
> Communication, language and literacy
>
> Mathematical development
>
> Knowledge and understanding of the world
>
> Physical development
>
> Creative development

If you cover all the main activities in this file, you will have touched upon every Early Learning Goal (see Early Learning Goal, Strand and Theme matrix p.vii).

How is each theme explored?

> Each theme carries an introductory page with the headings:
>
> How can you prepare for this activity?
>
> What are the starting points?
>
> What resources do you need to collect for the focus activity?
>
> Display suggestions
>
> Similar topics to explore
>
> Home links

A main activity sheet follows which relates to a specific Early Learning Goal, giving a detailed planned activity with learning objectives. The Stepping Stones toward the Early Learning Goal are given, together with examples of children's knowledge, skills and understanding at each stage of progress. The activity sheet also provides the opportunity to 'target' children for observation during the activity; key questions, key vocabulary and an evaluation section are also included.

Each theme, in addition to the detailed activity, offers ideas for other adult-led activities covering additional areas of learning: circle/review times, snack times and outdoor play; suggestions are also given for stories and rhymes and for special visitors/events. Learning objectives and additional resources are also listed for each supplementary activity.

Each theme is headed with the details of the Early Learning Goal, the strand of learning and the page reference to the relevant pages of _Curriculum guidance for the foundation stage_.

How long should each theme last?

There is no specific length of time for a theme to last. The age and maturity of the children will affect each theme's duration, as will the number and length of sessions. Above all, it will depend on the interest maintained by the children. Your setting can take some or all of the activities and use them as and when appropriate. Themes can run concurrently, or you could 'mix and match'. The planning sheet for supplementary activities for each theme can form the basis of a unit of adult-led activities linked to a particular theme over a period of time. A specimen medium-term plan shows the breadth of learning covered in a foundation stage theme.

Your planning will need to fit in with existing routines. You should review your planning on a regular basis, to ensure an appropriate balance of opportunity across the range of Early Learning Goals.

Sticking rigidly to the activities in this file is not necessary – the file is your resource book. You will also want to be able to respond to spontaneous learning opportunities and unexpected events that will arise.

What resources will I need when planning with The *LCP* Foundation Stage Resource File?

You will need to read each theme through in advance in order to collect the relevant detailed resources: these are given for the main activity and for supplementary activities. Resources recommended are items which are easily provided from within your setting or found at home.

When a camera is a recommended resource, this is indicated by the additional use of an icon.

The stories suggested are not an exhaustive list; you will, no doubt, have your own favourites to add to the lists. You can obtain all the books recommended from high street bookshops, from libraries, or via the Internet.

Many of the rhymes listed are traditional rhymes; others are mostly in a popular publication, *This Little Puffin. . .* (compiled by Elizabeth Matterson, Puffin Books). Once again, you may well have a rich source of rhymes of your own on which to draw.

What size should the activity groups be?

Group sizes for the activities will depend on your knowledge of the children. Some activities are more suitable for small groups and others can be carried out with large groups, i.e. circle time activities.

What health and safety issues arise in this file?

There are some instances in this file where Health and Safety issues are highlighted, e.g. the use of staplers, during food preparation etc. In these instances, the icon ⚠ is used as an indicator.

However, it is important that you follow the Health and Safety Policy of your own setting, since it is a fundamental responsibility of all practitioners working with children to ensure their safety at all times.

Assessment of children

The evidence you collect during the activities covered by **The *LCP* Foundation Stage Resource File**, through observation, notes, photographs and children's work, will form a significant part of the continuous assessment process.

Your observations and assessments should be noted both in your own records and those kept for inspectors/managers/owners. Students should also keep detailed evaluations for their college records. You may choose to record your observations on the Main activity sheets, or on the detailed assessment sheet for which a template is provided. Evaluations should also be recorded on the Planning sheets for supplementary activities, and examples of these are given. All sheets in this file may be photocopied for use in your setting.

Children will also need opportunities for spontaneous, supported play. Observation of children in this important aspect of their work will give you additional evidence of children's achievements which will support, or add to the information you have gathered in the adult-directed activities.

Songs

A lively collection of 13 new children's songs completes **The *LCP* Foundation Stage Resource File**.

These songs are a separate resource of CD, words, music and guitar chords, together with suggestions for the practitioner on using them with the children. You may choose to use these songs throughout the foundation stage, or to link them to themed activities within the Early Learning Goals.

Foundation

Early Learning Goal/strand/theme matrix

Early Learning Goal	Strand	Theme title
Personal, social and emotional development	Dispositions and attitudes Self-confidence and self-esteem Making relationships Behaviour and self-control Self-care Sense of community	My model Me! My friends Helping hands Shoes and socks Families
Communication, language and literacy	Language for communication (speaking) Language for communication (listening) Language for communication (vocabulary) Language for communication (language conventions) Language for thinking Linking sounds and letters Reading Writing Handwriting	What will I choose to play with today? The Gingerbread Man I don't want to go to bed! Teddy The fast food bar Hickory Dickory Dock The Little Red Hen Teddybears go shopping Washing line
Mathematical development	Numbers as labels and for counting Calculating Shape, space and measures	Treasure hunt Caterpillars Patterns
Knowledge and understanding of the world	Exploration and investigation 1 Exploration and investigation 2 Designing and making skills Information and communication technology Sense of time Sense of place Cultures and beliefs	Snails Water The Three Billy Goats Gruff On and off! Birthdays Little Red Riding Hood A new baby – what shall we call it?
Physical development	Movement 1 Movement 2 Sense of space Health and bodily awareness Using equipment Using tools and materials	Frogs We're all going on a bear hunt Spaced out! Healthy me! Games day The Queen of Hearts
Creative development	Exploring media and materials Music Imagination Responding to experiences and expressing and communicating ideas	Flowers Old MacDonald had a farm The wheels on the bus Jack Frost

Theme: *The wheels on the bus*
Focus area: *Creative development*

Specimen medium-term plan

Date: _____

Personal, social and emotional development	Communication, language and literacy	Mathematical development
Learning objectives To develop the feeling of belonging to a group To be aware of danger To develop a sense of their personal safety **Activities** Road safety	**Learning objectives** To take part in role-play with increasing confidence To make marks to communicate meaning To listen and respond to stories **Activities** Travel agent role-play	**Learning objectives** To recognise and understand cardinal numbers – 'how many?' To demonstrate 1:1 correspondence To recognise and name 2D shapes – circles **Activities** Counting people on the bus Collect and find circle shapes Print circle shapes Bubble prints
Knowledge and understanding of the world	**Creative development**	**Physical development**
Learning objectives To name forms of transport To observe closely and identify similarities and differences To classify according to certain criteria **Activities** Cut out pictures of cars/buses etc. Find and cut out pictures of things with wheels Make a car from a cardboard box Pack a bag for a journey	**Learning objectives** To individually re-enact situations imaginatively in character To respond to imaginative stimuli in co-operation with others **Activities** Role-play The wheels on the bus	**Learning objectives** To respond to imaginative stimuli in co-operation with others **Activities** Junk models of transport Make a roadway to follow and drive round on bikes Make a 'human bus' to travel along a roadway

The *LCP* Foundation Stage

Template for assessment and observation of targeted children, and evaluation of activity

Theme _____   Date _____

```
┌─────────────────────────────────────────────────────────┐
│  Targeted children                                        │
│                                                           │
│                                                           │
│                                                           │
│                                                           │
│                                                           │
│                                                           │
│                                                           │
│                                                           │
│                                                           │
│                                                           │
│                                                           │
└─────────────────────────────────────────────────────────┘
```

```
┌─────────────────────────────────────────────────────────┐
│  Evaluation                                               │
│                                                           │
│                                                           │
│  How did the activity go?                                 │
│                                                           │
│                                                           │
│                                                           │
│                                                           │
│  What evidence of children's learning have you collected? │
│                                                           │
│                                                           │
│                                                           │
│                                                           │
└─────────────────────────────────────────────────────────┘
```

Signed _____   Date _____

Shoes and socks (PSED)

Area of learning	Learning objective	Activity	Targeted children	Evaluation
PSED		Focus activity	Vicky, Hannah David, Carlos to be focus of observations all week	
CLL	To take part in role-play with increasing confidence To make marks to communicate meaning	Organise a shoe shop role-play area. Make signs for the shop and write captions and prices for all the shoes. Provide pads and pencils/pens to write receipts.	"	Both girls wrote prices on labels: correct numeral form.
Maths	To be able to match objects using a single criterion To demonstrate 1:1 correspondence	Provide a large selection of socks. Put them in a pile and ask the children to sort them out. Suggest the children peg them on a washing line in their pairs.	"	Found pairs OK. Discussed the pictures and patterns on socks.
KUW	To classify according to certain criteria To recognise and name some local buildings and what happens in them	Sort shoes according to how they fasten – laces, buckles, Velcro. Take the children to local shops to buy their own shoe-cleaning materials.	"	Sorted by fastening. Also chose to sort by colour.
Physical	To control refined hand movements and to develop eye/hand co-ordination	Show children how to tie knots. Encourage children to clean shoes. Show children how to lace a shoe.	"	C able to tie laces! D and H had difficulty controlling lace into hole. (Need bead-threading opps.)
Creative	To explore and experiment with materials through a variety of media, e.g. painting, printing, collage	Use old shoes to print with. Look at the soles of shoes and talk about the different patterns they can see. Collage 'An old woman who lived in a shoe'.	"	D needed help with printing. H & C talked about different patterns, wiggly lines and circles.
Snack times	To begin to use own language in everyday situations to talk about size, quantity, shape	With the children, make a large 'An old woman who lived in a shoe' cake.	"	C used language of more/less, full and empty.
Circle times	To interact with peers	Sentence starters 'My favourite shoes are…. I like them because… '	"	Vicky reluctant to speak in large group.
Outdoor play	To play sociably, to join in and to follow directions and instructions	Play 'follow the leader'. Take the children outside and encourage them to follow each other's footsteps.	"	Vicky needed lots of encouragement to join in. Others enthusiastic.
Stories & rhymes	To listen and respond to stories and rhymes	*Splosh* by Mick Inkpen. 'One, two, buckle my shoe' (traditional nursery rhyme). '"Splash," said a raindrop…. ' from *This Little Puffin. . .*	"	Vicky sat close to adult. Others joined in. D found '1,2' rhyme amusing.
Special visitors	To be aware of underprivileged children in their locality	Organise a sponsored fun walk to raise funds for a local children's charity.	"	

Adult role during spontaneous play sessions

Observing play ✓ observe H&C _____ Supporting play areas ☐ _____

Supporting individual play ☐ _____ Involvement in play area ✓ _____

Flowers (Creative development)

Area of learning	Learning objective	Activity	Targeted children	Evaluation
PSED	To respect and care for the environment	Children will be given the responsibility of caring for nursery plants. Children will take turns in being the monitor to water the plants.	Jak Aaron Maria	Aaron took great care watering plant. J and M needed help to control watering can.
CLL	To begin to write own captions	Take photographs of the Amaryllis as it grows, make a nursery book and add the photographs with captions. Support the children in writing their own labels and captions.	Sharon Lisa Mark Asif	S, L, A told me what marks meant. M reluctant to make marks on paper - needs more opps. for writing.
Maths	To begin to use standard measures of length appropriate to situations	Regularly measure the Amaryllis to see how it has grown, keeping a record of its growth. Add the information to the nursery book.	Ben	Said that it was really tall now.
KUW	To care for plants To recognise and name features of plants	Teach the children to name the main parts of the flower – stem, petals and leaves. Teach the children what a plant needs to grow – sunlight, warmth, soil and water.	Aaron Maria	Both could name flower and stem.
Physical	To control refined hand movements	Tear and cut activities. Encourage children to create their own collage flowers by sticking their 'shapes' on to a piece of card or paper.	Asif Mark	A made collage carefully. M could tear large pieces, used a lot of glue.
Creative		Focus activity		
Snack times	To be actively involved in a variety of experiences	A selection of fruit with pips or seeds such as oranges, apples, pears, melon, tomatoes.	Mark Asif Sharon	S chatted all through and took charge of giving out fruit.
Circle times	To gain confidence when speaking in familiar groups	The children will show and tell how they collaged or painted their picture.	Asif Mark	Asif gave clear explanation. M went shy.
Outdoor play	To be eager to explore new learning	Provide the tools and equipment for children to garden with, e.g. window boxes, tubs with soil, watering cans, gardening tools, seeds, bulbs, flowers, plants and plant pots.	Sharon Lisa	Both needed encouragement before touching soil.
Stories & rhymes	To listen and respond to stories and rhymes	*Titch* by Pat Hutchins. *Jack and the beanstalk.* Rhymes such as 'Oats and beans and barley grow', 'Mary, Mary'.	Maria	Noticed Maria really absorbed in Titch story.
Special visitors	To be aware of the different roles and jobs held by adults	Mother's Day. Invite families into nursery. Children will present them with small bunches of flowers and afternoon tea.		

Adult role during spontaneous play sessions

Observing play ☐ _____ Supporting play areas ✔ _____

Supporting individual play ☐ <u>Play alongside Mark</u> Involvement in play area ☐ _____

Personal, social and emotional development

- My model

- Me!

- My friends

- Helping hands

- Shoes and socks

- Families

Foundation

My model

How can you prepare for this activity?

- Organise the creative area so that the children can access some of the materials and tools they may need by themselves, e.g. label drawers or trays to show that they contain sticky tape, paper and crayons, hole punches etc.
- Establish ground rules for the creative area; for example, children should: wear an apron if they choose to paint or make a model; wait their turn if there are already children in the area; leave their finished painting to dry on the drying rack or any suitable surface; wash their hands when they have finished.
- Encourage the children to be as independent as possible. Let them wipe the tables clean themselves. Let them put out clean newspaper for the next child.
- Praise all children's efforts at being independent.

What are the starting points?

- During a group time, plan with the children what they would like to paint or what model they would like to make. Question them about the materials they will need. Encourage the children to make decisions for themselves.

What resources do you need to collect for the focus activity?

- Whether you are in purpose-built premises or a playgroup that has to tidy away at the end of every session, children need easily accessible resources. Ice-cream cartons, large margarine tubs, empty shoeboxes etc. are all ideal inexpensive storage containers that can be decorated, labelled and easily stored. The resource list depends entirely on your setting.
- Most creative resources can be built up over a period of time and are often a collection of 'junk' materials such as different sizes of boxes, cardboard tubes and tinfoil or polystyrene trays, washing-up liquid bottles, yoghurt pots, egg boxes, bottle tops, cake papers, wool, ribbon, yarn, string, material scraps, feathers, sequins, tinsel, matchsticks, pulses, rice, seeds, tea, lentils, toothbrushes, combs, grout scrapers, cotton reels, lolly sticks, twigs, sponges, paint rollers, different-textured papers such as tissue, Cellophane, shiny, crepe, and card, corrugated card. . . The list is endless! ⚠
- Teach children to access materials independently and to tidy them away independently at the end of each session.

Foundation

My model

Display suggestions

- If possible, have one display board where children can display their own works of art: some writing, a drawing, a painting, a collage or a picture from home. Also, if possible, leave a surface where children can display the models they have made.

Similar topics to explore

- Organise your curriculum areas so that children are able to make choices and can be independent learners.

Home links

- Encourage parents to value and take an interest in all paintings, models etc. that children take home.

Foundation

My model

Learning objectives

- To be eager to explore new learning
- To be actively involved in a variety of activities
- To make and express choices
- To ask for help when needed
- To be able to concentrate for increasing lengths of time

Activity

Set out the creative area with a selection of paint, brushes, paper, junk and collage materials.

Encourage children to explore their ideas in the creative area.

Ask questions, e.g. 'Would you like to paint?', 'What would you like to paint?'

Demonstrate how children could use their fingers, hands, brushes, toothbrushes etc. for painting.

Leave a tray of interesting 'bits' that children can choose to paint with.

Allow children time to experiment.

Support and advise when children ask for help.

Ask 'Would you like to make a model?' and 'What do you need?'

Show children various ways to join boxes etc. together. Suggest ways in which the model could be decorated. Ask older children to advise and support younger children. Value their opinion. Encourage children to work together on a project.

Encourage children to evaluate what they have made. Could they change or improve it in any way?

Praise and value all attempts.

Suggest they display their work with a label or caption.

Children should report back to their group at circle time about how they made their model.

What do the stepping stones look like?

 Step 1

Show curiosity.

Have a strong exploratory impulse.

Have a positive approach to new experiences.

Child spends time picking up, looking at and looking inside boxes. Will touch and pick up bits of collage materials. Will experiment randomly with the different brushes and paints.

 Step 2

Show increasing independence in selecting and carrying out activities.

Show confidence in linking up with others for support and guidance.

Having explored materials, child experiments with joining, fixing and attaching things. Will try out all brushes purposefully to see effects.

 Step 3

Display high levels of involvement in activities. Persist for extended periods of time at an activity of their choosing.

Take risks and explore within the environment.

Child will know what s/he needs to create a model or picture and will collect resources. Child continues until s/he is satisfied that it is complete.

 Step 4 (Early learning goal)

Continue to be interested, excited and motivated to learn.

Be confident to try new activities, initiate ideas and speak in a familiar group. Maintain attention and concentration and sit quietly when appropriate.

Child is proud of final result which, with support, could have taken more than one session to complete. Will tell others how model was constructed, in sequence, and why particular materials were chosen. Listens to others.

 5

My model

Key questions

- What have you made?
- How did you make it?
- What materials did you use?

Key vocabulary

- Paint, brush, collage, print, decorate, materials, model, construct

Targeted children

Evaluation

How did the activity go?

What evidence of children's learning have you collected?

My model

Planning sheet for supplementary activities

Area of learning	Learning objective	Activity	Targeted children	Evaluation
PSED				
CLL				
Maths				
KUW				
Physical				
Creative				
Snack times				
Circle times				
Outdoor play				
Stories & rhymes				
Special visitors				

Adult role during spontaneous play sessions

Observing play ☐ _____   Supporting play areas ☐ _____

Supporting individual play ☐ _____   Involvement in play area ☐ _____

 7

My model

Communication, language and literacy

Learning objectives

- To listen and respond to stories
- To interact verbally with peers and adults, using appropriate language
- To make marks to communicate meaning
- To recognise the different purposes of writing as a means of communication – labels, captions, lists etc.

Suggested activities

- Read stories that inspire children to draw, paint pictures or make models.
- Discuss with children how they will make their model, what they will use and so on. Encourage children to be creative.
- Support children in their emergent writing about their painting or model - it may be a label, a caption or a sentence about how they made it; it may be a list of materials they used.

Mathematical development

Learning objectives

- To choose and use resources related to task or activity
- To begin to use own language in play and everyday situations to talk about size, quantity, shape
- To use mathematical shapes in creative activities – 3D; 2D
- To make comparisons when exploring shape and space

Suggested activities

- When children are making their models, encourage them to use the correct mathematical language such as cube, cuboid, cylinder, square, rectangle, oblong, circle, bigger than, smaller than, the same size as, will fit together, won't fit together etc.
- Sort models for display purposes into groups such as 'these models all have wheels','these models all float'.

Additional resources

A selection of different-shaped boxes, with lids and tops of all different shapes and sizes

The *LCP* Foundation Stage

My model

Knowledge and understanding of the world

Learning objectives

- To ask relevant questions about why things happen and how they work
- To predict/guess what will happen – and test the prediction/guess
- To develop a sense of distance, direction and location
- To explore and investigate the natural and man-made environment
- To classify according to certain criteria

Suggested activities

- Make model boats. Firstly experiment with different materials to see if they sink or float. Talk to the children about how they will make their boats. Encourage children to test their boats in the water tray to see if they sink or float. If their boat sinks, suggest ways in which they could adapt it or how they could make another one using different materials.
- Take the children on a walk to the local park to collect natural materials for making models such as leaves, bark, twigs, pebbles, feathers etc. ⚠
- Ask children and parents to save junk items that are useful for making or decorating models such as sweet wrappers, yoghurt pots, tinfoil trays etc. Keep a large box ready for the children to put them in as they arrive each day and then sort them out at regular intervals with the children.

Additional resources

Polystyrene or tinfoil trays, lolly sticks, Plasticine, card, plastic bottles, scissors, glue etc.

Physical development

Learning objectives

- To gain control over fine motor skills – eye/hand co-ordination
- To be able to handle tools and materials safely and with increasing control

Suggested activities

- Encourage and support children at all times to have a go themselves at drawing and cutting out, at using sticky tape in a dispenser, using staplers, hole punches and any other tools they may need. ⚠

Additional resources

Gadgets and tools you have in your setting

 9

My model

Creative development

Learning objectives

- To evaluate and devise practical solutions to problems which arise in their creative work
- To listen, move and respond appropriately to music

Suggested activities

- Collect together cardboard boxes that children can sit in. They could design and make their own cars, boats, buses etc. They could design and make a robot. Encourage them to be imaginative.
- Find some music that best represents the sound machinery makes. Encourage children to move in a similar way, e.g. with strong, stiff, jerky movements.

Additional resources

Large cardboard boxes and collage materials, scissors, glue etc.

Cassette/CD player and music tapes/CDs

Snack times

Learning objectives

- To make and express choices
- To interact socially

Suggested activities

- Make sandwiches with the children. Encourage them to spread the bread with butter/margarine and the sandwich filling; they can then cut the sandwiches out themselves. Children could pour out drinks and share out sandwiches themselves. Encourage them to remind each other to say 'please' and 'thank you'.

Circle/review times

Learning objectives

- To increase the ability to listen, evaluate and reflect
- To use talk to question and reflect on experiences

Suggested activities

- During a review session encourage the children to tell each other about their models, how they made them, what materials they used etc. Encourage children to be complimentary about each other's models and to ask questions about how they made them.

My model

Outdoor play

Learning objectives

- To respond to imaginative stimuli in co-operation with others
- To ask relevant questions about why things happen and how they work

Suggested activities

- Collect together a couple of large boxes – the type a freezer or a cooker may come in. On a nice day take them outside and encourage the children to turn the boxes into 'houses'. The children could print brick shapes on the outside, cut out a door and windows, paint the roof etc.
- Encourage the children to play in the houses. They could take teddies and a teaset etc.outside.
- When the houses are beginning to get past their best, leave them out in the rain and watch what happens to the cardboard.
- Talk to the children about materials used for building houses. Why do we use bricks and not cardboard?

Additional resources

Large boxes, collage materials, scissors, etc.

Playhouse equipment

Stories and rhymes

Learning objectives

- To listen and respond to stories and rhymes

Suggested activities

Stories

Mr Wolf's Pancakes by Jan Fearnley (Tiger Tales)

Kipper's Toybox by Mick Inkpen (Hodder Children's Books)

The Three Little Pigs (Traditional story)

Harry and the Robots by Ian Whybrow and Adrian Reynolds (Gullane Publishing)

Special visitors/events

Suggested activities

- You may have a local artist in your area who would be prepared to come into nursery and paint alongside the children or who would paint suitable pictures on your outside walls or windows.
- You could have an afternoon when you turn your setting into an Art Gallery. Display the children's work and invite parents in to see it.

 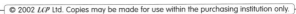

Me!

How can you prepare for this activity?

- Establish a comprehensive induction. Firstly, children should be visited in their own home before starting nursery, then the number of sessions a child attends nursery should be gradually built up. Whenever possible, encourage parents to stay with their children for the first few sessions. The induction policy will obviously depend on your setting and the work commitments of the parents.
- Ensure that each key practitioner has time to build up a relationship with the children in their care.
- Establish a grouping system whereby children sit with their key practitioner and the same children for story, circle or review time, giving them sense of familiarity and security.

What are the starting points?

- At the start of every session, i.e. morning and afternoon sessions, organise a selection of activities that the children are able to choose from and then play with independently. Practitioners should then be available to comfort any new or distressed children that arrive.
- Establish routines with the children and set ground rules such as being kind and friendly to each other, being polite and always saying 'please' and 'thank you', taking turns and sharing, not hurting each other - stress the importance of walking in the nursery so that children don't bump into each other. Explain to the children that you are all working together to create an environment where everyone feels safe and happy.

What resources do you need to collect for the focus activity?

- Organise the children's cloakroom so that every child has their own coat hook with their name and a picture label.
- If possible organise the bathroom so that each child has their name and the same picture label by their own toothbrush, flannel etc. Encourage children to be as independent as possible.

Display suggestions

- Organise an area where parents can read notices and letters when they arrive. If possible add photographs of the staff, giving their names and responsibilities. Parents will then know which adults to approach when they need information, support or advice.

Home links

- Provide parents with a nursery prospectus. Make sure parents feel welcome in the nursery and are aware of nursery routines, discipline strategies and daily or weekly planning. Encourage and welcome parental interest.
- Send home regular newsletters giving information about forthcoming events, updates on any ongoing projects, children's news, etc.
- Talk to parents at the end of the session about their child's day, giving a regular update on their child's progress.

Me!

Learning objectives

- To be able to respond to new routines and surroundings and to cope with change
- To be eager to explore new learning
- To build relationships with adults and other children

Activity

Welcome children into the nursery.

Encourage and support children to be independent in finding their own coat peg and hanging up their own coat.

Ask children which activity they would like to do.

Play alongside them, encouraging more settled and mature children to play with you also.

Talk to children about what they or other children are making, drawing etc.

Talk to each child about what they have done prior to coming to nursery. Talk to them about what they are wearing. Ask them how they got to nursery. Encourage conversation by asking open-ended questions.

When the activity is finished, encourage the children to tidy up for themselves, to put toys in the appropriate labelled boxes, find all the jigsaw pieces, hang up the dressing-up clothes and so on.

Encourage children to wipe tables clean themselves.

At tidy-up time encourage older children to act as role-models for the younger children.

At circle time, pass a teddy round the circle, with each child saying to teddy 'Hello, teddy, I feel….' or ask children to show a 'thumbs up' or 'thumbs down' depending on how they feel.

During group time discuss any topical issues, family or religious celebrations, anniversaries or any birthdays that have taken place.

At review time ask children what activities they have done. Encourage them to recall as many activities as they can. Suggest they try and remember one or two of their activities to tell their parents about.

What do the stepping stones look like?

Step 1

Separate from main carer with support.
Child takes practitioner's hand and waves good-bye to carer.

Step 2

Separate from main carer with confidence.
Have a sense of belonging.
Show care and concern for self.
Talk freely about their home and community.
Child hangs up own coat and leaves carer to join group.
Child tells practitioner about what s/he is doing.

Step 3

Have a sense of self as a member of different communities.
Express needs and feelings in appropriate ways.
Initiate interactions with other people.
Child asks adult to help resolve an argument over a toy.

Step 4 (Early learning goal)

Respond to significant experiences, showing a range of feelings when appropriate.
Have a developing awareness of their own needs, and the views and feelings of others.
Have a developing respect for their own cultures and beliefs and those of other people.
Child responds enthusiastically to birthday or other celebration of children in group.
Child is confident to show and express their own feelings and shows empathy with child who is unhappy.

Me!

Key questions

- Where does your coat go?
- Which is your picture/peg?
- What would you like to do?
- What have you been doing?
- Have you enjoyed yourself?

Key vocabulary

- Name, coat peg, picture, activity

Targeted children

Evaluation

How did the activity go?

What evidence of children's learning have you collected?

Me!

Planning sheet for supplementary activities

Area of learning	Learning objective	Activity	Targeted children	Evaluation
PSED				
CLL				
Maths				
KUW				
Physical				
Creative				
Snack times				
Circle times				
Outdoor play				
Stories & rhymes				
Special visitors				

Adult role during spontaneous play sessions

Observing play ☐ _____   Supporting play areas ☐ _____

Supporting individual play ☐ _____   Involvement in play area ☐ _____

Me!

Communication, language and literacy

Learning objectives

- To talk confidently about their experiences, ideas and feelings
- To join in and work as part of a group
- To take part in role-play with increasing confidence

Suggested activities

- Take individual photographs of the children. When they have been developed show them to the children. Talk to them about their features, their smile, their hair colour and style. Who do they look like? Be sensitive and aware of family background. Talk to them about how special and unique they are. Ask them about themselves, e.g. what is their favourite toy? What is their favourite dinner/colour/TV programme etc.?

- Make a nursery book. Display children's photographs with captions underneath, e.g. 'My name is…. I am 3/4 years old. I like…' Alternatively you could display the photographs on the wall so that parents and visitors could see them as they arrive.

- Collect together personal items for a 'Myself' feely bag such as a toothbrush, a flannel, soap, a hairbrush and comb, a teddy, a book etc. Sit the children in a circle and ask them to tell everyone what they can feel in the bag. Talk to the children about things that are 'theirs' like a toothbrush. You could also use the same items to play 'Kim's Game' in which all the items are placed on a tray and the children look at them for a short time; you then cover them over with a cloth, remove one item, take the cloth off and see if the children know which item is missing.

- The role-play area could become the doctor's surgery.

Additional resources

Camera and films

Items for feely bag/Kim's Game

Role-play items such as a Doctor's and Nurse's uniform, bandages, medical bag and instruments, weighing scales, height measurer, note pads, diaries, pens, pencils, telephone, computer keyboard, a desk, chair and bed, eye charts and posters for the wall

Me!

Mathematical development

Learning objectives

- To explore practical mathematical activities in a variety of everyday situations
- To choose and use resources related to a task or activity
- To be able to sort objects using a single criterion

Suggested activities

- Play in the role-play area with the children. Measure the children. Compare heights. Who is the tallest? The smallest?
- Use paper plates and collage materials such as pasta to make faces. ⚠ Discuss the number of eyes, noses, mouths etc. you will need.
- Sort Smarties and talk about favourite colours. Are there more red than green/more yellow than green? etc. Suck them to see who can suck theirs for the longest!
- Paint handprints and count the fingers. Sing finger rhymes such as 'Two Little Dicky Birds'.

Additional resources

Paper plates, collage materials, Smarties, paints and paper

Knowledge and understanding of the world

Learning objectives

- To recognise and name parts of the human body
- To observe closely and identify similarities and differences
- To become aware of the feeling of uniqueness

Suggested activities

- Teach children the names of body parts. Sing simple songs such as 'Head, shoulders, knees and toes', 'Simon says put your hands on your head' etc.
- Read *Funnybones* stories by Janet and Allan Ahlberg (Puffin).
- Talk to the children about skeletons; name some of the bones with the children.
- Use mirrors; encourage the children to look closely at themselves. What can they see? How are they the same as their friend? How are they different?
- Emphasise again how special the children are. No one else looks exactly like them!
- Talk about reflections. Ask where else can we see our reflection - on a shiny surface, in a pond etc. Let the children look at themselves on a spoon. What happens to their reflection?
- Tell them a simplified version of the story of *The Ugly Duckling*. This is a good opportunity to discuss how we are all different in appearance and how we all feel hurt and upset when people aren't kind to us or when they call us names.

Additional resources

Mirrors, sheets of aluminium foil, stainless steel trays, shiny teapots, large spoons

Funnybones stories, a copy of *The Ugly Duckling*

Me!

Physical development

Learning objectives

• To gain control over gross motor skills

• To begin to move with confidence

Suggested activities

• Play games where children have to run, jump, skip, hop, gallop etc. As children develop their skills, celebrate with 'I can ......' charts displayed in the nursery or with certificates to take home. Encourage children to be proud of their achievements. Be sensitive, however, with children who are still developing their gross motor skills, making sure they get lots of opportunities to practise and improve their skills.

Additional resources

Skipping ropes, balls, beanbags, hoops etc. 'I can....' charts, certificates

Creative development

Learning objectives

• To explore and experiment with materials through a variety of media – e.g. painting, drawing, collage

• To observe their own features and represent these observations

• To enjoy singing a range of familiar songs and action rhymes

Suggested activities

• Show children pictures from the *Funnybones* books. Talk about bones such as the ribs and the skull, and about the shapes of the bones. Talk about the spine and how it holds the body together; get the children to run their fingers along each other's spine. Tell them about the 'spine' of a book and how that spine holds the pages together. If you can, show the children an old x-ray from a hospital.

• Collage skeletons. Use white chalk or white paper art straws. Encourage children to glue them on to black paper in a skeleton shape.

• Encourage children to paint pictures of themselves. Suggest they look in a mirror first. What do they look like? What colour is their hair? What are they wearing?

• Make hand puppets using strong brown paper bags. Encourage children to decorate them with faces on the front and hair on the back. Ask children how their puppet feels: happy/sad/frightened/angry/excited/sleepy.

• Sing action songs such as 'Here we go round the Mulberry bush', adding verses like 'this is the way we wash our hands', 'this is the way brush our teeth', 'this is the way we comb our hair' etc.

• Sing 'If you're happy and you know it', 'Hokey-Cokey' etc.

Additional resources

Black paper, white art straws and white chalk

An old x-ray

Painting paper, paint and mirrors

Collage materials such as sticky paper shapes, pasta, scraps of material, felt, lace, wool etc.

The *LCP* Foundation Stage

Me!

Snack times

Learning objectives

- To actively be involved in a variety of activities
- To make and express choices

Suggested activities

- Children can make funny-face biscuits, cakes, sandwiches, jellies etc. to eat at snack time

Circle/review times

Learning objectives

- To interact with peers
- To use talk to express feelings and talk about experiences

Suggested activities

- Use sentence starters 'I feel happy when…', 'I feel sad when…', 'I get cross when…', 'I get frightened when…'

Outdoor play

Learning objectives

- To show confidence and self-esteem
- To be able to use a range of small and large equipment

Suggested activities

- Encourage and support children to learn how to ride a bike or a scooter, throw or kick a ball, throw and catch a beanbag, jump over a skipping rope or through a hoop.
- Again, celebrate children's achievements and give plenty of opportunities for children to practise their gross motor skills.

Me!

Stories and rhymes

Learning objectives

- To listen and respond to stories and rhymes

Suggested activities

Stories

Look What I Can Do! by Catherine and Laurence Anholt (Mammoth)

On your Potty! by Virginia Miller (Walker Books)

Eat your Dinner! by Virginia Miller (Walker Books)

Be Gentle! by Virginia Miller (Walker Books)

Bad Baby by Nanette Newman (Picture Lions)

Please be quiet by Mary Murphy (Mammoth Irish)

Pushchair Polly by Tony Bradman (Ladybird Book)

Rhyme

'All the little milk teeth standing in a row….' from *This Little Puffin . . .* (Puffin Books)

Special visitors/events

Suggested activities

- Organise regular parents' meetings to discuss children's progress.
- Organise coffee mornings where children make and serve up their home-made cakes and biscuits. The children could perform songs and action rhymes for the parents.
- Ask parents who don't work if they would like to help out at nursery occasionally. Maybe some of the parents have particular talents such as cookery, sewing, woodwork; they could help out with small groups of children working alongside a nursery practitioner.

My friends

How can you prepare for this activity?

- If children are not familiar with circle time activities, you will need to spend more time on the starting point activity, emphasising appropriate handling of and behaviour with the soft toys.

What are the starting points?

- Talk about the toys and how they want to be part of a game that you are going to play.
- Explain to the children that they need to look after the toys and hold them carefully.
- Practise passing the toys round the circle, encouraging the children to be gentle.

What resources do you need to collect for the focus activity?

- Two soft toys.

Display suggestions

- You could take photos to form part of a general display with a caption 'How we work and play in Nursery'.

Similar topics to explore

- Feelings.
- Taking turns.

Foundation

My friends

Learning objectives

- To play sociably, conforming to class/group requirements, and join in/follow directions and instructions
- To build relationships with adults and other children

Activity

Play the game 'All Change'.

The children and adults sit in a circle.

One child is to be chosen to be in the centre of the circle and to hold one of the soft toys.

The other children and adults pass the other soft toy round the circle and sing:

'Katy is in the ring, Tra-la-la-la-la,

Katy is in the ring, Tra-la-la-la-la,

Katy is in the ring, Tra-la-la-la-la,

And now she'll change with ....'

(Tune: Brown Girl in the ring)

At this point, Katy swaps with the child holding the toy at the end of the song. In this way the toy 'swaps places' as well!

It is important that all children have a turn in the centre, in order to learn about taking turns.

Some children may be reluctant to take a turn in the centre. If this is the case, allow them to pass the toy to another child.

A reluctant child may respond if an adult takes their place or goes with them.

As children become familiar with the activity, you could allow the child in the centre to choose who they swap with.

What do the stepping stones look like?

You need to be aware of any child who is insecure and feels more comfortable if next to an adult. Some children may not feel secure enough to join in.

 Step 1

Feel safe and secure and demonstrate a sense of trust.

Seek out others to share experiences.

Relate and make attachments to members of their group.

Child likes to sit next to a particular friend.

 Step 2

Demonstrate flexibility and adapt their behaviour to different events, social occasions and changes in routine.

Child accepts that s/he can't sit by a particular friend/adult. You may need to promise a change round 'next time' to support the child.

 Step 3

Value and contribute to own well-being and self-control.

Child understands that there is need to wait for their turn if practitioner takes time to reassure them that their turn will come.

 Step 4 (Early learning goal)

Form good relationships with adults and peers. Work as part of a group or class, taking turns and sharing fairly, understanding that there needs to be agreed values and codes of behaviour for groups of people, including adults and children, to work together harmoniously.

Child joins in the game with confidence, accepting that their turn will come. Will show an awareness of children who have not had a turn.

My friends

Key questions

- Whose turn is it now?

Key vocabulary

- Turn, fair, choose, swap

Targeted children

Evaluation

How did the activity go?

What evidence of children's learning have you collected?

My friends

Area of learning	Learning objective	Activity	Targeted children	Evaluation
PSED				
CLL				
Maths				
KUW				
Physical				
Creative				
Snack times				
Circle times				
Outdoor play				
Stories & rhymes				
Special visitors				

Adult role during spontaneous play sessions

Observing play ☐ _____   Supporting play areas ☐ _____

Supporting individual play ☐ _____   Involvement in play area ☐ _____

My friends

Communication, language and literacy

Learning objectives

- To explore and experiment with sounds
- To begin to associate sounds with syllables
- To develop attentive listening

Suggested activities

- Pass teddy round the circle; as teddy is passed to each child, everyone says that child's name.
- Introduce the idea of clapping the name as it is said. Clap children's names using one clap for each syllable as the name is spoken. Start with the child's first name and, as children gain confidence, extend to saying and clapping the first and family name, e.g. Kirindip Kaur.
- Choose four children and make up rhythm patterns with their names, e.g. Laura, Stephen, Jonathan, Beth.
- To extend this, add the syllable clap as before. You could re-order the children's names and see if the pattern is the same.
- Children need to listen carefully to the rhythm of the clap, to match the spoken words.

Additional resources

A teddy

Mathematical development

Learning objectives

- To begin to consider ways to solve problems
- To begin to show awareness of halves
- To use counting in a real-life context

Suggested activities

- The children should be in a circle. You need half the number of satsumas in a basket as there are children in the group. Discuss what is in the basket, and whether there are enough for everyone. How would the children find out?
- Try all the suggestions.
- Introduce the idea of sharing a fruit with someone, if this is not suggested by a child. Organise the children so that they each have a partner to share a satsuma. How can they make sure that this is fair?

Additional resources

Satsumas, basket

My friends

Knowledge and understanding of the world

Learning objectives

- To have confidence in using ICT in everyday situations
- To know how to use simple equipment

Suggested activities

- Make a tape recording of some individual children's voices saying something like 'Good morning, everybody'.
- Play the tape to the group. Can the children identify their own voices?
- Record staff members' voices. Can the children identify these?
- Show the children how to use the tape-recorder to record. (You might want to mark the buttons with bright coloured stickers.)
- Each day two or three children could tape–record their plans for the free choice or activity time. This recording will be used to review the children's activities. Play back the recording. Did the children carry out their planned activity?

Additional resources

Tape recorder and blank tape

Physical development

Learning objectives

- To work with a partner
- To gain control of body through small fine motor activities

Suggested activities (children work in pairs)

- Give each pair a long shoe lace and some beads. The children thread the beads on to the lace, each starting from a different end, until they have filled the lace.
- Children build a wall together for a toy to sit on.
- Give each pair a large box such as a cereal box and provide a variety of collage materials and glue. The children can decorate the box in any way they like.

Additional resources

Shoe laces and threading beads

Construction toys and soft toys

Cereal boxes, glue and collage materials

My friends

Creative development

Learning objectives

- To enjoy and appreciate music
- To listen, move and respond to music

Suggested activities

- Start with the children in a circle. Play the chosen music and listen to it.
- With the children, move in response to the music – on the spot, then moving round in a circle. Encourage the children to reach high and low, to reach to the side, to turn/bend/change direction etc.
- Play 'Follow the Leader' in which children copy the movements you make in response to the music.
- Let one of the children be the Leader.

Additional resources

Tape player and a lively piece of music of your choice

Snack times

Learning objectives

- To form good relationships with other children
- To take turns and share fairly

Suggested activities

- Put the children into pairs. One child in each pair has to 'look after' the other, e.g. by pouring or fetching drinks for them, or by sharing a plate of biscuits or crisps or fruit with them. The next time, they swap roles.

Circle/review times

Learning objectives

- To begin to take turns
- To be aware of others in the group

Suggested activities

- Sit the children in a circle. One child rolls a ball to a friend, saying 'I am rolling the ball to . . .' as s/he rolls the ball to the friend, who then chooses a friend to roll the ball to.
- When children are confident with this, see if they can make sure the ball is rolled to someone who has not received it before.

My friends

Outdoor play

Learning objectives

- To be aware of and to control the body
- To be able to balance
- To show awareness of others
- To be able to take turns

Suggested activities

- Draw a variety of lines in chalk on the ground outside for children to walk along. Make the lines wavy, zig-zag, straight, long and short. Initially you could ensure that there are more lines than the number of children.
- In order to encourage turn-taking and waiting, chalk fewer lines than there are children and support negotiation!

Stories and rhymes

Learning objectives

- To listen and respond to stories and rhymes

Suggested activities

Stories

The Ugly Duckling (traditional)

Moving Molly by Shirley Hughes (Red Fox)

It's My Turn! by David Bedford and Elaine Field (Little Tiger Press)

Rhymes

'If you're happy and you know it, clap your hands'

'My friend Sarah'

'Where is Thomas?' all from *This Little Puffin. . .* (Puffin Books)

Helping hands

How can you prepare for this activity?

- You will need a small soft toy that the children have not seen before and an attractive box that the toy will fit inside. You can include a special blanket for the toy if you like.
- Attach an address label to the box with your Nursery's address.
- Take a photo of the toy.

What are the starting points?

- The week before you start this theme, tell the children that you are having a special visitor coming to the Nursery, who will need looking after.

What resources do you need to collect for the focus activity?

- Soft toy, an attractive box, address label.
- Camera.
- Children's names on individual cards.

Display suggestions

- Photographs of the toy engaged with children's activities, with simple captions, e.g. 'Lee helped Floppy to play in the sand'.

Similar topics to explore

- People who help us.

Home links

- Prepare parents for the possibility that their child might bring the 'special visitor' home with them. The visitor will have a notebook with it. Ask parents to write in the notebook anything that their child 'helped the visitor' to do.

Foundation

Helping hands

Learning objectives

- To develop responsible attitudes
- To respect and care for others and the environment
- To deal with conflict situations by negotiating and reasoning without resorting to antisocial behaviour

Activity

Show the children the box, and tell them that there is a visitor coming to join the group inside the box, but s/he is very shy.

Gently open the box to reveal the 'visitor' and introduce him/her to the children (e.g. 'This is Floppy; he/she has come to visit our Nursery.').

Ask the children how they are going to help Floppy to feel welcome.

Show the children how Floppy likes to be held and stroked.

Pass Floppy round the group with each child stroking the toy and saying 'Hello, Floppy, my name is …'

Then explain that Floppy needs to be helped to play in the Nursery.

Ask the children what they could tell Floppy that will help him/her to have a happy time.

Children who want to contribute should hold Floppy and talk to him/her. Ideas will range from 'You can play in the sand…' to 'You can't fight'.

Each day a different child is to take responsibility for Floppy and help Floppy have a happy time in the Nursery.

At first, you will probably need to be in charge of Floppy and take him/her with you as you play with the children during the session, helping Floppy to play and behave as expected!

You might contrive a situation where Floppy misbehaves! Talk with the children involved about what to do.

Set up lots of situations where you can praise Floppy.

Use the circle time activity to discuss the behaviour of Floppy and how to deal with him/her.

It is important to focus on the good behaviour, e.g. 'Floppy built sandcastles in the sand with Ryan. They tidied up together' rather than on negative behaviour.

What do the stepping stones look like?

 Step 1

Begin to accept the needs of others, with support.
Child will need to be shown how to handle the toy.

 Step 2

Show care and concern for others, for living things and the environment.
Child may be very protective of the 'visitor'.

 Step 3

Show confidence and the ability to stand up for own rights.
Have an awareness of the boundaries set and behavioural expectations within the setting.
Child will probably tell Floppy off when s/he misbehaves.

 Step 4 (Early learning goal)

Understand what is right and wrong, and why.
Consider the consequences of their actions for themselves and others.
Child will tell Floppy the appropriate behaviour if s/he misbehaves.
Child will also praise the good behaviour.

Helping hands

Key questions

- How can we help Floppy to settle in?
- How should s/he play in…?
- What do we do if s/he is naughty?
- How can we show Floppy that we are pleased with him/her?

Key vocabulary

- Help, behave, well done, good, great, etc.

Targeted children

Evaluation

How did the activity go?

What evidence of children's learning have you collected?

Helping hands

Planning sheet for supplementary activities

Area of learning	Learning objective	Activity	Targeted children	Evaluation
PSED				
CLL				
Maths				
KUW				
Physical				
Creative				
Snack times				
Circle times				
Outdoor play				
Stories & rhymes				
Special visitors				

Adult role during spontaneous play sessions

Observing play ☐ _____

Supporting play areas ☐ _____

Supporting individual play ☐ _____

Involvement in play area ☐ _____

The LCP Foundation Stage

Helping hands

Communication, language and literacy

Learning objectives

- To make marks in different media
- To explore the forms that make letter patterns
- To practise writing names in different media
- To enjoy using sand and fingers as writing tools!

Suggested activities

- Provide children and yourself with individual small trays of wet sand. Allow the children to explore the sand and make marks with their fingers. Show them how to smooth the sand to refresh the surface. Children will need to be given time just to explore the sand in a small container with just their hands as tools. When you feel it is appropriate, show the children how to make patterns in the sand with a finger and encourage them to copy you. Practise writing names, letters, individual words and drawing pictures.
- Try the same sort of activity with dry sand.

Additional resources

Small trays of wet sand

Mathematical development

Learning objectives

- To develop the concept of how many fit in a space
- To count an irregular arrangement of objects
- To use language of more/fewer

Suggested activities

- Children need to work in pairs. Allow the children to explore and play with the pebbles if they have not used them before. One child holds his/her hand flat, whilst the other places a layer of small objects such as pebbles on the first child's hand. Discuss how many they think will fit on, and how they will check. The children can then swap roles.
- For some children it will be appropriate to think of ways in which to record their findings.

Additional resources

Small items such as pebbles from the garden (which have been washed) or coloured decorative stones

Helping hands

Knowledge and understanding of the world

Learning objectives

- To explore, investigate and be curious about themselves as living things
- To observe carefully features of their body
- To talk about what they observe

Suggested activities

- Talk to the children about their hands - how many they have, and how many fingers. Look at and discuss knuckles, nails, the front and back of the hands, the colour of their hands etc.
- Compare sizes of hands and consider why your hands are larger than theirs. Look at similarities and differences of each other's hands.
- Ask the childen to look at the palm of their hands and trace the lines with a finger.
- Use magnifying glasses to investigate the patterns, lines and texture of children's hands, fingers, nails, hairs etc.
- Support the children in making hand and thumb prints using an inkpad. Look at the prints with a magnifying glass.
- An alternative to this is to cover each child's thumb with chalk, take a print with sticky tape and stick the tape on to black paper.
- Some children could draw round their hands and, after looking at their hands with a magnifying glass, add lines and whirls to their drawing.

Additional resources

Magnifying glasses, ink pad, chalk, sticky tape, white or black paper

Physical development

Learning objectives

- To develop throwing, catching and rolling skills
- To develop hand-eye co-ordination

Suggested activities

- Play catching and throwing games in pairs. Beanbags or balls made by the children with newspaper (see Additional resources) will be easier to use for children who have difficulty catching balls.

Additional resources

Beanbags, a range of different-sized newspaper balls (screw up a piece of newspaper into a ball shape, and tape it firmly; add layers in this way until you have a ball of the size you want)

Helping hands

Creative development

Learning objectives

- To explore and experiment with texture and media

Suggested activities

- Spread liquid paint thinly on to a piece of polythene. Let the children explore this with their fingers, drawing and tracing etc.
- You could take a print by placing a piece of paper on top of the pattern, transferring the child's pattern or picture from the polythene on to the paper.
- Some children will just want to experience the medium!

Additional resources

Liquid paint, individual polythene sheets, paper

Snack times

Learning objectives

- To develop responsible attitudes
- To take on a role with responsibility

Suggested activities

- Children take turns to be the 'helper' for preparing the group snack. They can also be responsible for distributing the snack, and for helping to clear up and wash-up afterwards.
- The daily helper could have a special badge to wear.

Circle/review times

Learning objectives

- To build relationships with other children and adults
- To gain confidence and develop self-esteem

Suggested activities

- Pass a handshake! Sit the children in a circle, and ask them if have noticed what grown-ups do when they meet? Sometimes they might kiss; sometimes they will shake hands. Discuss what they do, and why. Show the children how to shake hands. In order to help children remember which hand to use, give each child a soft hair bobble to wear round their right wrist. Go round the circle and shake hands with each child. Then shake hands with the child next to you; that child then shakes hands with the next child and the handshake is passed round the circle.
- You could encourage children to shake your hand as they arrive each day.

Additional resources

Soft hair bobbles

Helping hands

Outdoor play

Learning objectives

- To enjoy using different media and tools outside the classroom
- To develop gross motor movements
- To take responsibility for appropriate behaviour and care of resources

Suggested activities

- Children can be painters and decorators, using water to paint the outside walls of the classroom with a variety of tools!

Additional resources

Lots of different sized brushes, rollers, sponges, waterproof clothing

Buckets of water

Stories and rhymes

Learning objectives

- To listen and respond to stories and rhymes
- To begin to consider behaviour of characters in familiar stories
- To add fun to tidy-up time

Suggested activities

Stories

The Little Red Hen (traditional)

Goldilocks and the Three Bears (traditional)

The Three Little Pigs (traditional)

Mr Gumpy stories by John Burningham (Red Fox)

The Teddy Robber by Ian Beck (Picture Corgi)

Rhymes

Use a familiar tune such as the tune to 'The farmer's in his den' to sing to accompany a tidy-up activity, for example:

> 'Put the bricks in here
> Put the bricks in here,
> One, two, three, four,
> Put the bricks in here.'

Helping hands

Special visitors/events

Learning objectives

- To recognise and acknowledge appropriate and helpful behaviour
- To develop an understanding of expected behaviour, and requirements of the Nursery

Suggested activities

- Hold a celebration session of helpful children. This could become a daily or weekly event. Throughout the day/week, reward children who show caring and helpful behaviour as it is observed. Small stickers are useful to reward good behaviour.
- At the end of the day/week, in circle time, talk about why these children have received stickers and give them all a clap.

Shoes and socks

How can you prepare for this activity?

- Collect together old shoes for the role-play shoe shop, old shoes to print with and different types of shoes to sort.

What are the starting points?

- Ask another member of staff to sit down with the children for group/circle/quiet time. You arrive a minute or two later in odd shoes - maybe a 'party' shoe and a trainer! See how many children notice your 'mistake', while you make a great show of not understanding the problem!

- Ask the children relevant questions such as 'Why don't they match?' 'Why do they need to match?' Ask the children if **their** shoes match. Produce a bag with the partners of each of the shoes in. Let the children decide which pair most suits the outfit you are wearing. Put them on, but on the wrong feet! Make it obvious to the children that your shoes are on the wrong feet by walking strangely! Make this into a game. This activity requires you to overact, putting the children in a position of teacher and you as child! Let them direct you. Introduce the vocabulary **left** and **right**. Thank the children for helping you.

- Use this activity as the starting point for a discussion about shoes. Get the children to look closely at their own shoes. What colour are they? Do they have laces? Velcro? Buckles? Which side are the buckles on? What are they wearing under their shoes? Do their socks match? Encourage them to look at each other's shoes. Are they all wearing the same shoes or different ones? Why?

- Ask the children to take off their shoes and socks. Encourage them to put one sock inside each shoe. Ask children to wiggle their toes. Encourage them to look closely at their toes. Ask them to count their toes – do they all have the same number of toes? Look at their toenails. Who cuts them? Why do we need to cut them? Look closely at each other's feet - are they all the same? Are some bigger than others? Are their toes all the same shape? Sing 'This Little Piggy went to Market'.

- Use this activity as a starting point on several occasions. You could wear a pair of shoes that are far too big or that are totally unsuitable such as wellies or football boots. Encourage the children to explain what is wrong. Alternatively bring in a baby's shoe, a ballet pump or a football boot and say you found it and you are not sure to whom it might belong!

What resources do you need to collect for the focus activity?

- A selection of paints, trays, rollers, an old roll of wallpaper or a roll of white fabric.
- Bowls of warm, soapy water, soap and towels.
- Camera and films.

Foundation

Shoes and socks

Display suggestions

- A tabletop shoe display.
- A large wall display of 'The Old Woman who lived in a Shoe'.

Similar topics to explore

- Hands.

Home links

- Ask parents to send in old pairs of shoes for the role-play area.
- Ask parents to sit with their children and compare feet! Whose are bigger? Have they got the same number of toes?

Foundation

Shoes and socks

Learning objectives

- To manage own personal needs with increasing independence
- To make and express choices

Activity

Ask the children who have chosen this activity to remove their shoes and socks.

Encourage the children to be independent.

Help those children who ask for assistance and also those who are obviously struggling (ask first if they need your help).

Talk through the process with the children who asked for help.

Praise all children's efforts.

Encourage children to select their own colour of paint, to squirt a small quantity on to a tray and then to use a roller to spread the paint out.

Encourage each child to step on to the paint and then on to the rolled-out wallpaper or white cloth which could later be used in the display. Let them walk along the paper or cloth looking at the prints their feet have made. Discuss with the children how the paint runs out. Would they like to repeat the process? Would they like to change their colour? They could try hopping, jumping, giant steps, tiptoes etc. on the paper. Take photographs.

Provide bowls of warm, soapy water for the children to wash their feet in. Encourage them to wash their feet themselves. Provide a bar of soap.

Are their feet clean? Has all the paint gone?

Provide towels and encourage the children to dry their own feet, making sure they dry between their toes, and then put their own socks and shoes back on.

Support and praise the children's efforts at all times but also be ready to assist if and when necessary. Encourage children to put their shoes back on the right feet using correct terminology such as 'left' and 'right'.

Encourage children to help each other.

What do the stepping stones look like?

 Step 1

Show willingness to tackle problems and enjoy self-chosen activities.
Demonstrate pride in own achievement.
Child perseveres to remove shoes, probably without undoing fastenings. Will need help with replacing socks.
Can put shoes on with help.
May show reluctance to step in paint.

 Step 2

Take initiatives and manage developmentally-appropriate tasks.
Child walks in paint and then on the paper, tentatively at first, if holding adult's hand.
Will have a go independently after first try.
Has a go at washing and drying feet. Needs to be 'finished off'.
May find difficulty getting socks on, but has a go.

 Step 3

Operate independently within the environment and show confidence in linking up with others for support and guidance.
Child enjoys carrying out activity. Washes own feet, but needs help drying feet properly.
Can get socks on but may need help straightening them up.

 Step 4 (Early learning goal)

Dress and undress independently and manage own personal hygiene.
Select and use activities and resources independently.
Child can wash and dry own feet. S/he responds to reminders to make sure to dry between toes.
Can put own socks and shoes back on. May need help with fastenings.

Shoes and socks

Key questions

- Can you take your shoes and socks off yourself?
- Are your feet clean?
- Are they dry?
- Can you put your shoes and socks back on by yourself?

Key vocabulary

- Feet, toes, toenails, shoes, socks, print, wash, clean, dry, left, right

Targeted children

Evaluation

How did the activity go?

What evidence of children's learning have you collected?

Shoes and socks

Planning sheet for supplementary activities

Area of learning	Learning objective	Activity	Targeted children	Evaluation
PSED				
CLL				
Maths				
KUW				
Physical				
Creative				
Snack times				
Circle times				
Outdoor play				
Stories & rhymes				
Special visitors				

Adult role during spontaneous play sessions

Observing play ☐ _____

Supporting play areas ☐ _____

Supporting individual play ☐ _____

Involvement in play area ☐ _____

The LCP Foundation Stage

Shoes and socks

Communication, language and literacy

Learning objectives

- To take part in role-play with increasing confidence
- To make marks to communicate meaning
- To begin to write own captions/labels
- To use ICT

Suggested activities

- Organise a shoe-shop role-play area. Make signs for the shop and write captions and prices for all the shoes. Provide a till and money, a shoe-size measure, old shoe boxes to stack the shoes in and pads and pencils/pens to write receipts.
- Write to a leading shoe manufacturer and ask them to send you posters and leaflets to put in your shoe shop. If you have a computer, write a letter on the computer and involve the children in what you are doing. Let them see you put the letter in an envelope and address it. Take a small group of children to the post office with you to buy the stamp and post the letter. ⚠

Additional resources

A selection of both children's and adult shoes and equipment for the role-play area

Mathematical development

Learning objectives

- To explore practical mathematical activities in a variety of everyday situations
- To be able to match objects using a single criterion
- To demonstrate 1:1 correspondence
- To talk about patterns
- To begin to use non-standard measures of length

Suggested activities

- Collect together a large selection of socks. Put them in a large pile and ask the children to sort them for you. Suggest the children peg them on a washing line in their pairs. Provide templates of sock shapes and encourage children to draw round them, cut them out and then decorate them so that they make a pair.
- Count in sets of two.
- Sort other pairs of objects like shoes and gloves.
- Discuss why we say 'a pair' of scissors, pants, trousers etc.
- Measure children's feet and draw round them. Let them draw round your feet. Encourage the children to cut the drawings out and display them on a size chart.

Additional resources

Washing line, pegs, sock templates, selection of socks and gloves, scissors, foot-size measure

Shoes and socks

Knowledge and understanding of the world

Learning objectives

- To observe closely and identify similarities and differences
- To classify according to certain criteria
- To be aware of the passing of time
- To recognise and name some local buildings and what happens in them
- To select appropriate materials and to experience the skills involved in assembling and joining them

Suggested activities

- Collect together a selection of shoes such as summer sandals, flip-flops, trainers, football boots, roller skates, ballet pumps, wellies, walking boots, party shoes, men's shoes, baby shoes, shoes from other cultures. Encourage the children to sort them according to their own criteria. Suggest groups they could sort them into - winter shoes, summer shoes, sports shoes, adult's shoes and children's shoes. Talk about any shoes you have collected from other cultures such as wooden clogs from Holland.
- Talk to the children about the different materials the shoes are made from.
- Sort shoes according to how they fasten: laces/buckles/Velcro.
- Talk to the children about the types of shoes people used to wear. Show them any photographs or pictures you may have from the past showing 'old fashioned' footwear.
- If you have a shoe shop in your locality take the children in small groups to look at the selection of shoes the shop provides. If you have a charity shop in your locality take the children to buy some shoes for their role-play area. Take the children to local shops to buy their own shoe-cleaning materials. ⚠
- Make sock puppets. Provide a selection of old socks and collage materials to make the puppets. Encourage the children to make their own selections and to decorate the puppet how they want. Value their interpretation.

Additional resources

A good selection of shoes

Photographs of old-fashioned footwear

Old socks to make puppets

Collage materials

Shoes and socks

Physical development

Learning objectives

• To control refined hand movements and to develop eye/hand co-ordination

Suggested activities

• Show children how to tie knots. Provide a selection of lengths and thicknesses of string, wool and laces and demonstrate how to tie a knot. These knots could be displayed on card. Show more able children how to tie laces.

• Show children how to clean shoes. Provide a selection of black or brown leather shoes, polish, brushes and dusters and encourage the children to clean the shoes. They may like to clean their own!

• Provide some shoes without laces and show the children how to lace a shoe. Encourage them to have a go themselves. Leave this activity out as an ongoing activity.

Additional resources

String of various thickness, laces

Shoe cleaning materials such as black or brown polish, brushes, dusters and newspaper to clean shoes on

Creative development

Learning objectives

• To explore and experiment with materials through a variety of media – e.g. painting, printing, collage

Suggested activities

• Look at the soles of shoes and talk about the different patterns the children can see. Use old shoes to print with. Cut out the prints and display them alongside a shoe display.

• Teach the children the nursery rhyme 'There was an old woman who lived in a shoe'.

• Collage a large shoe and encourage the children to paint pictures of themselves. Cut the pictures out and encourage the children to attach them to the display themselves. Call the display: 'The old woman who lived in a shoe'.

Additional resources

Old shoes to print with, thick paint, paper collage materials

Snack times

Learning objectives

• To begin to use own language in everyday situations to talk about size, quantity, shape

Suggested activities

• Make shoe-shaped biscuits and use liquorice laces.

• With the children, make a large 'An old woman who lived in a shoe' cake. Use two large Swiss rolls. Place one lengthways and one standing up so they form the basis of the boot shape. Cover with butter icing, made previously with the children. Decorate with sweets of different shapes.

Shoes and socks

Circle/review times

Learning objectives

- To interact with peers
- To use talk to recall ideas and experiences

Suggested activities

- Use the sentence starter 'My favourite shoes are… I like them because…'

Outdoor play

Learning objectives

- To play sociably, to join in and to follow directions and instructions
- To be eager to explore new learning

Suggested activities

- Play 'follow the leader', with you being the old woman who lived in the shoe.
- If the weather is snowy, take the children outside and encourage them to follow each other's footsteps.
- If the weather is wet, put wellies on and splash in the puddles.
- If the weather is hot, take buckets of water outside and let the children step in the water in their wellies and then make footprints. What happens to the footprints in the sunshine?

Stories and rhymes

Learning objectives

- To listen and respond to stories and rhymes

Suggested activities

Stories

Paddington Bear stories by Michael Bond (Various)

Sonny's Wonderful Wellies by Lisa Stubbs (Piccadilly Press)

Splosh! by Mick Inkpen (Hodder Children's Books)

Rhymes

'Paddling in the puddles….'

'"Splash," said a raindrop….' both from *This Little Puffin. . .* (Puffin Books)

'One, two, buckle my shoe' (traditional nursery rhyme)

Special visitors/events

Suggested activities

- Talk to the children about the importance of exercise and how walking can help them to keep fit and healthy.
- Organise a sponsored walk to raise funds for a local children's charity.
- Ask parents to walk their children to Nursery.

Families

How can you prepare for this activity?

- You will need individual photographs of the children and yourself. Preferably, these would be taken in the Nursery or you could ask parents to provide them.
- Make a microphone: attach a small ball to a cardboard tube and cover it all in silver foil.

What are the starting points?

- This activity would link in well if you have a regular photographer taking children's photos at a point in the year.
- Bring in a photo of yourself and talk about it. Tell the children when it was taken, how you were feeling at the time, why it was taken and why it is important to you. Explain to the children that you are going to take their photos as they play and work in the Nursery. Show them the camera and talk about how it works.
- Take individual photographs of the children at play. Discuss with the children what will happen to the film in the camera.
- If possible, take the children to the local film processing agent for the film to be developed. Talk about the price, the day you can collect the film and how long you have to wait.
- Collect film canisters, old cameras, film envelopes, negatives, old photographs you don't need, photograph envelopes, photograph albums, photo frames etc.

What resources do you need to collect for the focus activity?

- Camera, photographs, prepared microphone.

Display suggestions

- Display all the photos and pictures of the children labelled with their names (the labels can be written in the **Communication, language and literacy** activity).
- Set up a photographer's 'studio' or a film-developing shop.

Similar topics to explore

- My family at home.
- People who help us - the school photographer.

Home links

- Ask parents to provide photos of the children, with suitable captions, which can be added to the display.

Families

Main activity

Learning objectives

- To experience the feeling of belonging to a wider community

Activity

Sit in a circle with the children.

Talk about this being our special group and that everyone is part of it. If you have special names to identify groups, then talk about your special name, e.g. the Rabbits.

Using the microphone to pass round and talk into, start with yourself and say 'I am … and I belong to the Rabbits group.' Continue round the group. Any shy children could just be allowed to smile and pass on the microphone.

Talk about the photos of the Rabbits group. Remind children that they are special pictures, and ask how they can help to look after them.

Put all the photos in the centre and ask children to find their own photo.

Children can swap photos with the person next to them and look at that photo.

Put the photos back in the middle.

Can the children find their friend's photo now?

They might need to ask their friend to help.

As the children become familiar with the activity and with recognising each other from photos, you could ask 'Who can find Alya?'

You could remove a photo and see if the children can work out whose photo is missing.

Talk about everyone belonging to the Rabbits group and that it is a special group to be in.

This may lead into discussions about other special groups.

Key questions

- Who is in this photo?
- What is s/he doing?
- Can you find a photo of…?
- Do you know who is in our group?
- Do you know anyone in another group?

Key vocabulary

- Special, care, important, I, me, friend, family, group

What do the stepping stones look like?

 Step 1

Make connections between different parts of their life experience.
Child will recognise photos of self in Nursery and from home.

 Step 2

Show a sense of self as a member of different communities, such as their family or setting.
Child will recognise other members of group from the photos.

 Step 3

Have a positive self-image and show they are comfortable with themselves.
Child will talk about what they are doing in the photos and is eager to show photo to others in the group.

 Step 4 (Early learning goal)

Understand that people have different needs, views, cultures and beliefs that need to be treated with respect.
Understand that they can expect others to treat their views, cultures and beliefs with respect.
Child listens to other children's contributions.

Targeted children

Evaluation

How did the activity go?

What evidence of children's learning have you collected?

Families

Planning sheet for supplementary activities

Area of learning	Learning objective	Activity	Targeted children	Evaluation
PSED				
CLL				
Maths				
KUW				
Physical				
Creative				
Snack times				
Circle times				
Outdoor play				
Stories & rhymes				
Special visitors				

Adult role during spontaneous play sessions

Observing play ☐ _____ Supporting play areas ☐ _____

Supporting individual play ☐ _____ Involvement in play area ☐ _____

49

Families

Communication, language and literacy

Learning objectives

- To make marks in a variety of media
- To be aware that marks communicate meaning
- To begin to write own name

Suggested activities

- Ask the children to draw a picture of themselves for the display.
- The children should write their own names in felt pen on a prepared piece of paper or card. Encourage the children to write their name independently. For some children you may want to write their name with them, by writing each letter and talking through the formation of the letters. Older or more able children may be able to write a sentence about themselves.
- Add the names to the photograph and picture display.
- Ask a child to draw a picture of you! Add your name to the picture and ask the children to suggest a caption for you to write.

Additional resources

Felt pens, card/paper for name labels, paper

Mathematical development

Learning objectives

- To be able to match objects using a single criterion
- To be able to sort objects by a single criterion

Suggested activities

- Prepare two identical sets of cards with pictures, numbers or patterns on. You need enough for one card per child. Distribute the cards and encourage the children to find their partner – i.e. the child whose card has the same picture/pattern.
- Alternatively, prepare three or four sets of cards, e.g. with domino spots. Children can sort the cards according to the number of spots on them.
- Prepare two sets of picture, spot or pattern cards. Place them all face down on the carpet or table. Ask a child to pick up two cards. If the cards are the same, the child keeps them; if not, the cards are put back where the child found them and turned face down again. The aim is to remember and find all the pairs.

Additional resources

Sets of cards with identical pictures, spot patterns, numbers, colours or patterns

Families

Knowledge and understanding of the world

Learning objectives

- To have the opportunity to experience the skills involved in shaping, assembling and joining materials
- To select appropriate materials and equipment to construct and make
- To describe what they made, and evaluate and adapt where necessary

Suggested activities

- Look at a re-usable camera, talk about the features and what buttons are for.
- Provide materials for children to have a go at making their own cameras, supporting them in deciding how to join materials and suggesting any additional resources they might need. Make cameras with re-cycled goods.
- Show the children some photo envelopes from a photo shop. Carefully disassemble one to show how it is constructed. Demonstrate how to make a simple photo envelope, showing children where and how to fold and glue the paper to make the envelopes. Children can decorate their envelopes as they wish. Children can use the photo envelopes in the role-play area, which can become the photo-processing shop.

Additional resources

Cheap re-usable cameras, photo envelopes from a photo-processing shop

Small boxes, parts of cylinders/tubes, small circular pieces of card, string, postcard-size card, A4 paper

Physical development

Learning objectives

- To work co-operatively
- To be aware of their own body and gain control over their movements

Suggested activities

- Children need to be spaced round a blanket/sheet, holding the edge of it with both hands.
- Explore what happens when they hold the edge and shake the blanket/sheet.
- Make big movements up and down. Make small movements up and down.
- Place a ball on to the blanket/sheet. Explore what happens to the ball when the children shake their part of the blanket up and down. Can they toss and catch the ball in the blanket? Can they toss the ball out? Can they roll the ball round and round?
- Explore with different sized balls.
- Try using two balls.

Additional resources

A blanket/sheet and balls

Families

Creative development

Learning objectives

- To work together co-operatively
- To listen to instructions
- To listen and respond to music

Suggested activities

- Make a circle with the children, all holding hands.
- When the circle is formed, practise walking in one direction, and then on the signal 'change', all change direction and walk in the other direction.
- Try different speeds.
- Try this to some favourite music.
- When children are confident moving in a circle whilst holding hands, explore ways to dance round in a circle to the music, changing direction on the signal.
- You could add other instructions like 'dance with hands up high/down low', 'turn' etc.

Additional resources

Favourite taped music. You need a variety of types of music to dance to, e.g. pop, reggae,

brass band music, marches, classical music, music that reflects the cultures represented in your group

Snack times

Learning objectives

- To take turns
- To build relationships with other children
- To experience and develop social conventions

Suggested activities

- Whatever snack you are having, place it on a plate or in a bowl, and pass it round the circle so that children offer the snack to each other.

The LCP Foundation Stage

Families

Circle/review times

Learning objectives

- To develop trust in other members of their group
- To take turns

Suggested activities

- Try a 'Trust pass' activity in which pairs of children, facing each other, pass a toy to their partner. Then ask the children to try this with their eyes closed.
- When children are confident in the pair work, extend this to a circle activity. Pass a toy round the circle. Then ask the children to close their eyes and pass the toy round the circle again. Initially children may 'cheat', but as they become familiar with the activity, they will develop trust and wait their turn.

Additional resources

A toy to pass to each other

Outdoor play

Learning objectives

- To work co-operatively
- To have fun with a simple game

Suggested activities

- Play an 'Under and Over' game. Children need to be in groups of four. Children hold hands with a partner and one pair walks in front of the other pair. At a point that they decide, the first pair makes an arch for the second pair to go through. The second pair then makes an arch for the first pair to go through. Keep going!

Families

Stories and rhymes

Learning objectives

- To listen and respond to a range of stories and rhymes

Suggested activities

Stories

Stories about children in a family.

Teddybears stories by Susanna Gretz (A&C Black)

Peace at Last by Jill Murphy (Macmillan Children's Books)

All Kinds of People by Emma Damon (Tango Books)

Eat Up, Gemma by Sarah Hayes (Walker Books)

Alfie series of books by Shirley Hughes (Red Fox)

Ring games

'Hokey-cokey'

'Ring-o-Ring-o-Roses'

'In and out the dusty bluebells'

'We all clap hands together' all from *This Little Puffin. . .* (Puffin Books)

Special visitors/events

Learning objectives

- To be aware of different jobs within the community

Suggested activities

- The visit of the school photographer.

Communication, language and literacy

- What will I choose to play with today?

- The Gingerbread Man

- I don't want to go to bed!

- Teddy

- The fast food bar

- Hickory Dickory Dock

- The Little Red Hen

- Teddybears go shopping

- Washing line

Foundation

What will I choose to play with today?

How can you prepare for this activity?

- You will need to have a favourite puppet or teddy.
- Prepare cards with children's names on.
- Prepare a chart with photographs of each area in your setting, e.g. home corner, sand, water, creative etc.

What are the starting points?

- This activity is carried out just before children go to their self-selected activities.

What resources do you need to collect for the focus activity?

- Puppet or teddy.
- Children's name cards.
- Chart with pictures of areas in your setting.

Display suggestions

- The chart can stay as a 'working display'. As children become familiar with this activity as a routine, they will use it more independently.

Home links

- Ask children to bring in their favourite toy from home to talk about.

Foundation

What will I choose to play with today?

Learning objectives

- To articulate personal needs
- To interact verbally with peers and adults, using appropriate language
- To speak clearly

Activity

Children need to sit in a circle.

The children are going to show or tell teddy where they are going to play today.

When they have made their choice, they can put their name on the chosen place on the chart.

You may need to help a child choose where to play by suggesting that teddy has a look round the room before choosing.

If children just gesture to indicate, you will need to 'tell teddy' for them.

Older or more confident children should be encouraged to say what they are going to do in the area.

For these children you could write their plans for them, as a reminder.

At the end of the activity time, gather the children back into the circle and, using the teddy, ask children about what they did/made when they were playing in their chosen area.

If you wrote down the plan for a child, read this to them to remind them of what they chose to do.

Key questions

- What would you like to do today?
- Can you show/tell teddy?
- What do you need to help you?
- What will you do/make?
- Can you find the picture of the area on the chart?
- Can you put your name on the chart?
- Which area did you choose to play in?
- What did you do/make in there?
- Who was playing there with you?

What do the stepping stones look like?

 Step 1

Use words or gestures, including body language to communicate.
The child may point to the area or the picture on the chart or use teddy to point.

 Step 2

Use simple sentences linked to gestures. Use intonation to make their meaning clear to others.
The child may look at the area or the picture on the chart and tell you that s/he will play (e.g.) in the sand.

 Step 3

Have emerging self-confidence to speak to others about wants and needs.
The child may tell you that s/he wants to play with the cars and make a traffic jam.

 Step 4 (Early learning goal)

Interact with others, negotiating plans and taking turns in conversation.
Child may tell you that s/he wants to play in the home corner with a friend and that they will dress up and make tea for all the teddies.

Targeted children

Evaluation

How did the activity go?

What evidence of children's learning have you collected?

What will I choose to play with today?

Planning sheet for supplementary activities

Area of learning	Learning objective	Activity	Targeted children	Evaluation
PSED				
CLL				
Maths				
KUW				
Physical				
Creative				
Snack times				
Circle times				
Outdoor play				
Stories & rhymes				
Special visitors				

Adult role during spontaneous play sessions

Observing play ☐ _____   Supporting play areas ☐ _____

Supporting individual play ☐ _____   Involvement in play area ☐ _____

59

What will I choose to play with today?

Personal, social and emotional development

Learning objectives

- To make and express choices

Suggested activities

- Children take turns to fetch an item from the area they wish to play in. They can then tell teddy about what they want to do in the area.

Mathematical development

Learning objectives

- To use numbers in everyday situations
- To count
- To recognise some numerals

Suggested activities

- After children have made their choices, count the number of children who have chosen each area.
- Write the numeral on a sticky note and place on the chart.
- Where possible, encourage individual children to write the numeral for you.
- Provide a large sheet of paper, and large felt pens, and sit the children round the paper. Children can practise the numerals on the part of paper close to them.

Additional resources

Sticky notes

Large sheet of paper (which could be cut from a wallpaper roll) and large felt pens

The LCP Foundation Stage

What will I choose to play with today?

Knowledge and understanding of the world

Learning objectives

- To be aware of the purpose of a tape recorder
- To use a tape recorder to record
- To plan what s/he is going to do and choose resources

Suggested activities

- Show the children how to operate the tape recorder and explain that you will record what they plan to play with. You will need to demonstrate this, e.g. 'Today I want to make a model. I will need some boxes and sticky tape…'
- Tape record children's choices. Tell shy children that if they whisper to teddy, teddy will say it for them. You will then need to say the sentence for the child. Allow the children to operate buttons.
- Play back the recording.

Additional resources

Tape recorder and tapes

Physical development

Learning objectives

- To develop hand-eye co-ordination

Suggested activities

- Sit the children in a circle and explain that you will throw a beanbag to a child. When they catch the beanbag, it is their turn to choose where to play.

Additional resources

Beanbag

What will I choose to play with today?

Creative development

Learning objectives

- To represent their chosen activity by drawing

Suggested activities

- Children draw a picture of themselves playing today. Provide each child with a clipboard to rest paper on.

Additional resources

Paper and crayons, clipboards

Snack times

Learning objectives

- To talk about their play activities
- To interact verbally with adults and peers
- To listen to others and respond appropriately

Suggested activities

- This informal time gives children the opportunity to talk about their activities. If it is not possible for all children to contribute, keep a chart of children who have had a turn at reviewing their activities. This could be used to identify whose turn it is 'today'.

Circle/review times

Learning objectives

- To speak clearly, using appropriate language

Suggested activities

- Put some objects from around the room into a bag. Play some music or sing a song as the bag is passed round the circle. When the music stops, the child holding the bag takes out an object from the bag. In response to the question 'You have a ......; where does it go?' the child indicates or tells you where it belongs.
- If this activity is repeated often enough, children will join in with the question.

Additional resources

Bag for passing the objects round

What will I choose to play with today?

Outdoor play

Learning objectives

- To interact verbally with peers and adults
- To speak clearly

Suggested activities

- Encourage the children to indicate/tell you about which bike they want to play on.
- Set up a route to follow on the bikes. Draw the route with chalk and set up some obstacles to go round and between.
- Take children round the route and talk about it using directional vocabulary.

Stories and rhymes

Learning objectives

- To enjoy and join in with rhymes and songs

Suggested activities

Rhyme

'What do we do when we go to nursery?' from *This Little Puffin. . .* (Puffin Books)

Special visitors/events

Learning objectives

- To explore their local environment

Suggested activities

- ⚠ Plan a visit to the local park. Discuss what the children will do when they get there. Depending on the time of year, make collections, play on equipment, play games on the grass etc.
- Take photos of the visit. Use the photographs to make a book about the visit.

Additional resources

Camera

The Gingerbread Man

How can you prepare for this activity?

- Collect together ginger biscuits, gingerbread men, ginger root, ginger powder.
- Create a simple gingerbread man recipe card.
- List the measures in cups and spoons.
- Use photographs or draw pictures to show the ingredients.
- Write simple instructions to show the method, using a combination of numbers and pictures.
- Prepare a tape recording of the story which relates to the version that you use. When the page is turned, indicate this by a bell signal on the tape.

What are the starting points?

- Taste gingerbread men, biscuits and ginger. Talk about what each thing tastes and smells like.
- Read the story to the children.

What resources do you need to collect for the focus activity?

- Gingerbread men, ginger biscuits and ginger.
- The story, *The Gingerbread Man* (in big book version if possible) (traditional).
- Tape recording of the story.

Display suggestions

- Make a frieze of gingerbread men that the children have painted. Add a caption with a refrain from the story, e.g. 'You can't catch me!' or 'Run, run, as fast as you can!'

Similar topics to explore

- The story, *The Enormous Turnip* (traditional).

Home links

- Ask the children to look for ginger biscuits at home or when out shopping.
- Allow the story to be a 'take home' story to share with parent or carer.

Foundation

The *LCP* Foundation Stage

The Gingerbread Man

Learning objectives

- Listen and respond to a traditional story
- Join in with the refrain
- Talk about the story and characters

Activity

Taste the gingerbread men.

Before reading the story, talk about the cover of the book and what the book might be about.

Go through the book, pointing out the main characters in the story.

Read the story to the children and encourage them to join in with the 'Run, run, as fast as you can…' refrain.

Role-play the story, with the children as key characters.

Invite the children to tell you what happens in the story. Encourage them to respond in sentences. Where they give one word, put this into a sentence for them, e.g. 'Yes that's right, the old woman made a gingerbread man.'

Make the tape-recorded version available in the book area.

Key questions

- Who was the story about?
- Why did the old woman make a gingerbread man?
- Which animals were chasing the gingerbread man?
- What did the gingerbread man say to them as he ran?
- Why did they all want to catch him?

Key vocabulary

- run, fast, catch

What do the stepping stones look like?

 Step 1

Listen to favourite stories. Join in with repeated refrains.
Child will begin to join in as story develops.

 Step 2

Listen to stories with increasing attention and recall. Describe main characters, events and setting.
Child will talk about the characters and what happens to the gingerbread man.

 Step 3

Initiate conversations…
Child will take on the role of a character and will mimic the words used in the story.

 Step 4 (Early learning goal)

Listen with enjoyment and respond to stories. Make up their own stories.
Child responds enthusiastically to the story and could make up other characters or alternative endings.

Targeted children

Evaluation

How did the activity go?

What evidence of children's learning have you collected?

The Gingerbread Man

Planning sheet for supplementary activities

Area of learning	Learning objective	Activity	Targeted children	Evaluation
PSED				
CLL				
Maths				
KUW				
Physical				
Creative				
Snack times				
Circle times				
Outdoor play				
Stories & rhymes				
Special visitors				

Adult role during spontaneous play sessions

Observing play ☐ _____ Supporting play areas ☐ _____

Supporting individual play ☐ _____ Involvement in play area ☐ _____

The LCP Foundation Stage

The Gingerbread Man

Personal, social and emotional development

Learning objectives

- To develop an awareness of feelings: **sad** and **happy**

Suggested activities

- Talk about **happy** and **sad**. Ask what made the gingerbread man happy/sad. Ask the children what makes them happy/sad.
- Children can make a happy and sad gingerbread puppet by using a cardboard outline of a gingerbread man. They can draw a happy face on one side and a sad face on the reverse. Attach these to large lolly sticks.
- Use these puppets throughout the week in circle time.

Additional resources

Gingerbread men outlines

Lolly sticks

Materials to decorate, e.g. wool (for hair), sticker shapes (for eyes, nose and mouth)

Mathematical development

Learning objectives

- To use the vocabulary of **more/less**
- To count reliably
- To put numbers in order

Suggested activities (small group)

- Make 10 different-sized gingerbread shapes out of card. Arrange them on a baking tray. Explain that some gingerbread men are going to escape. Throw a dice (marked with 1 or 2 spots) to decide how many will escape at a time. Let 1 or 2 escape and refer to **1** or **2 less**. Discuss how many escape and how many are left.
- Play the game in reverse: throw the dice and 'find' **1** or **2 more**.
- Number the card gingerbread men 1–10. Ask the children to put the correct number of buttons on each gingerbread man, so that the number of buttons corresponds to the numeral.
- Ask the children to put them in numerical order.
- Compare the sizes of different cut-out gingerbread men.

Additional resources

Card gingerbread men shapes, baking tray

Dice (marked with 1 or 2 spots)

Buttons

The Gingerbread Man

Knowledge and understanding of the world

Learning objectives

• To observe the changes to ingredients as they are mixed together and after cooking

Suggested activities

• Make a simple gingerbread men recipe card which uses cupfuls/spoonfuls as measures. Encourage the children to follow the list as the ingredients are added. Wherever possible, encourage the children to measure, add and mix the ingredients themselves.
• Roll out and cut with cutters.
• Allow the children to add currants and candied peel for eyes, mouth and buttons independently.
• Count how many gingerbread men go in the oven. ⚠
• Set a timer for the cooking time and talk about this as you do it.
• Discuss the ingredients in their natural states and when they are mixed.
• Count how many gingerbread men come out of the oven.

Additional resources

Simple recipe for gingerbread men

Ingredients for gingerbread men

Baking tray, mixing bowls, spoons, cutters, oven timer

Cups and spoons to measure out

Physical development

Learning objectives

• To handle tools safely and with confidence
• To develop fine motor skills

Suggested activities

• Children practise making gingerbread men with play dough: rolling, cutting, arranging on tray to 'bake'.
• Children could use sieves or a garlic press to make hair out of the dough.

Additional resources

Play dough, cutters, round-ended knives, fish slices, rolling pins, sieves, flour sprinklers

Various tools to mark eyes/nose/mouth/buttons

Baking trays

The Gingerbread Man

Creative development

Learning objective

- To reproduce colour, line, shape, etc. using pictures from the story as a stimulus

Suggested activities

- Look carefully at the gingerbread man in the story and talk about him.
- Each child could paint his/her own gingerbread man independently. Make a picture available for children to refer to.
- Talk about the characters in the story and look at the pictures of them closely.
- Children can paint pictures of a chosen character.

Additional resources

Paints and brushes of different thicknesses

Snack times

Learning objectives

- To make and express choices
- To use please and thank-you

Suggested activities

- Eat the gingerbread men (made in **Knowledge and understanding of the world** activity)!

Circle/review times

Learning objectives

- To develop the ability to express their feelings

Suggested activities

- Use the happy/sad puppets made in **Personal, social and emotional development** activity. Let the children talk about what makes them feel happy/sad, e.g. 'I feel happy when…'
- Ask the children to hold up a happy or sad puppet to show how they feel.

Additional resources

Card gingerbread men puppets

The Gingerbread Man

Outdoor play

Learning objectives

- To explore their outside environment
- To use different spaces and levels

Suggested activities

- Have a gingerbread man hunt: hide cardboard shapes for the children to find.

Additional resources

Card gingerbread men shapes

Stories and rhymes

Learning objectives

- To explore and experiment with words

Suggested activities

- Make up variations on the 'Run, run…' refrain, e.g. 'Step, step, as slow as you can, You can't catch me, I'm the tortoise man…'
- Write these versions down for the children.

Special visitors/events

Learning objectives

- To be aware of purpose of different buildings and people who work in them
- To handle money to buy goods

Suggested activities

- Visit a local baker or supermarket to buy some gingerbread men.

Additional resources

Some money with which to buy the gingerbread men!

I don't want to go to bed!

How can you prepare for this activity?

- Collect together a selection of story and information books about animals that live in the wild in jungles.
- Collect together posters and pictures of wild animals. Laminate them if possible, so that the children can handle them, trace over them and draw on them if they want to.
- Organise a visit to a zoo or a safari park. ⚠

What are the starting points?

- Dress up a doll or a teddy in bedclothes, a sleepsuit or pyjamas. Ask the children why teddy is dressed the way he is. Discuss bedtime. Why do we need sleep? Why do babies have naps during the day? How do we feel when we wake up?
- Read *I don't want to go to bed!* by Julie Sykes and Tim Warnes (Little Tiger Press).

What resources do you need to collect for the focus activity?

- Story and information books about animals that live in the wild in jungles.

Display suggestions

- Tabletop display of night-time objects such as pyjamas, teddy, a book, a cup, a hot water bottle, a night light, a toothbrush, a flannel or sponge, bubble-bath, soap, shampoo, a plastic duck etc.

Similar topics to explore

- Other routines that children have first-hand experience of and will be able to talk about, e.g. getting up in the morning, going shopping and mealtimes.

Home links

- Encourage parents to accompany their children on the Nursery visit to the zoo or safari park.
- If a Nursery visit to a zoo or safari park is not possible, suggest that parents themselves take their children.

Foundation

I don't want to go to bed!

Learning objectives

- To articulate personal needs and feelings
- To explore and experiment with words
- To talk confidently about their experiences and ideas
- To have an increasing and extended vocabulary

Activity

After reading the story *'I don't want to go to bed!'* discuss with the children their bedtime routines.

Do they wash or have a bath before going to bed?

Do they have a drink or supper; do they clean their teeth?

Do they have a bedtime story? Who reads it?

Do they sleep by themselves or with a brother or sister?

What is their bed like? Is it big or small?

Do they sleep in bunk beds?

What is their quilt cover like? Did they choose it? Does it match the wallpaper?

Do they have the light on when they go to sleep or do they prefer sleeping in the dark?

Do they like going to bed or are they naughty like Little Tiger?

Do they take a teddy or a special blanket to bed with them?

What do their pyjamas or nightie look like? Encourage the children to describe their nightclothes.

Who usually takes them to bed? Some of the children may know what time they go to bed. Look at a clock and put the hands at the appropriate time.

Name the animals in the story and gather together other story or information books that name other jungle animals.

Re-read the story then sequence the events. Who did Little Tiger visit first? Next? What did every animal parent say to Little Tiger?

Explore the vocabulary used in the story.

The animal parents: **roared, growled, bellowed, trumpeted, whispered, yawned**. Explore other words that could replace the word 'said' in stories.

Little Tiger: **skipped, splashed, scurried, bounced, tiptoed** away. Use this vocabulary during movement activities.

What do the stepping stones look like?

 Step 1

Use familiar words, often in isolation, to identify what they do and do not want.
Use vocabulary focused on objects and people who are of particular importance to them.
Child will use 2-3 words to respond to questions.

 Step 2

Build up vocabulary that reflects the breadth of their experiences.
Begin to experiment with language describing possession.
Child will talk about their bedtime routines, e.g. 'Mummy tells me a story when I go to bed'.

 Step 3

Extend vocabulary, especially by grouping and naming.
Use vocabulary and forms of speech that are increasingly influenced by experience of books.
Child will add the vocabulary from the story.

 Step 4 (Early learning goal)

Extend vocabulary, exploring the meanings and sounds of new words.
Child will show enjoyment of the words used in the stories and will enjoy saying words like 'growled' in a growly voice.

I don't want to go to bed!

Key questions

- Why was Little Tiger naughty?
- Which friends did he visit?
- Did they play with him?
- Do you think Little Tiger would be naughty again?

Key vocabulary

- Night, morning, awake, asleep, tired, sleepy, yawn, nap

Targeted children

Evaluation

How did the activity go?

What evidence of children's learning have you collected?

I don't want to go to bed!

Planning sheet for supplementary activities

Area of learning	Learning objective	Activity	Targeted children	Evaluation
PSED				
CLL				
Maths				
KUW				
Physical				
Creative				
Snack times				
Circle times				
Outdoor play				
Stories & rhymes				
Special visitors				

Adult role during spontaneous play sessions

Observing play ☐ _____

Supporting individual play ☐ _____

Supporting play areas ☐ _____

Involvement in play area ☐ _____

I don't want to go to bed!

Personal, social and emotional development

Learning objectives

- To develop the ability to express their feelings
- To develop a knowledge of what is right and wrong, and why
- To begin to recognise the consequences of their own actions

Suggested activities

- Talk to the children about being naughty. What makes them naughty? What happens when they are naughty? How do they feel when they have been naughty? Talk about the ways in which their parents (or carers) look after them - feed them, cuddle them when they are upset or hurt, buy them clothes etc. Have they ever been lost like Little Tiger?

Mathematical development

Learning objectives

- To verbalise numbers by counting
- To be able to sort objects by a single criterion
- To begin to be aware of ordinal numbers in everyday situations
- To distinguish between day and night
- To begin to show an awareness of number operations such as subtraction

Suggested activities

- Count and paint the different animals in the story *'I don't want to go to bed!'* Use sets of plastic jungle animals to sort. Encourage the correct use of ordinal numbers: first he visited his best friend the lion, then he visited his second-best friend the hippo etc.
- Discuss day and night with the children. Talk about the things we do during the day and things that happen at night while we are asleep.
- Sing the song 'There were ten in the bed…' Make a bed and use teddies to 'act' out the song. Every time you sing 'one fell out', take a teddy away.

Additional resources

Sets of wild animals, in two sizes if at all possible, so that the children can sort them into mothers and babies as well as into animal types

A bed and 10 teddies

I don't want to go to bed!

Supplementary activities

Knowledge and understanding of the world

Learning objectives

- To develop the imagination
- To develop an awareness of the wider world
- To explore and name features of living things by looking at similarities, differences, pattern and change

Suggested activities

- Read stories and information books about animals in the jungle. Capture children's imagination with descriptions of wild animals; talk about their size and skin colours and patterns - stripes or spots. Name the adult animals and tell the children what their young are called.
- If possible organise a visit to a zoo.

Additional resources

A good selection of both story and information books about jungle animals

Posters and pictures of animals displayed on the Nursery walls

Physical development

Learning objectives

- To use self-expression in movement
- To begin to show movement in imaginative ways
- To develop refined hand movements during imaginative play

Suggested activities

- Play animal inspired music such as excerpts from 'Carnival of the Animals' by Saint-Saëns. Encourage the children first to listen to the music and then move like the appropriate animal.
- Provide small-world toys and natural resources so that the children can create their own jungle in the sand tray.

Additional resources

Tape recorder or CD player and music

Small-world jungle animal toys, lots of twigs, leaves and greenery

I don't want to go to bed!

Creative development

Learning objectives

- To explore and experiment with colour and texture through a variety of media e.g. collage, printing, painting
- To explore sound with fun and pleasure
- To initiate and create sound
- To enjoy singing

Suggested activities

- Collage, print and paint a large jungle scene. Use bright, vivid colours. Tear and cut unusual-shaped leaves. Paint and collage a selection of jungle animals. Value the children's interpretation. Display in a wild and wacky way! Involve the children in putting up the display.
- Make animal masks from paper plates. Make animal puppets from old socks or from strong paper bags, sew or stick on small pieces of material, felt, buttons, beads or sequins.
- Print stripes and spots on large sheets of paper using a selection of materials such as fingers, toothbrushes, chalk, felt-tip pens and string, and display them.
- The children could paint 'day' and 'night' pictures.
- Encourage the children to use musical instruments to create jungle sounds, e.g. beating a drum to create the sound of an elephant.
- Sing songs such as 'Down in the jungle where nobody goes'.

Additional resources

Paper of different thicknesses and textures. Brightly coloured paint mixed with different media such as salt, sugar, sand, flour, glue, wood shavings, pulses and rice. Paint brushes of different thicknesses. Tools that give texture such as combs, twigs and lolly sticks

Paper plates for masks

Old socks or paper bags for puppets and materials to decorate them with

Musical instruments

Collage materials, felt, buttons, beads, sequins, material

Large sheets of paper, materials for printing

Snack times

Learning objectives

- To develop an awareness of food grown and eaten in other countries and by other cultures
- To make and express choices

Suggested activities

- Introduce the children to a selection of tropical fruits and juices such as bananas, kiwis, mangoes etc. at snack time.

I don't want to go to bed!

Circle/review times

Learning objectives

- To develop the ability to express their feelings
- To gain confidence when speaking in a familiar group
- To begin to develop the ability to listen whilst others are speaking

Suggested activities

- Use sentence starters such as 'My Mum gets cross when I . . .', 'It is naughty to . . .', 'I like being good because . . .'

Outdoor play

Learning objectives

- To develop gross motor skills – climbing, balancing, creeping and crawling

Suggested activities

- Create an obstacle course using old tyres, boxes, climbing nets, benches etc. You and the children could design your own jungle.

Additional resources

Obstacle course equipment

The *LCP* Foundation Stage

I don't want to go to bed!

Stories and rhymes

Learning objectives

• To listen and respond to stories and rhymes

Suggested activities

Stories

Dear Zoo by Rod Campbell (Cambell Books)

Walking through the Jungle by Julie Lacome (Walker Books)

I'm Sorry by Sam McBratney (Picture Lions)

A Lion at Bedtime by Debi Gliori (Scholastic)

Rhymes

'If you should meet a crocodile'

'An elephant goes like this and that'

'Three little monkeys were jumping on the bed' all from *This Little Puffin. . .* (Puffin Books)

Special visitors/events

Learning objectives

• To know that all places are not the same
• To name and categorise different animals

Suggested activities

• A trip to a zoo or a safari park. ⚠

Teddy

How can you prepare for this activity?

- If possible take photographs of Teddy at home, in the garden, in bed – any places of interest that will engage the children in conversation about Teddy.

What are the starting points?

- Introduce Teddy to the children. Explain that he is very shy and a little bit lonely as this is his first day at Nursery.
- Tell the children his name and a few details about him, such as where he lives, how old he is and so on. Show the children any photographs you have taken of Teddy. These photographs could be put in an album and later displayed alongside Teddy.
- Explain to the children that it will be their job to look after Teddy.
- Pack Teddy a bag of his own. Put in a few of his personal possessions such as a toothbrush, a book, a diary etc.

What resources do you need to collect for the focus activity?

- A Teddy new to the setting, preferably one that is washable.
- A disposable camera so you can take photographs of Teddy with the children.

Display suggestions

- Display a photograph of Teddy with a caption saying 'My name is.... and I like….' and display Teddy's favourite items such as his breakfast cereal, his baseball cap, his favourite book etc.
- Ask the children to bring in their teddies and display them.

Similar topics to explore

- Similar activities with any soft toy or puppet.

Home links

- Ask parents if they would be prepared to take it in turns to take Teddy home for a weekend.
- Ask them if they could keep a diary about Teddy's weekend, noting down everything he has done during the weekend.
- Ask parents if they have an old teddy they could bring into Nursery to show the children.
- Ask parents who are going on holiday if they would take Teddy with them and then send Nursery a postcard from Teddy.

Teddy

Learning objectives

- To interact verbally with peers and adults, using appropriate language
- To talk confidently about their experiences, ideas and feelings
- To speak clearly

Activity

Ask the children to sit in a circle and pass Teddy around the circle. As they pass Teddy round, ask them to say 'Hello Teddy, my name is...', If a child does not wish to speak, just ask them to smile at Teddy to make Teddy feel better.

Sit with the children in small groups and ask them to tell Teddy about Nursery: the routines, the names of members of staff, where things belong, where the bathroom/toilet is etc.

Ask the children if they will keep an eye on Teddy.

Suggest they take it in turns to be his friend.

Discuss ways in which Teddy can be included in the children's activities.

Make Teddy a name card. Find him a chair to sit on at snack time. Sit him by the painting table and put an apron on him. Ask children to read him a story.

Children can take turns to take Teddy home. Ask parents to take photos of Teddy's visit.

After children have taken Teddy home for either a night or a weekend, ask them to tell the rest of the group about Teddy's adventures!

Suggest Teddy writes a 'thank you' letter after his visits home to thank parents for taking care of him.

Discuss with children why we say 'thank you'.

Talk to the children about any other times when they might say 'thank you'.

Key questions

- How did Teddy feel when he started Nursery?
- How did we make him feel better?
- What does being shy feel like?

Key vocabulary

- lonely, shy, excited, happy, quiet, frightened

What do the stepping stones look like?

 Step 1

Use isolated words and phrases and/or gestures to communicate with those well known to them.
Child will respond just with own name.

 Step 2

Begin to use more complex sentences.
Use a widening range of words to express or elaborate ideas.
Child will be using 3-4 word sentences.

 Step 3

Link statements and stick to a main theme or intention.
Use language for an increasing range of purposes.
Child will be able to give several sentences to talk about what Teddy is doing.

 Step 4 (Early learning goal)

Speak clearly and audibly with confidence and control and show awareness of the listener, for example by their use of conventions such as greetings, 'please' and 'thank you'.
Child will be able to hold a conversation with adult or other child about what Teddy is doing.

Targeted children

Evaluation

How did the activity go?

What evidence of children's learning have you collected?

Teddy

Planning sheet for supplementary activities

Area of learning	Learning objective	Activity	Targeted children	Evaluation
PSED				
CLL				
Maths				
KUW				
Physical				
Creative				
Snack times				
Circle times				
Outdoor play				
Stories & rhymes				
Special visitors				

Adult role during spontaneous play sessions

Observing play ☐ _____   Supporting play areas ☐ _____

Supporting individual play ☐ _____   Involvement in play area ☐ _____

Teddy

Personal, social and emotional development

Learning objectives

- To develop the ability to express their feelings

Suggested activities

- Discuss with the children what it feels like to be shy. Talk about their first day at Nursery. Do they remember it? How did they feel?

Mathematical development

Learning objectives

- To demonstrate 1:1 correspondence
- To make comparisons according to size

Suggested activities

- Ask the children to bring in their own teddy bears.
- The children could sort their bears according to size, colour etc. They could weigh them to see which is the heaviest/lightest.
- Read the children the story of *Goldilocks and The Three Bears* (traditional). Emphasise the language – big, medium, small. Set up a 'three bears' role-play area.

Additional resources

Children's own teddies, weighing scales, cups, plates, spoons etc., the story *Goldilocks and The Three Bears*

Knowledge and understanding of the world

Learning objectives

- To understand the differences between the past and the present

Suggested activities

- Ask staff and parents if they have an old teddy they could bring into Nursery. Talk to the children about what makes a teddy 'old' – lots of love and cuddles!! Tell the children about the first teddies - how their arms and legs moved and that they were stuffed with wood shavings.
- Make teddy-shaped biscuits to eat at snack time.

Additional resources

A selection of old teddies

The ingredients and equipment to make biscuits

Teddy

Physical development

Learning objectives

- To control refined hand movements, e.g. threading
- To begin to write own name

Suggested activities

- Cut out templates of small teddies; punch holes around the outside edge and give the children lengths of wool to thread around the edge. Encourage the children to 'write' their names on them and suggest they take them home.

Additional resources

Teddy templates, wool or laces

Creative development

Learning objectives

- To explore and experiment with colour and texture
- To represent in models, paintings, drawings and other media

Suggested activities

- Make 'feeling' faces. The children could use a selection of pasta or pulses and any other collage materials to produce their 'feeling' face – happy, sad etc.
- The children could also decorate biscuits with 'feeling' faces.

Additional resources

Paper plates, sticky paper shapes, pasta, pulses ⚠, wool, ribbon, tissue paper etc.
Round biscuits, chocolate buttons, marshmallows, melted chocolate, jelly sweets etc.

Snack times

Learning objectives

- To interact socially
- To be aware of and use social greetings

Suggested activities

- Eat the biscuits made in the **Knowledge and understanding of the world** and **Creative development** activity.
- Eat teddy-shaped crisps.
- Invite children's teddies to join them for snack time.
- Always encourage the use of 'please' and 'thank you' at snack time and all meal times.

Teddy

Circle/review times

Learning objectives

- To increase the ability to listen and reflect
- To articulate feelings
- To talk confidently about their experiences and ideas

Suggested activities

- This is an excellent topic to introduce other circle time activities. To begin with, the children need to sit in fairly small groups so that they are not sitting for too long waiting for their turn. Children enjoy circle time so much that eventually they enjoy the 'listening' aspect of circle time as much as the 'speaking'.
- Establish circle time rules: take turns; children only speak when they are holding the teddy and it is a listening time. Start circle time with gestures such as passing a smile, passing a hug, passing a 'thumbs-up' or 'thumbs-down' depending on how you feel - happy or sad.
- Pass around different objects such as a shell, a feather, a pine cone, a piece of fruit, any interesting object a child may bring into Nursery.
- Pass an object that makes a noise such as a bunch of keys or a tambourine and see how quietly the children can pass it around. Encourage children to sit quietly and listen.
- Pass the teddy. Start with 'Hello Teddy, my name is….' and go on eventually to 'Hello Teddy, I feel…./I like...' and so on. Be sensitive and allow children to sit out or not speak if they are not very confident or are particularly quiet children.

Additional resources

A teddy, interesting objects to pass around

Outdoor play

Learning objectives

- To gain independence in accessing resources and choosing materials and equipment

Suggested activities

- Suggest that the children set up their own teddy bears' party. Ask the children what they need and encourage them to find things themselves.

Additional resources

Provide sets of cups, plates, bowls, spoons etc. and a large blanket

Teddy

Stories and rhymes

Learning objective

- To listen and respond to stories and rhymes

Suggested activities

Stories

Bear by Mick Inkpen (Hodder Children's Books)

My Friend Bear and *Where's Teddy?* by Jez Alborough (Walker Books)

Let's Go Home, Little Bear by Martin Waddell (Walker Books)

I feel sad by Brian Moses (Hodder Wayland)

Freddy's Teddies by Peter Melnyczuk (Scholastic)

Rhyme

'Round and round the garden like a teddy bear…' (traditional)

Special visitors/events

Suggested activities

- If you live in an area where there is a Teddy Museum, organise a visit.

The *LCP* Foundation Stage

The fast food bar

How can you prepare for this activity?

- Visit the local fast food outlet.
- Note:
  What food is served
  The type of surroundings
  What staff are wearing
  Is music played in the background?
  Are newspapers provided?
- Talk to the manager about the possibility of organising a visit with children.
- Ask about the possibility of him/her donating cups/straws/cartons etc. for role-play.

What are the starting points?

- Take in some cartons/cups from the fast food outlet and talk to children about where you have been.
- Do the children recognise where they came from?
- If possible, take the children in small groups, to visit the outlet. ⚠ Encourage children to observe their surroundings.
- Listen to the children's conversations.

What resources do you need to collect for the focus activity?

- Props for setting up the role-play area, camera.

Display suggestions

- Use photographs taken at various stages of setting up the activity and display them with suitable captions, e.g. 'Visit our . . . .' in an area which children and parents can see.

Similar topics to explore

- Other role-play areas such as the supermarket, hairdresser, shoe-shop, pet-shop etc.

Home links

- Ask parents to take children to visit a fast food outlet and to talk to them about it.

The fast food bar

Learning objectives

- To talk confidently about their experiences, ideas and feelings
- To take part in role-play with increasing confidence

Activity

Set the scene: show children the empty burger carton, and ask them if they know where you've been for your lunch.

Ask questions such as:

Have you ever been to…?

What do you like to eat at…?

Which is your favourite fast food bar and why?

When do you go?

Set up a fast food bar, starting with donated containers.

Use children's ideas and suggestions.

Make a list of all the suggestions they make for what they need for the role-play.

What food will they need?

What equipment will they need - tables, chairs, counter, uniforms, cartons, cups, straws etc?

What will the fast food bar be called?

Discuss how many customers/attendants are needed to play.

Take photographs at various stages of setting up the role-play area.

Key questions

- Where will we set it up?
- How can we make uniforms/hats etc?
- Will we have background music and what type?
- How can we make burgers, chips etc?

Key vocabulary

- Play, share, imagine, pretend, ideas

Evaluation

How did the activity go?

What evidence of children's learning have you collected?

What do the stepping stones look like?

 Step 1

Use action, sometimes with limited talk, that is largely concerned with the 'here and now'.
Child will tell you what s/he likes to eat at e.g. McDonalds and will want to have his/her favourite foods in role-play area.

 Step 2

Talk activities through, reflecting on and modifying what they are doing. Use talk to give new meanings to objects and actions, treating them as symbols for other things.
Use talk to connect ideas, explain what is happening and explain what might happen next.
Child will take an active role in setting up area, moving things around and trying out ideas. May adapt home corner equipment to represent grill/fryer etc.

 Step 3

Begin to use talk to pretend imaginary situations.
Child plays with others in the fast food bar assuming the roles of customer and attendant, imitating vocabulary and language of fast food outlet.

 Step 4 (Early learning goal)

Use language to imagine and create roles and experiences.
Use talk to organise, sequence and clarify thinking, ideas, feelings and events.

Targeted children

The fast food bar

Planning sheet for supplementary activities

Area of learning	Learning objective	Activity	Targeted children	Evaluation
PSED				
CLL				
Maths				
KUW				
Physical				
Creative				
Snack times				
Circle times				
Outdoor play				
Stories & rhymes				
Special visitors				

Adult role during spontaneous play sessions

Observing play ☐ _____   Supporting play areas ☐ _____

Supporting individual play ☐ _____   Involvement in play area ☐ _____

The fast food bar

Personal, social and emotional development

Learning objectives

• To recognise and solve problems

Suggested activities

• Set up a party for four teddies with four of everything - chairs, cups, hats etc.
• A fifth teddy wants to join the party. What do we do?

Additional resources

5 teddies

Mathematical development

Learning objectives

• To choose and use resources related to a task
• To understand the concept and use specific language of long/long enough/too short in order to compare

Suggested activities

• Make hats: provide hat bands, and show children how to measure head sizes to create hats that fit. Allow children to explore measuring. Children need to be allowed to make mistakes so that they can find out for themselves about the need to adjust, e.g. hat too big that it falls off; hat too small that it won't fit!!

Additional resources

Provide children with a selection of resources to decorate their hat independently

Provide selection of tools for assembling the hat e.g. sticky tape, glue, stapler, ⚠ hole punch, string

Knowledge and understanding of the world

Learning objectives

• To recognise and name some features and buildings in the local area

Suggested activities

• Visit a local fast food outlet or snackbar.
• Use local bus service.
• Talk about what you see on the journey with the children.
• Discuss road safety.

Additional resources

Check adult/child ratio

The fast food bar

Creative development

Learning objectives

- To explore shape, form and space in 2 and 3 dimensions
- To represent in models, paintings and other media
- To select appropriate materials for a purpose

Suggested activities

- List the foods that children want to make. Provide a selection of resources and allow children to use their imagination to recreate burgers, chips, pizza, cakes, ice-creams etc.

Additional resources

Yellow foam, corrugated card, paper plates, plastic cups
Pieces of coloured tissue paper and crepe paper, salt dough

Physical development

Learning objectives

- To develop fine motor skills and hand-eye co-ordination

Suggested activities

- Design menus, captions and signs (show opening times!).
- Make price tags.

Additional resources

Felt pens, card (suitable for laminating)

Snack times

Learning objectives

- To understand the importance of keeping healthy

Suggested activities

- Provide healthy snacks and discuss alternatives to 'junk' food.

The fast food bar

Circle/review times

Learning objectives

- To gain confidence in speaking in familiar groups
- To make and express choices

Suggested activities

- Use Circle time sentence starter: 'I go to McDonalds when…'

Outdoor play

Learning objectives

- To take part in role-play with increasing confidence and imagination

Suggested activities

- Recreate a 'Drive-In' with bikes, scooters etc.

Stories and rhymes

Learning objectives

- To join in with familiar rhymes

Suggested activities

Rhymes

'Jelly on the plate'

'Ten fat sausages'

'Old MacDonald had a shop, e-i-e-i-o' all from *This Little Puffin. . .* (Puffin Books)

Special visitors/events

Suggested activities

- Give the children their lunch in a bag. Ask canteen staff to provide a 'take-away' style lunch one day.

Hickory Dickory Dock

How can you prepare for this activity?

• You need to make a 'Grandfather clock' from an old shoe box. Make the face from a paper plate, and attach clock hands with a brass split pin.

• Make a simple finger mouse puppet with a small piece of material. Add tail, ears and whiskers!

What are the starting points?

• The rhyme 'Hickory Dickory Dock'.

What resources do you need to collect for the focus activity?

• Collect pictures of clocks and watches.

• Bring in a selection of clocks and watches.

Display suggestions

• Children can make a large grandfather clock.

• Children can make their finger mice (made in **Mathematical development** activity) run up and down the clock.

• Set up a clock and watch shop.

Similar topics to explore

• Other traditional rhymes such as 'Twinkle, twinkle, little star'.

Home links

• Ask children to look for clocks and watches at home.

Foundation

Hickory Dickory Dock

Learning objectives

- To explore and experiment with patterns and rhymes
- To enjoy using language
- To explore initial and final sounds in words

Activity

Learn the rhyme 'Hickory Dickory Dock' using the clock and finger mouse to act it out.

Encourage the children to take a turn with the finger mouse running up/down the clock.

When the children are confident with the rhyme, introduce variations,

e.g. 'Hickory dickory dare,

    the mouse ran under the chair …'

or

    'Hickory dickory dock

    the mouse ran up the clock.

    The clock struck two,

    the mouse went BOO…'

Make up real and nonsense words to rhyme with 'clock'.

Play with the tick/tock rhythm, e.g. saying it at different speeds.

Try other possibilities e.g. lick/lock, sick/sock

Key questions

- What sound can you hear at the beginning/end/ middle of these words?

Key vocabulary

- rhyme, sound, beginning sound, last sound, sound in the middle, listen

What do the stepping stones look like?

 Step 1

Enjoy rhyming and rhythmic activities.
Child will join in and will move with the tick/tock pattern.

 Step 2

Recognise rhythm in spoken words.
Child will begin to recognise and enjoy the alternative rhymes. May begin to add an alternative word themselves.

 Step 3

Continue a rhyming string. Hear and say initial and final sounds in words.
Child will create strings of rhyming words including some nonsense words.
Child will show awareness in the changed initial letters as in e.g. tock, sock, rock.

 Step 4 (Early learning goal)

Hear and say initial and final sounds in words and short vowel within words.

Targeted children

Evaluation

How did the activity go?

What evidence of children's learning have you collected?

Hickory Dickory Dock

(Planning sheet for supplementary activities)

Area of learning	Learning objective	Activity	Targeted children	Evaluation
PSED				
CLL				
Maths				
KUW				
Physical				
Creative				
Snack times				
Circle times				
Outdoor play				
Stories & rhymes				
Special visitors				

Adult role during spontaneous play sessions

Observing play ☐ _____   Supporting play areas ☐ _____

Supporting individual play ☐ _____   Involvement in play area ☐ _____

Hickory Dickory Dock

Personal, social and emotional development

Learning objectives

- To be interested and be able to express themselves
- To respect property of others

Suggested activities

- Look at the collection of clocks and discuss the care needed when handling them.
- Children draw their favourite clock/watch, being careful when handling it.

Additional resources

Real clocks and watches

Mathematical development

Learning objectives

- To understand the concept of long and short, and use the specific language of long and short
- To be able to compare

Suggested activities (small group)

- Children make a simple finger mouse from a cone of paper, decorating it and attaching a tail from wool. Where possible encourage children to cut their own wool to make the tail.

Additional resources

Paper, wool, scissors, materials to decorate, sticky tape

Knowledge and understanding of the world

Learning objectives

- To select appropriate resources for constructing
- Describe and evaluate what they have made

Suggested activities

- Talk about different clocks and watches. Use pictures and real objects. Examine the clock faces and cases carefully.
- Offer the children the resources they might need to make a clock or watch themselves.
- Encourage the children to think what they want to use.

Additional resources

Allow children to select from a range of recycled and collage materials

The *LCP* Foundation Stage

Hickory Dickory Dock

Physical development

Learning objectives

- To be aware of their body and the space around them
- To begin to show movement in imaginative ways

Suggested activities

- Play a cat and mouse game. Children start in a mouse house (a mat or hoop). When all is quiet, children can pretend to leave the mouse house and creep out and about like mice.
- Now tell the children to watch out for the cat. When the cat comes, e.g. on signal of tambourine being shaken, children run back to the mouse house.

Additional resources

A musical instrument to represent a cat, e.g. shaking a tambourine

Mats or hoops to use as mouse houses

Creative development

Learning objectives

- To explore sound with fun and pleasure
- To initiate and create sounds

Suggested activities

- Record the rhyme on to a tape.
- Accompany the tape with a basic 'tick tock' rhythm using rhythm sticks or clapping.

Additional resources

Tape recorder and tape

Rhythm sticks - two pieces of wood which can be tapped to make a steady beat

Hickory Dickory Dock

Snack times

Learning objectives

- To show an awareness of the passage of time and the order of events during the day

Suggested activities

- Talk about at what time of the day the children have their snack, and about what happens before and after snack time.
- Make a simple clock face which shows the order of activities through the day. Use just one 'hand' to indicate 'time of day'.
- Eat small cubes of cheese.

Circle/review times

Learning objectives

- To develop ability to express feelings

Suggested activities

- Use a toy mouse to hold and stroke.
- Use sentence starter: 'I feel frightened when…..' Pass the mouse to the next child to continue with their sentence.
- Finish off with 'pass a hug' to make you feel better.

Additional resources

Toy mouse

Outdoor play

Learning objectives

- To explore and have fun

Suggested activities

- Have a 'Mouse-tail Hunt'. Hide lots of small pieces of wool in the outside area. The children are to collect as many as they can. Sort by length/colour. Count how many each child has found.

Additional resources

Lengths of wool

Hickory Dickory Dock

Stories and rhymes

Learning objectives

- To enjoy the rhythm, pattern and rhyme in familiar songs
- To control the sound of their voices to create expression in rhymes

Suggested activities

Stories

The Lion and the Mouse (traditional)

Rhymes

'Three blind mice' (traditional)

'Creep, mousie, creep' from *This Little Puffin. . .* (Puffin Books)

'Up the tall white candlestick' from *This Little Puffin. . .* (Puffin Books)

Special visitors/events

Learning objectives

- To care for small animals

Suggested activities

- If possible, bring a pet mouse in for children to look at, handle and talk about.
- Care for a small animal in the Nursery.

The Little Red Hen

Preparation

How can you prepare for this activity?

- Ask parents if any of their children are allergic to products containing wheat.
- Arrange with local baker/cake shop for small groups of children to visit. ⚠ Often supermarkets with their own bakeries will show the children how bread is actually made.
- This is a good springtime topic as the children may be able to plant seeds of their own.

What are the starting points?

- Read the story of *The Little Red Hen* (traditional).
- Ask children where they think bread comes from!
- Talk to the children about how bread is made.
- Make bread with the children. Use a cookery book and show the children the pictures of other recipes. Explain that it is an 'information' book as opposed to a storybook.

What resources do you need to collect for the focus activity?

- The story *The Little Red Hen*.
- The ingredients and equipment you will need to make your own bread.

Display suggestions

- Display the ingredients and equipment needed to make bread: flour, yeast, water, baking tin etc.

Similar topics to explore

- Other familiar or traditional stories that have well-known characters and plots.

Home links

- Ask parents if they will cook with their children.
- Tell parents that the children have been looking at cookery books; if there are cookery books at home, perhaps parents could look at them with their children.

Foundation

The *LCP* Foundation Stage

The Little Red Hen

Learning objectives

- To listen and respond to stories
- To increase the ability to listen with understanding and enjoyment and the ability to evaluate and reflect
- To have an increasing and extended vocabulary
- To recall stories and sequence events

Activity

Read the story of *The Little Red Hen* to the children several times, showing them the illustrations in the book and pointing to the words as you read them. Each time you read the story encourage the children to join in with the repetitive phrases 'Who will help me?' '"Not I," said the pig' etc. Use your voice to portray the different animals. Encourage the children to help you.

Sequence the story: what did the Little Red Hen do first, . . . next? Discuss the end of the story. Would the children have shared the hot, tasty bread? If not, why not?

Use masks or puppets to re-enact the story, giving different children different characters each time.

Discuss the different characters with the children. Why did they behave in such a way? Could the children think of a way in which they could change the ending? Maybe the animals could say how sorry they were and the Little Red Hen might change her mind.

Display pictures of the characters around the Nursery with captions such as 'Will you help me?' and '"Not I," said the pig'. Encourage children to read the captions back to you.

Put the book in the book corner and sit with individual children and encourage them to read you the story.

Read the story of *The Little Yellow Chicken* by Joy Cowley (The Wright Group). In it, the Little Red Hen's granddaughter has a party and her friends won't help her prepare the food, but she does invite them to the party.

Read other stories with refrains so that the children can join in with them.

Write 'sorry' letters to the Little Red Hen.

Use a recipe book and follow the instructions to make bread with the children.

What do the stepping stones look like?

 Step 1

Listen to and join in with stories and poems one-to-one and also in small groups. Show interest in illustrations and print in books and print in the environment. Begin to be aware of the way stories are structured.

Child will join in the refrain '"Not I," said...'

Child is interested in and will talk about pictures.

 Step 2

Have favourite books. Handle books carefully. Suggest how the story might end. Know that information can be relayed in the form of print. Hold books the correct way up and turn pages. Understand the concept of a word.

Child will pretend to read the story, turning the pages as the story develops, using different voices.

 Step 3

Enjoy an increasing range of books.

Begin to recognise some familiar words.

Child will recognise repeated words and some familiar words. Will follow the print with finger.

The Little Red Hen

Key questions

- Why did the Little Red Hen make the bread herself?
- Were her friends kind and helpful?
- Would you have helped her?

Key vocabulary

- Story, word, print, beginning, end, next, after, then

Targeted children

Evaluation

How did the activity go?

What evidence of children's learning have you collected?

Step 4 (Early learning goal)

Explore and experiment with sounds, words and texts. Re-tell narratives in the correct sequence, drawing on language patterns of stories. Read a range of common words and simple sentences independently. Know that print carries meaning and, in English, is read from left to right and top to bottom. Show an understanding of the elements of stories, such as main characters, sequence of events, and openings, and how information can be found in non fiction texts to answer questions about where, who, why and how.

Child can re-tell the story in sequence and will begin to put expression into ""Not I," said the...' Will be able to read some of the story and can make up similar story using Little Red Hen structures.

The Little Red Hen

Planning sheet for supplementary activities

Area of learning	Learning objective	Activity	Targeted children	Evaluation
PSED				
CLL				
Maths				
KUW				
Physical				
Creative				
Snack times				
Circle times				
Outdoor play				
Stories & rhymes				
Special visitors				

Adult role during spontaneous play sessions

Observing play ☐ _____   Supporting play areas ☐ _____

Supporting individual play ☐ _____   Involvement in play area ☐ _____

The Little Red Hen

Personal, social and emotional development

Learning objectives

- To develop a sense of what is right and wrong and a sense of fair play
- To develop an awareness of their own culture and a respect for the customs of other cultures
- To express and make choices

Suggested activities

- Discuss with the children the attitudes of the animals towards the Little Red Hen. Emphasise the need to help and support one another.
- Buy a selection of breads from other cultures and try them.
- Discuss with the children feeding the birds or going to a pond where there are ducks and feeding them with breadcrumbs.

Additional resources

French baguettes, pitta bread, naan bread, chapattis, soda bread, bagels, ciabatta etc.

Mathematical development

Learning objectives

- To explore practical mathematical activities in a variety of everyday situations
- To begin to use own language in play and everyday situations to talk about size, quantity, shape

Suggested activities

- Make sandwiches and cut them in halves and quarters. Cut them in different shapes, e.g. squares and triangles. Count them. Share them out. Are there enough? Match one to one.
- Set up a class Baker's Shop. Use the bread and cakes made during **Knowledge and understanding of the world** activity. Sort them into trays. Price all the bread and cakes. Use a till and money.

Additional resources

Bread, butter, and jam

Salt dough models of cakes and bread, till and money

The Little Red Hen

Knowledge and understanding of the world

Learning objectives

- To observe closely and identify similarities, differences and change
- To talk about what they have seen, are doing, seeing, tasting and touching
- To predict/guess what will happen, and to test the prediction/guess
- To recognise and name buildings in the local area
- To know that tools (knives) must be handled carefully

Suggested activities

- Make toasted sandwiches with the children; discuss the changes that take place when bread is toasted.
  ⚠ Leave slices of bread in a sealed plastic food bag to go hard and mouldy. Encourage the children to observe the changes that take place.
- Make pizzas, bread pudding or bread-and-butter pudding with the children; talk about washing hands etc. before starting.
- Go to the local bakery and buy a selection of breads to try. ⚠
- Read *Pass the Jam, Jim* by Kaye Umansky and Margaret Chamberlain (Red Fox) and make jam sandwiches.

Additional resources

Bread for toast and a toaster, sandwich fillings

Ingredients for any cooking you may decide to do

The story *Pass the Jam, Jim*, bread and jam

Physical development

Learning objectives

- To be aware of the differences in materials by touching
- To control refined hand movements, e.g. rolling, squeezing, shaping, kneading

Suggested activities

- Use salt dough to make a selection of bread shapes, e.g. cottage loaves, plaited loaves, French sticks etc.
- Make cake shapes and bake them in cake papers. Decorate them by painting on cherries etc.
- Butter some bread and roll the slices, then cut into wheel shapes. Eat at snack time.

Additional resources

Salt dough, paint, cake cases

Bread and butter

The Little Red Hen

Supplementary activities

Creative development

Learning objectives

- To explore and experiment with colour and texture
- To explore shape, form and space in 2 and 3 dimensions
- To explore and experiment with materials through a variety of media e.g. painting, printing and collage
- To enjoy saying/singing a range of familiar rhymes and songs

Suggested activities

- Children could paint or collage the Little Red Hen and all the animals. Display with captions on the wall.
- Make masks of the animals' faces and put them on sticks; the children can use them when they re–enact the story.
- Sing 'Five Currant Buns'.

Additional resources

A selection of collage materials, paint, printing materials

Snack times

Learning objectives

- To make and express choices
- To interact socially

Suggested activities

- Eat any food made by the children during the activities. Talk about shape and size, e.g. circular pizzas, triangle-shaped toast, square sandwiches. Discuss quantity, e.g. Have we enough? Do we need more? Buy unsliced bread and slice it with the children. ⚠
- Give the children healthy options at snack time such as whole-wheat bread as opposed to white sliced bread.

Circle/review times

Learning objectives

- To increase the ability to listen and reflect
- To articulate feelings and preferences

Suggested activities

- Use the sentence starter 'If I had been the Little Red Hen, I would have…'
- Discuss with the children their favourite bread and why they preferred it.

The *LCP* Foundation Stage

The Little Red Hen

Outdoor play

Learning objectives

• To plant seeds, observe them as they grow and watch them eventually decay

Suggested activities

• If you have an area in your Nursery grounds that would be suitable, give the children a patch of ground where they could dig, and plant some vegetable seeds of their own!

Additional resources

The children may need to wear Wellingtons. They will need small spades, watering cans and packets of seeds

Stories and rhymes

Learning objectives

• To listen and respond to stories and rhymes

Suggested activities

Story

Farmer Duck by Martin Waddell (Walker Books)

Rhyme

'I went to the kitchen and helped Mummy cook….' from *This Little Puffin. . .* (Puffin Books)

Special visitors/events

Learning objectives

• To recognise some local features and buildings
• To be aware of different jobs held by adults

Suggested activities

• ⚠ Visit a local cake/bread shop. Talk about the variety of bread/cakes on sale. Talk about the uniforms being worn and why they are worn.
• Talk about washing hands when handling food.
• Buy something to eat for snack time!

Teddybears go shopping

How can you prepare for this activity?

- Make each child a name card. Write the initial letter in a different colour. If you have more than one child with the same initial letter, give children their own colour. Laminate the name cards.
- Make sure you have labelled children's coat pegs etc. with both their name and their own picture.
- Prepare an area to become your 'supermarket'.
- Organise a writing area.

What are the starting points?

- Talk to the children about their name. Emphasise how their name has been chosen especially for them. Show them their name card. Count how many letters are in their name. Is it a short name or a long name? Look at the initial letter. Discuss its shape.
- Play games with the name cards such as Pass the Name Cards: children sit in a circle and pass the cards until they get their name back. Play Musical Names – put the names in the centre of the circle and play music; when the music stops, children have to find their name.
- Read the story *Teddybears go shopping* by Susanna Gretz (A&C Black). Discuss the bears' names, which bear is wearing yellow and so on. This could become a memory game.

What resources do you need to collect for the focus activity?

- Collect together empty packets and play-shop tins ready for children to label.
- You will need a till, play or real coins, a shopping trolley or baskets if you have them, shopping posters, cut-out pictures of food items from magazines, and any other items you may wish to 'sell' in your supermarket.
- A selection of paper and writing materials for the writing area.
- Camera and film.

Display suggestions

- A tabletop display of the children's favourite shopping items. The children should label all the items. All attempts at writing should be valued.
- A tabletop display of all the things you would need to care for a dog, e.g. dog food, dog biscuits, a lead, a basket, a brush, a ball or toy to play with etc.
- A wall display of a supermarket with captions and labels written by the children.

Similar topics to explore

- Any role-play situation whereby the children can write labels and captions, write lists and use note pads, e.g. The Flower Shop, The Baker's Shop etc.

Home links

- Ask parents if they will take their children shopping with them. Ask them to point out items that are stocked together, e.g. the frozen foods, the fruit and vegetables, biscuits and cakes etc.

Teddybears go shopping

Learning objectives

- To make marks in a variety of media with enjoyment
- To make marks to communicate meaning
- To recognise the different purposes of writing as a means of communication – lists, captions, labels etc.
- To begin to recognise and write own name
- To begin to write own captions/labels

Activity

On all pieces of work, whether it is a painting or drawing, encourage children to write their own name. Accept and value all attempts at name writing. Give children lots of opportunities to copy their name with paper and pencils/pens/felt tips and with magnetic, plastic or sponge letters.

Read the story *Teddybears go shopping*. Discuss the names of the bears. Talk about their characteristics, e.g. Robert is yellow, Sara is orange etc.

Sit with the children in the writing area and model how to write a shopping list. Ask the children what food items the bears put on the list. Make this into a memory game: write the items down and keep checking with the storybook to see what you have forgotten. Make sure there are plenty of pads and notebooks in the writing area.

Organise a 'Supermarket' in the role-play area. Decide on a name for it, preferably one the children are used to seeing in their local area, e.g. 'Sainsbury's'.

Encourage the children to write their own labels and captions for the packets, tins etc. for the supermarket.

Make a 'Teddybears go shopping' book or posters. Encourage the children to paint or draw pictures of the bears. Act as a scribe and write sentences for the children, ask them what you could write, e.g. Louise wears a spotty coat; John had the list in his hat. Sequence the story with the children.

Take photographs of the children in the creative area painting the bears, in the writing area, and in the supermarket. Ask children to write sentences about the activities seen in the photographs and display both the photographs and the captions written by children in an area where they can be seen by the children and their parents as a means of promoting the range of activities taking place in the Nursery.

Make a tape-recorded version available in the book area.

What do the stepping stones look like?

Step 1

Draw and paint, sometimes giving meaning to marks.
Child makes marks which they will tell you is writing and may tell you what it says.

Step 2

Ascribe meaning to marks.
Child makes marks which may have some letter shapes or features of letters. They will tell you what it says.

Step 3

Begin to break the flow of speech into words. Use writing as a means of recording.
As you write, the child will dictate what s/he wants you to scribe for them.
Will copy captions and labels for their role-play.

Step 4 (Early learning goal)

Use their phonic knowledge to write simple regular words and make phonetically plausible attempts at more complex words.
Attempt writing for different purposes, using features of different forms such as lists, stories and instructions.
Write own name and other things such as labels and captions and begin to form simple sentences, sometimes using punctuation.
Child will be able to write simple sentences with familiar words/3 letter words spelt correctly. They will make a recognisable attempt at longer, more complex words.
They may put a capital letter at the start of their sentence and finish with a full stop.

Teddybears go shopping

Key questions

- Why did the bears go shopping?
- What was on their list?
- Who had the list?

Key vocabulary

- Name, write, draw, copy, picture, caption, label, sentence, list, letter, read

Targeted children

Evaluation

How did the activity go?

What evidence of children's learning have you collected?

Teddybears go shopping

Planning sheet for supplementary activities

Area of learning	Learning objective	Activity	Targeted children	Evaluation
PSED				
CLL				
Maths				
KUW				
Physical				
Creative				
Snack times				
Circle times				
Outdoor play				
Stories & rhymes				
Special visitors				

Adult role during spontaneous play sessions

Observing play ☐ _____   Supporting play areas ☐ _____

Supporting individual play ☐ _____   Involvement in play area ☐ _____

Teddybears go shopping

Personal, social and emotional development

Learning objectives

- To build relationships with other children
- To play sociably, interacting verbally with their peers and adults, using appropriate language
- To share and take turns
- To think about and care for others

Suggested activities

- Encourage children to play together in the role-play area.
- Talk to the children about caring for a pet. In the story, the bears forgot to buy the dog food. What could they feed him on instead? Discuss a pet's needs, emotional as well as physical.
- Keep a pet at Nursery and encourage the children to take turns to look after it.

Additional resources

Role-play equipment

A selection of the things a dog would need to be properly cared for

Mathematical development

Learning objectives

- To know that clocks are used to mark time
- To have an understanding of the progression of the days of the week
- To have an understanding of, and an ability to use, the language of weight – heavy/light
- To verbalise numbers by counting
- To demonstrate 1:1 matching

Suggested activities

- Set up a Nursery supermarket price all the items and display them, provide a till and money, weighing scales and telephone. Play in the supermarket with the children, modelling mathematical language. 'How much is this?' 'How many would you like?' 'Here is your change.' Put an open/closed sign on the door with a clock saying what time the supermarket opens and closes. Put a sign up saying which days of the week it is open and closed.
- Use teddybears to represent the bears in the story. Plan one-to-one matching activities such as giving each bear a scarf, hat etc.

Additional resources

Role-play equipment

Seven teddy bears

Teddybears go shopping

Knowledge and understanding of the world

Learning objectives

- To make marks to communicate meaning
- To become more aware of their immediate environment
- To know that all places are not the same

Suggested activities

- ⚠ Take small groups of children to the local supermarket to buy snack-time treats. Before you go ask the children to write a list of the items you need to get. If your Nursery is near a shopping centre or supermarket this activity should take place all year long. The children should be involved in buying anything that they will eat or use in the Nursery.

Additional resources

Notepads for writing lists, money for treats

Physical development

Learning objectives

- To develop fine motor skills and hand-eye co-ordination
- To develop independence and self-help skills

Suggested activities

- Make hats with shopping list holders. Provide the children with a selection of resources. Give help when children ask for it.

Additional resources

Strips of card or paper, sticky tape, glue, staples and a stapler, ⚠ scissors, sticky shapes, felt pens, crayons etc.

Teddybears go shopping

Creative development

Learning objectives

- To explore with colour and texture
- To have the opportunity to experience the skills involved in assembling and joining materials

Suggested activities

- Collage, print or paint the bears. Number them and ask children to write their names on them.
- Display the bears in numerical order.
- Make teddy mobiles.
- Make moving teddies: cut out each body part separately, encourage the children to decorate them and then join them together with split pins.
- Collect together a selection of teddy action songs and rhymes for children to sing and dance to.

Additional resources

Paint and collage materials

Card and fishing wire to hang mobiles and split-pins for assembling the teddies

Tapes and tape recorder

Snack times

Learning objectives

- To make and express choices

Suggested activities

- Try different kinds of ice-cream at snack time. Talk to the children about their preferences. If possible make your own ice-cream with the children.

Circle/review times

Learning objectives

- To develop increasing levels of concentration

Suggested activities

- In small groups play 'I went shopping and I bought…' Each child tells you something they have bought from the shops but they must also try and remember the items the rest of the group bought as well.

Teddybears go shopping

Supplementary activities

Outdoor play

Learning objectives

• To be aware of their own body parts

Suggested activities

• Play 'Teddy says…' (a version of 'Simon says…').

Stories and rhymes

Learning objectives

• To listen and respond to stories and rhymes

Suggested activities

Stories

Alone in the Woods by Ian Beck (Scholastic)

We're Going on a Bear Hunt by Michael Rosen and Helen Oxenbury (Mantra Publishing)

Rhymes

'Teddy bear, teddy bear, touch your toes . . .'

'When Goldilocks went to the house of the bears, what did her blue eyes see…?'

'If you go down to the woods today . . .'

Washing line

How can you prepare for this activity?

- Collect together various items of clothing which have patterns on them.
- Set up a washing line.

What are the starting points?

- Read the story: *Mrs Mopple's Washing Line* by Anita Hewett (Red Fox).

What resources do you need to collect for the focus activity?

- Items of clothing: t-shirts, gloves, socks, scarves etc, which have distinct patterns, e.g. stripes, spots, zig-zags.
- Laundry basket.
- Washing line and pegs.
- Paper shapes of t-shirts/gloves/socks/bow-ties etc. prepared for the children, paint or felt pens.

Display suggestions

- Keep the washing line on display with items pegged on.
- Put the laundry basket in the home corner for children to sort clothes, match them and peg them on the line.
- The children's own washing line of decorated paper shapes can be displayed.
- Try switching the items round or removing an item ('the wind has blown it away') and use this as a discussion point.

Similar topics to explore

- The patterns on wrapping paper.

Home links

- Ask children to find things from home with patterns on which they could talk about in Circle time.
- Ask parents to sort the washing basket with the children at home, e.g. finding pairs of socks, and to talk about any patterns on the clothing.
- Ask parents to allow children to help to load the washing machine and to switch it on.

Washing line

Learning objectives

- To create patterns using some features of letter formation
- To hold a brush or felt pen efficiently
- To practise letters in their name

Activity

After reading the story of Mrs Mopple, look at the washing in the washing basket.

Talk about the patterns on the items of clothing.

Peg the clothes on the washing line.

Draw the patterns in the air with the children.

Use fingers to draw the patterns on the floor.

Help the children by talking through the action as you do it with them.

Ask the children which is their favourite pattern.

Provide the children with a choice of t-shirt/glove/sock/scarf paper shapes which they will decorate with their favourite pattern.

Designs can be made using paints or felt pens depending on the fine motor skills of the child.

Allow the children to cut out their shapes and peg them on the washing line.

Encourage children to write their name on the back of their shape.

Key questions

- Can you tell me about the pattern?
- Can you make a pattern like it in the air?
- How can we paint these stripes/circles/spots?

Key vocabulary

- Pattern, repeat, stripes, spots, zig-zag, colours

What do the stepping stones look like?

 Step 1

Engage in activities requiring hand-eye co-ordination.
Child will demonstrate some control over their marks and is seen to be concentrating hard.

 Step 2

Draws lines and circles using gross motor movement.
Child's efforts demonstrate concentration and recognisable up/down and circular movements.

 Step 3

Begin to use anti-clockwise movement and vertical lines. Begin to form recognisable letters.
Will produce some letters of own name. Will produce vertical stripes and make circles with felt pen or paint brush.

 Step 4 (Early learning goal)

Use a pencil and hold it effectively and form recognisable letters.
The child produces a recognisable pattern using up/down and circular features.
Child will write own name independently.

Targeted children

Evaluation

How did the activity go?

What evidence of children's learning have you collected?

Washing line

Planning sheet for supplementary activities

Area of learning	Learning objective	Activity	Targeted children	Evaluation
PSED				
CLL				
Maths				
KUW				
Physical				
Creative				
Snack times				
Circle times				
Outdoor play				
Stories & rhymes				
Special visitors				

Adult role during spontaneous play sessions

Observing play ☐ _____   Supporting play areas ☐ _____

Supporting individual play ☐ _____   Involvement in play area ☐ _____

Washing line

Personal, social and emotional development

Learning objectives

- To develop an awareness of other cultures

Suggested activities

- Consider the variety of clothing worn by people in the local community who are from different cultures.
- Bring in clothing worn by people of different cultures and discuss the patterns and colours in them.
- Add the items to the role-play dressing-up box.

Additional resources

Lengths of sari material

Shalwar kamees suits

Mathematical development

Learning objectives

- To talk about patterns
- To be able to match objects – pairing

Suggested activities

- Bring in lots of pairs of clean socks or gloves to go in the laundry basket.
- Can the children talk about the patterns on them?
- Give each child a sock or glove and ask them to find another the same. Check that they know what they are looking for.

Additional resources

Lots of different pairs of socks or gloves

Washing line

Knowledge and understanding of the world

Learning objectives

- To explore what happens when washing powder is added to warm water
- To introduce the simple concept of evaporation by drying clothes
- To understand how to operate everyday household equipment

Suggested activities

- Hand wash dolls' clothes, and hang out to dry outside. Discuss how they dry.
- Wash clothes in a washing machine and tumble dry them.
- Talk about how to make the washing machine work. Discuss how the machine washes the clothes. Watch the action of washing.
- Discuss how the tumbler dries the clothes. What are the clothes like when you take them out of the machine?

Additional resources

Washing powder/liquid, dolls' clothes

Outdoor washing line and pegs

Physical development

Learning objectives

- To co-ordinate their own body
- To be aware of body movements

Suggested activities

- Make 'Twirlies': attach lengths of ribbon or long strips of crepe paper to the end of a stick. Use them to make big circle shapes, up-down patterns, zig-zags, smooth/curvy patterns. This can be an inside or outside activity!

Additional resources

Short sticks, e.g. rulers

Ribbons or strips of crepe paper/material

The LCP Foundation Stage

Washing line

Creative development

Learning objectives

• To explore and experiment making patterns in paint

Suggested activities

• Spread liquid paint on to a large piece of polythene. Allow the children to explore circular and up-down and zig-zag movements in the paint.
• The children can write their name in the paint.
• You could take a 'magic' print of their work by placing a piece of paper on the work and gently pressing down, then peeling the paper away from the polythene.

Additional resources

Liquid paint, sheets of polythene, paper for printing

Snack times

Learning objectives

• To control small, refined hand movements

Suggested activities

• Give the children small 'finger foods' to pick up with fingers to help with fine motor development.
• Allow children to pour their own drinks.

Outdoor play

Learning objectives

• To explore and experiment with different tools
• To handle tools confidently with increasing control

Suggested activities

• Provide children with a large bowl of water and different sizes of paint brushes and paint rollers. They can use them to make water patterns on the wall and ground.
• Children can fill washing-up liquid bottles with water and write their names with them on the ground.

Additional resources

Bowl of water, paintbrushes and rollers, washing-up liquid bottles

Washing line

Stories and rhymes

Learning objectives

- To enjoy and experiment with rhymes and sounds in familiar songs
- To listen and respond to stories appropriately and with pleasure

Suggested activities

Story

Mrs Lather's Laundry by Allan Ahlberg & André Amstutz (Puffin Books)

Rhyme

'This is the way we wash our clothes...' from *This Little Puffin. . .* (Puffin Books)

Special visitors/events

Learning objectives

- To be aware that people have different clothing and customs

Suggested activities

- The festivals of Diwali or Eid provide the opportunity to look at clothing worn by people of different cultures.
- At this time, you could also make mendhi patterns with children.

Mathematical development

- Treasure hunt

- Caterpillars

- Patterns

Foundation

Treasure hunt

How can you prepare for this activity?

- You need to gather together collections of small objects for 'treasure', e.g. shells, shiny pebbles, buttons.
- Each child will need a small container, e.g. foil dish.
- Prepare numbered cards, e.g. 1-5 or 1-10 depending on ability of children.
- Hide the treasure in the sand tray.

What are the starting points?

- Show the children some of the treasure and tell them that Teddy has hidden some more in the sand tray.

What resources do you need to collect for the focus activity?

- Objects for treasure, Teddy, foil containers, number cards.

Display suggestions

- Make a collection of attractive boxes with treasure inside, e.g. necklaces, bangles.
- Allow children to make treasure and jewels to add to the treasure trove.
- Make 'gold coins' and add to a treasure box.
- Display treasure and boxes on a table draped with rich coloured or textured cloth.

Similar topics to explore

- You can use anything to add to the sand tray for a similar hunt.
- You could set up a similar activity using fishing nets in the water tray.

Home links

- Ask parents or carers to play treasure hunts with their children.
- Give each child a card with a number on; the child needs to find that number of treasure items at home.
- Children can draw pictures of the items they have found and bring them into Nursery.

Foundation

Treasure hunt

Learning objectives

- To recognise numbers
- To be able to count a group of objects

Activity

Hide the treasure in the sand. You will need to hide about five objects for each person in the group.

Everyone should have a container and hunt for treasure, including the adults!

When all the treasure has been found, count your treasures by showing the children how you line them up as you count them.

The children then count their treasures in the same way.

Count the total number of objects each child has in his/her container and encourage the children to find the correct number card.

Children can practise writing the number in the sand. You will need to demonstrate this first for correct formation.

Some children could be asked to record their results. Allow them to choose how they do this.

Hide the treasure again.

Key questions

- How many have you found?
- How many have you got now?
- Can you find the right number?
- Can you write the number?

Key vocabulary

- Count, number names, how many?

Evaluation

How did the activity go?

What evidence of children's learning have you collected?

What do the stepping stones look like?

 Step 1

Show an interest in numbers and counting. Use some number names and language spontaneously.
Child may use number names but not in 1:1 correspondence.

 Step 2

Uses some names accurately. Willingly attempts to count, with some numbers in the correct order.
Child counts along with the practitioner and uses some number names correctly.

 Step 3

Counts up to 3 or 4 objects, saying one number name for each. Recognises some numerals of personal significance. Begins to represent numbers using marks on paper or pictures. Recognises numerals 1-5 or more.
Counts out up to 6 objects. Selects the correct numeral 1-5 or beyond. Can count an irregular arrangement of objects.
Child can count treasures up to 10, but may need some assistance. Can recognise most numerals.

 Step 4 (Early learning goal)

Say and use number names in order. Count reliably up to 10 objects. Can recognise the numerals 1-10.
Child counts objects independently to 10 and beyond.
Can recognise all numerals to 10.
Can draw the correct number of items found and write the numeral.

Targeted children

Treasure hunt

Planning sheet for supplementary activities

Area of learning	Learning objective	Activity	Targeted children	Evaluation
PSED				
CLL				
Maths				
KUW				
Physical				
Creative				
Snack times				
Circle times				
Outdoor play				
Stories & rhymes				
Special visitors				

Adult role during spontaneous play sessions

Observing play ☐ _____   Supporting play areas ☐ _____

Supporting individual play ☐ _____   Involvement in play area ☐ _____

Treasure hunt

Personal, social and emotional development

Learning objectives

- To have respect for feelings of others and their property

Suggested activities

- Each day ask a child to bring in a special treasure from home to show the group. Talk about why it is special to the child.
- Talk about how we look after special things.

Additional resources

You could start this off with a special object of your own

Communication, language and literacy

Learning objectives

- To build up children's vocabulary when describing familiar objects
- To interact and negotiate with others
- Use language to imagine roles

Suggested activities

- Set up a 'Kings and Queens' prop box. Use descriptive words such as shiny, sparkly, golden etc. to describe the items in the box.

Additional resources

Crowns, jewellery, chains, silver trays, capes, cloaks, special tea-sets (spray plastic cups and paper plates with gold spray), throne draped with velvet cloth

Boxes of 'gold' and 'silver' coins

Knowledge and understanding of the world

Learning objectives

- To select appropriate resources and tools for a purpose

Suggested activities

- Make treasure boxes from recycled boxes. Let the children paint or decorate them with a variety of materials of their choice. Encourage them to talk about what they are doing and the materials they are using.

Additional resources

A variety of boxes for children to make into treasure boxes and materials for decorating

Treasure hunt

Physical development

Learning objectives

- To be able to control movement, speed and sound

Suggested activities

- Practise creeping very quietly.
- Practise listening to the sound made when a bag of treasure is moved.
- Play the game 'King's Treasure': children sit in a circle and one child is selected to guard the bag of treasure for the king. This child is blindfolded. Choose a child to try to creep up to collect the treasure bag without being heard. The blindfolded guard tries to point at the direction of any sounds.

Additional resources

Scarf for blindfold, bag of objects that rattle if moved!

Creative development

Learning objectives

- To explore and experiment with materials

Suggested activities

- Children draw a numeral in glue on black sugar paper, then shake glitter over the glue to make sparkly numerals.

Additional resources

Black sugar paper, glitter

Snack times

Learning objectives

- Use counting and numbers for a real-life purpose

Suggested activities

- Count how many children there are for drinks/biscuits at snack time.
- Ask a child to write the number and collect the correct number of cups/biscuits.

Treasure hunt

Supplementary activities

Circle/review times

Learning objectives

- To give a context for counting
- To review their activities and take turns

Suggested activities

- Pick a number for the day, e.g. 4. Pass a teddy round the circle and count as he is passed on. The child where the count stops at number 4 can review his/her activities. Carry on round the circle.

Outdoor play

Learning objectives

- To recognise numerals in real-life situations

Suggested activities

- Give the bikes numerals so that children start to identify their chosen bike to ride.
- Create numbered bike parks so that the bikes are parked in the corresponding bay.

Stories and rhymes

Learning objectives

- To listen to and respond to traditional stories and rhymes

Suggested activities

Story

Jack and the Beanstalk (traditional)

Rhyme

'There was a princess long ago' from *This Little Puffin...* (Puffin Books)

Special visitors/events

Learning objectives

- To explore the environment
- To talk about their experiences

Suggested activities

- Hold a treasure hunt in your setting. Hide a variety of interesting objects for the children to find inside and outside.
- The children can then talk about what items they found, and where they found them.

Caterpillars

How can you prepare for this activity?

- You will need to prepare some green and yellow playdough or Plasticine.
- Collect some large green leaves from the garden (or make some from green sugar paper).
- If possible, collect some caterpillars in a covered fish bowl with their source of food.

What are the starting points?

- Read the story *The Very Hungry Caterpillar* by Eric Carle (Mantra).

What resources do you need to collect for the focus activity?

- Playdough or Plasticine.
- Leaves: 1 for each child.
- 1 very large leaf.
- Dice: this could be a conventional 1-6 number or spot dice, or make your own using just 0, 1, 2.
- Small circles of card to make a face for the caterpillar!

Display suggestions

- When the children have made the caterpillars, they can be used in a display on a shelf, with a simple caption, e.g. 'James has made a caterpillar with 5 segments'.

Similar topics to explore

- Read *The Bad-Tempered Ladybird* by Eric Carle (Puffin Books) and adapt the activities.

Home links

- Look for caterpillars and butterflies in the garden.

Foundation

Caterpillars

Main activity

Learning objectives

- To use the language of counting and addition
- To develop strategies for counting: showing 1:1 correspondence
- To be aware of quantity
- To be able to recognise some numerals

Activity

After sharing the story *The Very Hungry Caterpillar* with the children, talk about the caterpillar and how, as it eats, it grows bigger. Compare the size and number of segments of the caterpillar through the book.

The following activity involves children making caterpillars of their own.

You will need to show them how to roll the playdough to make the segments, join them together and place the caterpillar on the leaf.

As you do this, talk through and count the number of segments: 'and here is one more, so that makes …'

Encourage the children to count with you.

Some children will want to and should be allowed to then play with the playdough, whilst you talk it through for them, giving them the mathematical language and counting with them.

For some children this can be developed into a game:

Make lots of segments of playdough which can be kept on a large leaf in the centre.

Each child rolls a dice and collects the number of segments represented on the dice to add to their caterpillar on their leaf.

Count the number of segments together each time.

Children can make a face for their caterpillar.

Talk about how many segments are left in the centre store.

Key questions

- How many have you got?
- How many more are you putting on?

Key vocabulary

- Counting names: one, two, etc.
- more, another, and…
- …altogether, total

What do the stepping stones look like?

 Step 1

Compare two groups of objects, saying when they have the same number.
Child playing with the dough comments 'I've got more than you' or asks for more.

 Step 2

Shows an interest in number problems.
Child talks about number of segments on caterpillar with some accuracy of counting and use of number names. Will talk about 'another one' or 'one more'.

 Step 3

Finds the total by counting items in the group. Says with confidence the number that is one more than a given number.
Child knows s/he has 4 segments on caterpillar and that another one will make 5.

 Step 4 (Early learning goal)

In practical activities and discussion begin to use the vocabulary involved with adding and subtracting.
Use language such as more/less to compare two numbers.
Begin to relate addition to combining two groups of objects.
Child will talk about having more than another child.
Will keep counting as s/he adds more segments.

Targeted children

Evaluation

How did the activity go?

What evidence of children's learning have you collected?

Caterpillars

Planning sheet for supplementary activities

Area of learning	Learning objective	Activity	Targeted children	Evaluation
PSED				
CLL				
Maths				
KUW				
Physical				
Creative				
Snack times				
Circle times				
Outdoor play				
Stories & rhymes				
Special visitors				

Adult role during spontaneous play sessions

Observing play ☐ _____

Supporting play areas ☐ _____

Supporting individual play ☐ _____

Involvement in play area ☐ _____

Caterpillars

Personal, social and emotional development

Learning objectives

- To show curiosity
- To experience a sense of awe and wonder
- To respect and care for living things and the environment

Suggested activities

- If possible, watch a caterpillar and talk about being gentle when handling it, and staying quiet so as not to frighten it.
- Watch it move and feed.
- Talk about why you need to return the caterpillars back to their own environment.
- In *The Very Hungry Caterpillar* story, the caterpillar gets fatter and fatter and then gets tummy ache. Talk about what it feels like when the children have tummy ache, and what makes them feel better.

Additional resources

Caterpillars in a transparent container, with the source of food

Communication, language and literacy

Learning objectives

- To listen and respond to stories and rhymes
- To be aware that print carries meaning
- To enjoy using language when talking about a story
- To be aware of how books are organised

Suggested activities

- Read the story of *The Very Hungry Caterpillar* to the group, using the big book version.
- Talk about what happens to the caterpillar as he eats and eats and gets bigger and bigger.
- Talk about what he eats each day and how he feels.
- Make a book with the children: 'The very, very, very hungry caterpillar' making up other food items that he could eat. The children could draw or cut out pictures from magazines for this. Add a simple caption, e.g. 'The caterpillar ate a huge banana.'
- Allow children to write their own captions where possible.

Additional resources

Pictures of the food eaten by the caterpillar
The Very Hungry Caterpillar by Eric Carle – big book version

Caterpillars

Knowledge and understanding of the world

Learning objectives

- To explore and investigate the natural world
- To observe and talk about caterpillars
- To take care of caterpillars

Suggested activities

- When talking about the story, follow what happens to the caterpillar from egg→caterpillar→chrysalis →butterfly.
- In small groups, use a magnifying glass to look at a caterpillar and talk about it – what it looks like, how it moves, where it moves.
- From observations, children can draw a caterpillar. Remind the children to look carefully at different features.

Additional resources

Magnifying glasses

Creative development

Learning objectives

- To represent in paintings, models, and other media

Suggested activities

- Children make caterpillars with egg-boxes/collage/paint.
- Children could cut out leaves for the caterpillars to climb/rest on/hide under etc.
- Make caterpillar food with salt dough and paint it.
- Print caterpillars with sponges or circular objects.
- Paint butterflies.
- These models and paintings could be used to make a display.

Additional resources

Collage materials, recyclable materials, sponges, salt dough, paint

Caterpillars

Physical development

Learning objectives

- To move in different ways and different directions
- To be able to move at different speeds
- To be aware of own and others' personal space

Suggested activities

- Set up a caterpillar trail: children have to move over, under, through, along obstacles as if they were a caterpillar hunting for its favourite food.
- Curl up in a space to sleep as a chrysalis.
- Emerge from the chrysalis as a beautiful butterfly.
- Flit and flutter like butterflies.

Additional resources

Small equipment that children can slide under, along, over, through, round

Snack times

Learning objectives

- To be aware of healthy food
- To be aware that food helps us to grow

Suggested activities

- Try different fruit and vegetables each day. Talk about whether the children like them and how we all need food to grow.

Circle/review times

Learning objectives

- To be able to take turns
- To talk about their feelings when they are unwell

Suggested activities

- Use the caterpillar puppet to pass round to identify whose turn it is to talk.
- Use the caterpillar puppet to talk about feeling poorly and what we can do if someone is unwell.

Additional resources

Caterpillar puppet made from a spare green sock!

Caterpillars

Stories and rhymes

Learning objectives

- To listen to stories and rhymes
- To join in with familiar rhymes

Suggested activities

Rhymes

'Caterpillar' by Delphine Evans from *First Verses* (Oxford University Press) compiled by John Foster.

'Little Arabella Miller' from *This Little Puffin...* (Puffin Books)

'Who's that tickling my back?' from *This Little Puffin...* (Puffin Books)

Patterns

How can you prepare for this activity?

- Collect together patterned wrapping paper, wallpaper pattern books, clothing with patterns on, patterned fabrics.
- Collect lots of patterned socks.
- Bring household objects with patterns on, e.g. mugs, plates, etc.
- Make sets of squares, triangles, circles and rectangles from wrapping paper and mount on cards. Laminate or cover them in sticky-backed plastic.

What are the starting points?

- Look at the variety of patterns on children's clothing and on objects brought from home. Talk about patterns such as stripes, spots, zig-zags (known as geometric patterns) and repeating patterns.
- Draw these patterns in the air with the children.

What resources do you need to collect for the focus activity?

- You will need some sheets of patterned wrapping paper – two of each pattern.
- Make some shapes, e.g. circles, squares and triangles from wrapping paper for matching and sorting.
- Cut paper into shapes, e.g. sock, t-shirt, glove, hat, etc.

Display suggestions

- A washing line of patterned clothes made by the children.
- A collection of patterned objects brought from home.

Similar topics to explore

- Patterns in nature.

Home links

- Ask parents to help children to look for patterns at home: on tiles in the bathroom or kitchen, on curtains and on clothing, bedding, household objects.
- Suggest that children help to sort the washing and to pair up socks.
- The children could bring in some patterned items from home to add to the pattern display.

The *LCP* Foundation Stage

Patterns

Main activity

Learning objectives

- To talk about patterns
- To recognise pattern in a variety of situations
- To recognise and continue a sequential pattern

Activity

Talk about patterns on the children's own clothing.

Look at sheets of patterned wrapping paper.

Talk about the prepared shapes and match them to the corresponding wrapping paper sheet.

Sort all the shapes by pattern.

Play games such as 'pairs' and 'snap'.

If you have made a variety of shapes from the paper, you could make simple repeating patterns for the children to copy and continue. Some children could make their own repeating patterns, e.g. circle, triangle, circle, triangle….

Sort clothing according to patterns.

Children can paint patterns on the paper clothes shapes; these could be pegged on to a washing line to make a display.

Key questions

- What can you tell me about the pattern on your…?
- What shapes can you see?
- What comes next in the pattern?
- How can we sort these…?
- Can you find another that matches this?

Key vocabulary

- Pattern, sort, match

What do the stepping stones look like?

 Step 1

Show awareness of similarities in shapes in the environment.

Child can talk about shapes and how they are arranged. S/he will talk about geometrical patterns (stripes/spots) on their clothing.

 Step 2

Show interest by talking about arrangements.

Child will recognise and talk about a repeated pattern. S/he is able to recognise, find and talk about geometric patterns on wrapping paper.

 Step 3

Show awareness of symmetry.

Children can recognise and continue a pattern started for them.

 Step 4 (Early learning goal)

Talk about, recognise and recreate simple patterns.

Child can make up own simple repeating pattern.

Targeted children

Evaluation

How did the activity go?

What evidence of children's learning have you collected?

Patterns

Planning sheet for supplementary activities

Area of learning	Learning objective	Activity	Targeted children	Evaluation
PSED				
CLL				
Maths				
KUW				
Physical				
Creative				
Snack times				
Circle times				
Outdoor play				
Stories & rhymes				
Special visitors				

Adult role during spontaneous play sessions

Observing play ☐ _____

Supporting play areas ☐ _____

Supporting individual play ☐ _____

Involvement in play area ☐ _____

Patterns

Personal, social and emotional development

Learning objectives

- To develop an awareness of other cultures and beliefs

Suggested activities

- Look at clothing from different cultures, e.g. saris, shalwar kamees.
- Look at patterns on fabrics from other countries, e.g. Jamaica. Link to stories such as *Handa's Surprise*.
- Talk about mendhi and rangoli patterns.
- Draw round children's hands and make mendhi patterns on the drawings with felt pens.

Additional resources

Fabrics and clothing, felt pens

The story *Handa's Surprise* by Eileen Browne (Walker Books)

Communication, language and literacy

Learning objectives

- To explore and experiment with words and sounds
- To enjoy using language
- To associate sounds with patterns and rhymes

Suggested activities

- Make up patterns with sounds or words, e.g.

  shhh, pop, shhh, pop, shhh, pop . . .

  Tick, tock, tick, tock . . .

  Oo, ah, oo, ah . . .

Patterns

Knowledge and understanding of the world

Learning objectives

- To be aware of patterns in the environment
- To be able to use a computer programme to make own pictures

Suggested activities

- Look at pictures of tigers, zebras, fish etc. and talk about the patterns you can see.
- Children could do paintings of either tropical fish or jungle animals. Add these to the pattern display.
- Read a simple version of the story *101 Dalmatians* by Dodie Smith (Ladybird Books).
- Use a basic paint programme on the computer to generate patterns of stripes/spots or repeating patterns.

Additional resources

Books showing wild animals

Computer programme such as 'paintspa'

The story *101 Dalmatians*

Physical development

Learning objectives

- To be able to co-ordinate own body
- To move with confidence

Suggested activities

- Explore patterns and sequences of movements for the children to copy, e.g. marching to a rhythmic left-right chant; jumping in/out of hoops.
- Singing games such as 'Skip to my Lou', 'In and out the dusty bluebells', 'Hokey-cokey', 'There was a princess long ago', all of which have repeated lines.

Additional resources

Hoops, marching music

Patterns

Creative development

Learning objectives

- To reproduce colour and patterns
- To explore and experiment with paint
- To select tools to use

Suggested activities

- Provide shapes cut out of paper, e.g. squares, rectangles, triangles and circles. Each child is to choose a shape to use. Allow child to select thickness of paintbrush and colour of paint, and to paint a pattern such as stripes, spots, zig-zags on the paper shape.
- Give each child a sheet of polythene and provide thick paint for the child to paint all over the polythene. Children then choose a tool to use to make a pattern with in the paint. When each child is happy with the result, take a print of the pattern on a sheet of paper.

Additional resources

Pieces of thick polythene and thick paint

Tools such as sticks, wide/narrow tooth combs, forks, or just fingers!!

Paintbrushes of different thickness and paper for printing

Paper shapes

Snack times

Learning objectives

- To explore pattern in everyday objects
- To make repeating patterns

Suggested activities

- Provide patterned paper plates and cups.
- Use different coloured cups and put them out in a repeating pattern.

Additional resources

Patterned paper plates and cups; different coloured cups

Circle/review times

Learning objectives

- To be able to take turns

Suggested activities

- Make patterns with words. Start with a word, e.g. 'run' and go round the circle with each child saying the word in turn.
- Introduce another word, e.g. 'walk'. Go round the circle with the children saying 'run', 'walk' alternately.
- Let the children choose new words to pass round.

Patterns

Outdoor play

Learning objectives

- To explore pattern in environment

Suggested activities

- Have a pattern hunt round the Nursery. Encourage the children to look for patterns outside, e.g. on the brickwork.
- Provide large building blocks for children to build walls outside.

Additional resources

Large building blocks for wall building

Stories and rhymes

Learning objectives

- To explore patterns in repetitious stories and rhymes
- To look for patterns in the pictures of favourite stories
- To recognise repeated words and phrases in stories and rhymes

Suggested activities

Stories

Dear Zoo by Rod Campbell (Campbell Books)

Mrs Mopple's Washing Line by Anita Hewitt (Red Fox)

Peace at Last by Jill Murphy (Macmillan Children's Books)

We're Going on a Bear Hunt by M. Rosen and H. Oxenbury (Mantra Publishing)

Stripe stories by Joanne Partis (Oxford University Press)

Rhymes

'The wheels on the bus go round and round'

Any other stories and rhymes that have repetition in them.

Special visitors/events

Learning objectives

- To be aware that different people have different customs

Suggested activities

- Explore the Festival of Divali and the Rangoli/mendhi patterns linked to Divali.

The *LCP* Foundation Stage

Knowledge and understanding of the world

- Snails

- Water

- The Three Billy Goats Gruff

- On and off!

- Birthdays

- Little Red Riding Hood

- A new baby – what shall we call it?

Foundation

Snails

How can you prepare for this activity?

- It would be best to plan this activity for September after a rainy spell.
- Tell the children not to pick up any other mini-beasts or plants without asking because they could get bitten or stung.
- Talk to the children about the places they might find snails - in the long grass, under leaves or stones, at the side of walls or in holes in walls.
- Before taking the children out on your walk, talk to them about caring for the environment - not walking all over plants and flowers, not dropping litter.
- Explain that they must handle any snails they find gently, and that they will be returning the snails back to their home later.
- Make sure you collect enough greenery to feed the snails while they are in the Nursery.
- ⚠ Make sure the children wash their hands when they have finished handling the snails.

What are the starting points?

- Take the children on a snail hunt in the Nursery gardens or in a local park.

What resources do you need to collect for the focus activity?

- Large containers to carry snails in, magnifying glasses and a camera.

Display suggestions

- Make a garden collage.
- Display photographs taken on the snail hunt. Display children's observational drawings or paintings of snails. Make a tabletop display of magnifying glasses, stones, leaves etc.

Similar topics to explore

- Ladybirds, worms, caterpillars, spiders etc.

Home links

- Ask parents if anyone has a tortoise they could bring into Nursery for the children to observe.

Snails

Learning objectives

- To explore and investigate the natural environment
- To observe closely and identify similarities, differences, patterns and change
- To classify according to certain criteria, e.g. creatures that live inside shells
- To talk about what they have seen
- To talk about what they are doing, seeing and touching
- To treat living things with care

Activity

Take children on a snail hunt and take photos.

Take the snails back to Nursery and allow the children lots of time to observe the snails closely.

Talk to them about their observations.

Use the magnifying glasses and discuss the body features they are observing. Can they name the body parts they are observing?

Talk about where snails live, what they eat and how they move.

Talk about the shell and look at the patterns on the shell.

Tell the children how the shell becomes the snail's home and its protection from predators.

Find information books and pictures about other creatures that live in shells such as tortoises, crabs, and sea urchins.

Set up a fish tank with pond snails for the children to observe.

Key questions

- Where did we find them?
- What does it feel like?
- How does it move?
- Has it got legs?
- Where is its home?

Key vocabulary

- Shell, body, spiral, pattern, stalks, feelers, slimy, slither, trail, move, live

Evaluation

How did the activity go?

What evidence of children's learning have you collected?

What do the stepping stones look like?

 Step 1

Show curiosity and interest by facial expression, movement or sound.
Child shows excitement by pointing at the snail, peering closely at it.

 Step 2

Show curiosity, observe and manipulate objects. Describe simple features of objects and events.
Child wants to touch the snail/shell, talks about it to others, points out its mouth, nose etc.

 Step 3

Examine objects and living things to find out more about them.
Child talks about the unusual features, its eye-stalks, shell, trail, movement; asks questions, wants to know where it came from, where it is going; looks for books about snails.

 Step 4 (Early learning goal)

Investigate objects and materials by using all of their senses as appropriate.
Find out about and identify some features of living things, objects and events they observe.
Child will talk about the shell and feelers. S/he will comment on the way snails move and the trail of slime left behind.

Targeted children

The LCP Foundation Stage

Snails

Area of learning	Learning objective	Activity	Targeted children	Evaluation
PSED				
CLL				
Maths				
KUW				
Physical				
Creative				
Snack times				
Circle times				
Outdoor play				
Stories & rhymes				
Special visitors				

Adult role during spontaneous play sessions

Observing play ☐ _____ Supporting play areas ☐ _____

Supporting individual play ☐ _____ Involvement in play area ☐ _____

Snails

Personal, social and emotional development

Learning objectives

- To care for living things

Suggested activities

- Talk to the children about careful handling of the snails. Demonstrate careful handling. Explain why the snails need to be returned to their natural habitat.
- Talk about the shell being the snail's home. Discuss the children's homes, as somewhere they feel safe and secure.

Communication, language and literacy

Learning objectives

- To use talk to plan, question and reflect on experiences
- To sequence events
- To recognise the different purposes of writing as a means of communication
- To make marks in a variety of media with enjoyment

Suggested activities

- Take photographs on the snail hunt. When they have been developed, sequence them with the children. Ask the children what they did first, next, etc. Make a book about the snail hunt with the children and stick the photographs in. Scribe captions for the children or encourage them to write their own. Decide on a title for your 'information' book and display it where parents can see it.
- Encourage children to make snail-trail patterns in wet sand, with shaving foam, in paint on a table surface with their fingers, or in the writing area with pens, crayons, felt pens etc.

Additional resources

A selection of writing materials in the writing area, shaving foam, paint, sand

Snails

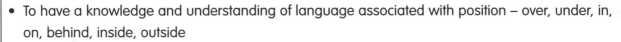

Mathematical development

Learning objectives

- To have a knowledge and understanding of language associated with position – over, under, in, on, behind, inside, outside
- To be able to match and sort
- To make comparisons when exploring shape - circles

Suggested activities

- Use positional language, e.g. the snail puts his head **in/out** of the shell etc. Discuss size - how small mini-beasts are in comparison to the children and how small the children are in comparison to an elephant for instance.
- Use sets of plastic mini-beasts for sorting.
- Cut out a selection of circles in different colours, sizes and textures and encourage the children to glue them one on top of another starting with the largest, ending with the smallest, and creating a spiral shape.

Additional resources

Sets of plastic mini-beasts, pre-cut circles of different colours, sizes and textures

Physical development

Learning objectives

- To begin to move with confidence
- To gain control over their own body
- To begin to show movement in imaginative ways

Suggested activities

- Plan lots of slow movement activities – slithering and sliding, creeping and crawling, over and under, in and out, curling and stretching.
- Draw pathways on the floor with chalk; encourage the children to imagine they are following the slimy trail a snail has left behind.

Additional resources

Chalk

Snails

Creative development

Learning objectives

- To explore and experiment with colour and texture
- To explore shape, form and space in 2 and 3 dimensions
- To observe features of snails and represent these observations
- To plan and produce work in different forms

Suggested activities

- Use salt dough, clay or Plasticine to create models of snails. Encourage children to paint or draw pictures of snails. Tell them to look closely, using magnifying glasses, to observe the patterns and lines on the shell. Talk to the children about the type of lines they can see: straight or curved. Encourage the children to paint pictures with lots of spiral movements; use a painting turntable if you have one. A cake display plate can be used if not!
- Collage snails, using tissue paper, pasta shapes or wool wound round in a spiral shape. Use pipe cleaners for the eye stalks.
- Use string dipped in white paint and make snail trails on black or coloured paper.
- Make snail paperweights as presents to take home. Paint, decorate and varnish large stones, wrap in tissue paper and send home.

Additional resources

A selection of malleable materials, collage materials, different thicknesses and textures of paint, string, large stones etc.

Snack times

Learning objectives

- To make children aware of healthy options

Suggested activities

- Prepare, with the children, crunchy snacks e.g. carrot, cucumber and celery sticks. Make some mayonnaise dips, adding a small drop of green food colouring to the dip. Ask the children to suggest their own names for the dip!

Circle/review times

Learning objectives

- To initiate, share and sustain conversation with others

Suggested activities

- Show snail paperweights made in **Creative development** activity. Encourage the children to tell each other how they were made and whom they are for.

Snails

Outdoor play

Learning objectives

- To be aware that small creatures live in the local environment

Suggested activities

- Designate a wildlife area outside for mini-beasts; collect logs, plant pots, roof tiles etc. to provide shelter for them.
- Regularly visit the area. Dig up a square of turf; examine it with a magnifying glass, looking for insects and bugs. Lift up pots and tiles and examine any creatures underneath them.

Stories and rhymes

Learning objectives

- To listen and respond to stories, songs and rhymes

Suggested activities

Stories

The Best Bug Parade by Stuart J. Murphy (Harper Collins Publishers)

The Bad-Tempered Ladybird by Eric Carle (Puffin)

The Hungry Caterpillar by Eric Carle (Mantra Publishing)

Rhyme

'Under a stone where the earth was firm' from *This Little Puffin. . .* (Puffin Books)

Special visitors/events

Suggested activities

- Organise a visit to a nature reserve if there is one in your locality.

Water

How can you prepare for this activity?

- Water play should be a well-resourced ongoing activity in a nursery setting. Any focused activities may need extra resources and these should be collected together well in advance.
- This topic should be planned for the summer months so that some of the activities could take place outside.
- Organise a visit to an aquarium.

What are the starting points?

- Talk to the children about water, and what we use water for: drinking, cooking, to wash with, in the bath, in a swimming pool etc.
- Read *Swim, Polar Bear, Swim!* by Joan Stimson (Scholastic).
- Discuss with the children where water comes from. Talk about clouds and the rain.

What resources do you need to collect for the focus activity?

- A large water tray and plastic aprons.
- A selection of water toys, all sorted and clearly labelled in separate boxes –
  1. Objects that will float or sink, such as corks, sponges, plastic bottles - some with their lids on and some with their lids off - foil containers, table-tennis balls, pieces of wood, Plasticine balls, plastic bricks, cotton reels, plastic egg trays etc.
  2. Objects that will move the water, such as spoons, whisks, funnels, water-wheels, siphons, jugs, squeezy bottles, sieves, potato mashers, slotted spoons, measuring spoons, different widths and lengths of plastic tubing, straws etc.
  3. Different materials such as paper, card, plastic, foil etc. to make boats.
  4. Small-world toys such as boats, shells, pebbles, people, fish and sea creatures.
  5. Objects that water runs through such as sieves, colanders, a watering can and plastic containers with holes in etc.
- A selection of food colourings, nice-smelling oils and soap flakes to add to the water.
- Ice cube trays, containers to freeze water in, ice lolly moulds.
- Jellies and jelly moulds.
- Tea-leaves, kettle, teapot, tea-strainer, cup/mug.

Water

Display suggestions

- A 'seaside' collage.
- A display of bubble prints.
- A tabletop display of objects that float and objects that sink, with captions.
- A display of photographs of children playing in different-coloured water or with bubbles, all with captions explaining what the children are doing, for parents to see.

Similar topics to explore

- There are many aspects of the water theme to explore; you could look more closely at the seaside, ponds, rain, snow etc.

Home links

- Suggest to the parents that they take their children swimming or that they arrange swimming lessons for their children.
- Ask them to discuss the dangers of water with their children.

Foundation

Water

Main activity

Learning objectives

- To observe closely and identify similarities, differences, pattern and change
- To talk about what they have seen
- To talk about what they are doing, seeing, hearing, tasting, touching
- To ask relevant questions about why things happen and how things work

Activity

Fill the water tray with warm water and soap flakes to make bubbles. Ask the children to move the water. Suggest blowing. Suggest they move their hands from side to side and backwards and forwards, with their fingers open and then shut. Can they make ripples? Can they think of other ways to move water? What happens? How does the water feel?

Give the children a selection of objects that move the water, e.g. water-wheels etc.

Allow the children time to play and experiment.

Give the children a selection of objects that sink and float. Talk about which objects float and which ones sink. Can the children make objects that sink?

Can they make objects that float? Can they make boats using different materials and containers?

Add different scented oils for the children to smell.

Change the colour of the water. Add two colours to find out what colour they make.

Make different-coloured ice cubes. Look at the patterns made by the food colouring in the ice cubes.

Empty the ice cubes into the water tray and watch them melt. Discuss with the children the changes taking place. Fill other containers such as yoghurt pots, rubber gloves or a balloon with water and freeze them. Look at the strange shapes they make and watch them melt. Make ice-lollies.

Make jellies.

Make a cup of tea. Show the children the tea-leaves. Encourage them to touch and smell them. ⚠ Boil a kettle away from the children and add to the teapot. Use a tea-strainer and pour out a cup of tea. Talk to the children about the changes that have taken place.

What do the stepping stones look like?

 Step 1

Explore objects.
Show an interest in why things happen and how things work.
Plays and splashes in the water. Gets excited when sees effect of action.
Watches other children and adults as they explore boat making.
Wants to help make jelly etc.

 Step 2

Sort objects by one function.
Talk about what is seen and what is happening.
Child explores and will be able to talk about which objects go to the bottom and those that stay on the top whilst demonstrating effects to you.
Will notice the ice melting and comment.

 Step 3

Notice and comment on patterns.
Show an awareness of change.
Is fascinated by changes, e.g. watching the ice melt and asks about what happens. Will comment on what happens when colouring is added to water or when tea is strained.

 Step 4 (Early learning goal)

Look closely at similarities, differences, pattern and change.
Ask questions about why things happen and how things work.
May show an interest in the tea-strainer and will want to try other similar situations, e.g. sifting stones from sand.
Will make links between water and ice and the process water has gone through when making tea. May ask why the ice melts.

The LCP Foundation Stage

Water

Key questions

- Does it float? Sink?
- Can you move the water?
- How does it feel?
- What happens when….?

Key vocabulary

- Splash, ripple, trickle, soak, full, empty, spill, pour, melt, hot, cold, float, sink, bubbles, changes

Targeted children

Evaluation

How did the activity go?

What evidence of children's learning have you collected?

Water

Planning sheet for supplementary activities

Area of learning	Learning objective	Activity	Targeted children	Evaluation
PSED				
CLL				
Maths				
KUW				
Physical				
Creative				
Snack times				
Circle times				
Outdoor play				
Stories & rhymes				
Special visitors				

Adult role during spontaneous play sessions

Observing play ☐ _____

Supporting play areas ☐ _____

Supporting individual play ☐ _____

Involvement in play area ☐ _____

The *LCP* Foundation Stage

Water

Personal, social and emotional development

Learning objectives

- To be aware of danger
- To develop a sense of their own safety
- To be aware of personal hygiene

Suggested activities

- Discuss water safety – taking care by canals, at the seaside, at the swimming pool etc. Why do we learn to swim? If we can't swim, what should we wear in the water: arm bands, rubber rings, life jackets etc.
- Discuss bath time. Do the children like having a bath? What do they take in the bath with them? Collect together a selection of soaps. Smell them and test them. Make lather with them. Do they make a better lather with hot or cold water? What do we dry our hands on? Test different materials for absorbency.

Additional resources

A selection of soaps

A selection of materials for drying hands such as a towel, paper, plastic, a woollen garment etc.

Communication, language and literacy

Learning objectives

- To listen and respond to rhymes
- To interact verbally with peers and adults
- To explore and experiment with words and learn new vocabulary

Suggested activities

- Sing and learn the actions to 'I'm a Little Teapot' and ' Polly, put the kettle on'.
- Talk about the seaside. Collect together pictures of sea creatures and spend time naming different fish, sea animals and shells. Buy a fish such as a mackerel and let the children feel and smell it. Question them about how it feels and smells. Dissect it with the children. Name the body parts such as fins, gills, eyes, scales, bones.

Additional resources

A fresh fish

A collection of shells and pictures of the seaside

Water

Mathematical development

Learning objectives

- To have an understanding of, and the ability to use, the language of capacity – full/empty
- To verbalise numbers by counting
- To begin to show an awareness of number operations, e.g. subtraction
- To begin to show an awareness of 'pairs'

Suggested activities

- Put a selection of pouring jugs in the water tray and encourage the children to discuss 'full' and 'empty'.
- Sing 'Five Little Ducks' with the children. Use the water tray and place plastic ducks on the water; fish one duck out each time a duck swims away.
- Tell the children the story of *Noah's Ark*. Talk about the animals being grouped in twos.

Additional resources

A selection of pouring jugs, cups and containers

One large plastic duck and five smaller ones

Noah's Ark story (traditional)

Physical development

Learning objectives

- To develop refined hand movements
- To take part in role-play with increasing confidence and imagination

Suggested activities

- Wash the dolls and dolls' clothes. Put up a washing line and help the children to peg the washing on the line. Use language such as squeezing, wringing, rubbing and scrubbing.
- Role-play a 'Car Wash' scenario and encourage the children to wash all the bikes, scooters, prams and any other large toys that are outside.

Additional resources

A washing line, pegs, washing bowls, soap powder, sponges, cloths, scrubbing brushes

Water

Creative development

Learning objectives

- To develop an awareness of colour and how it is created
- To explore and experiment with different media and materials

Suggested activities

- Encourage the children to mix their own paint, using powder paint and small amounts of water.
- Make pots of different-coloured paint and mix with washing-up liquid. Encourage the children to use straws to blow bubbles. Press paper on to the pots to create bubble prints.
- Use wet paper and let the children sprinkle powder paint on to the wet paper. Discuss the effects with the children.
- Make salt dough with the children and encourage them to create their own models of shells or sea creatures.
- Create a collage of an under-water scene.

Additional resources

Powder paint, washing-up liquid, ingredients to make salt dough, collage materials, paper

Snack times

Learning objectives

- To develop independence

Suggested activities

- Let the children make and pour out their own squash. Talk to them about diluting – how much squash/water do we need to make it taste nice?
- Eat the jellies made by the children in the **Main activity**.

Circle/review times

Learning objectives

- To express their feelings

Suggested activities

- Use the sentence starter 'My favourite drink is…'
- 'I like bath time because…'/'I don't like bath time because…' Give the children the choice.

Water

Outdoor play

Learning objectives

- To be eager to explore new learning
- To be actively involved in a variety of activities
- To observe closely and identify patterns and change

Suggested activities

- On nice days put the water tray outside and do the focus activities outside.
- Put a paddling pool outside and either organise small groups to play in the pool or organise a fishing game using small plastic fish and fishing nets. ⚠
- Provide the children with a selection of paintbrushes, water pistols or water sprays. Encourage them to paint the floor with water and then watch how long it takes to dry.
- On a rainy day dress the children in macs and Wellington boots and go outside to splash in the puddles.

Additional resources

A paddling pool or a large bowl, plastic fish and fishing nets

A selection of paint brushes, water pistols/water sprays etc.

Stories and rhymes

Learning objectives

- To listen and respond to stories and rhymes

Suggested activities

Stories

Daisy and the Egg by Jane Simmons (Orchard Books)

Five Minutes' Peace by Jill Murphy (Walker Books)

Special visitors/events

Suggested activities

- Organise a family day out to the seaside or a waterpark.
- Go for a walk to splash in puddles.

The Three Billy Goats Gruff

How can you prepare for this activity?

- This activity requires a good selection of resources, most of which are 'junk' items that should be collected together in advance. Some of the resources may need to be ordered, bought or borrowed!

- This activity requires children to experiment with resources. They should be encouraged to try out different methods of constructing and joining materials. They should be shown how different tools work and be encouraged to use them independently. They should be taught the correct names of the tools and encouraged to use them.

- Wherever possible, materials should be readily available, clearly labelled and stored in separate boxes. Empty shoeboxes are very useful as they can be stacked with lids on when not in use. The shoeboxes themselves can be painted in different colours and decorated so that the children can easily identify the box they need.

- Organise a 'green' day when everyone, including the Nursery staff, comes to Nursery wearing something green.

What are the starting points?

- Read the story of *The Three Billy Goats Gruff* (traditional).

- Discuss with the children other ways in which the Billy Goats may have got to the other side of the bridge.

- Talk to the children about bridges. Where and why do we use and need bridges? Have the children ever crossed a bridge? What sort of bridge? Over a road/a railway/a river?

- Discuss the safety aspects of bridges. Why do they need to be strong?

What resources do you need to collect for the focus activity?

- Construction kits which contain a variety of shapes and interlocking pieces such as Duplo/Lego, Stickle Bricks, wooden bricks, Mobilo, Popoids etc.

- Clay, playdough, Plasticine.

- Junk items such as egg boxes, empty packets, kitchen-roll tubes, yoghurt pots, newspaper rolled diagonally into tubes etc.

- Paper clips, elastic bands, scissors, sticky tape, glue, Blu–Tack, paper fasteners, string, stapler and staples, hammer and nails, hole punch, Velcro, moulds, masking tape.

The Three Billy Goats Gruff

Display suggestions

- Make a tabletop display of the models of the bridges the children have made. Add a caption such as 'We made models'.
- Display a collage of the Three Billy Goats and the Troll.

Similar topics to explore

- The stories/rhymes *The Three Little Pigs*, 'Humpty Dumpty' and 'The Queen of Hearts' offer similar designing and making opportunities.

Home links

- Ask parents if they could take their children over a bridge either in a car or on foot.

Foundation

The Three Billy Goats Gruff

Learning objectives

- To select appropriate materials and equipment to build and construct
- To describe what they have made, evaluating and adapting where necessary
- To devise practical solutions to problems which arise in model-making, construction and imaginative play

Activity

Encourage children to play with construction kits and small-world toys, making bridges for cars on the road mat or over the railway track.

Suggest that the children use a selection of materials and small-world construction kits to recreate the story of *The Three Billy Goats Gruff*. Offer a choice of resources.

Encourage the children to select their own resources. Question the children. Will they paint a river, use tissue paper scrunched up or could they find a small piece of blue material?

Which construction kit is best suited to building the bridge? Would they prefer to make a bridge using tubes, yoghurt pots, packets, rolled-up newspapers etc.? Which construction holds up the best? Encourage children to evaluate and revise their constructions if necessary.

Imagine that the goats have decided to cross the river by another means such as by boat. Children can design and make boats and float them on the water tray.

Collage a troll. Make a large face and attach material for the body.

Make a stick puppet or mask of each of the Billy Goats.

Re–enact the story giving different children turns at being the Troll.

Make a river using kitchen foil or paint large pieces of paper blue and green.

Find ways of crossing the river without 'falling in'!

Use nursery furniture to make a large bridge.

What do the stepping stones look like?

 Step 1

Investigate construction materials.
Child builds a model and will choose and discard blocks to suit purpose. Will explore objects which form a bridge, looking through the shape made.

 Step 2

Join construction pieces together to build and balance.
Begin to try out a range of tools and techniques safely.
Will make models which they attribute to being a bridge.
Will explore tools and resources, selecting more by trial and error than by informed choice.
Will use available resources to fix model and will need guidance to choose tape rather than glue.

 Step 3

Construct with a purpose in mind, using a variety of resources.
Use simple tools and techniques competently and appropriately.
Child will choose or reject resources to refine model. Will explore ways to make boats that will float and will suggest some ideas.

 Step 4 (Early learning goal)

Build and construct with a wide range of objects, selecting appropriate resources and adapting their work where necessary.
Select the tools and techniques they need to shape, assemble and join materials they are using.
Child will recognise need to modify models and will persevere until s/he thinks it is right. S/he knows which material does the job, e.g. masking tape is more substantial than glue.

The Three Billy Goats Gruff   Main activity

Key questions

- Why did the goats want to cross the river?
- Who went first? Next? Last?
- What did the troll want to do? Why?

Key vocabulary

- Bridge, river, goats, grass, troll, over, under, on, by, the other side

Targeted children

Evaluation

How did the activity go?

What evidence of children's learning have you collected?

The *LCP* Foundation Stage

The Three Billy Goats Gruff

Planning sheet for supplementary activities

Area of learning	Learning objective	Activity	Targeted children	Evaluation
PSED				
CLL				
Maths				
KUW				
Physical				
Creative				
Snack times				
Circle times				
Outdoor play				
Stories & rhymes				
Special visitors				

Adult role during spontaneous play sessions

Observing play ☐ _____ Supporting play areas ☐ _____

Supporting individual play ☐ _____ Involvement in play area ☐ _____

167

The Three Billy Goats Gruff

Personal, social and emotional development

Learning objectives

- To develop the ability to express their feelings and explore relationships

Suggested activities

- Discuss with the children things they are frightened of. Would they help their younger brothers or sisters if they were in trouble? Would their older brothers and sisters help them?

Communication, language and literacy

Learning objectives

- To recall stories and sequence events
- To show awareness of variety of language patterns in stories
- To show an understanding of the main elements of a story – characters/the setting/beginning and ending

Suggested activities

- Read the story of *The Three Billy Goats Gruff* several times, emphasising language such as **first, next, last, before, when, under, over**.
- Encourage the children to join in with the refrains. Discuss the characters. Were they brave? Discuss alternative endings.

Mathematical development

Learning objectives

- To be able to order a given set of objects by size or number
- To identify the ordinal position in sequence – first, second, third

Suggested activities

- Ordering - find sets of objects which the children can order into sizes from big to small such as Russian dolls, cardboard boxes that fit one into another, pencils, cups, teddies etc.
- Emphasise ordinal numbers - first, second, third; first, last.

Additional resources

Sets of objects that are ordered by size

The Three Billy Goats Gruff

Physical development

Learning objectives

• To control refined hand movements
• To be able to co-ordinate the whole body

Suggested activities

• Use pre-cut cardboard shapes of goats. Give the children balls of thick wool and encourage them to wind the wool around the goat's body.
• Use skipping ropes or long pieces of ribbon which are attached to bangles on wrists to create the swirling movements of the river. Encourage the children to see if they can cross the river without standing on the rope or the ribbon.
• Use appropriate music and encourage the children to skip around like goats or make giant steps like a troll, pulling faces as they do so.

Additional resources

Wrist bangles with long pieces of ribbon tied to them
CD/cassette player and music
Pre-cut cardboard goat shapes, balls of thick wool

Creative development

Learning objectives

• To have opportunities to practise the skills involved in shaping, assembling and joining materials
• To explore and experiment with materials through a variety of media – e.g. collage, painting

Suggested activities

• Make pop-up trolls. Cut out bridge and troll shapes. If the children are able to cut their own shapes encourage them to do so. Collage both the front of the troll and the front of the bridge. With masking tape, attach a wide-holed straw to the back of the bridge and a thin stick to the back of the troll, and thread the stick through the straw. Pop the troll up behind the bridge. Encourage the children to say 'Who's that trip-trapping over my bridge?' as they play with the troll and the bridge.

• Collage a forest of green trees. Use a selection of green materials to collage the trees. Encourage the children to cut and tear the materials themselves.

• Allow the children to mix their own green paint using small quantities of yellow and blue paint. They could paint one hand yellow and the other hand blue; then suggest they rub their hands together and look at the changes. What has happened? Encourage them to print with their hands. Look at the shades of green. Suggest the children add white paint to the green to create lighter shades of green.

Additional resources

Card, thick straws, sticks, masking tape
A selection of green materials such as tissue paper, crepe paper, Cellophane, ribbon etc.
yellow and blue paint

The Three Billy Goats Gruff

Supplementary activities

Snack times

Learning objectives

• To make and express choices

Suggested activities

• Eat monster-style potato snacks.

• Eat green snacks such as cucumber and celery sticks, or green jelly.

• Make peppermint creams using icing sugar, peppermint essence and green food colouring.

Circle/review times

Learning objectives

• To develop the ability to express their feelings

Suggested activities

• Use the sentence starter 'I am frightened of…'

Outdoor play

Learning objectives

• To respond to imaginative stimuli in co-operation with others

Suggested activities

• Draw chalk lines on the playground to make a river and play 'Please Mr Troll, may we cross your rickety bridge?' (A version of ' Please, Mr Crocodile, may we cross your golden river?')

The *LCP* Foundation Stage

The Three Billy Goats Gruff

Stories and rhymes

Learning objective

- To listen and respond to stories, poems and rhymes
- To increase the ability to listen with understanding and enjoyment

Suggested activities

Make up a rhyme, e.g:

> 'I'm a troll, foll-de-roll,
>
> I'm a troll, foll-de-roll,
>
> I sing a 'trolly' song,
>
> and I catch who comes along.
>
> Who goes trip trap over my bridge?
>
> (Jake) goes trip trap over my bridge.
>
> Too late… he's gone.'

On and off!

How can you prepare for this activity?

- Look at items of equipment (e.g. toaster, washing machine, microwave) in the setting and talk about how they work. If safe to do so, allow children to operate equipment; if not, demonstrate how it works. ⚠
- Prepare a story tape to use on the tape recorder.

What are the starting points?

- Listen to a story on a tape recorder.

What resources do you need to collect for the focus activity?

- Tape recorder, story tape.

Display suggestions

- Make a display of everyday electrical objects, e.g. telephones, radios, etc.
- Talk about how they work, and whether they use batteries or need to be plugged in.

Similar topics to explore

- Robots.

Home links

- Ask parents and carers to talk to the children about electrical equipment at home.

Foundation

On and off!

Learning objectives

- To have confidence in the use of a variety of information and communication technology

Activity

Listen to the taped story. Show the children how to stop the tape and rewind to the beginning.

Demonstrate how to use the tape recorder to record a song the children can sing.

Place the tape player in the book corner for the children to use to listen to favourite songs or stories.

What do the stepping stones look like?

 Step 1
Children show an interest in ICT.
Child is interested in the tape player and wants to try to work it.

 Step 2
Know how to operate simple equipment.
Child can operate buttons on tape player with support (e.g. coloured sticker).

 Step 3
Perform simple functions on apparatus.
Child is able to use tape player without help.

 Step 4 (Early learning goal)
Find out and identify the uses of everyday technology.
Child knows that buttons and switches control the machine.

Key questions

- Can you switch the tape player on?
- Can you make the sound quieter/louder?
- Can you switch the player off?

Key vocabulary

- On/off, switch, control, turn/press

Targeted children

Evaluation

How did the activity go?

What evidence of children's learning have you collected?

On and off!

Planning sheet for supplementary activities

Area of learning	Learning objective	Activity	Targeted children	Evaluation
PSED				
CLL				
Maths				
KUW				
Physical				
Creative				
Snack times				
Circle times				
Outdoor play				
Stories & rhymes				
Special visitors				

Adult role during spontaneous play sessions

Observing play ☐ _____   Supporting play areas ☐ _____

Supporting individual play ☐ _____   Involvement in play area ☐ _____

The LCP Foundation Stage

On and off!

Personal, social and emotional development

Learning objectives

- To be confident to try new activities
- To gain confidence when speaking in a group

Suggested activities

- Children tape record themselves choosing their activities.
- They should operate the on/off switch and play back their recording.

Additional resources

Blank audio tapes

Communication, language and literacy

Learning objectives

- To use imagination in role-play

Suggested activities (small group)

- Set up a role-play area as a dark place and provide torches to be used inside. Talk about when you use torches. Talk about what it is like inside the dark place and how the children feel in the dark.
- Talk about the batteries in the torch, and about the switches which turn the torches on and off.

Additional resources

A blanket to make a dark area

Torches

Mathematical development

Learning objectives

- To develop an understanding of language associated with position and direction

Suggested activities

- Use a programmable toy, and programme it to knock down a pile of bricks or small boxes.
- Talk about what the children want the toy to do and the direction they want it to go in.

Additional resources

Programmable robot/toy

On and off!

Physical development

Learning objectives

- To be aware of directional and positional language

Suggested activities

- Play a game to try to throw bean bags into a bucket.
- Talk about how many landed in the bucket and how some landed outside it - some were close, some not close.

Additional resources

Bean bags, bucket

Creative development

Learning objectives

- To explore position when making a decision about where to place materials in collage
- To make models to represent everyday electrical equipment

Suggested activities

- Find pictures of electrical equipment in catalogues and encourage children to cut them out and stick them on to paper to make a large group collage. Allow children to make the decisions about where to place their pictures as this will give insight as to their spatial understanding.
- Make 'household electrical equipment' from recycled resources. Encourage children to make switches or control knobs. Talk children through what they need to make their models. You will need to offer support to make doors for microwaves that open!

Additional resources

Boxes and materials to make knobs and switches; catalogues showing electrical equipment

Snack times

Learning objectives

- To use ICT in everyday situations

Suggested activities

- Use a toaster to make toast for children. Let them watch you using the toaster and if the toaster has a control for how dark you can make the toast, demonstrate this to the children.
- Allow children to spread their own toast with their choice of topping. This is a good activity to enable children to explore some of the properties of shapes; talk to them about spreading right to the edges and corners.

Additional resources

Toaster, knives, bread and choice of toppings

On and off!

Circle/review times

Learning objectives

- To use words relating to position
- To listen carefully and follow instructions

Suggested activities

- Use the rhyme: 'Teddy bear, teddy bear, turn around,

    Teddy bear, teddy bear, touch the ground,

    Teddy bear, teddy bear, reach up high,

    Teddy bear, teddy bear, ……… ' (add your own action here!)
- Offer the opportunity for children to take the turn to be the 'leader' and give the final instruction.

Outdoor play

Learning objectives

- To follow a route
- To investigate their environment

Suggested activities

- Hide a small parcel. Set up a trail of small pieces of bread for children to follow outside to reach it. Talk about how they followed the trail. What would happen if the birds had found the bread crumbs?
- You could repeat this on different days with different finds.
- You could devise a simple map with the children.

Additional resources

A small parcel, bread for trail

On and off!

Stories and rhymes

Learning objectives

- To listen to and join in with stories and rhymes that use positional and directional language

Suggested activities

Stories

Rosie's Walk by Pat Hutchins (Red Fox)

We're Going on a Bear Hunt by Michael Rosen (Mantra Publishing)

Inside, Outside, Upside Down by S&J Berenstain (Picture Lions)

Where's Spot? by Eric Hill (Frederick Warne)

Rhymes

'The Grand Old Duke of York'

'The Wheels on the Bus'

Special visitors/events

Learning objectives

- To be aware of the use of ICT in everyday life

Suggested activities

- ⚠ Visit the local shops to buy some items for snack time. Look at the bar codes on packets and talk about the way the tills are operated in the shop.
- Look at the electrical equipment in the shop, e.g. fridges/freezers.
- Look to see if there is a closed circuit TV in the shop.

Additional resources

Money for purchases

Birthdays

How can you prepare for this activity?

- Ask children to bring in photographs of themselves and their parents as babies or toddlers.
- Ask Nursery staff also to bring in photographs of themselves as small children.
- Make appropriate provision for any Jehovah's Witness children who don't celebrate birthdays.

What are the starting points?

- Read the story *Birthday Bear* by Joan Stimson (Ladybird).
- Talk to the children about birthday surprises. Ask what they do for their birthday.
- Talk to the children about how old they are. Ask how old they will be next birthday. Look at the birthday/baby photographs with the children. How have they changed?
- Show the children photographs of members of staff as children. Do the children recognise them?
- Talk to the children about your memories of being 4 years old, your family, your favourite toy and fashions etc. Ask the children if you have changed!!
- Look at the children's photographs of their parents; can they see any similarities between themselves and their parents?

What resources do you need to collect for the focus activity?

- Birthday cards, wrapping paper, balloons, a birthday cake, candles, candle holders.
- Story books about birthdays, photographs.

Display suggestions

- Make a tabletop display of birthday cards, wrapped presents, wrapping paper, blown-up balloons, banners, books and maybe a model of a birthday cake.
- Make birthday posters saying 'I am 3' and 'I am 4'. Stick the children's photographs or their paintings of themselves on the appropriate poster, and transfer them to the next poster on the day of their birthday.
- Display children's paintings of themselves at a birthday party. Add paintings of balloons, presents and a cake.
- Display all the photographs with a caption, written by a child, 'Can you guess who this is?'

Birthdays

Similar topics to explore

- Other family celebrations such as weddings or religious festivals.
- Look at old toys or the clothes that people used to wear.

Home links

- Ask parents to send in photographs of themselves as small children.
- Ask parents if a grandparent would be willing to come into Nursery to talk to children about their memories of being a small child.
- Enquire if there is an older person in the community whose birthday you could celebrate; if not, plan a party for a member of staff or a special occasion.

Foundation

The LCP Foundation Stage

Birthdays

Learning objectives

- To understand the differences between past and present events in their own lives and in those of their families

Activity

Look at the photographs of themselves which the children have brought into school.

Can they remember being a baby?

Discuss with the children how they have changed since they were babies. What can they do now that they couldn't do then?

Look at the photographs of their parents. Do the children look like their parents? In what ways? Do they have the same hair colour/straight hair or curly hair?

Talk to the children about things their parents can do that they can't do themselves.

Ask them about the things they want to be able to do when they are grown up.

Celebrate a birthday. Organise a party.

Make a birthday cake adding icing and the appropriate number of candles, or make small cakes.

Key questions

- How old are you?
- How old will you be next birthday?
- How have you changed since you were a baby?

Key vocabulary

- Old, past, then, before, used to, different, remember, now

What do the stepping stones look like?

 Step 1

Remember and talk about significant things that have happened to them.
Child will acknowledge their own baby photo and be interested in it!

 Step 2

Show an interest in the lives of people familiar to them.
Begin to differentiate between past and present.
Children are interested in the photographs of themselves and others. They will talk about what they did as babies (mum has probably told them a story about them as a baby).
Child is fascinated by pictures of familiar adults as babies.

Step 3

Not applicable.

 Step 4 (Early learning goal)

Find out about past and present events in their own lives and in those of their families and other people they know.
Can talk about things they can do now which they couldn't do as a baby. Can tell you about some toys parents used to play with.

Targeted children

Evaluation

How did the activity go?

What evidence of children's learning have you collected?

Birthdays

Planning sheet for supplementary activities

Area of learning	Learning objective	Activity	Targeted children	Evaluation
PSED				
CLL				
Maths				
KUW				
Physical				
Creative				
Snack times				
Circle times				
Outdoor play				
Stories & rhymes				
Special visitors				

Adult role during spontaneous play sessions

Observing play ☐ _____ Supporting play areas ☐ _____

Supporting individual play ☐ _____ Involvement in play area ☐ _____

The LCP Foundation Stage

Birthdays

Personal, social and emotional development

Learning objectives

- To be actively involved in a variety of experiences
- To develop an awareness of healthy eating

Suggested activities

- Encourage children to plan and work together. Discuss the healthy options you could add to your party.
- Discuss health issues when making cakes – washing your hands, being careful with electrical equipment such as a mixer and not having wet hands.
- Discuss with children why we give and receive presents, and how it makes us feel. Talk about how we can give in other ways, like helping at home to tidy up.

Communication, language and literacy

Learning objectives

- To recognise the different purposes of writing as a means of communication
- To begin to recognise initial sounds

Suggested activities

- Use the writing table to write invitation letters or birthday cards. This activity could be modelled by an adult or left as a play activity.
- The children could write their own shopping lists prior to being taken shopping to buy the ingredients for the cakes or party food.
- Play sound games, e.g. 'Odd Sound Out'. Make sure everything on a table begins with 'c' – candles, cards, cake, crisps. Explain that all the items begin with the same sound, then add an 'odd man out'. Change the 'odd man out' regularly and see if any children spot the odd sound out and can tell you why it is different from the others.

Additional resources

Card, pencils, felt-tips, sticky shapes, sequins, glitter, glue, Sellotape, scissors, old birthday cards to cut up
Paper for shopping lists
Items for 'Odd Sound Out' game

Birthdays

Supplementary activities

Mathematical development

Learning objectives

- To begin to use own language in play and everyday situations to talk about quantity
- To verbalise numbers by counting
- To demonstrate and match 1:1

Suggested activities

- Provide play dough to make cakes, candle holders and candles for play activities; model the activity and give the children time to play.
- Make a collection of birthday cards with different age stickers on them and in small groups sort them (this activity should first be modelled by an adult).
- Draw pictures of cakes with numbers from 1 to 4 on them. Cut out paper candles and encourage the children to stick the right number of candles on each cake. Alternatively, the older children could paint or draw their own cakes and candles.

Additional resources

Play dough

A selection of birthday cards with different ages on

Paper for candles

Physical development

Learning objectives

- To gain control over fine motor skills

Suggested activities

- Using a selection of empty boxes and toys as presents, children wrap presents using their own wrapping paper made in **Creative development**, sticky tape, string and ribbon. Write gift tags.
- These presents could be used for a guessing game 'Can you guess what this is?'

Additional resources

Selection of boxes and small toys such as teddy bears, cars, building blocks

Birthdays

Creative development

Learning objectives

- To experiment with a variety of media by printing and painting

Suggested activities

- Children make wrapping paper by printing a pattern on to large sheets of paper.
- Make paper hats and paper chains for the party.
- Print/collage birthday cakes.
- Children could paint pictures of themselves, presents and balloons; these could make a party display.

Additional resources

Sponges, cotton reels, boxes, tubes etc. for printing

Paint, paper, collage materials

Snack times

Learning objectives

- To take turns and share fairly
- To develop an awareness of routine
- To make and express choices
- To interact socially
- To begin to describe an awareness of terms such as halves and quarters

Suggested activities

- Make either a large cake or fairy cakes. Share out cakes. Ask 'Do we have we enough? Do we need more?'
- Cut the cakes into halves and quarters.

Additional resources

Recipe, ingredients and equipment for making cakes

Circle/review times

Learning objectives

- To develop the ability to express feelings

Suggested activities

- Use sentence starters such as 'When I was a baby, I needed help to…', 'When I grow up I will be able to…'

Birthdays

Outdoor play

Learning objectives

- To use self-expression in movement
- To interact socially

Suggested activities

- Play traditional/party games such as 'The farmer's in his den', 'Hokey-Cokey', 'Ring-o-Ring-o-Roses', 'Hop Scotch', 'Here we go Looby Lou' etc.

Stories and rhymes

Learning objectives

- To listen and respond to stories/rhymes/poetry
- To increase the ability to listen with understanding and enjoyment

Suggested activities

Stories

Getting up and *The Toys' Party* by Rod Hunt (OUP)

P.B. Bear's Birthday Party by Lee Daris (Dorling Kindersley)

Birthday Bear by Joan Stimson (Ladybird)

Happy Birthday, Lulu by Caroline Uff (Orchard Books)

You'll soon grow into them, Titch by Pat Hutchins (Red Fox)

The Little Yellow Chicken by Joy Cowley (The Wright Group)

Kipper's Birthday by Mick Inkpen (Hodder Children's Books)

Rhymes

'These are Grandmother's glasses'

'Five little candles' both from *This Little Puffin. . .* (Puffin Books)

Special visitors/events

Suggested activities

- Celebrate a member of the community's birthday - preferably an older person who could talk to the children about their memories of being a small child.

Little Red Riding Hood

How can you prepare for this activity?

- Organise a 'red' day when everyone, including the staff, comes to Nursery wearing something red.

What are the starting points?

- Talk to the children about their journey to school. Who brings them? How do they get there? Do they walk or go by car or bus? What do they see on the way – shops, a park, a post box? Do they cross over any roads? Do they use a zebra crossing?
- Read the children the story of *Little Red Riding Hood* (traditional).
- Discuss the ways in which Little Red Riding Hood might have travelled to her granny's, e.g. bike, car, taxi, bus. Do the children visit their grannies?
- Do they enjoy walking? Where do they walk to?

What resources do you need to collect for the focus activity?

- Small-world toys.
- A play mat.
- Twigs, stones, leaves, pieces of wood, wooden blocks etc.
- Clipboard and camera.
- Litter pickers and disposable gloves.

Display suggestions

- A tabletop display of items Little Red Riding Hood could take to her Granny's house. Make them 'caring' items such as a piece of fruit to make her feel better, a book to read while she is in bed, some nice smelly soap to have a wash with etc.
- A 'red' display – see **Creative development**.
- A wall display of the children's houses. Children should write their own captions such as 'This is my house. It has a blue door.' etc.
- Display photographs you took on your walk of the local area with a caption, 'Guess where we are'.

Little Red Riding Hood

Similar topics to explore

- My street, my Nursery, homes, transport.
- The story *The Three Little Pigs*.

Home links

- Ask parents if they have a photograph of their home that they could send into Nursery.
- Talk to the parents about road safety. Do they teach their children about crossing the road/Zebra crossings/Pelican crossings etc?

Little Red Riding Hood

Learning objectives

- To know that not all places are the same
- To know about some of the features in the town and the countryside
- To become aware of the need to take responsibility for caring for the environment

Activity

After reading the story of *Little Red Riding Hood*, set up a play mat with small-world people, trees, houses, twigs, leaves etc. Encourage the children to act out the story through the small-world toys. Suggest they add paths, a pond and a play area. Help children gather together the resources they may need. Encourage the children to plan the 'map' themselves.

Talk to the children about where Little Red Riding Hood lived. Was it a park or the woods she had to walk through? Would it be nice to live by a park?

⚠ Take children for a walk around the Nursery locality. Are there any shops? Is there a local park? Take a clipboard with you and write down all the significant landmarks you see.

Take a camera with you to record your walk. 📷

⚠ Take small groups outside the Nursery and observe the traffic. How many cars pass by? Do any buses pass the Nursery? Is it on a busy road or a quiet road?

Go on a litter walk. Take a bag with you and pick up litter in the immediate environment. ⚠ (Adult to be responsible for picking up litter.) Talk to the children about the kind of litter they find. Who do they think it might belong to?

Ask the children to record their observations by drawing or painting what they have seen.

Key questions

- Where did Little Red Riding Hood live?
- How did she get to her Granny's?
- Should she have talked to the Big Bad Wolf?

Key vocabulary

- Woods, park, path, trees, plants, flowers, fences, fields, ponds, gardens, bus stops, post boxes, shops, litter, cars, buses, lorries, bikes

What do the stepping stones look like?

 Step 1

Show an interest in the world in which they live. *In their play, will add familiar features such as shop, park, trees.*

 Step 2

Comment and ask questions about where they live and the natural world.
Notices differences between features of the local environment.
Will notice features such as road signs and crossings on their walk. If taking photographs, will point out some features to photograph. May comment on unpleasant aspects such as litter.

 Step 3

Not applicable.

 Step 4 (Early learning goal)

Observe, find out about and identify features in the place they live and the natural world.
Find out about their environment and talk about those features they like and dislike.
Can recognise features in their area from photographs.
Will comment on nice gardens and dog mess and litter which improve or are unpleasant. They will begin to express their opinion about litter.

Targeted children

Evaluation

How did the activity go?

What evidence of children's learning have you collected?

Little Red Riding Hood

Planning sheet for supplementary activities

Area of learning	Learning objective	Activity	Targeted children	Evaluation
PSED				
CLL				
Maths				
KUW				
Physical				
Creative				
Snack times				
Circle times				
Outdoor play				
Stories & rhymes				
Special visitors				

Adult role during spontaneous play sessions

Observing play ☐ _____

Supporting play areas ☐ _____

Supporting individual play ☐ _____

Involvement in play area ☐ _____

Little Red Riding Hood

Supplementary activities

Personal, social and emotional development

Learning objectives

- To develop a sense of personal safety and become aware of the dangers of traffic
- To begin to develop responsible attitudes towards people other than themselves

Suggested activities

- Discuss road safety with the children. Talk about zebra crossings, the Green Cross code, crossing the road behind vehicles, etc.
- Discuss with the children the dangers of talking to strangers.
- Talk to the children about their Granny and how they help her. Do they visit her? Do they ever take her flowers or little treats?

Communication, language and literacy

Learning objectives

- To show an understanding of the main elements of the story – characters/the setting/beginning and ending
- To recognise the different purposes of writing as a means of communication – letters, lists etc.

Suggested activities

- Discuss the story of *Little Red Riding Hood*. Discuss the characters and the ending. Ask the children if they can think of an alternative ending. Read the story several times and encourage the children to join in the refrains.
- Model writing a letter to Granny telling her you are going to visit. Encourage the children to write their own letters. Provide writing paper and envelopes in the writing area.
- Read *The Shopping Basket* by John Burningham (Red Fox).
- Write lists of the items you might put in the shopping basket.
- Read *Rosie's Walk* by Pat Hutchins (Red Fox).

Additional resources

A selection of writing materials in the writing area, including envelopes

Books: *The Shopping Basket* and *Rosie's Walk*

Little Red Riding Hood

Supplementary activities

Mathematical development

Learning objectives

- To begin to use own language in play and everyday situations to talk about size, quantity, shape, weight

Suggested activities

- Place items in a shopping basket. Change them daily. Each day count how many items there are today. Is the basket heavier or lighter today? What shapes have you put in? Sort all the solid shapes. One day they could all be tins (cylinders), the next day packets (cuboids); another day they could all be apples and oranges (spheres) then a basket of mixed shapes. Do the children notice? Which shapes stack together better? Why?

Additional resources

A large shopping basket and a selection of items to fill it

Physical development

Learning objectives

- To respond to imaginative stimuli in co-operation with others

Suggested activities

- Play 'Hide and Seek'.
- Play 'What's the time, Mr Wolf?'

Creative development

Learning objectives

- To explore and experiment with materials through a variety of media – e.g. painting, drawing, collage, printing

Suggested activities

- Sort red things and make a 'red' table. Make red collage pictures. Collect together materials that are red and encourage the children to create their own picture.
- Give the children red paint to mix with other colours, e.g. with yellow to make orange, with blue to make purple, with white to make pink. Talk about shades. Talk about red being thought of as a hot colour.
- Make prints with children's shoes and follow Red Riding Hood's tracks around the Nursery.

Additional resources

Selection of red materials such as tissue paper, crepe paper, Cellophane, ribbon etc.
Paint and paper

Little Red Riding Hood

Snack times

Learning objectives

- To make and express choices

Suggested activities

- Eat red food all week, e.g. red jam sandwiches, red jelly. Decorate biscuits with red icing sugar.

Circle/review times

Learning objectives

- To develop the ability to express their feelings

Suggested activities

- Encourage the children to show their red collages.
- Use the sentence starters 'We walk to the……', 'I live near…….'

Outdoor play

Learning objectives

- To be aware of directional and positional language e.g. backwards, forwards, sideways, up and down

Suggested activities

- Devise an obstacle race.
- Create a road outside. Make a zebra crossing. Put up road signs. Encourage children to use their bikes, scooters etc. on the play road.

Little Red Riding Hood

Stories and rhymes

Learning objectives

- To listen and respond to stories, songs and rhymes

Suggested activities

Stories

The Enchanted Wood by Gerald Hawksley (Treehouse Children's Books)

Little Rabbit Foo Foo by Michael Rosen *et al.* (Walker Books)

Special visitors/events

Suggested activities

- Invite the local crossing man/lady into Nursery to talk about road safety.

A new baby - what shall we call it? (Preparation)

How can you prepare for this activity?

- It is quite likely that one of your children will be welcoming a new baby brother or sister into their family at some time during the year! With all the adults around them being very excited about the new arrival, this can be a time when young children can become very confused and may be experiencing very mixed emotions.

- This theme opens up opportunities for children to talk about and express their feelings. It will also support children in developing their self-esteem whilst understanding the importance of giving names to new babies. Finding out about their own names, what they mean and why they were chosen, can help in the development of the child's sense of identity.

- You have the opportunity to look at how different religions represented in your group celebrate the naming of a new baby. You will need to have information about the cultural mix of the children in your setting and which religions are represented.

- All the major religions attach significance to the naming of children and some have particular naming ceremonies. This is a brief outline of some rituals associated with naming of children.

Christianity: A baby is usually taken to the Church where s/he is baptised with Holy Water. Promises are made by parents and godparents on behalf of the child. The child is named by his/her parents and s/he is welcomed into the Church family. The family usually holds a party with presents for the baby.

Islam: At birth, special prayers are whispered into the child's ears to ensure that the first words s/he hears are words of Allah. At 7 days old, the child is given a name which has a special religious meaning and is a significant part of the identity of being a Muslim.

A spot of honey is rubbed on the baby's tongue to symbolise that life will be sweet. Muslims will usually hold a feast to celebrate.

Sikhism: All male Sikhs take the title Singh, meaning 'lion'. All female Sikhs take the title Kaur, meaning 'princess'. These titles show that all Sikhs are of one family of God.

When the baby is a few weeks old, there is a ceremony held in the Gurdwara and special prayers are said with readings from the Holy Work Guru Granth Sahib. This is opened randomly and the first letter of the first word on the page becomes the initial letter of the child's name. The name is announced to all present and the baby is welcomed into the whole family of Sikhs. The baby's family gives a gift of a new cloth to cover the Holy Work Guru Granth Sahib.

Hinduism: The child is given a name at 12 days old. Hindus believe that the right name will bring the child luck. In the naming ceremony, the priest will choose the initial letter of the child's name. Then, the eldest woman of the family will announce the chosen name. The father will sing the name into the baby's ear. The new baby is welcomed with singing and a sharing of specially prepared sweets.

A new baby - what shall we call it? (Preparation)

What are the starting points?

- Ideally this will lead on from a child's news of a new baby brother or sister.
- Read a story about the arrival of a new baby in a family.

What resources do you need to collect for the focus activity?

- Collect together baby items to use in a role-play area: clothes, feeding-bottles, empty baby-milk tins, baby bath, baby toys, dolls' pram, etc.
- 'Baby' dolls including those which represent different cultures.
- Books about babies; non-fiction as well as stories.
- Books about babies' names. If you have children from different cultures, ask parents if they can help with this.
- Pictures of babies.

Display suggestions

- Display current photos of children alongside their photos of themselves as babies.
- The activity in **Communication, language and literacy** will provide cards with children's names and their meanings which can be added to the display.

Similar topics to explore

- Weddings.
- Birthdays.

Home links

- Ask children if they can find and bring to Nursery photographs of themselves as babies and, if possible, those taken at a naming ceremony.

Foundation

A new baby - what shall we call it? (Main activity)

Learning objectives

- To be aware of special events such as a naming ceremony and the importance they have in family life

Activity

If one of the children has recently had a new baby in the family, encourage them to talk about choosing the name for the baby and whether they have had a special ceremony, e.g. christening, for the baby.

Otherwise, read a story about the arrival of a new baby.

If you have children from different cultures, talk about the ways babies are named.

Using a doll, talk about needing to name the doll. Discuss possible names and how to make the decision.

Look up the meanings of some of the names suggested.

When a name is decided on, talk about how you need to make it a special occasion.

You could then perform a very simple naming ceremony in which you give the doll the name and welcome it into the Nursery family. You could pass the newly-named doll round to each child who says 'Welcome, ..., to our Nursery.'

You do not need to enact a 'christening' as such.

Key questions

- What shall we name our baby?
- How shall we decide on the name?
- Why do we need to name the baby?

Key vocabulary

- name, baby, ceremony, special

What do the stepping stones look like?

Step 1

Express feelings about significant personal events.
The child will tell you that s/he has a new baby.

Step 2

Describe significant events for family or friends.
Will talk about the arrival of new baby, and some of the needs of a new baby. Will talk about the naming ceremony.

Step 3

Gain awareness of the cultures and beliefs of others.
Will show interest in naming ceremony and talk about experiences in own family.

Step 4 (Early learning goal)

Begin to know about their own cultures and beliefs and those of other people.
Will talk about naming ceremonies they have experienced and is aware of the importance attached to giving a new baby a name.

Targeted children

Evaluation

How did the activity go?

What evidence of children's learning have you collected?

A new baby - what shall we call it?

Planning sheet for supplementary activities

Area of learning	Learning objective	Activity	Targeted children	Evaluation
PSED				
CLL				
Maths				
KUW				
Physical				
Creative				
Snack times				
Circle times				
Outdoor play				
Stories & rhymes				
Special visitors				

Adult role during spontaneous play sessions

Observing play ☐ _____   Supporting play areas ☐ _____

Supporting individual play ☐ _____   Involvement in play area ☐ _____

A new baby - what shall we call it?

Supplementary activities

Personal, social and emotional development

Learning objectives

- To develop respect for each other

Suggested activities

- You will need to set up a role-play area as 'looking after baby' with all the baby paraphernalia that you have collected.
- Play with the children in the area, talking about the needs of a new baby.
- Encourage the boys as well as the girls to take part in this.
- You will need to be aware that some children may demonstrate negative feelings towards the dolls. This will need careful and sensitive handling.
- In the role-play, show the children how they need to handle the 'babies' carefully and gently.

Additional resources

- Any baby equipment you have collected

Communication, language and literacy

Learning objectives

- To use information books
- To have a go at writing their name
- To see writing used for a purpose

Suggested activities

- Use the baby name books and information you have collected to look up the meanings of children's names.
- Make a special name card for each child. Each child is to write his/her own name and decorate the card themselves.
- With each child, talk about the meaning of their name and write the meaning on a separate card to display alongside the child's name card.
- You could also make name cards for the dolls in the role-play area.

Additional resources

Special resources to decorate the name card: sequins, glitter etc.

Books about children's names

A new baby - what shall we call it?

Mathematical development

Learning objectives

- To solve problems in their play, involving comparing, matching and counting
- Use the language of money in role-play

Suggested activities

- Set up a 'Baby Shop'; make lists and 'go shopping' for things the baby needs.

Additional resources

Items (priced) in a 'Baby Shop', toy money

Physical development

Learning objectives

- To be able to use refined hand movements to manipulate fastenings

Suggested activities

- Dressing and undressing dolls.

Additional resources

Dolls and appropriate sized dolls' clothes

Creative development

Learning objectives

- To enjoy a range of familiar songs
- To control sounds they make with their voices

Suggested activities

- Sing lullabies together. These could be recorded and children allowed to play them back in the role-play area.
- Talk about why lullabies are sung quietly.
- Make up quiet sounds, e.g. humming.
- Have a day when all your singing is in quiet voices.

Additional resources

Tape recorder, blank tapes

The LCP Foundation Stage

A new baby - what shall we call it?

Supplementary activities

Snack times

Learning objectives

- To explore and experience different foods
- To be aware of the differences between their needs as a baby and now

Suggested activities

- Eat Marmite soldiers - children could help with cutting these up.
- Have soft foods like bananas to cut up as finger foods.
- Provide rusk fingers.
- Talk about the sort of foods babies eat and why, and compare these with the foods the children like to eat now.

Circle/review times

Learning objectives

- To develop the children's sense of self-esteem

Suggested activities

- Carefully pass a doll round. Start with a sentence starter: 'When I was a baby, I…(cried a lot/crawled/needed a nappy etc.)., Now I can….(talk to mummy/run/use a toilet by myself etc.).' Encourage children to make a contribution, but if children are shy or embarrassed, they can just carefully pass the doll on to the next child.
- Give lots of positive comments which reinforce the message that the children are really grown up now and should be proud of themselves.

Additional resources

A doll to pass round

Outdoor play

Learning objectives

- To explore real-life situations through role-play

Suggested activities

- Use outside area to 'take the babies to the park'.
- Take the shop outside.
- Use prams and pushchairs.
- Ask the children how the 'babies' need to be prepared for an outing.

A new baby - what shall we call it?

Supplementary activities

Stories and rhymes

Learning objectives

- To hear stories about a familiar situation
- To sing familiar and new songs and rhymes

Suggested activities

Stories

The Baby by John Burningham (Red Fox)

Busy Baby by Stephen Cartwright (Blackie Children's Books)

My baby sisters by Donna Bailey (Heinemann Young Books)

Our Baby by Tony Bradman & Lynn Breeze (Collins Toddler Books)

A New Baby - I'm still important by Jen Green (Collins Toddler Books)

This Baby! by Rod Campbell (Macmillan Children's Books)

Mummy Laid an egg by Babette Cole (Red Fox)

Rhymes

'Baby Peter' from *This Little Puffin. . .* (Puffin Books)

'Rock a bye baby'

'Miss Polly had a dolly'

Special visitors/events

Learning objectives

- To be aware of the significance of buildings used for worship and special events

Suggested activities

- Visit a local church to see a font. You could ask the vicar/priest/minister to show how a baby is named in Christian families.

Physical development

- Frogs

- We're all going on a bear hunt

- Spaced out!

- Healthy me!

- Games day

- The Queen of Hearts

Foundation

Frogs

How can you prepare for this activity?

- Sing the rhyme 'Five Little Speckled Frogs'.
- Talk about frogs and how they jump.
- Children need to be dressed for an active session, preferably in shorts and t-shirts and without socks or shoes.
- Begin with a warm-up activity; this is an important part of physical activity.

What are the starting points?

- Sing the rhyme: 'Five Little Speckled Frogs'.
- Adapt the rhyme to make your own version, e.g.

'We are the speckled frogs,

Sat on a speckled log,

Eating the most delicious bugs, yum! yum!

We jumped into the pool

Where it is nice and cool.

Swimming is most tremendous fun, splish! splash!'

What resources do you need to collect for the focus activity?

- Mats for lilypads.
- You may want to use taped music such as Paul McCartney's 'Frog Song'.

Display suggestions

- Display the pond scene made by the children in the **Creative development** activity.

Similar topics to explore

- Other animals, e.g. rabbits could be explored in a similar manner.

Home links

- Send a copy of the basic rhyme home for carers to sing with the child.

Frogs

Learning objectives

- To begin to move with confidence
- To be able to co-ordinate and control the whole body
- To be aware of directional and positional language

Activity

Warm-up time:

Make a circle with the children and ask them to wriggle their fingers. Imagine fingers are spiders crawling to the top of a wall. Go right to the top; stand on tippy-toes if necessary.

Bring the spiders down the wall, to the bottom, then make the spiders run around their feet.

Take the spider fingers up legs, round their tummies, over shoulders and up and down arms. Tell children to watch the spider fingers as they go travelling over their body.

Main activity:

Sing 'Five Little Speckled Frogs' with the children.

Show the children how to make froggy jumps.

Ask the children to copy you.

Practise froggy jumps in different directions. On a signal, children must find a lilypad (mat) to sit on.

Children will need a change in activity as their legs get tired.

When the frogs 'jump into the pool', the children could try 'breast stroke' movements to pretend to swim in the pool.

Put together a simple role-play based on the adapted rhyme which will put together the movements practised.

Key questions

- How do frogs move when they jump?
- How do they swim?
- Can you froggy jump so that you don't bump into another frog?
- Can you froggy jump backwards?
- How can you make sure you don't bump into another frog?

Key vocabulary

- Jump, move, forwards/backwards/sideways direction, space, safely

What do the stepping stones look like?

 Step 1

Moves spontaneously within available space. Can stop.
Child copies adult, and will move freely in space, stopping when asked. May not yet be aware of space between them and others.

 Step 2

Moves freely with pleasure and confidence. Can move in range of ways. Negotiate space successfully.
Child can do froggy hops around the room.

 Step 3

Can go backwards, forwards, sideways. Experiments with different ways of moving.
Child responds to instructions initially, and will experiment with jumping forwards, backwards and sideways.

 Step 4 (Early learning goal)

Moves with confidence, imagination and safety.
Child moves confidently and with enthusiasm, being aware of others and able to avoid bumping into them.

Targeted children

Evaluation

How did the activity go?

What evidence of children's learning have you collected?

Frogs

Planning sheet for supplementary activities

Area of learning	Learning objective	Activity	Targeted children	Evaluation
PSED				
CLL				
Maths				
KUW				
Physical				
Creative				
Snack times				
Circle times				
Outdoor play				
Stories & rhymes				
Special visitors				

Adult role during spontaneous play sessions

Observing play ☐ _____   Supporting play areas ☐ _____

Supporting individual play ☐ _____   Involvement in play area ☐ _____

Frogs

Personal, social and emotional development

Learning objectives

- To take turns

Suggested activities

- Play Tiddlywinks or a commercial frog-flip game!
- Flick the counter into the 'pool'.

Additional resources

Frog-flip game, counters, shallow bowl with water in

Communication, language and literacy

Learning objectives

- To make marks on paper in a variety of media
- To produce controlled marks

Suggested activities

- Using a paint brush, paint 'jumps' on a large piece of paper. Take the paintbrush in a series of curved movements along the paper to represent springy jumps being made by the frog. You could have a picture of a frog on the left side of the paper and a picture of a pond on the right. Show the children and talk it through e.g. 'Start here and jump into the pond…'

Additional resources

Various colours of paints, brush, paper

Frogs

Mathematical development

Learning objectives

- To begin to understand language in the development of simple mathematical ideas and concepts
- To enjoy the experience of using numbers in simple contexts
- To be able to find one more and one less than a given number

Suggested activities

- Sing the rhyme 'Five Little Speckled Frogs' with the children.
- Choose five children to be the frogs and act out the rhyme.
- Talk about how many frogs are on the log, and how many are in the pool.
- Talk about the numbers in the rhyme. Children could find the appropriate number on the number line.

Additional resources

Frog masks, a piece of blue material to represent the pool, numerals 0 to 5 on individual cards displayed in order as a number line

Knowledge and understanding of the world

Learning objectives

- To observe closely and identify change
- To recognise and name features of living things
- To care for living things

Suggested activities

- Collect some frog spawn from a garden pond along with some of the pond-weed. (It is illegal to collect spawn from the wild.)
- Over time, observe the changes as the spawn turns into tadpoles. When the tadpoles grow legs, provide a rock for them to climb out of the water. Feed with fishfood as tadpoles develop legs.

  ⚠ **Health & Safety note**: Do not allow children to handle tadpoles.
- Use a magnifying glass for observing.
- The children can record their observations with drawings.

Additional resources

Shallow tank, frog spawn, pond weed, magnifying glasses

'Be Safe' booklet from The Association for Science Education (Tel. 01707 267411)

Frogs

Creative development

Learning objectives

- To explore and experiment with colour and texture
- To represent in models, paintings, drawings and other media

Suggested activities

- Make a pond scene:

  The background should be made by children with large decorators' brushes and different shades of blue. Let them go for it!

  Frog spawn can be made with bubble wrap.

  Children can cut long strips of different types of green paper to make pond-weed.

  Lily pads: children can cut these out from green sugar paper or crepe paper. A 3D effect can be gained if you slightly gather the part to be attached to the stem.

- Children can do paintings of frogs.

Additional resources

Decorators' brushes and blue paint, bubble wrap, different types of green paper

Find pictures of ponds and frogs as the stimulus if you can't visit a pond

Snack times

Learning objectives

- To understand about using tools safely
- To control fine hand movements

Suggested activities

- Children can use plastic knives to cut up slices of banana for a snack.

Circle/review times

Learning objectives

- To join in activities involving taking turns
- To follow instructions

Suggested activities

- Play 'Pass the frog' (toy frog or bean bag):

  In a circle, start the activity by e.g. passing the frog under a leg to the next person; all the children continue to pass the 'frog' in the same way.

  If you can play music while passing the frog, this adds to the fun!

Frogs

Outdoor play

Learning objectives

- To develop attentive listening and to respond appropriately

Suggested activities

- Play a game: 'Please, Mr Frog, can I cross your flowing river?'

  Chalk a river on the ground which children can jump over. Children chant 'Please, Mr Frog, can I cross your flowing river?' to you. You can reply with e.g. 'Only if you are wearing the colour red'. The children wearing red can jump to the other side. Repeat with remaining children using different colours.

Stories and rhymes

Learning objectives

- To explore and enjoy rhymes and songs

Suggested activities

Rhymes

'Five little froggies'

'Little Tommy Tadpole'

'A little green frog' all from *This Little Puffin. . .* (Puffin Books)

Special visitors/events

Learning objectives

- To explore the local environment

Suggested activities

- Visit a pond in a local park. You will need additional adults for safety reasons.

We're all going on a bear hunt

Preparation

How can you prepare for this activity?

- This activity requires the practitioners in the setting to collect a wide selection of resources in advance. The resource list is endless; it depends entirely on the children's and your imagination to adapt everyday objects and furniture. All the resources can be begged or borrowed then returned or stored depending on the cupboard space in your Nursery.
- All the resources need to be health/safety checked before the children use them.
- The activity can take place either inside or out. It would be preferable to hold it outside, but again it depends on the space and facilities available to you.
- This is an exciting activity that lends itself to a good imagination and everyone's ability to scrounge!
- Organise a 'brown' day when everyone, including the staff, comes to Nursery wearing something brown.

What are the starting points?

- Read the children the story *We're going on a Bear Hunt* by Michael Rosen and Helen Oxenbury (Mantra Publishing) several times, until the children begin to join in the catchy phrases.
- Discuss the story with the children. What was the weather like? What did the family see/hear/feel? Why were they scared?

What resources do you need to collect for the focus activity?

- Undo large cardboard boxes and attach them together with sticky tape to make a tunnel.
- Torches.
- Old blankets, drapes/curtains, sheets and a clothes horse.
- Carpet pieces, old mattresses.
- A washing line with strips of white sheeting pegged to it to represent snow.
- Paddling pool/old baby baths/bowls of water for the river.
- Sturdy crates, bales of hay/straw, logs; old tyres/inner tubes.
- Play tent/wigwam for a cave.
- Benches, short stepladders, large plastic boxes to climb on and step over.

Display suggestions

- Make a tabletop display of brown things.
- Display a collage of a big brown bear.

Home links

- Ask parents to contribute any of the above resources. They may have suggestions of their own depending on the line of work they are in.

We're all going on a bear hunt

Learning objectives

- To be aware of their own body parts, body shapes and body movements
- To begin to move with confidence
- To gain control over their own body
- To develop skills such as climbing, sliding, balancing, rolling
- To be aware of positional language such as on, over, under, through

Activity

Read *We're going on a Bear Hunt.*

Clear as large a space as possible.

Introduce the children to various body movements: e.g. on tiptoe, creeping, crawling, sliding, rolling, tiny steps, giant steps, slow steps, running steps, large sweeping arm movements, curling and stretching.

With the children discuss and plan an obstacle course that sequences the story.

Talk about and demonstrate movements such as:

Sliding or crawling **through** the tunnels, the tyres, the clothes horse draped with a blanket, table legs or chair legs.

Climbing **on** and **over** boxes, crates, logs etc.

Sweeping **through** strips of sheeting hanging on the line and stepping through the bowls of water.

Climbing **up and down** the rungs or bars on the climbing frame or a pair of small stepladders.

Encourage children to use alternate feet.

Encourage children to be adventurous and to challenge themselves.

Support and praise achievement.

Encourage the children to chant the expressive language from the story – **Swishy-swashy, swishy-swashy, swishy-swashy** etc. as they progress through the obstacle course.

What do the stepping stones look like?

 Step 1

Manage body to create intended movement. Combine and repeat a range of movements. *Child will copy movements shown by the practitioner and enjoys the different ways of moving. Will probably need assistance with climbing over boxes.*

 Step 2

Sit up, stand up and balance on various parts of the body.
Demonstrate the control necessary to hold a shape or fixed position.
Mount stairs, steps or climbing equipment using alternate steps.
Child shows confidence and enjoys trying to balance independently. When using alternate feet to climb, will need some assistance.

 Step 3

Not applicable.

 Step 4 (Early learning goal)

Move with control and co-ordination.
Travel around, under, over and through balancing and climbing equipment.
Child will explore apparatus with confidence and approaches activity independently.

We're all going on a bear hunt

Main activity

Key questions

- Why were the children scared?
- How did they get to the cave?
- Where was the bear?
- Why was the bear scared?
- Why did they run all the way back home?
- What did they do when they got there?

Key vocabulary

- Bear, hunt, grass, river, mud, forest, snowstorm, cave, tiptoe, home, hide

Targeted children

Evaluation

How did the activity go?

What evidence of children's learning have you collected?

We're all going on a bear hunt

Planning sheet for supplementary activities

Area of learning	Learning objective	Activity	Targeted children	Evaluation
PSED				
CLL				
Maths				
KUW				
Physical				
Creative				
Snack times				
Circle times				
Outdoor play				
Stories & rhymes				
Special visitors				

Adult role during spontaneous play sessions

Observing play ☐ _____   Supporting play areas ☐ _____

Supporting individual play ☐ _____   Involvement in play area ☐ _____

We're all going on a bear hunt

Supplementary activities

Personal, social and emotional development

Learning objectives

- To demonstrate appropriate range of feelings
- To develop the ability to express those feelings

Suggested activities

- Discuss with the children how it feels to be scared. Who in the story was more scared - the children or the bear? Talk to the children about the last page of the story when the bear goes back home to the cave. How does he feel? Did he just want to be friends? Was he just a lonely bear? What must it be like to feel lonely?

Communication, language and literacy

Learning objectives

- To listen and respond to stories
- To recall stories and sequence events
- To make marks to communicate meaning
- To begin to recognise their own name
- To recognise names other than their own

Suggested activities

- Read the story several times. Learn the refrain, 'We can't go over it. We can't go under it. Oh no! We've got to go through it!' Encourage children to join in the descriptive language…'Swishy-swashy' etc. Begin each line quietly and get louder.
- Talk about how the bear felt. In the writing area make cards to send to him or write letters to say you are sorry for disturbing him.
- Make the role-play area into the bear's cave. Use a tent or play house if you have one. Put a large bear inside and encourage the children to find him all the things he may need.
- Have a bear hunt: draw round templates of bears and cut them out. Write a child's name on each one and hide them in the Nursery. Children have to find their own name. If they find one that isn't theirs they have to put it back.

Additional resources

A writing area with a selection of paper, envelopes, card, sticky shapes, stamps and ink, pencils, pens etc.

Teddy bear templates, a large bear

We're all going on a bear hunt

Mathematical development

Learning objectives

- To have a knowledge and understanding of language associated with position – over, under, in, on, behind, inside, outside
- To recognise number symbols
- To identify the ordinal position in sequence – first, second, third

Suggested activities

- Have a Nursery 'Bear Hunt'. Hide a small bear in the room. Tell the children the bear is **behind** something, then let them find the bear. The next time, tell them it is **under** something.
- Use other terms such as below, above, on top of, next to, in front of, etc.
- Play the 'bear' game. The children roll a dice to create their own bear. A number 6 represents the body, a number 5 the head, the number 4 the legs, the number 3 the arms, the number 2 the ears and number 1 the eyes, nose and mouth. The children can stick on pre-cut bear shapes or draw the bear body parts themselves if they prefer, after they have rolled the dice. You can use either a numbered dice or a spotted one. This game can be altered according to the age or ability of the children.
- Position bears in a line. Which one is first, second, last?

Additional resources

Bears

Dice with either spots or numbers, pre-cut bear body parts, glue and paper

Knowledge and understanding of the world

Learning objectives

- To be able to name different animals, where they live and what they eat
- To be aware of a variety of weather conditions

Suggested activities

- Talk to the children about real bears. Show them pictures of polar bears, big brown bears, black bears, pandas and koalas. Talk about where they live and what they like to eat.
- Discuss with the children what we think of as 'a beautiful day'. In the story the sun was shining and the children were wearing summer clothes but they met with a snowstorm. Did they feel cold? Did they wish they had taken coats? Do we plan for weather changes? Do we take clothes with us 'just in case'?

Additional resources

A selection of pictures of bears

We're all going on a bear hunt

Supplementary activities

Creative development

Learning objectives

- To explore and experiment with colour and texture
- To explore and experiment with materials through a variety of media

Suggested activities

- Collage a big brown bear, make it as large as you can and display it. Collect together as many different brown materials as possible to make the bear. Add a shiny wet nose, two big furry ears and two big goggly eyes.
- Encourage the children to mix paint and make their own 'brown'. This can be done on a piece of paper, on a wipe-clean table surface, or by painting their hands with a selection of colours and rubbing them together. The 'brown' they make can then be 'hand' printed on to paper. Talk to the children about the shades they have made.

Additional resources

Collage materials, paints and paper

Snack times

Learning objectives

- To make and express choices

Suggested activities

- Have brown snacks such as:
  brown bread with chocolate spread
  jacket potatoes cut into small portions
  sausages or cocktail sausage rolls
  chocolate squares
  chocolate coated cereals.

Circle/review times

Learning objectives

- To increase the ability to listen and reflect
- To articulate feelings

Suggested activities

- Use the sentence starter 'I get scared when...'
- Pass a teddy round the circle as the children say 'I think the bear felt...'

We're all going on a bear hunt

Outdoor play

Learning objectives

• To respond to imaginative stimuli in co-operation with others

Suggested activities

• Organise a bear hunt. If the weather is good, hide teddy bears around the outside area and encourage the children to find them.

Stories and rhymes

Learning objectives

• To listen and respond to stories, songs and rhymes

Suggested activities

Stories

Mr Bingley's Bears by Gabrielle Vincent adapted from the French by Anthea Bell (Hutchinson)

Big Panda, Little Panda by Joan Stimson (Scholastic)

Little Teddy Left Behind by Anne Mangan (Little Tiger Press)

Home Before Dark by Ian Beck (Scholastic)

Goldilocks and the Three Bears (Traditional)

Stories about Paddington Bear by Michael Bond (Various)

Special visitors/events

Suggested activities

• If possible take the children to an adventure playground where there are ropes to climb, swings, slides etc. Local parks often have areas where children can play safely. ⚠

Spaced out!

How can you prepare for this activity?

- Children don't naturally know how to position themselves so that they have their own personal space.
- Children need lots of guidance to position themselves in a line or in a circle comfortably.
- You could make some space ships from pieces of material, for the children to sit on in different arrangements.

What are the starting points?

- You could use this rhyme to play the game inside:

  'Here are the spacemen flying round the moon,

  In and out and round about, they'll get there very soon.

  Out come some aliens to block their way - OH NO!

  So back to their spaceships the spacemen go.' (rhyme authors' own)

What resources do you need to collect for the focus activity?

- Box to represent spaceship and some Lego men to represent spacemen.
- Chalk or hoops.

Display suggestions

- Display the spaceships and rockets made by children in **Knowledge and understanding of the world** activity on the moonscape made in **Creative development** activity.
- Encourage children to decide on the position of their work.

Similar topics to explore

- Traffic jams.

Home links

- Ask children to bring in lots of different boxes for the **Mathematical** and **Creative development** activities.

Spaced out!

Learning objectives

- To be aware of space in relation to themselves and others

Activity

In the playground draw some 'spaceships' with chalk on the ground - enough for each child and maybe one or two more so that there is always more than enough. Alternatively, place hoops on the ground.

Each child starts in their 'spaceship'.

On a signal the children pretend to be spacemen and have to run around in 'space' until a given signal, when they have to land in a spaceship. Only one person is allowed in a spaceship. Children must keep their fingers and toes inside their spaceship.

Repeat the activity, but this time they have to land in a different spaceship.

Tell the children to take care not to bump into another spaceman.

Play 'Follow the Leader' round all the spaceships.

Take turns to be the leader.

Add some more spaceships to bring the spaceships closer together.

Jump from spaceship to spaceship (only one spaceman to a spaceship!).

Key questions

- Can you find a spaceship that is empty?
- Can you move so that you don't bump into someone?

Key vocabulary

- space, round, avoid, run

Evaluation
How did the activity go?

What do the stepping stones look like?

 Step 1

Negotiate an appropriate pathway when walking or running.
Judge body space in relation to spaces available.
Tends to stay close to 'own' spaceship.

 Step 2

Show respect for other children's personal space when playing among them.
Avoids the spaceships when running round, and looks for empty one on signal.

 Step 3

Move body position as necessary.
Child adjusts position in readiness to move again on the signal.

 Step 4 (Early learning goal)

Show awareness of space of themselves and of others.
Thinks about what others are doing/where they are going, and can make alternative choices of spaceship.

Targeted children

What evidence of children's learning have you collected?

Spaced out!

Planning sheet for supplementary activities

Area of learning	Learning objective	Activity	Targeted children	Evaluation
PSED				
CLL				
Maths				
KUW				
Physical				
Creative				
Snack times				
Circle times				
Outdoor play				
Stories & rhymes				
Special visitors				

Adult role during spontaneous play sessions

Observing play ☐ _____   Supporting play areas ☐ _____

Supporting individual play ☐ _____   Involvement in play area ☐ _____

Spaced out!

Personal, social and emotional development

Learning objectives

- To work collaboratively with others

Suggested activities

- Sit the children round the parachute/sheet and tell them to take hold of the edge.
- Children gently raise and lower the chute/sheet and experience the effect.
- Put a light ball on the chute/sheet. The task is to try to keep it on the sheet.

Additional resources

Parachute, or old sheet cut into a circle

Communication, language and literacy

Learning objectives

- To listen and respond to stories/songs/music/rhymes/poetry
- To recall stories and sequence events
- To take part in role-play with increasing confidence

Suggested activities

- Read a story such as *Whatever next?* by Jill Murphy (Macmillan Children's Books).
- Act out the story with children.

Additional resources

Teddy bear, large grocery box, colander, wellies, play food

Mathematical development

Learning objectives

- To use the language of position
- To explore space, and talk about things that fit or don't fit

Suggested activities

- Give each child a piece of paper which has been cut to form any irregular shape.
- Show the children how you want them to fill the shape with boxes, so that they fit on the shape but are not piled up.
- If you have a range of sizes of cut-out shapes, you can offer different challenges to the children.

Additional resources

Lots of different boxes which the children have brought from home (ensure you have a range of sizes and shapes), paper for shapes

Spaced out!

Knowledge and understanding of the world

Learning objectives

- To select appropriate materials and equipment to build and construct
- To describe what they have made, evaluating and adapting where necessary

Suggested activities

- Children use boxes to make spaceships and rockets.
- Show children how to make a cone shape to use as the nose cone on a rocket (cut a slit to the centre of a circle of paper/card, then curve the paper round to fit).

Additional resources

Recycled boxes, paper/card, scissors, sticky tape

Creative development

Learning objectives

- To explore and experiment with texture and materials

Suggested activities

- Make a moonscape. The children can glue egg boxes, lumps of screwed-up newspaper etc. on to a base board.
- When children are not in the vicinity, spray with silver paint. ⚠
- Make moon rocks with screwed-up newspaper; cover them with foil.
- Make a night sky with children.
- Use this as part of the display for the space rockets.

Additional resources

Silver spray, silver foil, newspapers, egg cartons, glue, baseboard

Snack times

Learning objectives

- To begin to use mathematical understanding and language in practical tasks
- To be aware of space when arranging objects

Suggested activities

- Children take turns to set out cups, place-mats etc. for the group.

Spaced out!

Circle/review times

Learning objectives

- To make and express choices
- To take turns
- To conform to rules of a game

Suggested activities

- In the circle, pass the Space Ted round. Play music as Ted is passed around. When the music stops, the child he 'lands' at is to say: 'When he goes to the moon, Ted will take…' and suggest something for Ted to take.

Additional resources

You will need a teddy with a colander covered in silver foil on his head to become Space Ted!

Outdoor play

Learning objectives

- To initiate ideas
- To take part in role-play

Suggested activities

- Set up a role-play area outside for flying into space. Involve children in the decisions about resources.

Stories and rhymes

Learning objectives

- Listen to stories and rhymes with interest

Suggested activities

Collect books about space travel, both fiction and non-fiction.

Rhymes

'There were five little spacemen' from *This Little Puffin . . .* (Puffin Books)

'Twinkle, Twinkle, Little Star' (traditional)

'Five small stars' from *This Little Puffin . . .* (Puffin Books)

Special visitors/events

Learning objectives

- To be aware of colours in their environment

Suggested activities

- Have a 'White and Silver' day when everyone, including the staff, comes to Nursery wearing something white or silver.

Healthy me!

How can you prepare for this activity?

- You need to make streamers with the children: use strips of material attached to a piece of dowel.

What are the starting points?

- Activities to raise children's awareness of their bodies.
- Use an activity rhyme, e.g.
  'Head, shoulders, knees and toes …'
  'Teddy Bear, Teddy Bear, touch your toes…'
  'Simon says…..touch your nose'.

What resources do you need to collect for the focus activity?

- Strips of material/ribbons/crepe paper.
- Dowel or rolled-up newspaper.
- Water to drink.

Display suggestions

- Display the hands and feet drawings made during the **Mathematical development** activity.
- Make a display of things we need to keep ourselves clean and healthy.

Similar topics to explore

- Healthy foods.
- Feeling poorly.

Home links

- Ask parents/carers to help their children to draw round the hands and feet of everyone in their family and to bring the drawings into the Nursery. These can be cut out and put in size order with the child's own hands and feet drawings. Display the hands and feet drawings of the children alongside those of their families.

Healthy me!

Learning objectives

- To understand the importance of keeping healthy
- To be aware of some of the changes in the body during physical exercise

Activity

Sit the children down and ask them to think about how they feel, how they are breathing, whether they are feeling hot or cold or just right.

Give the children a streamer each to run around with outside.

Talk about how they feel after the activity.

The children should be breathless, hot and sweaty. They may say they feel tired. They will probably be aware of their heart beat. They should also be excited and have enjoyed the activity.

You will need to explain that this is because their muscles are working hard, which warms them up.

Their bodies need to have more air, so their lungs have to work harder for a while. The heart is also working harder, so they can feel the beat.

You will need to explain that if they feel 'puffed out' or their legs ache, then their body is telling them they need a rest for a while.

Let the children rest for a while and repeat the exercise. The children will soon become fascinated by the changes they experience.

This is a good time to talk about not wearing lots of warm clothes when running around as this will make them too hot.

After a very active session, give the children a drink of water, and talk about how their bodies are asking for water when they feel hot and sweaty and thirsty.

Key questions

- What do you feel like?

Key vocabulary

- Breath, hot, temperature, puffed-out, sweaty, tired, heart, lungs, achy, air, water

What do the stepping stones look like?

 Step 1

Show awareness of needs.
Child will say s/he is too hot, but may not realise the need to remove a layer of clothing!

 Step 2

Observe the effects of activity on their bodies.
Child comments on feeling tired or out of breath.

 Step 3

Show some understanding that good practices with regards to exercise can contribute to good health.
Child will recognise that being puffed out, s/he needs a rest.

 Step 4 (Early learning goal)

Recognise the changes that happen to their body when they are active.
Child comments on how they feel after very active experiences. S/he will rest, and recognise need to remove a jumper if too hot.
Will ask for a drink of water after very physical activity.

Targeted children

Evaluation

How did the activity go?

What evidence of children's learning have you collected?

Healthy me!

Planning sheet for supplementary activities

Area of learning	Learning objective	Activity	Targeted children	Evaluation
PSED				
CLL				
Maths				
KUW				
Physical				
Creative				
Snack times				
Circle times				
Outdoor play				
Stories & rhymes				
Special visitors				

Adult role during spontaneous play sessions

Observing play ☐ _____   Supporting play areas ☐ _____

Supporting individual play ☐ _____   Involvement in play area ☐ _____

Healthy me!

Personal, social and emotional development

Learning objectives

- To take care of personal needs
- To be aware of what helps them to grow and be healthy

Suggested activities

- Introduce Teddy who is going to stay overnight with a friend. What will he need and why?
- Collect together items needed to keep clean e.g. flannel, soap, toothbrush etc.
- Pack Teddy's bag. He can then spend a night with each child.
- During the day, children can take turns looking after Teddy; they are responsible for his well-being. Children could ensure he uses wet wipes before a snack etc.

Additional resources

Teddy bear, small bag containing flannel, toothbrush, towel, wet wipes etc.

Notebook and pencil

Communication, language and literacy

Learning objectives

- To make marks to communicate meaning
- To recognise the different purposes of writing as a means of communication

Suggested activities

- When Teddy goes to stay overnight, the host child and carer should record what they do together in the notebook (Teddy's diary).
- Spend time the following day for the child to share with the group. Read the diary.
- As the children plan their activities for the session, discuss what Teddy plans to do.

Additional resources

As for **Personal, social and emotional development** activity

Healthy me!

Mathematical development

Learning objectives

- To understand the concept of, and to use specific language of big/small, tall/short in order
- To be able to compare and to use language such as longer/shorter

Suggested activities

- Draw round children's hands and feet. Draw round your own hand and foot. Cut the drawings out for the children to decorate.
- Compare your hands and feet drawings with the children's. You could put them in size order.
- If carers have sent in drawings of hands and feet from home, cut them out and help the child to put them in order on a piece of paper. These can then be displayed.
- Measure the children: you do not need a commercial height chart for this. A large piece of paper on the wall is sufficient. Mark each child's height with the name alongside. If this is left up, children will return to it to compare themselves and insist they have grown!
- This activity should be repeated every few months to show that children have grown.

Additional resources

Paper, pencils, scissors, crayons or felt pens

Large sheet of paper for height chart

Knowledge and understanding of the world

Learning objectives

- To talk about what they are seeing, hearing, tasting, doing
- To observe closely and identify change
- To talk about use of ICT in everyday situations

Suggested activities

- Children can chop up bananas. Talk about the bananas and what they look like/smell like/taste like. Look at texture of outside and cut surface.
- Add to blender, with the milk. Ask children what they think it will look like when it has been blended.
- After a quick whiz, look at the mixture, observing texture/lumps/colour. ⚠
- When completely blended, look carefully at the mixture and talk about what has happened to the bananas and milk. You will also see bubbles of air.

Additional resources

Bananas, milk, blender, plastic knives

Healthy me!

Creative development

Learning objectives

- To explore and experiment with paint
- To develop awareness of their body functions

Suggested activities

- Make bubble pictures: you need a small container of liquid paint. With the children, add some washing-up liquid, and mix. Show what happens when you blow gently into the paint with a straw. Make a huge bubble and place the paper on the top.
- Talk to the children about what makes the bubbles, and emphasise the importance of blowing, NOT sucking!! ⚠ It is worth practising with straws, away from the paint.

Additional resources

Washing-up liquid, small containers of paint, straws for each child, paper

Snack times

Learning objectives

- To manage their own personal needs
- To develop a sense of routine

Suggested activities

- Use different soaps to wash hands. Discuss how the different soaps smell and what happens to the soap as water is added.
- Talk about why we have to wash our hands before handling food.
- Children could take turns to wipe the table clean each day.
- Provide the banana milk-shake made in **Knowledge and understanding of the world** activity.

Circle/review times

Learning objectives

- To be aware of their own body and move with confidence

Suggested activities

- Sing the song 'Here we go Looby Lou' from *This Little Puffin. . .* (Puffin Books). Provide each child with a stretchy hair bobble to wear on their right wrist to help them remember their right hand.

Additional resources

Stretchy hair bobbles

Healthy me!

Outdoor play

Learning objectives

- To be able to co-ordinate their body
- To be aware of body changes after exercise

Suggested activities

- Play 'Follow the leader'.

Stories and rhymes

Learning objectives

- To enjoy familiar songs and rhymes
- To handle books appropriately
- To be aware that books contain information

Suggested activities

- Collect a range of children's non-fiction books relating to health.
- Use action songs/rhymes such as:

  'This is the way we wash our hands …'etc. (to tune of 'Here we go round the Mulberry Bush')

  'Hokey-cokey'

  'Here we go Looby Lou'

  'Head, shoulders, knees and toes'.

Special visitors/events

Learning objectives

- To develop awareness of the need to look after their bodies

Suggested activities

- Invite a nurse or dental practitioner to talk to the children about an aspect of keeping healthy.

Games day

How can you prepare for this activity?

- This is a day when favourite games are set up outside. It could be adapted to use as a 'fun-day' to which families are invited.
- It is important to incorporate activities which will help children develop throwing/catching/balancing/ dribbling/climbing and riding skills, rather than to have the competitive element of a 'sports day'.

What are the starting points?

- Talk to the children about the idea of having a games day.
- Take suggestions from them as to what activities they would like.
- List these ideas down on a large piece of paper. This can be added to as the children think of them.
- You could plan the games day with the children, again writing the suggestions down as children come up with them.

What resources do you need to collect for the focus activity?

- Skittles - these can easily be made with plastic bottles weighted with sand or water; they could be labelled with numbers if appropriate – and a bean bag.
- Equipment for playing 'Beanies in the Bowl': bean bags and a large bowl, e.g. baby bath or empty paddling pool.
- Equipment for playing 'Hit the Spot': buckets of water, sponges, and faces chalked on the wall as targets.
- For a weaving activity: traffic cones and a large ball.
- Slide.
- For stepping stones use reclaimed carpet tiles.
- For wibbly-wobbly activity: chalk for drawing a wiggly line on the ground.
- For egg and spoon games: large spoons, a variety of stones, a bucket.
- Equipment for any other favourite games of your own.

Games day

Display suggestions

- Display photos of the games day.
- The lists and plans made with the children could also be displayed.

Similar topics to explore

- Holding an indoor games day, using variety of simple board games.

Home links

- Invite families/carers to join you for the games day.

Foundation

The *LCP* Foundation Stage

Games day

Learning objectives

- To gain control over their own body: climbing, sliding, walking, balancing, catching, throwing, kicking
- To be able to use a range of small and large equipment

Activity

This is best set up outside.

You will need a variety of favourite activities such as:

Skittles.

Beanies in the Bowl.

Hit the Spot!

Weaving in and out of the cones, 'dribbling' the ball.

Set up a slide and/or a climbing frame.

Stepping Stones, set up in a route requiring children to take large steps or jumps.

Wibbly Wobbly activity - can the children walk along the chalk line without wobbling off?

Eggs and Spoons - can the children carry the stone on the spoon to the bucket?

Obstacle Course - bikes and prams can be ridden or pushed round a set course.

Key questions

- How far can you throw?
- Can you hit the target?
- Can you roll the ball to . . .?

Key vocabulary

- Roll, slide, throw, hit, ride, balance, step, jump, dribble, walk, hop, round, down, in, out

Evaluation

How did the activity go?

What do the stepping stones look like?

 Step 1

Operate equipment by means of pushing or pulling.

Child pushes pram or manoeuvres bike with feet round obstacle course.

Will have a go with smaller equipment and will need large target areas and larger objects to throw.

 Step 2

Show increasing control in using equipment for climbing, sliding etc.

Child is confident using larger apparatus, and is more accurate in using small equipment but still needs large targets.

 Step 3

Use increasing control over an object by pushing, patting, throwing, catching, kicking. Retrieve, collect and catch objects.

Rolling and throwing generally more controlled.

 Step 4 (Early learning goal)

Use a range of small and large equipment.

Child has the basic skills with reasonable control over their actions.

Targeted children

What evidence of children's learning have you collected?

Games day

Planning sheet for supplementary activities

Area of learning	Learning objective	Activity	Targeted children	Evaluation
PSED				
CLL				
Maths				
KUW				
Physical				
Creative				
Snack times				
Circle times				
Outdoor play				
Stories & rhymes				
Special visitors				

Adult role during spontaneous play sessions

Observing play ☐ _____   Supporting play areas ☐ _____

Supporting individual play ☐ _____   Involvement in play area ☐ _____

Games day

Personal, social and emotional development

Learning objectives

• To deal with conflict through negotiation

Suggested activities

• Make two teddies fight over whose turn it is to throw a ball at the skittles. One teddy 'dissolves in tears'.
• Ask children how they can help the teddies.
• The children can sit in the leader's seat to talk to the teddies and help resolve the problem.
• The children can take the teddies to join in their activities. Observe how the children make the teddies behave.

Additional resources

Two teddies, ball, skittles

Communication, language and literacy

Learning objectives

• To understand that writing is for a purpose

Suggested activities

• Children make invitations to invite carers to join the fun!
• Use plain cards: children can decorate one side and a message can be written on the other.
• Encourage children to sign the cards themselves.

Additional resources

Plain cards

Mathematical development

Learning objectives

• To be aware that numbers have a purpose in informal and formal situations
• To record numbers and show understanding of the use of numbers in practical activities and experiences
• To demonstrate 1:1 correspondence

Suggested activities

• Play a Skittles game:
  Set up the skittles; the children take turns to roll a ball and see how many they can each knock down.
• Talk to the children about how they want to record their scores.
• Each child could record their own scores on paper on a clipboard.
  It is important that children decide for themselves how to record their results. Some may draw the skittles,

Games day

some may make simple tally marks, e.g. | | | | representing 4, and some may want to write the numeral, e.g. 4. Any method is acceptable.
- Extend this activity by giving each skittle a number; children record the numbers on the skittles that they knock over each time.

Additional resources

Skittles (easily made from empty plastic bottles which can be weighted with some sand), ball

Clipboards (**Tip**! Card from the back of A4 paper pads and a paper clip make good clipboards.)

Knowledge and understanding of the world

Learning objectives
- To have confidence in the use of a variety of IT technology

Suggested activities
- Set up two skittles as a gate or goal.
- Use a programmable toy or remote control car. The children are to try to manoeuvre the toy between the skittles.

Additional resources

2 skittles, a programmable or remote control toy

Creative development

Learning objectives
- To respond to rhythm and repetitious nature of singing games

Suggested activities
- Sing circle games, e.g. 'In and out the dusty bluebells', 'Ring-o-Ring-o-Roses', 'Oranges and Lemons', 'Hokey–cokey'.

Snack times

Learning objectives
- To gain control of body, refining hand movements by pouring

Suggested activities
- Allow children to pour drinks into cups for others.

Games day

Circle/review times

Learning objectives

- To experience the feeling of belonging to a group

Suggested activities

- The children are to sit in a circle. Call the name of a child and roll a ball to the child. That child then names another, and rolls the ball to him/her.
- When children are used to the game, see if they can make sure the ball is passed to each person once only.

Outdoor play

Learning objectives

- To use a range of small and large equipment

Suggested activities

- See **Main activity**. Select any activity to play outside in the lead-up to the day.

Stories and rhymes

Learning objectives

- To join in with familiar rhymes with actions

Suggested activities

Action rhymes which children can join in physically, e.g.

'Humpty Dumpty'

'Hickory Dickory Dock'

'The Grand Old Duke of York'

Special visitors/events

Learning objectives

- To experience the feeling of being part of the community (Nursery)
- To begin to take responsibility
- To be involved in planning and preparing an activity

Suggested activities

- Invite families/carers to the games day. Provide drinks and refreshments. Children can be involved in making and selling refreshments.

The Queen of Hearts

How can you prepare for this activity?

- You will be making jam tarts; each step can be carried out by the children if the equipment is prepared beforehand.
- Mark on the scales where the arrow will point when there is enough flour/fat, then the children can weigh the ingredients reasonably accurately under supervision. Similarly, mark a line on the measuring jug to show how much liquid is needed.
- For about 24 tarts you will need: 100g plain flour, 50g margarine, water, jam and lemon curd.

What are the starting points?

- The rhyme 'The Queen of Hearts':

    'The Queen of Hearts,

    She made some tarts

    All on a summer's day.

    The Knave of Hearts,

    He stole those tarts

    And took them right away.'

- Say the rhyme and discuss words such as Queen, Knave, tarts. Show the children the pictures of The Queen and Knave of Hearts from a pack of playing cards.

What resources do you need to collect for the focus activity?

- Ingredients for pastry, a variety of jams and lemon curd.
- Equipment: clear mixing bowl, kitchen scales, pastry cutters, rolling pins, teaspoons, flour in a shaker, bun tins, aprons.

Display suggestions

- Display the 'Queen of Hearts' paintings made in **Creative development** activity.
- Find and display Valentine cards, wrapping paper with hearts on, heart-shaped boxes etc.

Similar topics to explore

- Valentine's Day.

Home links

- Ask children to look for pictures with hearts on.

The Queen of Hearts

Learning objectives

- To control refined hand movements
- Use simple tools appropriately and safely

Activity

Talk to the children about the ingredients that you will be mixing together. Allow the children to feel the texture of the flour.

Explain that the children need to measure the amount of flour, fat and liquid to make the pastry. Tell the children how the scales work and demonstrate what happens when something is placed on the weighing pan. Show the children the mark to which the arrow will point when there is the right amount of flour.

Children can then spoon out the flour until the arrow points to the mark.

Repeat with the fat.

The children should enjoy the experience of mixing the flour and fat with fingers when you have shown them how to do this.

Allow the children to gradually add liquid until it mixes to the right consistency.

Turn out on to floured surface and knead. Each child could then have a small piece of dough to knead and roll out, then cut with a pastry cutter.

Place carefully in bun tin. It is worth cooking a piece of pastry without jam to look at how it changes.

Allow each child to decide on their favourite jam to add with a teaspoon.

⚠ Bake in moderate oven (150-160°, Gas 3–4) for 10-15 minutes. Set a timer to ring when the tarts should be ready. Eat when cool enough.

Key questions

- What can you see happening to the mixture?
- What does the flour/mixture/dough feel like?
- Can you roll out the pastry?
- What shape has the cutter made?
- What has happened to the pastry when it comes out of the oven?
- Can you still stretch it?

Key vocabulary

- Mix, rub, weigh, measure, scales, measuring jug, carefully, roll, stretch, twist, pull, pat, cut, shape

What do the stepping stones look like?

 Step 1

Engage in activities requiring hand-eye co-ordination. Use tools and equipment. *With support child will pour flour, with concentration, with some accuracy; some spillage.*

 Step 2

Understand that tools and equipment have to be used safely. *Child understands that the oven and baking trays will be hot. Understands need to be careful using the cutters.*

 Step 3

Explore malleable materials, use simple tools to effect changes to the materials. *Child explores the textures of ingredients and can roll out the pastry and comment on what happens. Uses cutter and can carefully transfer the resulting shape into the bun tray.*

 Step 4 (Early learning goal)

Handle tools and malleable materials safely and with increasing control. *Child can use the provided tools safely and effectively with independence. S/he will be able to choose size of spoon required to scoop jam.*

Targeted children

Evaluation

How did the activity go?

What evidence of children's learning have you collected?

The Queen of Hearts

Planning sheet for supplementary activities

Area of learning	Learning objective	Activity	Targeted children	Evaluation
PSED				
CLL				
Maths				
KUW				
Physical				
Creative				
Snack times				
Circle times				
Outdoor play				
Stories & rhymes				
Special visitors				

Adult role during spontaneous play sessions

Observing play ☐ _____   Supporting play areas ☐ _____

Supporting individual play ☐ _____   Involvement in play area ☐ _____

The Queen of Hearts

Personal, social and emotional development

Learning objectives

- To be aware of their own feelings
- To consider the effect of their actions on others

Suggested activities

- This links with **Circle time** activity. Use two dolls dressed as the Queen and Knave of Hearts to dramatise the rhyme.
- Talk about what the Knave of Hearts did and what the Queen felt like. Can the children show you by their facial expressions?
- Talk about why the Knave stole the tarts. What should the Knave do?
- Make the Knave refuse to say sorry. Explore this with the children.
- What will happen if the Knave says sorry? What will the Queen do?
- Finish with a positive ending, e.g. the Queen will share the tarts if the Knave is sorry.

Additional resources

Two dolls dressed to be Queen and Knave of Hearts - just a gold crown and a cloak for the Queen and a white piece of cloth with a red heart for the knave (old baby vests are useful for this)

tray of tarts

Communication, language and literacy

Learning objectives

- To take part in role-play with increasing confidence

Suggested activities

- Set up a 'Queen of Hearts' role-play area with the children.
- Talk to the children about what they think they need to make a castle.
- Large construction bricks could form the castle walls.
- You will need lengths of bright and shiny materials for cloaks.
- Provide some crowns made from gold card.
- Spray cheap paper cups, plates and plastic cutlery with gold spray.
- Children could make tarts using circles of card and painting a dollop of jam.
- A simple tabard with a large red heart could become the Knave's outfit.
- Wherever possible, encourage children to talk about how the items for the castle could be made/found.

Additional resources

Lengths of material, tabard with heart on

Sparkly bracelets, necklaces etc.

Cheap paper cups and plates and plastic cutlery all sprayed gold

Baking trays and cake tins

The Queen of Hearts

Mathematical development

Learning objectives

* To be able to sort objects using a single criterion
* To be able to match objects using a single criterion
* To begin to have an awareness of symmetry

Suggested activities

* Look at cards from a pack of cards.
* Ask the children to find all the ones which have heart shapes on them.
* Talk about the Queen of Hearts card. Talk about what happens if you turn it 'head to tail'! Use a mirror across the middle and discuss what the children can see.
* Extract the cards with Ace – 5 of hearts, and look at the pattern/layout of the hearts on the cards.
* Remove the same set of hearts from another pack, and use both sets of cards to find matching pairs.
* You could add the picture cards from the two sets, or more of the number cards, to extend the matching activity.

Additional resources

Two packs of playing cards

Mirror

Knowledge and understanding of the world

Learning objectives

* To know that tools should be handled safely and carefully
* To have opportunities to practise the skills involved in shaping, assembling and joining materials
* To understand the concept of length and size and use specific language of 'long/short, longer/shorter, too small/big'

Suggested activities

* The children make King and Queen crowns for themselves. Provide strips of card for children to decorate as they wish with shiny paper, tissue, etc. They should be encouraged to cut pieces of coloured or shiny paper themselves to decorate their crown.
* Initially, join the ends of the crown together with a paper clip.
* Discuss whether the crown would fit, and what would need to be done to make it fit the child's head.
* When the crown has been adjusted to fit, you should staple the ends together. If you feel confident enough, allow the child to use the stapler under supervision. ⚠

Additional resources

Prepared long strips of card, tissue paper, coloured shiny paper, e.g. sweet wrappers

Glue, paper clips, stapler, staples

The Queen of Hearts

Creative development

Learning objectives

- To begin to have an awareness of symmetry
- To explore and experiment with materials through painting

Suggested activities

- Look carefully at the Queen of Hearts picture on the playing cards and discuss what it looks like when it is turned the other way round.
- Fold a piece of paper in half and keep it folded. Place it with the folded edge nearest the child.
- The children are to paint a picture of their face, with a crown like the Queen of Hearts, on the paper.
- Open the paper and fold on to the wet paint. Open the paper up again and Hey Presto! - children have their own Queen of Hearts pictures.

Additional resources

Playing cards, paper, paints, brushes

Snack times

Learning objectives

- To make and express choices

Suggested activities

- The children can eat the jam tarts they have made in the **Main activity**. Talk about which tarts the children chose.

Circle/review times

Learning objectives

- To know the difference between right and wrong

Suggested activities

- Use a favourite soft toy or teddy to pass round the circle.
- Tell the children that you are going to tell the toy something that you don't like happening to you.
- Start the circle time with 'I don't like it when . . .' (e.g. 'people write on my work').
- Pass the toy to the next child who uses the starter and adds their own ending. Allow children to simply pass the toy if they feel uncomfortable.
- When everyone has had a turn, talk about some of the issues raised. Encourage children to talk about what should happen when someone has done something wrong.
- Finish the session either by passing a hug to each other, or by passing the toy and giving it a hug. The children should leave feeling good about themselves.

Additional resources

Soft toy or teddy

The Queen of Hearts

Outdoor play

Learning objectives

- To understand the concept of big and small

Suggested activities

- Cut out heart shapes of different sizes to hide outside.
- The children are to hunt for a big and a small heart each.
- More able children should hunt for 3 different sizes.

Additional resources

Heart shapes made from paper/card

Stories and rhymes

Learning objectives

- To listen and respond to stories and rhymes

Suggested activities

Stories

I'm sorry by Sam McBratney (Collins)

Sorry, Miss! by Jo Furtado and Frederic Joos (Andersen Press)

Goldilocks and the Three Bears (traditional)

Special visitors/events

Learning objectives

- To be aware that there are some special days that people celebrate

Suggested activities

- For Valentine's Day, make Valentine cards for a friend.

Creative development

- Flowers

- Old MacDonald had a farm

- The wheels on the bus

- Jack Frost

Foundation

Flowers

How can you prepare for this activity?

- This theme should ideally take place during the spring.
- If possible, plan a visit to a Garden Centre. ⚠
- Buy a selection of seeds in packets.
- Buy some sunflower seeds, cress seeds and bean sprouts.
- Check to see if you have a watering can, plant/yoghurt pots, compost, a trowel or an old spoon and magnifying glasses, camera and films. 🗔
- Check that any flowers or plants you buy are safe for children to touch and smell. ⚠
- Buy an Amaryllis bulb (in the shops in December and early January) and keep it until you are ready to plant it at the start of the topic.

What are the starting points?

- Sing the nursery rhyme 'Mary, Mary, quite contrary…'
- Plant the Amaryllis bulb with the children. These plants are excellent to watch growing as they literally 'grow before your very eyes'.

What resources do you need to collect for the focus activity?

- A selection of flowers and plants in season for observational drawing, painting and discussion.
- A selection of collage materials such as string, wool, yarn, ribbon, matchsticks, confetti, glitter, sequins, fabric scraps, tissue paper, crepe paper, coloured paper, wax paper, shiny paper, tinsel, newspaper etc.
- Textured paper such as corrugated paper, wallpaper, paper bags and paper doilies.
- Paints of various colours, thicknesses and textures. Mix these with the children. Add flour, glue, sawdust, sugar, sand, rice etc. to the paint to give texture.
- A range of painting materials such as sponges, twigs, lolly sticks, combs and toothbrushes for the children to create their own texture.
- Objects to print with such as tubes, Duplo bricks, cotton reels, leaves, sponges etc.
- A copy of the painting 'The Sunflower' by Van Gogh.
- Pebbles, twigs, coloured stones, compost etc. for miniature garden

Display suggestions

- Make a tabletop display of gardening equipment such as a plant pot, trowel, seeds, a watering can, gardening gloves, gardening books, pictures of flowers etc.
- Make a large wall display of a garden using all the children's work on flowers.
- Display a nature table with a selection of plants and flowers all named, together with a selection of gardening books with pictures or photographs of flowers in.

Flowers

Similar topics to explore

- The Seaside, Minibeasts or the Jungle.

Home links

- Ask parents to accompany their children on a visit to the Library.
- Suggest parents let their children help them in the garden if they have one.

Foundation

Flowers

Learning objectives

- To explore and experiment with colour and texture
- To explore shape and form
- To explore and experiment with materials through a variety of media, e.g. painting, drawing and collage

Activities

Encourage the children to paint flowers in a variety of colours, textures and thicknesses of paint using their fingers, toothbrushes etc. as well as paintbrushes. Always value their interpretation.

Provide the children with a selection of flowers to observe; encourage them to gently touch and smell the flowers. Talk about the size of the flower, the shape of the petals, the colours they can see. Encourage children to draw or paint what they see. Talk to the children about their observations.

Look at and discuss 'The Sunflower' by Van Gogh. Encourage the children to collage their own flowers. The techniques for this activity may need to be demonstrated first. Show children how to tear and cut petal shapes from the selection of paper, card, tissue and wallpaper etc.

Print the centre of the flower with the resources provided such as kitchen-roll tubes, sponges etc.

Glue the petals around the centre.

Encourage the children to have several attempts using different media. The children will have their own ideas; encourage them to be creative.

Display all the flowers as a beautiful garden. Encourage the children to help put the display on the wall.

Collect flowers, press them and when ready, glue them on to either card or paper. Ask the children to write their name on the card and then, if possible, laminate it. These could then be used as individual place mats for children at snack time or lunchtime or as a present to take home.

Design and make a miniature garden. Collect together pebbles and coloured stones, lolly sticks, compost, twigs etc. and plant seeds. Carrot tops are ideal as they grow into realistic trees, and cress can be used for growing into grass.

What do the stepping stones look like?

 Step 1

Begin to differentiate colours.
Use their bodies (fingers, hands) to explore texture and space.
Child enjoys experimenting with different tools. They can name most colours and enjoy experience of touching and smelling flowers.

 Step 2

Differentiate marks and movement on paper.
Begin to describe the texture of things.
Use lines to enclose a space, and then begin to use these shapes to represent objects.
Child may use favourite colours and make recognisable flower shapes. Will select appropriate objects to make centre of flowers.

 Step 3

Explore what happens when they mix colours.
Understand that different media can be combined.
Choose particular colours to use for a purpose.
Experiment to create different textures.
Work creatively on a small or large scale.
Child will choose different resources to make collages and pictures.
S/he will take delight in seeing effect of mixing red and yellow to make orange.
Will select an appropriate colour for the flowers based on observation.

 Step 4 (Early learning goal)

Explore colour, texture, shape, form and space in two and three dimensions.
Child is able to decide on resources s/he wants for their collage and is happy to use a variety of media on one piece of work! S/he takes great care in placing petal shapes where s/he wants and is capable of sustained concentration on task.

Flowers

Key questions

- What do the flowers feel like/smell like?
- What patterns can you see?
- How many petals are there?

Key vocabulary

- Smooth, soft, prickly, patterned, bumpy, silky,
  lighter, darker, thicker, thinner, smooth, lumpy

Targeted children

Evaluation

How did the activity go?

What evidence of children's learning have you collected?

Foundation

Flowers

Planning sheet for supplementary activities

Area of learning	Learning objective	Activity	Targeted children	Evaluation
PSED				
CLL				
Maths				
KUW				
Physical				
Creative				
Snack times				
Circle times				
Outdoor play				
Stories & rhymes				
Special visitors				

Adult role during spontaneous play sessions

Observing play ☐ _____   Supporting play areas ☐ _____

Supporting individual play ☐ _____   Involvement in play area ☐ _____

Flowers

Supplementary activities

Personal, social and emotional development

Learning objectives

• To respect and care for the environment

Suggested activities

• Give the children the responsibility of caring for any Nursery plants. Children could take turns in being the 'monitor' who waters the plants.

• Discuss what a plant needs to grow. Talk about what children need to grow. Discuss how love and care make us all feel happier.

• Talk to the children about the occasions when we send flowers: when babies are born, to say sorry, to say thank you etc. Maybe a group of children could visit someone who has been ill and take them a bunch of flowers or a plant.

Communication, language and literacy

Learning objectives

• To gain pleasure and enjoyment from pictures, books and print
• To know that print carries meaning
• To begin to write own captions
• To take part in role-play with increasing confidence

Suggested activities

• Read *Koala and the flower* by Mary Murphy (Egmont Children's Books). Discuss with the children how interesting it is to visit a library. Invite a librarian in to Nursery to tell the children a story. Visit a library in small groups; encourage parents to come along with you. ⚠

• Take photographs of the Amaryllis as it grows; make a nursery book and add the photographs with captions. Support the children in writing their own captions. Make the finished book available for parents to see.

• The role-play area could become either The Flower Shop or The Garden Centre.

Additional resources

Camera and films

A selection of plastic, silk, paper or real flowers

Tissue or kitchen paper to wrap flowers in

Plastic plant pots, seed packets, watering cans

A till and play money

A small café area if the role-play area becomes a Garden Centre

Flowers

Mathematical development

Learning objectives

- To begin to use standard measures of length appropriate to situations
- To verbalise numbers by counting
- To copy a simple sequential pattern
- To be able to sort using a single criterion

Suggested activities

- Regularly measure the Amaryllis to see how it has grown, keeping a record of its growth. Add the information to the nursery book.
- Take photographs of the Amaryllis as it grows and add these to the nursery book.
- Measure the children and display their heights with strips of paper on the wall.
- Count the petals on different flowers. Which flowers have the most?
- Cut out petals in two different colours and begin sticking them around a centre in a pattern; see if the child can continue the pattern on their own.
- Use empty seed packets and encourage children to sort by their own criteria, e.g. by colour, type, size of petals etc.

Additional resources

Camera and film

Seed packets

Coloured paper, scissors

Flowers

Knowledge and understanding of the world

Learning objectives

- To recognise the changes in seasons
- To plant seeds and bulbs and observe them grow
- To care for plants
- To recognise and name features of plants
- To predict/guess what will happen, and to test the prediction/guess
- To observe closely and identify similarities, differences, patterns and change

Suggested activities

- Read the story *The Tiny Seed* by Eric Carle (Puffin Books). Discuss what happens to the little seed. Talk about how winter changes to spring, then summer, then autumn.
- Grow cress. Plant sunflower seeds. Watch beans grow in a jar, by placing some wet kitchen roll in the jar and placing the beans between the paper and the glass. Put the jar in a warm place.
- Go on a spring walk; take a camera with you to record the visit.
- Regularly take small groups of children to a flower shop to buy flowers.
- Teach the children to name the main parts of the flower – stem, petals and leaves.
- Teach the children what a plant needs to grow: sunlight, warmth, soil, water.
- Place a white flower in water with food dye in. Watch how the stalk and then the flower slowly change colour to that of the coloured water.
- Encourage the children to observe flowers and plants through a magnifying glass.

Additional resources

Cress seeds, sunflower seeds, bean sprouts, jars, kitchen roll, white flowers, food dye, magnifying glasses

The story *The Little Seed* by Eric Carle

Camera and film

Flowers

Physical development

Learning objectives

- To control refined hand movements

Suggested activities

- Thread beads in two or three colours to make a pattern, e.g. red, blue, red, blue etc.
- Tearing and cutting activities will improve the children's fine motor skills. Encourage children to create their own collage by sticking their torn or cut shapes on to a piece of card or paper.
- Use appropriate music so children can imagine they are plants growing. Start by curling up small then slowly stretching very tall. Reverse the process.

Additional resources

Beads in two or three colours and thread

Collage materials and card

Music for movement

Snack times

Learning objectives

- To be actively involved in a variety of experiences
- To build relationships with other children
- To interact socially

Suggested activities

- Have a selection of fruit with pips or seeds such as oranges, apples, pears, melons, tomatoes.
- Grow cress and make sandwiches.
- Have slices of poppy-seed bread.
- Decorate fairy cakes with sugar flowers.

Circle/review times

Learning objectives

- To show confidence and self–esteem
- To gain confidence when speaking in familiar groups
- To develop the ability to express their feelings

Suggested activities

- The children could show and tell how they collaged or painted their picture (see **Main activity**).

Flowers

Outdoor play

Learning objectives

- To be aware of directional and positional language, e.g. backwards, forwards, sideways, up and down
- To be eager to explore new learning

Suggested activities

- Play ring games outside e.g. 'Ring-o-Ring-o-Roses' and 'In and out the dusty bluebells'.
- Provide the tools and equipment for children to garden with, e.g. window boxes, tubs with soil, watering cans, gardening tools, seeds, bulbs, flowers, plants and plant pots.

Additional resources

Gardening tools and equipment

Stories and rhymes

Learning objectives

- To listen and respond to stories/songs/rhymes/poems
- To increase the ability to listen with understanding and enjoyment

Suggested activities

Stories

Titch by Pat Hutchins (Red Fox)

Jack and the beanstalk (traditional)

Rhymes

'Oats and beans and barley grow'

'There's a worm at the bottom of my garden'

'Five little leaves so bright and gay' all from *This Little Puffin...* (Puffin Books)

Special visitors/events

Suggested activities

- This unit could be planned around Mother's Day or Easter. The parents could be invited into Nursery and the children could present them with small bunches of flowers and maybe afternoon tea.

Old MacDonald had a farm

How can you prepare for this activity?

- Introduce the children to the idea of listening. Provide opportunities for children to listen to and talk about sounds they hear every day such as phones ringing, other children playing in the Nursery, taps running, toilets flushing, cars passing by.

- Introduce the children to the sounds that everyday objects make if they are banged, hit, shaken etc. such as spoons (both wooden and metal) tapping on saucepans, cake tins and tin cans.

- Teach the children to use their bodies to create sounds such as clapping, tapping their heads/shoulders/knees/the floor, stamping their feet, humming, clicking their fingers etc.

- Make your own instruments that can be shaken, blown, scraped, hit or plucked.

  Fill washing-up liquid bottles or yoghurt pots with old crayons, milk bottle tops, chopped-up straws, sand, rice, beans or pasta. Make cardboard trumpets. Place different-sized elastic bands around a tube at varying widths apart to create a range of sounds. Use coconut shells, keys, sandpaper blocks, tissue paper wrapped around a comb etc. ⚠

- Play different types of music in the Nursery such as orchestral, classical, chart music, jazz, opera, folk, reggae, music from other cultures. Encourage the children to sit quietly for short periods of time to listen and then talk about what they have heard. Did they hear any voices/musical instruments? Which ones did they hear? Did they hear any drums? To begin with, it may just be a guessing game but eventually the children will become more familiar with the sounds they are hearing and may be able to distinguish between styles.

- Introduce the children to a selection of musical instruments. Encourage careful handling of each instrument. Demonstrate how the instrument is played. Encourage the children to listen to the sound it makes and to understand how sounds can be quiet or loud, high or low, soft or hard, fast or slow. Give the children plenty of opportunities to play with and explore the instruments. Allow time for unstructured music sessions as well as organised ones.

What are the starting points?

- Talk to the children about animals that live on a farm. Make the noise that each animal makes. Repeat the activity several times so that the children feel more confident about making animal sounds.

- Read *Noisy Farm* by Rod Campbell (Puffin Books).

What resources do you need to collect for the focus activity?

- Instruments made in the Nursery.

- Untuned percussion instruments such as tambourines, bells, drums, wooden blocks, castanets and tuned percussion instruments such as chime bars and xylophones.

- Simple drawings or pictures of each instrument, laminated if possible. When you want the children to play a particular instrument these can be held up for the children to see; they will then know when it is their turn to play their instrument.

- Props for the characters in 'The Farmer's in his Den'.

Old MacDonald had a farm

Preparation

Display suggestions

- Make a tabletop display of musical instruments, with captions labelling each instrument.
- Make a wall display of farm animals.

Similar topics to explore

- Topics that include repetitive noises such as transport or the jungle.

Home links

- Suggest parents take their children to visit a farm.
- Ask parents to play records/tapes/CDs to their children and to talk to them about the music they have heard. Ask the parents if some of them would bring in their favourite pieces of music, particularly if they are from other cultures.

Foundation

Old MacDonald had a farm

Main activity

Learning objectives

- To explore sound with fun and pleasure
- To initiate and create sounds
- To listen perceptively and recall repeated sounds and sound patterns
- To share music with others
- To enjoy singing a range of familiar songs and rhymes

Activity

Sit the children in a circle. Sing a selection of familiar nursery rhymes including 'Baa, Baa, Black Sheep'. Whilst sitting in the circle the children can clap the rhythm, tap their knees, click their fingers etc. or they can skip around in a circle, holding hands.

Sing 'The Farmer's in his Den'. Choose a child to be the farmer – he/she wears a farmer's hat, chooses a wife etc. Let each character have a prop such as an apron for the wife, a teddy for the child etc.

Sing 'Old MacDonald had a farm'.

Ask the children which farm animals they would like to sing about and what noises they make. Vary the animals' noises each time you sing the song. Introduce a selection of instruments. Decide which instrument best represents each animal. Divide the children into small groups with each group representing one animal. Share out the instruments and give the same instrument to each child in that group.

Each time that animal's noise is made, the group of children play their instruments. When you want that child or group to play their instrument hold up the picture. (See **Resources**.)

Encourage the children to keep a beat and to follow the pictorial instructions. Practise stopping and starting on a signal.

Use the 'orchestra' approach to other songs and rhymes. Vary the instruments according to the song.

Key questions

- What instrument is this?
- What sort of sound does it make?
- Can you find an instrument that makes high sounds/low sounds/two that sound the same?

What do the stepping stones look like?

 Step 1

Join in favourite songs.
Respond to sound with body movement.
Enjoy joining in with dancing and ring games.
Child joins in with rhyme that is familiar. With encouragement and repetition, child will join in with the movements.

 Step 2

Sing a few simple, familiar songs.
Sing to themselves and make up simple songs.
Tap out simple repeated rhythms and make some up. Explore and learn how sounds can be changed.
Initiate and create movement in response to music.
Child enjoys the repetitive patterns with sound and making sounds with the instruments when accompanying 'Old MacDonald'.

 Step 3

Begin to build a repertoire of songs.
Explore the different sounds of instruments.
Begin to move rhythmically.
Sings these familiar songs confidently and moves rhythmically in time to the songs. (Observe whole-body movements as well as tapping, clapping.)
Begins to show a preference for an instrument. With support will respond to pictorial prompt to play instruments.

 Step 4 (Early learning goal)

Recognise and explore how sounds can be changed, sing simple songs from memory, recognise repeated sounds and sound patterns and match movements to music.
Recognises the repetitive elements to songs and enjoys. Anticipates when it is their turn to play when in the orchestra.
Responds to the pictorial instructions.

Old MacDonald had a farm

Main activity

Key vocabulary

- Fast, slow, high, low, quiet, loud, beat, rhythm, tune, song

Targeted children

Evaluation

How did the activity go?

What evidence of children's learning have you collected?

Foundation

The LCP Foundation Stage

Old MacDonald had a farm

Planning sheet for supplementary activities

Area of learning	Learning objective	Activity	Targeted children	Evaluation
PSED				
CLL				
Maths				
KUW				
Physical				
Creative				
Snack times				
Circle times				
Outdoor play				
Stories & rhymes				
Special visitors				

Adult role during spontaneous play sessions

Observing play ☐ _____ Supporting play areas ☐ _____

Supporting individual play ☐ _____ Involvement in play area ☐ _____

Old MacDonald had a farm

Personal, social and emotional development

Learning objectives

- To build relationships with other children
- To experience a sense of belonging
- To be actively involved in a variety of activities

Suggested activities

- Encourage the children to take part in the musical activity.
- Encourage, support and praise the children who join in and are able to recognise familiar tunes, songs and rhymes.
- Children who are feeling upset, angry or frustrated may be calmed by singing or listening to a gentle piece of music.

Communication, language and literacy

Learning objectives

- To listen and respond to stories
- To increase the ability to listen with understanding and enjoyment and to evaluate and reflect
- To show an understanding of the main elements of a story: characters/the setting/beginning and ending. To be able to talk about these

Suggested activities

- Read the story of *Farmer Duck* by Martin Waddell and Helen Oxenbury (Walker Books). Encourage the children to join in the refrain: '"How goes the work?" called the farmer. The duck answered "Quack".'
- Take time to look at the detail in the expressive illustrations. Look at the expressions on the animals' faces. How are the animals feeling? Before turning each page, ask the children what they think might happen next. Talk about how the animals feel about the duck. Talk about the farmer. Was he a good farmer?
- Play 'listening lotto' of farm animal sounds.

Additional resources

Cassette player, tape of farm animal sounds

The story *Farmer Duck*

Old MacDonald had a farm

Mathematical development

Learning objectives

- To join in and recite number rhymes
- To verbalise numbers by counting
- To recognise and understand cardinal numbers – 'how many?'
- To begin to show an awareness of number operations – subtraction

Suggested activities

- Chant: 'Five fluffy chicks were pecking in the sun.
  The old fox came and he caught one'.
- Play this as a ring game with the old fox waiting on the outside of the ring, coming in and taking a chick every time you sing …'the old fox came'.
- Change the numbers to e.g. Ten fluffy chicks. How many are left after the fox has been?
- Make a collage of farm animals and display them on the wall. Count how many there are of each animal and ask the children if there are more cows than sheep, more sheep than pigs, etc.

Additional resources

Masks/headbands for the chicks and the fox

Collage materials

Knowledge and understanding of the world

Learning objectives

- To know that not all places are the same
- To classify according to certain criteria – farm animals
- To recognise and name features of living things

Suggested activities

- Talk to the children about farm animals. Where do they live? Name their homes such as a pig/sty, horse/stable, cow/shed etc.
- Ask the children what we get from sheep/chickens/cows. Talk to the children about milk products – butter, yoghurt, cream and cheese.
- What are the different baby animals called? What are the Mummies and Daddies called?
- Sing 'Baa, Baa, Black Sheep', 'Chick, chick, chick, chick, chicken, lay a little egg for me' and 'This little piggy went to market'.
- Talk to the children about the crops that grow on a farm and the need to protect them from the birds.
- Sing 'Oats and beans and barley grow' and 'Two little dicky birds', adding the different actions or the finger movements to them.
- Watch what happens to a plastic container of milk when it is left to go sour. ⚠
- Set up a small-world play mat with a farm and farm animals.

Additional resources

Sealed plastic container of milk

Play mat, farm animals and buildings

Old MacDonald had a farm

Physical development

Learning objectives

- To begin to show movement in imaginative ways
- To gain control over fine motor skills – eye/hand co-ordination
- To be able to handle construction or small-world toys with increasing control

Suggested activities

- Sing 'When all the cows were sleeping' ('I'm a dingle-dangle scarecrow') (*This Little Puffin...*) adding all the actions.
- Encourage the children to complete animal jigsaws, starting with inset jigsaws. Can they remove/replace 6 pieces/12+ pieces? Can they complete simple fit-together puzzles with 6/8/10 pieces? Can they complete more complex puzzles? Record your observations on how able each child is and plan appropriately.
- Introduce the farm as a small-world activity.

Additional resources

Animal jigsaws of varying degrees of difficulty

Small-world farm buildings, fences, farm animals etc.

A Playmobil farm set

Snack times

Learning objectives

- To make and express choices
- To interact socially

Suggested activities

- Make different flavoured milk shakes or try a variety of flavoured yoghurts or ice–creams.
- Spread cream cheese on crackers. Encourage the children to do this themselves. Try different cheeses.
- Make egg sandwiches on brown bread.

Circle/review times

Learning objectives

- To express their opinions
- To join in with a group activity

Suggested activities

- Use the circle time sentence starter 'My favourite animal is…'
- Encourage the children to make a farm animal sound and see who can guess which animal they are pretending to be.

The *LCP* Foundation Stage

Old MacDonald had a farm

Supplementary activities

Outdoor play

Learning objectives

- To be eager to explore new learning
- To be actively involved in a variety of activities

Suggested activities

- Play ring games outside.

Stories and rhymes

Learning objectives

- To listen and respond to stories and rhymes

Suggested activities

Stories

Wibbly Pig stories by Mick Inkpen (Hodder Children's Books)

The Very Sleepy Pig by John Malam (Mustard)

Oh Dear! by Rod Campbell (Macmillan Children's Books)

Farmer George and the Lost Chick by Nick Ward (Pavilion Books Ltd)

Hungry Hen by Richard H. Waring (Oxford University Press)

Where's my Mummy? by Colin and Jacqui Hawkins (Walker Books)

Rhymes

'Higgledy, Piggledy, my black hen'

'To market, to market to buy a fat pig'

'I went to visit a farm one day' all from *This Little Puffin...* (Puffin Books)

Song books

Three Singing Pigs by Kaye Umansky (A&C Black)

It's time to wake up by Niki Davies (International Music Publications)

Special visitors/events

Learning objectives

- To share music with others

Suggested activities

- Arrange for the children to visit a live performance of a show or arrange for performers to visit the Nursery.
- Encourage children to appreciate live and recorded performances whenever possible.

The wheels on the bus

How can you prepare for this activity?

- If possible take the children, in small groups, on a bus journey or to visit a bus station.

What are the starting points?

- Talk to the children about bus journeys. Do the children ever catch a bus? Where do they catch them? Who do they go with? Where do they go? Why do people take buses? What colour are they? What is a single-decker bus? What is a double-decker bus? How do they know which is their bus?
- Talk to the children about traffic lights, zebra crossings and road signs. Do they know why we need road signs?
- Sing the song 'The Wheels on the Bus go round and round'. Sing the popular verses but also add any extra verses you or the children can make up. Use the children's suggestions!

What resources do you need to collect for the focus activity?

- Nursery chairs, coins and a till, dolls, baskets, a bus driver's hat, tickets, props for the passengers.

Display suggestions

- Make a wall display of a large bus painted by the children. Encourage the children to draw, paint or collage pictures of their own faces; suggest they look in a mirror and observe themselves. Do they have long or short hair? Is it curly or straight? Attach the faces to the windows of the bus. Encourage a child to write a number and the destination on the bus. Add the children's names in their own writing. Label the driver, the people, the wheels etc.
- Display the children's paintings of transport such as cars, bikes, lorries, vans etc. Encourage the children to write their own captions.
- Display a small-world play mat and add cars, buses, road signs, people etc.

Similar topics to explore

- Action rhymes such as 'When Goldilocks went to the house of the bears'.

Home links

- Ask parents who don't normally use the bus to take their child on a bus ride. Ask them to look out for the number on the bus and where the bus is going. Let the child choose where to sit.

The wheels on the bus

Learning objectives

- To individually re-enact situations imaginatively in character
- To respond to imaginative stimuli in co-operation with others

Activity

Sing 'The Wheels on the Bus'.

Encourage the children to create their own bus.

Suggest they use Nursery chairs. How many will they need? Do they need an aisle?

Which way should the chairs face – forwards or sideways?

Where will the driver sit?

What does the driver need – money/a till/tickets? Where will the driver put the till, the money, and the tickets? What should they use for tickets?

What number is the bus? Where is it going?

Help the children to find any resources they might need: a driver's hat, dolls and baskets for the mummies and daddies to carry on to the bus.

Play with the children. Allow the children to be in charge! Be a passenger on the bus.

Model appropriate language: 'Two adults, one child to London, please.'

Withdraw from their play when you feel the time is right.

Observe their play. Intervene only if necessary. Offer any other resources in the Nursery that could be used as props.

Help the children design and make a bus stop, traffic lights, a zebra crossing and any other road signs they suggest.

Use a large piece of card and design the front of a bus.

Key questions

- Where is the bus going?
- Who will be the driver?
- How many passengers will there be?

Key vocabulary

- Driver, passengers, tickets, seats, destination, journey, fare, number, please, thank you

What do the stepping stones look like?

 Step 1

Pretend that one object represents another, especially when objects have characteristics in common.

Notice what adults do, imitating what is observed and then doing it spontaneously when the adult is not there.

After this has been enacted with an adult, child will mimic the actions and use props in the same way as the adult did.

 Step 2

Use available resources to create props to support role-play.

Develop a repertoire of actions by putting a sequence of movements together.

Enjoy stories based on themselves and people and places they know well.

Engage in imaginative and role-play based on own first-hand experiences.

S/he will mimic adult acting and start to add ideas of own, e.g. where bus is going/organising others on the bus/pretending to drive.

 Step 3

Introduce a story line or narrative into their play. Play alongside other children who are engaged in the same theme.

Play co-operatively as part of a group to act out a narrative.

Child will extend into stories based on own bus journey experiences, including members of family. May take the lead in organising the others or may allow themselves to be organised by others. Note the roles taken by children.

 Step 4 (Early learning goal)

Use their imagination in art and design, imaginative and role-play and stories.

The role-play could develop into using quite sophisticated props and making journeys round the Nursery.

The wheels on the bus

Main activity

Targeted children

Evaluation

How did the activity go?

What evidence of children's learning have you collected?

Foundation

The wheels on the bus

Planning sheet for supplementary activities

Area of learning	Learning objective	Activity	Targeted children	Evaluation
PSED				
CLL				
Maths				
KUW				
Physical				
Creative				
Snack times				
Circle times				
Outdoor play				
Stories & rhymes				
Special visitors				

Adult role during spontaneous play sessions

Observing play ☐ _____   Supporting play areas ☐ _____

Supporting individual play ☐ _____   Involvement in play area ☐ _____

The wheels on the bus

Personal, social and emotional development

Learning objectives

- To develop the feeling of belonging to a group
- To be aware of danger
- To develop a sense of their personal safety

Suggested activities

- Encourage the children to work together as a group in the role-play situation.
- Discuss road safety. Emphasise how important it is to get on and off a bus only while it is stationary and to always sit down on a bus while it is moving.
- Talk about wearing seat belts when they are available.

Communication, language and literacy

Learning objectives

- To take part in role-play with increasing confidence
- To make marks to communicate meaning
- To listen and respond to stories

Suggested activities

- Organise a Travel Agents' role-play area. Collect together a selection of brochures and posters from travel agents. Provide pencils/pens and pads, old desk diaries, a computer keyboard, telephone, card for the children to make tickets etc.
- Talk to the children about holidays. Where do they go? How do they travel? Where do they stay?
- Make a list of all the clothes and any other items they might take on holiday with them.
- Show the children a holiday postcard you have received. Show them how to write their own postcard. Add a stamp.
- Change the writing area into a post office.
- Read stories, e.g. about *Postman Pat* by John Cunliffe (Scholastic) and *Thomas the Tank Engine* by Rev. W. Awdry (Random House Children's Books).

Additional resources

Provide travel brochures and posters, postcards, paper, envelopes, an inkpad and stamps

A till and money, a telephone, telephone directories, parcels, scales, etc.

Make a post box and add a notice stating collection times

Postman Pat and *Thomas the Tank Engine* stories

The wheels on the bus

Mathematical development

Learning objectives

- To recognise and understand cardinal numbers – 'how many?'
- To demonstrate 1:1 correspondence
- To recognise and name 2D shapes – circles

Suggested activities

- Count the people on the bus: are there enough chairs? Do we need more?
- Talk about the wheels. What shape are they?
- Look around the Nursery for other circular shapes.
- Collect together objects that are circles and make a shape display.
- Cut circle shapes and encourage children to print with circular objects such as cotton reels, cardboard kitchen-roll tubes, sponges etc.
- Make bubble prints. Cut them out and display them.

Additional resources

Paper/card for circle shapes, cotton reels, cardboard tubes, sponges etc.

Paper, liquid paint, washing-up liquid and straws for bubble paintings

Knowledge and understanding of the world

Learning objectives

- To name forms of transport
- To observe closely and identify similarities and differences
- To classify according to certain criteria

Suggested activities

- Discuss journeys and different forms of transport. Name all the forms of transport the children are aware of. Encourage the children to cut pictures of cars, buses, lorries, vans, bikes etc. out of catalogues and magazines.
- Talk to them about other things that have wheels such as prams, pushchairs, wheelie bins, supermarket trolleys, suitcases etc. Why do they need wheels?
- Collect together large cardboard boxes (big enough for a child to sit in!) and encourage the children to design and make their own bus, car, van, lorry etc. They could paint the box first and add their own 'extras'.
- Some of the children may prefer just to sit in the box and use their imagination.
- Provide a selection of clothes they might take on holiday and a suitcase. Show the children how to fold clothes and pack them into a suitcase. Encourage them to have a go themselves.

Additional resources

A collection of old car/motorbike/transport magazines

Large cardboard boxes, paints

Selection of holiday clothes and a suitcase

The wheels on the bus

Physical development

Learning objectives

- To respond to imaginative stimuli in co-operation with others

Suggested activities

- Encourage the children to pretend to be bus drivers. Holding an imaginary steering wheel, they can go slowly or fast or follow a road marked out with chalk. They could follow signals: green for go, amber for slow down and red for stop.
- Encourage the children to make transport junk models.

Additional resources

A collection of empty boxes of all shapes and sizes, masking tape, sticky tape, paint of all colours

Junk to decorate the models such as old bottle tops, cotton reels, polystyrene containers etc.

Snack times

Learning objectives

- To make and express choices
- To recognise and name 2D shapes – circles

Suggested activities

- Eat circular snacks such as biscuits, crackers and small cakes.
- Encourage the children to notice the shapes and to say 'circle'.

Circle/review times

Learning objectives

- To interact with peers
- To use talk to recall ideas and experiences

Suggested activities

- Encourage the children to show each other their junk models, and to tell each other how they made them.

The wheels on the bus

Outdoor play

Learning objectives

- To play sociably, to join in and to follow instructions and directions
- To take turns and share fairly

Suggested activities

- Make or buy traffic cones and plan a route.
- Encourage the children to ride their bikes, scooters etc. in the same direction following each other. Devise an overtaking lane!
- Make a bus stop sign. Encourage the children to wait at the bus stop for their turn. As bikes and scooters come round to the bus stop, children get off and allow another child their turn. The children could take it in turns to dress up as the crossing warden or a policeman or policewoman.

Additional resources

Traffic cones, bus stop sign, bikes, scooters etc., dressing up clothes

Stories and rhymes

Learning objectives

- To listen and respond to stories, songs and rhymes

Suggested activities

Stories

Dazzling Diggers by Tony Mitton and Ant Parker (Kingfisher Books)

The train who was frightened of the dark by Denis Bond (Scholastic)

Bumper to Bumper by Jakki Wood (Frances Lincoln)

Rhymes

'The wheels on my bike go round like this...'

'I'm driving in my car…'

'Come to the station early in the morning…'

'Piggy on the railway…'

'I had a little engine…'

'Here comes a big red bus…'

all from *This Little Puffin...* (Puffin Books)

Special visitors/events

Suggested activities

- If your Local Education Authority has a Playbus that visits schools, nurseries and playgroups, organise a visit from them.

Jack Frost

How can you prepare for this activity?

- This is a winter theme and should be planned during a frosty or snowy spell. It will probably have to be fairly spontaneous.
- During this theme ask parents to send their children to Nursery in warm coats, hats, gloves, scarves and warm boots.
- Organise a 'white' day when everyone, including the staff, comes to Nursery wearing something white.

What are the starting points?

- A spell of cold wintry weather/the day after a snow fall.
- Talk to the children about how they need to keep themselves and the Nursery warm when it is cold and frosty outside. Talk to the children about 'Jack Frost' and how he usually appears at night while we are sleeping. Talk to them about how nice it is to be cosy and warm in our beds on a cold winter's night. Read the story *Can't you sleep, little Bear?* by Martin Waddell (Walker Books) or any similar type of story.

What resources do you need to collect for the focus activity?

- A camera and films.
- A collection of objects that the children can use to decorate a snowman. Ask the children for their suggestions!
- White collage materials such as cotton wool, white tissue and crepe paper, white art straws, doilies, white textured wallpaper, silver and white glitter etc.
- A cassette player and the sound-track to *The Snowman* (based on the book by Raymond Briggs).
- A 'Snowman' role-play box including a dressing gown, a set of boy's clothes, hat, scarf, carrot, a Santa outfit and wellies.

Display suggestions

- A winter scene.
- A white collage.
- A tabletop display of things we need when it is icy: hat, scarf, gloves, boots, a window scraper, a can (empty) of de-icer, ⚠ a sledge etc.

Jack Frost

Similar topics to explore

• Autumn.

Home links

• Ask if any parent or grandparent could make a bird table for the Nursery garden.
• Ask parents if they could take photographs of their children in their garden, or anywhere outdoors when it has been snowing.

Foundation

Jack Frost

Main activity

Learning objectives

- To respond with enthusiasm to what they are seeing and doing
- To articulate their feelings in an expressive and imaginative way
- To be aware of a variety of weather conditions

Activities

Dress children in warm clothes.

Encourage children to be as independent as possible.

Take children outside and look at the patterns the frost makes on the grass, on leaves, in trees, on windows, doors, walls etc.

Look for spiders' webs and talk about how the frost glistens on the fine silver threads.

Crunch through the crispy frozen grass.

Look at the tracks their footprints make.

Encourage the children to breathe out and watch their warm breath.

Use descriptive vocabulary and encourage the children to talk about what they are doing and how they feel. Take photographs of the children in the snow. 📷

Keep sessions outside short so that the children don't get cold and are eager to return later.

If there is snow, make a snowman.

Inside the Nursery look through the windows with the children. Talk about how you feel about frost!

Suggest they make frosty pictures with collage materials.

Encourage them to paint snowy scenes using white paint mixed with different media. Some children may not like the cold and might prefer to paint a sunny picture. Ask them!

Listen to the music from the story of *The Snowman* by Raymond Briggs.

Provide a box of *The Snowman* articles of clothing and encourage the children to role-play the story.

What do the stepping stones look like?

Step 1

Show an interest in what they see, hear, smell, touch and feel.
Use body language, gestures, facial expression or words to indicate personal satisfaction or frustration.
Look for child's facial expressions and physical responses to indicate excitement and awe.

Step 2

Further explore an experience using a range of senses. Begin to use representation as a means of communication. Describe experiences and past actions, using a widening range of materials.
Child may show fascination with frosty breath and will talk about what s/he is doing. Will use photographs to talk about experiences.

Step 3

Try to capture experiences and responses with music, dance, paint and other materials or words. Develop preferences for forms of expression. Talk about personal intentions, describing what they were trying to do. Respond to comments and questions, entering into dialogue about their creations. Make comparisons.
Child will choose materials and resources from a variety offered, to express their ideas. Will act out 'The Snowman' story with props.

Step 4 (Early learning goal)

Respond in a variety of ways to what they see, hear, smell, touch and feel. Express and communicate their ideas, thoughts and feelings by using a widening range of materials, suitable tools, imaginative and role-play, movement, designing and making and a variety of songs and musical instruments.
Will draw from own experience of materials, tools and resources to make own pictures independently. Will ask for tools/resources they require, e.g. cotton wool or thread.

Jack Frost

Key questions

- What does frost look like/feel like?
- What kind of patterns does it make?
- When does it disappear?

Key vocabulary

- Frost, snow, ice, white, patterns, slippery, crunchy

Targeted children

Evaluation

How did the activity go?

What evidence of children's learning have you collected?

Jack Frost

Planning sheet for supplementary activities

Area of learning	Learning objective	Activity	Targeted children	Evaluation
PSED				
CLL				
Maths				
KUW				
Physical				
Creative				
Snack times				
Circle times				
Outdoor play				
Stories & rhymes				
Special visitors				

Adult role during spontaneous play sessions

Observing play ☐ _____   Supporting play areas ☐ _____

Supporting individual play ☐ _____   Involvement in play area ☐ _____

Jack Frost

Personal, social and emotional development

Learning objectives

- To manage their own personal needs with increasing independence
- To develop an awareness of their own personal safety
- To respect and care for others in the environment

Suggested activities

- Encourage children to dress themselves independently. Support them in doing up their own buttons and zips. Introduce correct vocabulary 'left' and 'right' when the children are putting on their gloves and their boots. Talk to them about wearing a hat and how important it is for maintaining body warmth; remind them how much heat is lost from their head if they don't wear a hat. Repeat this information regularly.
- Talk to the children about the safety aspect of ice on the pavement and on the road. Tell them how difficult it is for old people to walk on the ice and how the gritters have to come out at night time to grit the roads. Tell the children how the grit works.
- Talk to the children about birds in winter. Make seed cake with them and hang it outside on a tree or bird table. ⚠ Take photographs! 📷

Additional resources

Ingredients to make seed cake

Aprons, yoghurt pots, pieces of string

A bird table

Communication, language and literacy

Learning objectives

- To show an understanding of the main elements of a story: the characters, the setting, the beginning and ending
- To make marks in a variety of media with enjoyment

Suggested activities

- Watch *The Snowman* video by Raymond Briggs. Discuss the characters and sequence the story. What happened first/next/at the end?
- Cover a wipe-clean surface with shaving foam and encourage the children to draw 'Jack Frost' patterns in it. Sprinkle talcum powder on a surface and encourage the children to make patterns in it with their fingers or to make tracks with footprints.

Additional resources

The Snowman video, a can of shaving foam, talcum powder

Jack Frost

$$\boxed{\text{Supplementary activities}}$$

Mathematical development

Learning objectives

- To join in and recite number rhymes
- To verbalise numbers by counting
- To recognise and understand cardinal numbers – 'how many?'
- To begin to show an awareness of number operations – subtraction
- To demonstrate 1:1 correspondence

Suggested activities

- Chant the rhyme 'There were five little snowmen' from *This Little Puffin...* (Puffin Books)
- Act out the rhyme with the children: each time a snowman melts, a child sits down. How many are left? How many have melted? Change the number of snowmen: 'There were six little snowmen' etc. Change the number who melt – '. . . and melted two . . .'
- Sort mittens and wellies into pairs.

Additional resources

A collection of mittens and wellies to sort

Knowledge and understanding of the world

Learning objectives

- To be aware of a variety of weather conditions
- To observe closely and identify similarities and differences
- To recognise and name living things
- To predict/guess what will happen – and test the prediction

Suggested activities

- Discuss the weather with the children. Introduce appropriate vocabulary such as wind, rain, thunder, lightning, hail, snow, fog, cloud, cold, damp, wet, sun, dry, hot, warm. Make a weatherboard: laminate a set of weather symbols, stick Velcro on the back of each symbol and, after discussing the weather daily, change the weather symbol on the board. Encourage the children to 'watch' the weather and comment on it.
- Sort clothes into summer clothes and winter clothes.
- Talk to the children about animals that live in cold climates, such as penguins from the Antarctic and polar bears from the Arctic. Talk about where they live and what they like to eat.
- Experiment with the children on the best ways to melt ice. Use ice cubes and try melting them with different things such as salt, sand, water (hot or cold). Put ice into small bags and encourage children to crush the ice. How long does it take?
- Make 'ice-lollies' using paint. Paint with them. Tell the children not to lick them. ⚠

Additional resources

Equipment for making the weatherboard

Sunglasses, swimsuits, sunhats, shorts, T-shirts, sundresses, woolly hats, gloves, scarves, trousers, jumpers, thick socks, boots etc.

Pictures of penguins, polar bears, seals etc.

Ice cubes, sand, salt, small plastic bags etc. Lolly moulds and paint

Jack Frost

Physical development

Learning objectives

- To listen, move and respond appropriately to a variety of action rhymes
- To be able to handle malleable materials with increasing control
- To develop fine motor skills

Suggested activities

- Play ring games such as 'Here we go round the Mulberry Bush on a cold and frosty morning'.
- Encourage children to manipulate dough. Support them in stretching, pinching, rolling, pulling and shaping in order to model a snowman.
- Use an old pair of wellies and encourage the children to print with them – use thick white paint and black paper or vice versa, and then encourage the children to cut out the prints. Make a track to follow around Nursery.
- Have an indoor snowball fight! The children can make snowballs by crumpling up newspaper into balls and securing them with sticky tape.

Additional resources

Playdough, wellies, thick paint and sugar paper, newspaper and sticky tape

Snack times

Learning objectives

- To make and express choices
- To interact socially

Suggested activities

- Eat white food such as ice–cream, bananas, yoghurt, bread and butter, popcorn, white marshmallows, white chocolate buttons and meringues. Drink milk.

Circle/review times

Learning objectives

- To develop the ability to express their feelings
- To use talk to recall past experiences
- To participate in a game and take turns

Suggested activities

- Use the sentence starter 'I liked/didn't like going outside in the snow/frost because……'
- Play a circle game. Use a beanbag or small ball to throw or roll to each other. As you do this, call out the child's name so that they know it is their turn.

Jack Frost

Outdoor play

Learning objectives

- To respond to imaginative stimuli in co-operation with others
- To develop responsible attitudes

Suggested activities

- If it has been snowing, allow the children to play outside in the snow. Encourage them to roll the snow into balls and to make a snowman.
- Talk to the children about the safety aspects of throwing snowballs. Set some ground rules first.
- Make tracks in the snow and play 'Follow the Leader'.

Stories and rhymes

Learning objectives

- To listen and respond to stories and rhymes

Suggested activities

Stories

Camels don't ski by Francesca Simon (Gullane Publishing)

F-freezing ABC by Posy Simmonds (Alfred A. Knopf Inc.)

Rhymes

'One day we built a snowman'

'Who made the footprints in the snow?'

'A chubby little snowman' all from *This Little Puffin...* (Puffin Books)

Special visitors/events

Suggested activities

- This theme could be planned around Christmas if the weather is cold and frosty. The children could dress up and dance to the music from *The Snowman*. They could also sing a selection of their winter rhymes and perform for the parents.

Songs

These songs are a separate resource of CD, words, music and guitar chords, together with suggestions for the practitioner on using them with the children.

One of the songs is shown in two different keys for the benefit of guitar players.

You may choose to use these songs throughout the Foundation Stage, or to link them to themed activities within The Early Learning Goals.

Tidy up song

Words and music by Sanchia Sewell

Verse 1

Now it's time to tidy things away.

Let us tidy all the toys away.

Pick them up and put them over here,

So that ev'rything's tidy and clear.

Verse 2

Now it's time to tidy things away.

Let us tidy all the books away.

Pick them up and put them over here,

So that ev'rything's tidy and clear.

Verse 3

Now it's time to tidy things away.

Let us tidy all the pens away.

Pick them up and put them over here,

So that ev'rything's tidy and clear.

Verse 4

Things are tidy, all the jobs are done.

Singing songs makes everything such fun.

Now there's only one thing left to do,

To say thank you, thank you to you.

Using this song

Make a game of tidying up by singing this song. It encourages 'without telling' and may work on some of the children that need constant prompting in this area. Substitute your own words for the things that need to be tidied, and encourage the children to thank each other at the end of the song, in the same way as you have thanked them.

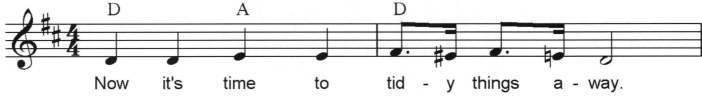

Now it's time to tid - y things a - way.

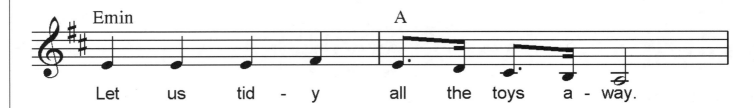

Let us tid - y all the toys a - way.

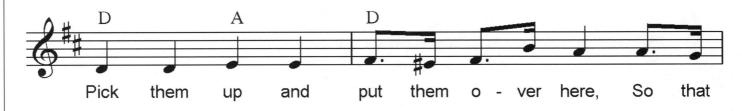

Pick them up and put them o - ver here, So that

ev' - ry - thing's ti - dy and clear.

Roll the ball away from you
Based on the tune 'Have you seen the Muffin Man?'

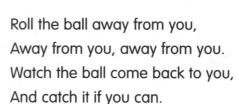

Roll the ball away from you,
Away from you, away from you.
Watch the ball come back to you,
And catch it if you can.

Ev'ryone shall have a turn,
Have a turn, have a turn.
Ev'ryone shall have a turn
To catch and roll the ball.

Throw and catch
Based on the tune 'Hot Cross Buns'

Words by Sanchia Sewell

Throw and catch.
Throw and catch.
Taking turns one at a time to
Throw and catch.
Throwing is quite easy,
Catching's hard to do.
Taking turns one at a time to
Throw and catch.

Repeat.

Using these songs

The children sit in a semi-circle while you roll (or throw) the ball to each one in turn. The ball is rolled (or thrown) back to you each time. Once familiar with the game, the children may roll (or throw) the ball to each other. At the end of each verse, ask the children to try and remember who has not yet had a turn.

The easy words and familiar tunes will encourage the children to sing along. This activity works well both in and outdoors. Smaller groups may work better with younger children, as they won't have long to wait for their turn to come round each time.

Roll the ball a - way from you, A - way from you, a - way from you.

Watch the ball come back to you, And catch it if you can.

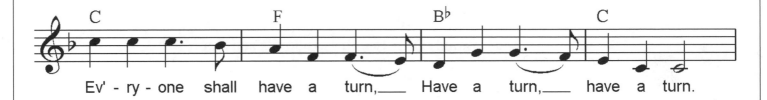

Ev' - ry - one shall have a turn,___ Have a turn,___ have a turn.

Ev' - ry - one shall have a turn, To catch and roll the ball.

Throw and catch

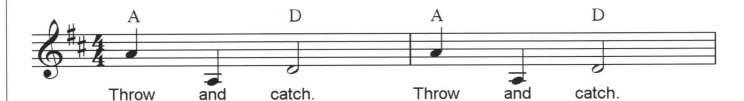

Throw and catch. Throw and catch.

Tak - ing turns one at a time to Throw and catch.

Throw - ing is quite ea - sy, Catch - ing's hard to do.

Tak - ing turns one at a time to Throw and catch.

Isn't it fun?

(**Words and music by Sanchia Sewell**)

Verse 1

Isn't it fun to walk out in the jungle?

Isn't it fun to jump up and down?

Isn't it fun to watch the lazy hippos

And to stand quite still and listen to the lions roar?

Verse 2

Isn't it fun to walk out in the jungle?

Isn't it fun to jump up and down?

Isn't it fun to see the silly monkeys

And to take a photo of a smiling crocodile?

Verse 3

Isn't it fun to walk out in the jungle?

Isn't it fun to jump up and down?

Isn't it fun to see the snakes a-slith'ring

And to look up in the trees for a chimpanzee?

Repeat first verse.

Using this song

Talk about the animals in this song. Look at pictures and ask the children to
think about how the animals move. Sing the song and use these
movements as actions. Try and use a big space and encourage big
movements. Repeat the first verse at the end of the song, so that everyone
can enjoy a long and sustained roar, but make sure you have an agreed-
upon signal for when the roar should end.

1. Is - n't it fun_____ to walk out in the jun - gle?

Is - n't it fun__ to jump up and down?

Is - n't it fun_____ to watch the la - zy hip - pos And to

stand quite still and lis - ten to the li - ons__ roar?

Foundation

Cat and mouse game

Words and music by Sanchia Sewell

Little mouse, softly creep.

Sh! be quiet, the cat's asleep.

Little mouse, softly creep.

Don't make a sound because the cat's asleep.

(spoken)

Oh no! The cat's awake.

Hurry, scurry, hurry, scurry,

There's no time to stop.

Running, skipping, jumping, sliding,

Going hop, hop, hop.

Watch out for that great big cat,

Who wants to catch the mouse,

Hurry, little mouse, and hide inside your house.

Using this song

This is a musical version of the classic cat and mouse game. Have an imaginary cat at first, and later take it in turns for one of the children to be the cat. Start off by all creeping around the room as softly as possible. After you say, 'Oh no! The cat's awake', the children then hurry-scurry and find a place to hide. You (as the imaginary cat) or the 'cat' then find the mice.

Lit - tle mouse, soft - ly creep. Sh! be quiet, the cat's a - sleep.

Lit - tle mouse, soft - ly creep. Don't__make a sound be - cause the cat's a - sleep.

(spoken) Oh no! The cat's awake. Hur - ry, scur - ry, hur - ry, scu - ry, There's no time to stop.

Run - ning, skip - ping, jump - ing, slid - ing, Go - ing hop, hop, hop.

Watch out for that great big cat, Who wants to catch the mouse.

Hur - ry lit - tle mouse and hide in - side your house.

Foundation

Shaky shake song

Words and music by Sanchia Sewell

Verse 1

I've got a head that goes shaky, shaky shake,

Shaky, shaky shake,

Shaky, shaky shake.

I've got a head that goes shaky, shaky shake,

And two hands that go clap, clap, clap.

Verse 2

I've got strong legs that march left, right, left,

Left, right, left,

Left, right, left.

I've got strong legs that march left, right, left,

And two hands that go clap, clap, clap.

Verse 3

I've got a body that can curl up small,

Stretch up tall,

Curl up small.

I've got a body that can curl up small,

And two hands that go clap, clap, clap.

Verse 4

I've got two eyes that look up and down,

Up and down,

Up and down.

I've got two eyes that look up and down,

And two hands that go clap, clap, clap.

Repeat verse 1.

Using this song

Emphasise the patterns by using actions as the words suggest. Make the children aware of the sequence of each verse by showing them that they always end with three hand claps. Children could make up their own verses for other parts of the body.

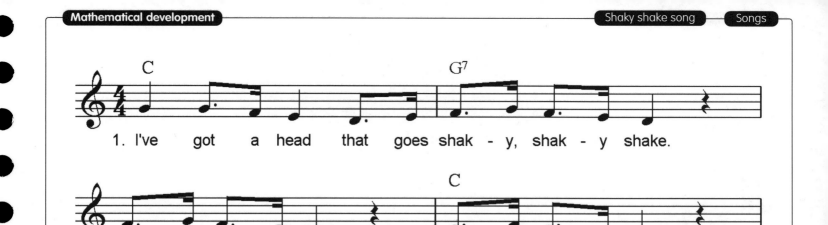

1. I've got a head that goes shak - y, shak - y shake.

shak - y, shak - y shake.   shak - y, shak - y shake.

I've got a head that goes shak - y, shak - y shake, And two

hands that go clap, clap, clap.

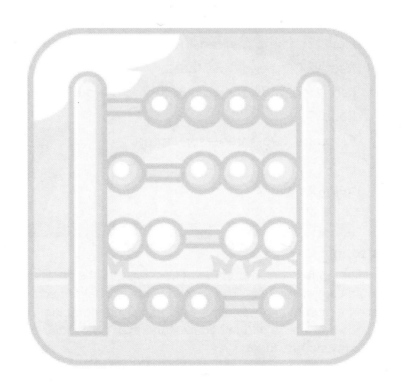

Foundation

Treasure count song

Words and music by Sanchia Sewell

In key of D flat major

Chorus

Searching for treasures – where can they be?

Hiding somewhere away from me!

Using my eyes I look all around.

That's the way that my treasures are found.

Verse 1

Counting up my treasures now, one, two, three.

One more makes four.

If I find another treasure then I will have five.

Count them,

One, two, three, four, five.

Repeat chorus.

Verse 2

Now I've found my treasure I can clap three times.

Ready? Clap one, two, three.

I can add another clap and then a great big stamp.

Ready?

Clap one, two, three, four, stamp.

Repeat chorus.

Using this song

You could line up the correct number of treasures for the children to count, or you could use your fingers. The second verse will help the children experience the numbers physically, by clapping and stamping. Ask how many sounds they made altogether (five) and then how many claps (four) and how many stamps (one).

Note

This song is sung in the key of D flat on the CD, but we have also included a second version in the key of D, especially for guitar players.

Treasure count song

Words and music by Sanchia Sewell

In key of D major (for guitar)

Chorus

Searching for treasures – where can they be?

Hiding somewhere away from me!

Using my eyes I look all around.

That's the way that my treasures are found.

Verse 1

Counting up my treasures now, one, two, three.

One more makes four.

If I find another treasure then I will have five.

Count them,

One, two, three, four, five.

Repeat chorus.

Verse 2

Now I've found my treasure I can clap three times.

Ready? Clap one, two, three.

I can add another clap and then a great big stamp.

Ready?

Clap one, two, three, four, stamp.

Repeat chorus.

Using this song

You could line up the correct number of treasures for the children to count, or you could use your fingers. The second verse will help the children experience the numbers physically, by clapping and stamping. Ask how many sounds they made altogether (five) and then how many claps (four) and how many stamps (one).

Note

This song is sung in the key of D flat on the CD, but we have also included a second version in the key of D, especially for guitar players.

In key of D major (for guitar)

(Chorus) Search - ing for trea - sures where can they be?

Hid - ing some - where a - way from me!

Us - ing my eyes I look all a - round. That's the

way that my trea - sures are found.

1. Count - ing up my trea - sures now, one, two,___ three.
2. Now I've found my trea - sure I can clap three___ times.

One more___ makes four. If I
Rea - dy?___ Clap one, two, three. I can

find a - no - ther trea - sure then I will have five.
add a - no - ther clap and then a great big stamp.

Count them, one, two, three, four, five.
Rea - dy?___ Clap one, two, three, four, stamp.

Foundation

Hip-hip hooray

Words and music by Sanchia Sewell

Verse 1

Hip-hip hooray,

It's my birthday today.

Today I'm turning one.

I sleep in a cot

And I cry quite a lot.

Hip-hooray, I'm turning one.

Verse 4

Hip-hip hooray,

It's my birthday today.

Today I'm turning four.

I can almost ride a bike

And I know my left from right.

Hip-hooray, I'm turning four.

Verse 2

Hip-hip hooray,

It's my birthday today.

Today I'm turning two.

I can walk and talk a bit,

I can stand and I can sit.

Hip-hooray, I'm turning two.

Verse 5

Hip-hip hooray,

It's my birthday today.

Today I'm turning five.

I can balance on one leg

And do sums up in my head.

Hip-hooray, I'm turning five.

Verse 3

Hip-hip hooray,

It's my birthday today.

Today I'm turning three.

I can throw a ball and catch it,

And I ask for it, don't snatch it.

Hip-hooray, I'm turning three.

Using this song

This song helps children to understand how they have changed, and will continue to change as they get older. Encourage them to hold up the appropriate number of fingers as they sing each verse, and use actions where you can. Muddle up the verses and instead of singing the number, hold up a number card for the children to read. Older children could make up their own verses of things that they can do, now that they are four or five.

The *LCP* Foundation Stage

1. Hip - hip hoo - ray, It's my birth - day to - day. To-

day I'm turn - ing one. I

sleep___ in a cot, And I cry___ quite a lot. Hip - hoo-

ray I'm turn - ing one.

Foundation

Here's a snail

Words and music by Sanchia Sewell

Verse 1   **Actions**

Here's a snail,   *One hand flat on ground*

Here's his shell,   *Make fist (shell) to go on top*

This is how he moves.   *Slowly move hands*

Slowly forward,

Slimy trail,

He hides away like this.   *Hide flat hand under fist*

He's not at all like a bunny rabbit,

Who likes to hop and jump, jump, jump.   *All jump*

He's not at all like an elephant,

Who waves his trunk and goes thump,   *Wave arm like a trunk*

thump, thump.   *Stamp feet*

Oh no, he's not like that.   *Shake head*

Verse 2

Here's a snail,   *As before*

Here's his shell,

His eyes on two long stalks.

Looks around,

Up and down,

He hides away like this.

He's not at all like a caterpillar,

Who wiggles on leaves so green.   *Wiggle whole body*

He's not at all like a crocodile,   *Extend arms, palms together*

With his sharp, sharp teeth and his great   *Lift one arm up*

big smile.   *Lower arm, clapping, on 'smile'*

Oh no, he's not like that.   *Shake head*

Verse 3

Here's a snail,   *As before*

Here's his shell,

He finds the winter cold.   *Hug self and shiver*

Sleeps quite soundly in his shell,   *Pretend to sleep*

Wakes up when it is warm.   *Yawn and stretch*

He's not at all like a bunny rabbit,   *As before*

Who likes to hop and jump, jump, jump.

He's not at all like an elephant,

Who waves his trunk and goes thump,

thump, thump.

Oh no, he's not like that.

1. Here's a snail, Here's his shell, This is how he moves.

Slow-ly for-ward, Slim-y trail, He hides a-way like this. He's

not at all like a bun-ny rab-bit, Who

likes to hop and jump, jump, jump. He's

not at all like an el-e-phant, Who waves his trunk and goes

thump, thump, thump. Oh no, he's not like that.

Using this song

Encourage the children to do as many diffrent actions as possible. The contrast between the slow movements of the snail (requiring more control and co-ordination and the bigger, faster movements of the other animals will appeal to the children and hold their interest.

You could also talk about other animals that sleep through winter and why it is useful to have eyes on stalks.

Foundation

Froggies

Words and music by Sanchia Sewell

Froggies jump so very high.

Caterpillars wriggle by.

Ants go rushing here and there.

Bunnies hopping ev'rywhere.

Repeat.

Actions

Froggies – jump from a crouching position.

Caterpillars – standing, make small wiggling movements.

Ants – pretend that fingers are ants, and let them 'scurry' on the ground.

Bunnies – jump around the room with feet together. Older children could hop.

Using this song

Encourage the children to move as much as possible since the contrasting actions help to gain control of both big and small movements. You could also let the children play along on tambourines, striking the tambourine for the frog and bunny jumps and shaking the tambourines for the caterpillar and ant movements.

Frog - gies jump so ve - ry high.

Cat - er - pil - lars wrig - gle by.

Ants go rush - ing here and there.

Bun - nies hop - ping ev' - ry - where.

Foundation

I can walk with giant steps

Words and music by Sanchia Sewell

Verse 1

I can walk with giant steps,

Giant steps, giant steps.

I can walk with giant steps,

Tra-la-la-la-la.

(spoken)

Let's all walk with giant steps.

Verse 2

I can walk with fairy steps,

Fairy steps, fairy steps.

I can walk with fairy steps,

Tra-la-la-la-la.

(spoken)

Let's all walk with fairy steps.

Verse 3

I can walk along the line . . .

Verse 4

I can walk all wobbly . . .

Verse 5

I can jump up very high . . .

Verse 6

I can curl up very small . . .

Using this song

Use this song as a 'follow-my-leader' game outside, or simply allow the children to enjoy doing the actions and exploring the space around themselves. Make up your own verses and let the children give ideas for different ways their bodies can move. The music between each verse is to provide more time for each action.

1. I can walk with gi - ant steps, Gi - ant steps, gi - ant steps,

I can walk with gi - ant steps, Tra - la - la - la - la.

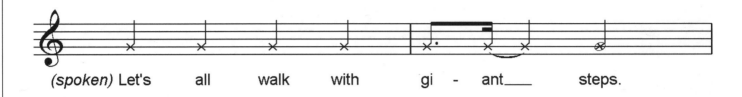

(spoken) Let's all walk with gi - ant___ steps.

Colours

Words and music by Sanchia Sewell

Chorus

Colours!

Sing a song of c-c-colours

And what happens when we mix them.

If we mix them we get something that could be
completely new.

Verse

Red and yellow make *(spoken)* orange.

Yellow and blue make *(spoken)* green.

Blue and red make *(spoken)* purple.

Yellow, red and blue make *(spoken)* brown.

Repeat chorus and verse.

Repeat chorus.

Using this song

Start off by looking at the flowers the children have made. Talk about all the different colours they have used and see how many they can name.

Remind them how they mixed the paint in order to get some of the colours. When singing the song it may be useful to hold up the various colours as you sing them (painted paper plates work well). When you repeat the song, leave out the words orange, green, purple and brown but still give visual clues. Once the children are familiar with the song you could start leaving out the visual clues.

309

Here is a bell

Words and music by Sanchia Sewell

Verse 1

Here is a bell,

It jingles, can you tell?

And when I shake it,

It goes ting-a-ling-a-ling-a-ling.

Verse 2

Let's play together

A jingle melody.

Don't stop, keep playing,

Ting-a-ling-a-ling-a-ling.

Verse 3

Here is a clapper,

How you play it, it doesn't matter.

In your hand, or on your leg,

Clap, clap, clack'ty, clack'ty, clack'ty, clap.

Verse 4

Here is a woodblock,

It sounds just like a ticking clock.

And when I play it,

It goes tick, tock, tick, tock.

Verse 5

Here is a tambourine,

Together we make quite a team.

And when I play it,

It goes ching-a-ling-a-ling-a-ling.

Using this song

This is a good way of introducing rhythmic instruments to children. It teaches them the correct name of each instrument and the type of sounds they make. Demonstrate how each instrument is held and played before you start.

The *LCP* Foundation Stage

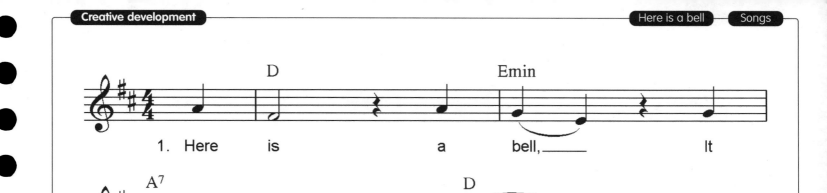

1. Here is a bell,_____ It

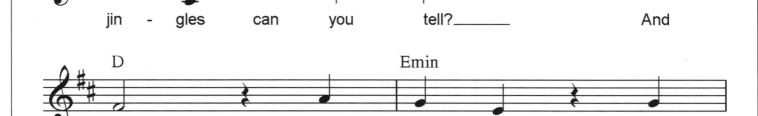

jin - gles can you tell?_____ And

when I shake it, It

goes ting - a - ling - a - ling - a - ling.

Foundation

Contents

Identifying more able mathematicians

What characteristics might gifted mathematicians display?

More able mathematicians are likely to have good powers of logic, reasoning and deduction, and will be able to hypothesise, experiment and categorise. This list of questions may be useful in establishing mathematical ability:

- Do they enjoy number puzzles?
- Do they show a good awareness of patterns and sequences?
- Do they ask interesting mathematical questions?
- Do they give explanations you may not have thought of?
- Are they good at solving problems?
- Are they good at applying knowledge in unfamiliar contexts?
- Do they like to choose their own methods?

This list is by no means exhaustive; there are many more characteristics that may be observed in gifted mathematicians, and many gifted children will display only some of these qualities. For example, a child who you believe to be a high achiever may not show advanced problem-solving skills. This may be because they don't yet know how to set about solving a problem, because they haven't learned the strategies required. You may find children who are gifted in just one or two areas of maths. For example, they may excel at calculation and number, but may not do so well at shape and space.

What about children who don't show any of these traits?

There may be gifted mathematicians in your class who do not display any of these characteristics. This could be due to one or more of these factors:

- lack of confidence
- unwillingness to stand out from their peers
- the desire to avoid 'extra' work
- an insufficiently stimulating learning environment
- lack of challenging activities
- lack of familiarity with basic number facts and skills
- language barriers
- problems with reading and/or writing.

What can be done to identify gifted mathematicians?

Here are a few suggestions of practical steps that can be taken:

- Ask parents and carers to supply information about any mathematical abilities they have noticed at home.
- Conduct a brief interview with children at the beginning of the school year to find out about their interests and anything they think they are especially good at.
- Keep a portfolio of particularly good work completed either at home or in school. This will help to assess progress and spot patterns.
- Testing can provide evidence of high ability, but you should be aware that some more able or gifted children may not perform well in tests, and many factors can affect children's performance in a test environment.

The identification–provision cycle

A two-way process of identification and provision is needed. You will not be able to observe exceptional abilities in children unless they are given the opportunity to demonstrate them. Activities must be provided that challenge children and allow them the scope to show what they can do. In this way, appropriate provision leads to identification, which in turn allows you to make better provision.

How can a stimulating learning environment be created?

It is important that more able children are asked probing and open-ended questions. These will allow you to assess and extend their understanding, get them to think more deeply, and lead them to continue their explorations. Here are some examples of the types of question you might ask:

- What do you think will happen if …?
- How many different ways can you …?
- Is it always true that …?
- Why?
- What patterns can you see?
- Why did you choose to work it out like that?
- Why do you think this happens?
- How do you know that?
- Can you make up a rule?

It is also important to create an atmosphere in which children feel they are able to ask questions, and have access to resources to find the answers. One practical thing you can do is to create a 'Challenge corner': an area of the classroom where you can set out maths resources, puzzles, prompts and questions for children to explore. This should be accessible by all children in the class, giving everyone the opportunity to challenge themselves.

What are 'challenge' activities?

'Challenging' work can be defined as something difficult that requires the learner to learn something new. For children to enjoy a challenging activity there must be something about it that motivates them. For example, it could be about a subject that they are particularly interested in, or it could be placed in a meaningful context, with a goal that has nothing to do with completing a page of calculations. The level of challenge must be just right – it must stretch them without being so difficult that children are demotivated and want to give up. The best challenge activities will allow different levels of outcome, so that a wide range of children can succeed at them.

More able or gifted children need to be given opportunities to:

- exercise their curiosity and explore new ideas
- choose their own ways of working and representing their results
- ask questions and find the answers
- make conjectures and test them out
- discuss their ideas with adults and other children
- reflect on their own work.

What thinking skills should more able children be using?

More able children need to be given opportunities to access their higher-order thinking skills. Bloom's Taxonomy identifies six levels of thinking:

- knowledge – the acquisition and recall of facts
- comprehension – the ability to describe what you know in your own words
- application – the application of what you have learned in context
- analysis – for example, categorising things and identifying patterns
- synthesis – the creation of new ideas or products
- evaluation – the evaluation of ideas, processes and products.

The first three are generally thought of as lower-order skills, although application requires a deeper level of thinking than the first two. If you can plan activities that incorporate the three higher-order thinking skills, children will be challenged.

Introducing *Abacus Evolve Challenge*

What is *Abacus Evolve Challenge*?

Abacus Evolve Challenge is designed to stretch and motivate more able mathematicians. The activities are creative and engaging, and offer opportunities for written, verbal and practical work. Using and applying skills are practised throughout, with plenty of open-ended investigations and problem solving. Speaking and listening skills are promoted through the high proportion of paired and group work.

Which children is *Challenge* for?

Challenge is not just for those children who would be classed as 'gifted'. The activities have been written with the whole of the 'top table' in mind. Differentiation by outcome is often possible because of the open-ended nature of the activities, and the teacher notes accompanying the activities usually suggest ways to differentiate further.

What types of enrichment and extension are provided?

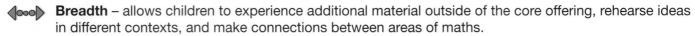 **Breadth** – allows children to experience additional material outside of the core offering, rehearse ideas in different contexts, and make connections between areas of maths.

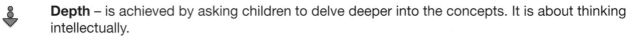 **Depth** – is achieved by asking children to delve deeper into the concepts. It is about thinking intellectually.

Pace – refers to speed in covering the curriculum and can result in achievement at a level exceptional for the age range.

What types of activity are provided?

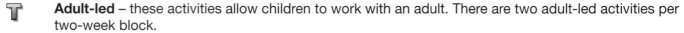 **Adult-led** – these activities allow children to work with an adult. There are two adult-led activities per two-week block.

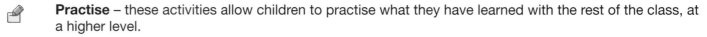 **Practise** – these activities allow children to practise what they have learned with the rest of the class, at a higher level.

Discover – these activities allow children to learn about things like famous mathematicians and ancient number systems.

Investigate – these activities allow children to explore a concept freely, asking questions, looking for patterns and drawing conclusions.

When should the *Challenge* activities be used?

There are 90 activities per Year; six for every two-week block. They are intended to be used by small groups of children in the part of the maths lesson when the class is split into groups for differentiated work. This allows the more able children to be included in the whole-class parts of the lesson.

What level of adult support is needed?

The *Challenge* resources have been designed with effective classroom management in mind. Four of the activities in each two-week block can be carried out by children without adult support, allowing you to focus on the other groups. Some of these will require a couple of minutes to get the group started on the activity, but after this children should be able to continue unaided.

Two of the activities in each two-week block require adult support, so that your able and gifted children have the benefits of adult input.

How does *Challenge* fit alongside the *Abacus Evolve* maths scheme?

The *Challenge* activities are organised using the same blocked structure as *Abacus Evolve*. You can use the *Abacus Evolve* weekly plans, and fit the *Challenge* activities into these. *Abacus Evolve* objectives are referenced for each activity, and these will help you to decide which core activities to run them alongside. If you also have the *Challenge* Module of I-Planner Online, you will be able to see the *Challenge* activities allocated to suitable days in the weekly plans.

It is intended that the more able children join in with the whole-class parts of the lesson: the mental oral starter, the main teaching activity, and the plenary. When the rest of the class is split up into 1-dot, 2-dot and 3-dot groups to do Textbook activities or practical activities, you can give your top group a *Challenge* activity that fits in well with what the rest of the class are doing.

Can I use *Challenge* with another maths scheme or my own planning?

Although the *Challenge* activities complement *Abacus Evolve* activities, they are not specifically linked to them, so there is no dependence on any part of the *Abacus Evolve* scheme. The *Challenge* activities can be used to accompany any other maths scheme or your own planning. You can search for *Challenge* activities that fit your teaching by looking at the Renewed Framework objectives in the Teacher Guide. All of the Renewed Framework objectives are covered by the *Challenge* activities.

What resources are in the *Challenge* range?

Each Year includes:

- a Teacher Guide
- a Textbook
- an I-Planner Online Module.

Teacher Guide

The Teacher Guide contains detailed notes to accompany each activity. The information provided includes:

- Suggested group size and adult support
- Resources required (Textbook pages, Photocopy Masters and other resources)
- *Abacus Evolve* objectives
- Renewed Framework objectives
- A description of the activity
- 'Extra help': ideas for differentiating at a lower level
- 'Further extension': ideas for differentiating at a higher level
- 'If you have time': ideas for continuing the activity
- Background maths information for the non-specialist teacher
- 'Be aware': things to watch out for, such as common misconceptions
- Outcomes for the activity, given in child-friendly language
- Ideas for other resources to support the activity, such as useful websites.

Textbook

There are five Textbook pages per two-week block, so nearly every activity has an accompanying Textbook page. The pages are colourful and engaging, and they include the following features:

- speech bubbles to indicate opportunities for discussion
- an Extra activity at the bottom of each page for children who finish early.

The Textbook pages are not just intended for children to use individually. They are often suitable for paired or group work.

I-Planner Online

The *Abacus Evolve* I-Planner is a powerful online tool that provides ready-to-use weekly, medium-term and yearly plans that are completely flexible. It can save hours of planning time, but allows you to adapt the plans to meet the exact needs of your class. The Challenge module of I-Planner for each Year includes an extra column in the weekly plans in which you can see all the Challenge activities allocated to suitable days. This allows you to plan the Challenge activities seamlessly into your maths lessons.

What support is provided for assessing the children?

The adult-led activities are ideal for day-to-day observational assessment, as they provide plenty of opportunities to work closely with the children and ask probing questions to ascertain their level of understanding.

The charts on pages 8–11 of this book show the Assessment Foci from the Assessing Pupils' Progress guidelines, and the Challenge activities that can be used to provide evidence towards this type of assessment.

On pages 106–115 of this book you will find three end-of-term investigative activities. These will allow you to assess how well children use and apply the skills they have built up over the term.

Icon guide

Group size

 Children working individually, without an adult

 Children working in pairs, without an adult

 Children working in groups, without an adult

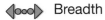 Children working in groups, with an adult

Type of resource

 Textbook

 Photocopy Master

Additional resources

Type of enrichment/extension

 Breadth

 Depth

 Pace

Type of activity

 Adult-led

Practise

Discover

Investigate

Support for Assessing Pupils' Progress

If you are using Assessing Pupils' Progress to assess children, you may find this chart helpful when deciding which of the *Challenge* activities could be used to provide evidence towards each Assessment Focus.

We do not recommend that you use every activity to make an assessment. It is also important to recognise that a full assessment cannot be made on the basis of the *Challenge* activities alone; you will need to draw on other sources of information as well. We would advise that in each block of work you use this chart as guidance towards choosing one activity to assess against APP criteria, to complement other day-to-day or periodic assessments.

The Year 5 *Challenge* activities should give children the opportunity to work at a high Level 4, and in some cases at a low or secure Level 5.

Ma1 Using and applying mathematics

	Problem solving	Communicating	Reasoning
Level 5	• B1.5 Parallel and perpendicular • C1.6 The best buy • A2.5 Investigating days and dates • C2.1 Stamp sizes • C2.2 Surface area • A3.6 Solving money matters • D3.1 The Shipping Forecast • D3.2 Interior angles • D3.4 How many are there? • E3.3 Ratio and proportion	• A3.6 Solving money matters • C3.2 Weather • C3.3 The best deal	• A1.3 Triangular and square numbers • B2.1 Multiplication investigation • C2.3 Area and perimeter • B3.1 Big addition game • C3.1 Probability • C3.4 Luggage sizes • D3.5 Using digit roots • D3.6 Equivalent calculations • E3.6 Factors and prime numbers
Level 4	• A1.1 Very large numbers • B1.3 Investigating number sequences • A2.2 Imperial and metric conversions • B2.3 Double up! • C2.5 Number patterns • C2.6 Schedules • D2.1 Perfect numbers • D2.4 Fair share • C3.6 Angles and degrees	• A1.2 Inequalities and symbols • A1.5 Recurring decimals • D1.1 In the mirror • D1.4 Find the rule	• B1.1 Multiplying and dividing even and odd numbers • C1.5 Rectangles and rhombuses • D1.1 In the mirror • D1.4 Find the rule • E1.4 Improper fractions game • D2.2 Adding with a difference • D2.4 Fair share • E2.6 Divisibility • B3.4 Subtraction game

Ma2 Number

	Numbers and the number system	Fractions, decimals, percentages, ratio and proportion	Operations, relationships between them
Level 5	• A1.3 Triangular and square numbers • A2.3 Rounding and estimating using place value • A2.6 Common multiples and prime factors • A3.1 Extreme temperatures • A3.3 Working with seconds • E3.6 Factors and prime numbers	• E1.5 Fractions • E3.1 Fractions to decimals • E3.3 Ratio and proportion	• B3.1 Big addition game
Level 4	• A1.1 Very large numbers • B1.2 Number sequences • A2.1 Rounding and converting distances • D2.1 Perfect numbers • E3.4 Square numbers • E3.5 Find the factor	• A1.6 Equivalent fractions • E1.4 Improper fractions game • E1.6 Finding proportions • E2.4 Fractional amounts • E2.5 Fractions problems • E3.4 Square numbers	• D2.3 Make the calculation • D2.5 Odd one out • D2.6 Money steps • B3.5 Football stadiums

9

Ma2 Number

	Mental, written and calculator methods	Solving numerical problems	Algebra
Level 5	• A1.4 Multiplying and dividing decimals • C1.6 The best buy • A2.3 Rounding and estimating using place value • B2.1 Multiplication investigation • C2.1 Stamp sizes • E2.1 Multiplication challenge • E2.2 Multiplication problems with time • E2.3 Decimal multiplication • E2.5 Fractions problems • A3.2 Using your calculator • A3.3 Working with seconds • A3.5 Cross the river • B3.1 Big addition game • B3.2 Decimal spin off • B3.6 Basketball throws • D3.6 Equivalent calculations • E3.2 Fruity percentages	• C2.1 Stamp sizes • A3.2 Using your calculator • B3.3 Heavy reading • C3.4 Luggage sizes • D3.4 How many are there? • D3.5 Using digit roots • E3.2 Fruity percentages	• A1.3 Triangular and square numbers • B2.4 Coordinates • B2.5 Reflecting with coordinates
Level 4	• E1.1 Doubling numbers • E1.2 Find my double • E1.3 Half price sale • B2.3 Double up! • D2.2 Adding with a difference • D2.3 Make the calculation • D2.5 Odd one out • D2.6 Money steps • E2.6 Divisibility • A3.4 A different way to multiply • B3.4 Subtraction game • B3.5 Football stadiums • E3.5 Find the factor	• D1.5 Will it divide? • D1.6 Cross-numbers • E1.3 Half price sale • E1.6 Finding proportions • A2.1 Rounding and converting distances • A2.2 Imperial and metric conversions • E2.2 Multiplication problems with time • E2.4 Fractional amounts	

Ma3 Shape, space and measures

	Properties of shape	Properties of position and movement	Measures
Level 5	• B1.5 Parallel and perpendicular • D3.2 Interior angles		• C2.2 Surface area • C2.3 Area and perimeter
Level 4	• D1.1 In the mirror • B2.6 Investigating diagonals • D3.3 Looking at triangles	• B1.4 Making quadrilaterals • B1.6 Making triangles on a pinboard • B2.4 Coordinates • B2.5 Reflecting with coordinates	• C1.5 Rectangles and rhombuses • C2.6 Schedules • C3.6 Angles and degrees

Ma4 Handling data

	Specifying the problem and planning, collecting data	Processing and representing data	Interpreting data
Level 5		• C3.1 Probability • C3.2 Weather • C3.3 The best deal	• C1.3 Averages
Level 4	• C3.1 Probability	• C1.1 Tables and graphs • C1.2 Line graphs and conversion graphs	• C1.1 Tables and graphs • C1.2 Line graphs and conversion graphs

Talk Maths Extra pupil software

Abacus Evolve *Talk Maths Extra* will reinforce key maths skills and get children talking about maths.

1 Place-value puzzle 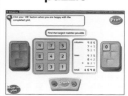	Create six 3-digit numbers, to make the largest and smallest totals possible.	**2 Find the remainders** 	Divide a 2-digit number by a 1-digit number to give a specified remainder.	**3 Always, sometimes, never** 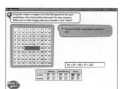	Investigate statements about sums of consecutive and adjacent numbers.
4 Shape properties 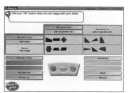	Place shapes onto a Carroll diagram, then choose labels to match.	**5 Cube nets** 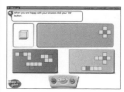	Work out which nets could make the open cube shown.	**6 Mystery number** 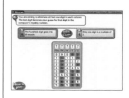	Find a mystery 5-digit number by eliminating digits based on clues.
7 Function machine 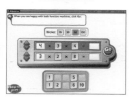	Make a product in two different ways by multiplying three numbers together.	**8 Make-a-shape** 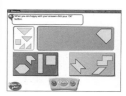	Work out which shapes could be made by fitting smaller shapes together.	**9 Area and perimeter** 	Describe a route to draw a rectangle with a given area and perimeter.
10 Magic square 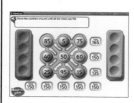	Place numbers so that each row, column and diagonal has the same total.	**11 Marble run** 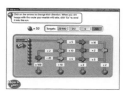	Make a number by selecting a path for a marble through × and ÷ calculations.	**12 Line graphs** 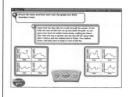	Choose the line graph that best represents what happens in a story.
13 Capacity dominoes 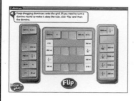	Place dominoes in a loop so that touching ends have equivalent capacities.	**14 Fractions and decimals** 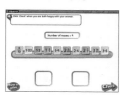	Place fractions and decimals on a rack, aiming to end up with the numbers in order.	**15 Carroll diagram** 	Create numbers for a Carroll diagram, then choose labels to match.
16 Symmetrical patterns 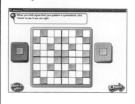	Complete a symmetrical pattern, and then create a symmetrical pattern of your own.	**17 Estimating an angle** 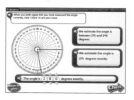	Estimate an angle, then measure the angle using a protractor.	**18 Measuring capacity** 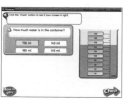	Complete the scale on a measuring beaker, then say how much water is in the beaker.

This chart shows which *Talk Maths Extra* activities could be used to extend some of the *Challenge* activities. The 4-dot version of each *Talk Maths Extra* activity is likely to be the most suitable for your children.

Challenge activity	Related *Talk Maths Extra* activities
A1.1 Very large numbers	1 Place value puzzle
A1.2 Inequalities and symbols	14 Fractions and decimals
A1.6 Equivalent fractions	2 Find the remainders
B1.1 Multiplying and dividing even and odd numbers	3 Always, sometimes, never
B1.4 Making quadrilaterals	4 Shape properties
B1.5 Parallel and perpendicular	4 Shape properties
B1.6 Making triangles on a pinboard	4 Shape properties, 8 Make-a-shape
C1.1 Tables and graphs	12 Line graphs
C1.2 Line graphs and conversion graphs	12 Line graphs
C1.4 Imperial or metric?	13 Capacity dominoes
C1.5 Rectangles and rhombuses	9 Area and perimeter
D1.1 In the mirror	16 Symmetrical patterns
D1.2 Polyominoes	5 Cube nets
D1.3 Platonic solids	5 Cube nets
D1.5 Will it divide?	6 Mystery number
E1.4 Improper fractions game	14 Fractions and decimals
E1.5 Fractions	14 Fractions and decimals
A2.2 Imperial and metric conversions	13 Capacity dominoes
A2.3 Rounding and estimating using place value	1 Place value puzzle, 6 Mystery number
A2.6 Common multiples and prime factors	15 Carroll diagram
B2.1 Multiplication investigation	7 Function machine, 11 Marble run
B2.5 Reflecting with coordinates	16 Symmetrical patterns
B2.6 Investigating diagonals	8 Make-a-shape
C2.1 Stamp sizes	9 Area and perimeter
C2.2 Surface area	9 Area and perimeter
C2.3 Area and perimeter	9 Area and perimeter
D2.1 Perfect numbers	6 Mystery number
D2.2 Adding numbers with a difference	10 Magic square
D2.3 Make the calculation	3 Always, sometimes, never
D2.5 Odd one out	7 Function machine
E2.6 Divisibility	6 Mystery number
A3.5 Cross the river	11 Marble run
C3.3 The best deal	12 Line graphs
C3.4 Luggage sizes	13 Capacity dominoes, 18 Measuring capacity
C3.6 Angles and degrees	17 Estimating an angle
D3.2 Interior angles	17 Estimating an angle
D3.3 Looking at triangles	17 Estimating an angle
D3.4 How many are there?	2 Find the remainders
E3.1 Fractions to decimals	14 Fractions and decimals
E3.4 Square numbers	15 Carroll diagram
E3.5 Find the factor	15 Carroll diagram
E3.6 Factors and prime numbers	15 Carroll diagram

Abacus Evolve *Solve the Problem* will challenge children with rich, open-ended problems that draw on a range of mathematical strategies.

Top team

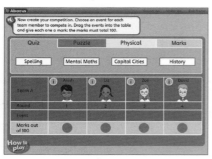

Children choose one of four teams, by comparing form in previous competitions. They then choose events from a choice of quizzes, puzzles and physical challenges, and allocate marks to each event. The aim is to choose the best event for each player and win the competition.

Cinema

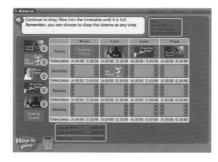

Children become the managers of a cinema. They decide when to open the cinema and which films to show at different times of the day. The aim is to plan a schedule that attracts customers and makes a good profit.

Marble factory

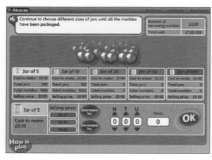

Children are asked to pack 4230 marbles into different-sized jars (5, 10, 20, 50 and 100), and then sell them. The aim is to maximise profits and/or to sell as many as possible. If they are priced too highly they may be left with stock; if they are priced too cheaply they may not make a profit. Jar sizes differ in popularity.

Theme park

Children visit a theme park. There are eight attractions: six rides, a burger bar and a shop, each of which can be visited twice during the day. Children plan their day returning to the entrance/exit gate at the end. Various challenges can be set, for example planning a day for a certain amount of money or minimising queuing time.

Farming fields

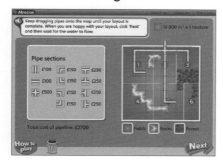

Children own a large amount of farmland for growing crops on. They need to install an irrigation system. Some of the land is rocky, some forest, some farmland. They need to decide which areas to water and how to lay the pipes. The aim is to make a profit from crops grown.

Kayak challenge

Children plan a route for a kayak across a stretch of water. The start and finish are already plotted. When they have plotted their route they direct the kayak along it, scoring points for passing the flags and incurring penalties for hitting land.

This chart shows which *Solve the Problem* activities could be used to extend some of the *Challenge* activities. The *Solve the Problem* activities are suitable for all ability levels, as children can set their own problems.

Challenge activity	Related *Solve the Problem* activities
C1.5 Rectangles and rhombuses	Farming fields
E1.5 Fractions	Top team
E1.6 Finding proportions	Farming fields
A2.1 Rounding up and converting distances	Theme park
B2.4 Coordinates	Kayak challenge
C2.1 Stamp sizes	Farming fields
C2.6 Schedules	Cinema, Theme park
D2.4 Fair share	Marble factory
D2.6 Money steps	Theme park
E2.2 Multiplication problems with time	Theme park, Kayak challenge
A3.6 Solving money matters	Cinema
C3.6 Angles and degrees	Kayak challenge
D3.1 The Shipping Forecast	Kayak challenge
D3.4 How many are there?	Marble factory
E3.2 Fruity percentages	Top team
E3.3 Ratio and proportion	Farming fields

Challenge Plan: Year 5

A1: reading and writing whole numbers; comparing and ordering numbers; multiplication facts; dividing with remainders

Summary

Y5 ⬠ **A1.1**

Very large numbers

Individuals, pairs or groups working independently

Year 5 Challenge Textbook page 3

Abacus Evolve objectives

- Read and write whole numbers in figures and words, and know what each digit represents

Framework objectives

- Explain what each digit represents in whole numbers and decimals with up to two places, and partition, round and order these numbers
- Plan and pursue an enquiry; present evidence by collecting, organising and interpreting information; suggest extensions to the enquiry

Teacher notes

Activity

Children work from page 3 of the Textbook. They will learn about the names of very large numbers such as trillion and quadrillion, and extremely large numbers such as googols.

Extra help

If children struggle to read large numbers correctly, explain: *We group numbers in sets of three, starting from the units and working to the left. This helps us to read very large numbers because we know that the sets of three digits are (from the right) ones, thousands, millions. So 123 456 789 is said as 'one hundred and twenty-three million, four hundred and fifty-six thousand, seven hundred and eighty-nine'.*

123	456	789
millions	thousands	ones

If you have time

Discuss the way we way say telephone numbers, and point out that saying integers in this way is not mathematically correct, but is in common usage. Discuss the use of the words 'oh' and 'zero' for the digit 0.

Explain the idea of writing multiples of ten by using powers of ten: $10 = 10^1$, $100 = 10^2$, etc. Point out that $1 = 10^0$. In fact, any number to the power 0 is 1!

Information

There are two different systems of referring to very large numbers, the short scale and the long scale.

For most of the 19th and 20th centuries, the UK used the long scale. However, in 1974 the UK abandoned the long scale, so that the UK now uses the short scale in mass media and official usage.

	Short scale (US)	Long scale (traditional UK)
million	1 000 000	1 000 000
billion	1 000 000 000	1 000 000 000 000
trillion	1 000 000 000 000	1 000 000 000 000 000 000

Be aware

- Saying numbers as separate digits e.g. three six five instead of three hundred and sixty five loses the value of the number.

Outcomes

- I can read, write and say very large numbers such as 4 823 944.

Supporting resources

Find out more about very large numbers here:
- http://www.isthe.com/chongo/tech/math/number/howhigh.html
- http://en.wikipedia.org/wiki/Googol
- *Mathematics and the Imagination* by Edward Kasner and James R. Newman (Penguin, 1940)

Challenge Plan: Year 5

A1: reading and writing whole numbers; comparing and ordering numbers; multiplication facts; dividing with remainders

Summary

Y5 ☆ A1.2

Inequalities and symbols

A small group working with an adult

Year 5 Challenge Textbook page 4

Eight sticky notes

Abacus Evolve objectives

- Use the vocabulary of comparing and ordering numbers, including symbols such as <, >, =
- Say one or more numbers lying between two given numbers (revise)
- Use decimal notation for tenths and hundredths

Framework objectives

- Explain what each digit represents in whole numbers and decimals with up to two places, and partition, round and order these numbers
- Understand the process of decision making

Teacher notes

Activity

In this activity, you will be introducing children to these symbols:

< is less than   > is greater than
= is equal to   ≤ is less than or equal to
≥ is greater than or equal to   ≠ is not equal to
≈ is approximately

- Write these four statements:
  $3 + 4 > 6$ $18 < 10 \times 2$ $50 + 23 < 73$ $5 \times 10 = 5 \times 5 \times 2$
  One of these statements is incorrect. Which one? (The third one.)
  Can you explain why?
  If necessary, discuss the meaning of the symbols, then show the correct solution on a number line.

- Draw a number line divided into tenths, and label the ends 3 and 4.
  Write this missing-number statement: $3 < n > 4$
  Discuss the possibility of *n* being any one of 3·1–3·9, to one decimal place.
  What if the missing number had two decimal places?
- Draw a number line divided into hundredths, and label the ends 3·0 and 4·0.
  Discuss the infinite number of possible values for n if we don't know how many decimal places it has.

- In the incorrect statement $50 + 23 < 73$, change the < symbol to the ≤ symbol.
  Discuss the meaning of ≤, and explain why it makes the statement true.

- Write each of the following numbers and symbols on a sticky note:
  22   60   28   38   +   −   >   ≥
  Ask children to choose any five sticky notes and make a correct statement.
  There is more than one solution. *Why did you choose your solution?*
  Discuss the possibility of reversing the statements by using the < and ≤ symbols instead.

Draw the ≠ and ≈ symbols. *What do you think these mean?*

If you have time

Children could work from page 4 of the Textbook. They solve the puzzle by finding which symbol belongs in each of the five spaces lettered a–e. They can then answer the questions at the bottom of the page.

Be aware

- The symbols < and > are easily misinterpreted. A way to remember which is which is that the point is always towards the smaller number.

Outcomes

- I can understand the symbols <, >, ≤, ≥, ≠ and ≈, and use them to solve equations.

Challenge Plan: Year 5

A1: reading and writing whole numbers; comparing and ordering numbers; multiplication facts; dividing with remainders

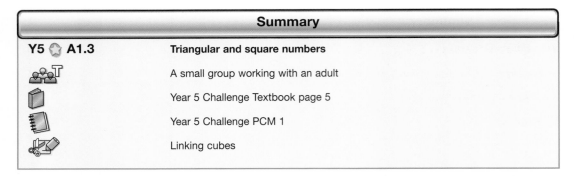

Summary

Y5 ⬡ **A1.3**

Triangular and square numbers

A small group working with an adult

Year 5 Challenge Textbook page 5

Year 5 Challenge PCM 1

Linking cubes

Abacus Evolve objectives

- **Y6** Know squares of numbers to at least 12 × 12
- **Y6** Calculate squares of larger numbers
- **Y6** Begin to recognise triangular numbers
- **Y6** Make and investigate a general statement about familiar numbers or shapes by finding examples that satisfy it
- **Y6** Explore patterns created by number sequences

Framework objectives

- **Y6** Use knowledge of multiplication facts to derive quickly squares of numbers to 12 × 12 and the corresponding squares of multiples of 10
- **Y6** Represent and interpret sequences, patterns and relationships involving numbers and shapes; suggest and test hypotheses; construct and use simple expressions and formulae in words then symbols, e.g. the cost of c pens at 15 pence each is 15c pence

Teacher notes

Getting started
Check and reinforce children's knowledge of the square numbers up to at least 12 × 12.

Activity
Explain what a triangular number is: *Triangular numbers are the sum of consecutive integers.*
The first triangular number is 1. The second triangular number is 1 + 2 = 3.
The third triangular number is 1 + 2 + 3 = 6. The fourth triangular number is 1 + 2 + 3 + 4 = 10.
Ask children to generate some more triangular numbers.

- Demonstrate building triangular numbers using linking cubes
- Start with one (1)
- Add two more (3)
- Add three more (6)
- Emphasise that we could go on adding cubes this way.

- Take the set of three cubes and a single cube, and demonstrate how they fit together.
What do you notice? (The two triangular numbers form a square number.)
What do you think will happen if we put the second and third triangular numbers together?
Any square number is the sum of two consecutive triangular numbers.
- Write some examples of this pattern:
4 = 1 + 3   25 = 10 + 15   64 = 28 + 36.
Allow children to explore with much bigger triangular numbers using linking cubes.

If you have time
Children could work from page 5 of the Textbook. They complete tables of triangular and square numbers on PCM 1, and look at the patterns in the two sequences.

Be aware

- Children may think that 1 × 1 = 2.

Outcomes

- I can explain how triangular and square numbers are linked.
- I can make up a rule to show this.

Supporting resources

Find out more about triangular numbers and other number sequences here:
- http://www.isallaboutmath.com/triangnum1.aspx
- http://mathforum.org/library/drmath/view/58729.html
- http://www.cut-the-knot.org/do_you_know/numbers.shtml#square

Challenge Plan: Year 5

A1: reading and writing whole numbers; comparing and ordering numbers; multiplication facts; dividing with remainders

Summary

Y5 ⭐ **A1.4**

Multiplying and dividing decimals

Individuals, pairs or groups working independently

Year 5 Challenge PCMs 2 and 3

Card; calculators (optional)

Abacus Evolve objectives

- **Y6** Use the relationship between multiplication and division to multiply and divide mentally
- **Y6** Use known number facts and place value to consolidate mental multiplication and division
- **Y6** Continue to multiply using closely related facts
- **Y6** Check with the inverse operation when using a calculator

Framework objectives

- **Y6** Use knowledge of place value and multiplication facts to 10 × 10 to derive related multiplication and division facts involving decimal numbers, e.g. 0·8 × 7, 4·8 ÷ 6
- **Y6** Use approximations, inverse operations and tests of divisibility to estimate and check results
- **Y6** Use a range of oral techniques to present persuasive argument

Teacher notes

Preparation
Photocopy PCM 2 onto card and cut out the numbers. Children will also need a copy of PCM 3.

Getting started
You may wish to give children calculators, but they are not necessary as all the calculations involve multiplication or division by 5, 2, 0·5 or 0·2.

Activity
Children place the cards in the correct positions on the multiplication and division grid.

Further extension
To make it harder, include the numbers from the last column on PCM 2 as red herrings, add or remove some of the correct cards so that children have to fill in the gaps themselves.

If you have time
If children finish early, you could give them a calculator and ask them to explore what happens when multiplying or dividing using a mixture of decimals less than 1, and whole numbers.

Information
Avoid statements such as 'multiplying makes a number bigger'. This only applies to calculations involving numbers greater than 1.

Be aware

- If children think that ÷ 0·5 means halving, explain that it means *How many halves in...?*
- If children struggle with calculations such as 5 ÷ 0·2, word it as *How many 0·2s in 5?* Ask them to first of all work out how many 0·2s in 1, and then multiply by 5.

Outcomes

- I can understand that multiplying by a decimal makes the number smaller.
- I can understand that dividing by a decimal makes the number larger.
- I can find pairs of calculations that give the same result, such as ÷ 2 and × 0·5.

Challenge Plan: Year 5

A1: reading and writing whole numbers; comparing and ordering numbers; multiplication facts; dividing with remainders

Summary

Y5 ○ **A1.5**

Recurring decimals

Individuals, pairs or groups working independently

Year 5 Challenge Textbook page 6

Calculators

Abacus Evolve objectives

- Begin to express a quotient as a fraction, or as a decimal when dividing an integer by 2, 4, 5 or 10, or when dividing £.p
- Recognise equivalence between fractions and decimals
- Relate fractions to division
- Recognise and explain patterns and relationships, generalise and predict

Framework objectives

- Express a smaller whole number as a fraction of a larger one, e.g. recognise that 5 out of 8 is $\frac{5}{8}$; find equivalent fractions, e.g. $\frac{7}{10} = \frac{14}{20}$, or $\frac{19}{10} = 1\frac{9}{10}$; relate fractions to their decimal representations
- Find fractions using division, e.g. $\frac{1}{100}$ of 5 kg, and percentages of numbers and quantities, e.g. 10%, 5% and 15% of £80
- Explore patterns, properties and relationships and propose a general statement involving numbers or shapes; identify examples for which the statement is true or false
- Explain reasoning using diagrams, graphs and text; refine ways of recording using images and symbols

Teacher notes

Getting started
Make sure each child has a calculator.

Activity
Children work from page 6 of the Textbook. They use a calculator to find the decimal equivalents of some vulgar fraction 'families', such as $\frac{1}{9}, \frac{2}{9}, \frac{3}{9}, \dots \frac{1}{11}, \frac{2}{11}, \frac{3}{11}, \dots$ They then explore fractions such as $\frac{1}{7}$ which have cyclical recurring digits. Children can then share their findings with another child or an adult.

If you have time
Show the correct notation for recurring decimals: draw a dot over the digits that are repeated. For example, $\frac{1}{9} = 0.\dot{1}$; $\frac{1}{6} = 0.1\dot{6}$; $\frac{1}{11} = 0.\dot{0}\dot{9}$. When more than two digits are repeated, draw a dot over the first and last digits in the repeating pattern. For example, $\frac{1}{27} = 0.\dot{0}3\dot{7}$.

Be aware

- The term vulgar fraction can be misinterpreted as an improper fraction. A vulgar fraction is simply any fraction presented as one integer over another, for example, $\frac{1}{2}$. We use the term vulgar fraction to distinguish from a decimal fraction such as 0·5.

Outcomes

- I know what a vulgar fraction is and I know how to find the decimal equivalent.
- I can present my results clearly.

Summary

Y5 ⭐ A1.6

Equivalent fractions

Individuals, pairs or groups working independently

Year 5 Challenge Textbook page 7

Year 5 Challenge PCM 4

Calculators

Abacus Evolve objectives

- Rehearse the concept of a remainder, when dividing
- Begin to express a quotient as a fraction, or as a decimal when dividing an integer by 2, 4, 5 or 10, or when dividing £·p
- Use fraction notation, including mixed numbers, and the vocabulary 'numerator' and 'denominator'
- Change an improper fraction to a mixed number, and vice versa
- Recognise when two simple fractions are equivalent
- Recognise and explain patterns and relationships, generalise and predict

Framework objectives

- Express a smaller whole number as a fraction of a larger one, e.g. recognise that 5 out of 8 is $\frac{5}{8}$; find equivalent fractions, e.g. $\frac{7}{10} = \frac{14}{20}$, or $\frac{19}{10} = 1\frac{9}{10}$; relate fractions to their decimal representations
- Explore patterns, properties and relationships and propose a general statement involving numbers or shapes; identify examples for which the statement is true or false
- Plan and pursue an enquiry; present evidence by collecting, organising and interpreting information; suggest extensions to the enquiry
- Understand the process of decision making

Teacher notes

Getting started
Make sure each child has a calculator.

Activity
Children work from page 7 of the Textbook. They find divisions that result in the same mixed number, and explore the patterns in the dividend and divisor and the numerator and denominator. They then complete the table on PCM 4 to find different ways to make 9·3 using division.

Extra help
If children need a visual representation of equivalent fractions, you could draw a counting stick with multiples of 2 labelled across the top and multiples of 3 along the bottom. Point to the division with 2 at the top and 3 at the bottom, and explain that this represents $\frac{2}{3}$. Then go along the divisions, pointing out $\frac{4}{6}$, $\frac{6}{9}$, and so on.
You could extend the counting stick to show equivalents such as $\frac{22}{33}$ and $\frac{30}{45}$.

Be aware

- Children do not always consider the possibility that there can be more than one correct answer to a question.

Outcomes

- I can cancel fractions to their lowest form.
- I know that some questions have more than one answer.

Challenge Plan: Year 5

B1: odd and even numbers; number sequences; parallel and perpendicular lines; classifying triangles

Summary

Y5 ⭐ **B1.1**

Multiplying and dividing even and odd numbers

Individuals, pairs or groups working independently

Year 5 Challenge Textbook page 8

 Calculators

Abacus Evolve objectives

- Make general statements about odd or even numbers, including their sums and differences
- Explain a generalised relationship (formula) in words
- Use knowledge of sums or differences of odd/even numbers to check calculations

Framework objectives

- Explore patterns, properties and relationships and propose a general statement involving numbers or shapes; identify examples for which the statement is true or false

Teacher notes

Getting started
Encourage children to recall the rules for adding and subtracting odd and even numbers:

$E \pm E = E$ $\qquad$ $O \pm O = E$ $\qquad$ $E \pm O = O$ $\qquad$ $O \pm E = O$

Activity
Children work from page 8 of the Textbook. Children predict what will happen when multiplying and dividing even and odd numbers. They first consider multiplying combinations of even and odd numbers. They should repeat this for at least three pairs of even numbers, three pairs of odd numbers and three pairs of even and odd numbers.

Children can discuss their results and look for further combinations to check the patterns they find.

Children repeat this for division and think about how similar division is to multiplication.

Information
Children should find that multiplication produces $E \times E = E$; $O \times O = O$; $E \times O$ or $O \times E = E$. They may (with prompting) relate this to results they have found previously for repeated addition of odd and even numbers.
With division children will notice that some numbers are not exactly divisible. Where numbers are exactly divisible, $O \div O = O$; $E \div O = E$; but $E \div E = O$ or E. An odd number is never exactly divisible by an even number.

Be aware

- Children may assume that when multiplying and dividing even and odd numbers they will get the same results as with adding and subtracting.

Outcomes

- I can understand what happens when even and odd numbers are multiplied together.
- I can explain what happens when even and odd numbers are multiplied or divided.
- I can show why this happens.

Summary

Y5 ☆ B1.2

Number sequences

A small group working with an adult

Year 5 Challenge Textbook page 9

1–100 square

Abacus Evolve objectives

- Recognise and extend number sequences formed by counting from any number in steps of constant size, extending beyond zero when counting back, including decimals
- Recognise and explain patterns and relationships, generalise and predict

Framework objectives

- Count from any given number in whole-number and decimal steps, extending beyond zero when counting backwards; relate the numbers to their position on a number line
- Explore patterns, properties and relationships and propose a general statement involving numbers or shapes; identify examples for which the statement is true or false
- Understand the process of decision making

Teacher notes

Activity

Write this sequence: *5   13   10   18   15*

- Ask the group the following questions. Children investigate one or two questions and feed back to the group.
  - *What are the rules for this sequence?* ($+ 8$, $- 3$)
  - *What will be the next four numbers in the sequence?* (23, 20, 28, 25)
  - *Can you predict which numbers on the 100-square will be in the sequence? Why?* (Numbers ending in 0, 3, 5 or 8; because effect of adding 8 and subtracting 3 means that 5 is being repeatedly added to the two starting numbers.)
  - *What if you continued to 200?*
  - *What if you ran the sequence backwards from the number five?* (It would go into negative numbers.)
  - *What if the same sequence began at the number four?* (Numbers ending in 4, 2, 9 and 7.)

Children look at the first part of page 9 of the Textbook.
Discuss the first sequence: 17   19   15   17   13   15

- *Will every number occur twice? Why?* (Yes because 2 is added while 4 is subtracted and 4 is a multiple of 2.)
- *Why are there no even numbers in this sequence?* (Because it starts on an odd number, and the difference between each term is always even.)

Discuss the second sequence: 19   28   26   30   39   37   41   50

- *Which multiples of ten appear in this sequence? Is there any pattern to this?* (30, 50, 70. After 70 the next multiples of 10 that occur will be 140, 160 and 180. Since the overall effect of the sequence ($+ 9$ $- 2 + 4$) is $+ 11$, the further multiples of 10 occur at intervals of 110 (i.e. 10×11) after the first three multiples of 10.)

Children complete the first part of Textbook page 9 by answering questions about a sequence with larger numbers.

Children then work from the second part of page 9 of the Textbook. Children look at sequences with fractions and decimals and work out the rule for each sequence. They can work in pairs or groups, or solve the sequences independently then discuss results with the group.

Extra help

During the activity, probe children's responses by asking questions such as: *How can you be sure? How many numbers do you need to generate to be sure?*
These questions will ensure that children make predictions, justify answers with reference to things that they have evidence for and make recordings in a concise way.

Be aware

- Children may look at sequences superficially with two or three numbers only. At this level it is important to generate a longer sequence before examining it for repeated patterns.

Outcomes

- I can find and continue sequences.
- I can make predictions and explain my findings.

Summary

Y5 ⭐ **B1.3**

Investigating number sequences

Individuals, pairs or groups working independently

 Year 5 Challenge Textbook page 10

Abacus Evolve objectives

- Construct number sequences
- Recognise and extend number sequences formed by counting from any number in steps of constant size, extending beyond zero when counting back, including decimals
- Recognise and explain patterns and relationships, generalise and predict

Framework objectives

- Count from any given number in whole number and decimal steps, extending beyond zero when counting backwards; relate the numbers to their position on a number line
- Plan and pursue an enquiry; present evidence by collecting, organising and interpreting information; suggest extensions to the enquiry
- Explore patterns, properties and relationships and propose a general statement involving numbers or shapes; identify examples for which the statement is true or false

Teacher notes

Activity

Children work from page 10 of the Textbook. They follow the rules at the top of the page:
- Start with a whole number between 10 and 100.
- If the number is even, halve it; if the number is odd, add 1 then halve it.
- Continue until they reach 1.

They investigate which start numbers generate the longest sequences. Children can work in groups, and collectively devise a strategy for covering a range of numbers and ways to record results.

If you have time

Ask questions such as: *What is a good number to start with? What happens towards the end of the sequence? Why will an odd start number need more steps? Why have you chosen that method to record your results?*

Information

The number between 10 and 100 which generates the longest sequence is 66 (12 steps).
Children may realise that longer sequences are produced when more odd numbers occur, and this fact can be used to work backwards from 1, alternately doubling and subtracting 1 to find maximum solutions.

Be aware

- Many children will be surprised that the start number below 1000 that produces the longest sequence is 513. They are likely to expect a larger start number.

Outcomes

- I can make predictions and explain my results.
- I can make a number sequence by following instructions.

Summary

Y5 ⭐ B1.4

Making quadrilaterals

Individuals, pairs or groups working independently

Year 5 Challenge Textbook page 11

Year 5 Challenge PCMs 5 and 6

3 × 3 pinboards; rubber bands; scissors; glue

Abacus Evolve objectives

- **Y6** Use the terms 'parallelogram', 'rhombus' and 'trapezium'
- **Y6** Begin to know the properties of parallelograms, rhombuses and trapezia
- **Y6** Begin to use the term 'kite'
- **Y6** Classify quadrilaterals, using criteria such as parallel sides, equal sides, equal angles

Framework objectives

- **Y6** Describe, identify and visualise parallel and perpendicular edges or faces; use these properties to classify 2D shapes and 3D solids
- **Y6** Understand and use a variety of ways to criticise constructively and respond to criticism

Teacher notes

Getting started
Make sure each child has a 3 × 3 pinboard, a rubber band, a copy of PCM 5 and PCM 6.
It would be useful to provide a few extra copies of the PCMs.

Activity
Children work from page 11 of the Textbook. They use 3 × 3 pinboards and rubber bands to explore how many different quadrilaterals they can make, not including rotations or reflections. They work in pairs or groups to compare quadrilaterals. This should help to eliminate any duplicates. Children draw each unique quadrilateral on the dotted grids on PCM 5, then cut out each quadrilateral. They use the Carroll diagram from PCM 6 to arrange the quadrilaterals in the correct sections of the diagram. Once they are sure they have positioned them correctly, they can glue them in place.

If you have time
Ask questions such as: *How can you be sure these two shapes are different? Which of your shapes have parallel lines? Which have perpendicular lines? Which section of the diagram should that one go in? How do you know?*

Information
There are 16 unique quadrilaterals that can be made on a 3 × 3 pinboard.

Be aware

- Some rotations and reflections can be difficult to spot. Encourage children to compare each new quadrilateral carefully to avoid duplicates.

Outcomes

- I can find different quadrilaterals.
- I can place quadrilaterals in the correct section of a Carroll diagram.

B1: odd and even numbers; number sequences; parallel and perpendicular lines; classifying triangles

Summary

Y5 ⬠ B1.5

Parallel and perpendicular

Individuals, pairs or groups working independently

Year 5 Challenge Textbook page 12

Linking cubes

Abacus Evolve objectives	Framework objectives
• **Y6** Recognise parallel and perpendicular faces and edges on 3D shapes • **Y6** Visualise 3D shapes from 2D drawings and identify different nets for a closed cube	• **Y6** Describe, identify and visualise parallel and perpendicular edges or faces; use these properties to classify 2D shapes and 3D solids • **Y6** Use a range of oral techniques to present persuasive argument

Teacher notes

Activity

Children work from page 12 of the Textbook.

They discuss the parallel and perpendicular faces and edges they can see in photos of four famous buildings.

Children then look at three drawings of different arrangements of five linking cubes. Children make these shapes themselves and work out which one has the most parallel faces, and which has the most perpendicular faces. Children should count the faces of the whole shape, not the faces of each cube.

They then use five linking cubes to find all the possible arrangements of cubes.

Be aware	Outcomes
• If children are used to finding parallel and perpendicular lines on 2D shapes they may find it hard to find parallel or perpendicular faces on 3D shapes.	• I can find parallel and perpendicular faces on buildings and on models.

Summary

Y5 **B1.6**

Making triangles on a pinboard

A small group working with an adult

Year 5 Challenge PCM 5

3 × 3 pinboards; rubber bands

Abacus Evolve objectives

- Classify triangles, using criteria such as equal sides, equal angles, lines of symmetry

Framework objectives

- Identify, visualise and describe properties of rectangles, triangles, regular polygons and 3D solids; use knowledge of properties to draw 2D shapes, and to identify and draw nets of 3D shapes
- Explain reasoning using diagrams, graphs and text; refine ways of recording using images and symbols

Teacher notes

Preparation
Photocopy PCM 5, at least two copies for each child. Provide each child with a pinboard and a rubber band.

Getting started
- Review triangle vocabulary with children, for example equilateral, scalene, isosceles, right-angled.

Activity
- Ask children to use their pinboards and rubber bands to find as many different triangles as they can. Explain that rotations and reflections don't count at this stage.
- After a few minutes, ask children to classify the triangles they have made according to their properties: *Which ones are right-angled? Which are scalene? Which are isosceles?*
- *Have any of you made an equilateral triangle?* Discuss why this is not possible on a 3 × 3 pinboard.
- Ask children to explain why this isn't an equilateral triangle, without measuring.
- Look at the triangles that children have made. Agree which ones are unique, and put these aside.
- Work as a group to try and make all the other triangles: there are eight in total.

- *What if rotations and reflections and translations of each triangle were allowed? How many triangles could we make then?* Discuss, using the pinboards to check assumptions.
- Give each child a copy of PCM 5. Challenge them to draw as many triangles as possible. Compare results.
- *Which of the eight unique triangles can be rotated and reflected and translated into the most positions? How about the least?*
- Ask children to discuss these questions in pairs, then compare results as a group.
- This triangle has the most unique positions:

- This triangle has the least unique positions:

Be aware

- Some children might overlook translations. Make sure that children are aware that translation is the same shape, shifted to another location on the board, without turning.

Outcomes

- I can find a range of triangles on a pinboard.
- I can find how many positions there are for any of these triangles.

Challenge Plan: Year 5

C1: frequency tables, pictograms and bar graphs; bar line graphs; units of length; units of weight

---

Summary

Y5 ⬡ C1.1

Tables and graphs

A small group working with an adult

Year 5 Challenge Textbook page 13

Year 5 Challenge PCM 7

Abacus Evolve objectives

- Draw and interpret frequency tables, pictograms and bar graphs
- Organise and interpret data represented in bar line graphs
- Draw and interpret a line graph

Framework objectives

- *Construct frequency tables, pictograms and bar and line graphs to represent the frequencies of events and changes over time*

Teacher notes

Preparation
Photocopy PCM 7, one for each child.

Activity
Ask children to think about different types of graphs and which one should be used depending on the data you have.
Children look at PCM 7.
These two graphs show similar data but one is a bar graph and the other is a line graph.
What does each graph tell you?
- Graph 1 shows that there was one relatively hot day and one relatively cold day. There were 10 days when it was 13 degrees. Point to 3·5 days. *What is the reading here? We cannot find a reading – we cannot interpret the intermediate points on a bar graph.*
- Graph 2 shows that it got warmer over the day but the temperature fell again towards the end of the day.
  Point to 12:30pm. *What does the graph show at 12:30pm? On a line graph the intermediate points have meaning. We can see that at 12:30pm the temperature was just below 14 degrees Celsius.*

- *What information can we get from both graphs? We can see the highest and lowest temperature.*
- *The bar graph shows the most common temperature over a month. The line graph shows a steady rise and then fall in temperature. The bar graph could not show this. Different graphs are drawn for different purposes.*
- *We would use a bar graph to show:*
  - *the number of children in people's families*
  - *favourite ice-cream flavours*
  - *the number of bicycles sold over a day.*
Can you think of any more information that we would show in a bar graph?
- *We would use a line graph to show:*
  - *A person's change in height over a period of time*
  - *The speed of a runner during a 500 m race.*
Can you think of any more information that we would show in a line graph?

Children work from Textbook page 13. They draw a bar graph and a line graph.

Information
Discrete data is normally counted, e.g. the number of puppies in a litter. A tally chart or frequency table is needed in order to draw a graph. Continuous data is normally measured, e.g. the weight of one puppy during its first month. There is no need for a tally chart but a table of measurements is needed.

Be aware

- Children may confuse discrete and continuous data.

Outcomes

- I can understand the difference between bar graphs and line graphs.
- I can interpret different types of graph.

Challenge Plan: Year 5

C1: frequency tables, pictograms and bar graphs; bar line graphs; units of length; units of weight

Summary

Y5 ⭐ C1.2

Line graphs and conversion graphs

Individuals, pairs or groups working independently

Year 5 Challenge Textbook page 14

Year 5 Challenge PCM 8

Abacus Evolve objectives

- **Y6** Construct and interpret line graphs in which intermediate values have meaning
- **Y6** Construct and interpret a conversion graph

Framework objectives

- **Y6** *Solve problems by collecting, selecting, processing, presenting and interpreting data, using ICT where appropriate; draw conclusions and identify further questions to ask*

Teacher notes

Preparation
Photocopy PCM 8, one for each child.

Getting started
Ensure that children are familiar with plotting data to draw a line graph.

Activity
Children work from Textbook page 14. They test a hypothesis about a set of data by drawing a line graph, and then answer questions about the graph. Children then answer questions about a conversion graph, and draw and interpret their own conversion graph.

Information
London was the most populous European Capital in 1801 and was the most populous city in the world from approximately 1831 to 1931. However, the population of London began to fall in the latter half of the twentieth century.

Be aware

- Children may need reminding that line graphs must only be used for continuous data. A quick way to test whether a line graph is based on continuous data is to check whether the intermediate points have meaning.

Outcomes

- I can draw and interpret line graphs and conversion graphs.
- I can solve problems using line graphs.

C1: frequency tables, pictograms and bar graphs; bar line graphs; units of length; units of weight

Summary

Y5 ⬠ C1.3

Averages

Individual, pairs or groups working independently

Year 5 Challenge Textbook page 15

Abacus Evolve objectives

- **Y6** Find the mode and range of a set of data
- **Y6** Begin to find the median and mean of a set of data
- **Y6** Calculate different types of average for a set of data

Framework objectives

- **Y6** Describe and interpret results and solutions to problems using the mode, range, median and mean
- **Y6** Understand and use a variety of ways to criticise constructively and take criticism

Teacher notes

Getting started

Ensure that children are confident with adding strings of numbers and dividing by 1- and 2-digit numbers.

Activity

Children work from Textbook page 15. They read about two children who are learning mode, mean, median and range. In each section, one child has understood the method and the other has misunderstood. Children work out who is correct in each case, and perform calculations using the right method. Children use their findings to reach a decision about what the data shows.

Extra help

Explain to children: *Mode, mean and median are three different ways of measuring average. When we are asked to work out the average of some numbers we tend to do the arithmetical average, which is the mean. The mode or modal average is the most common. The median is the middle average. Each of these averages has a use and they can all be used to compare data. For instance a shop would want to know the modal size of shoes bought so that they could stock more of the popular sizes.*

If you have time

Children could collect data from around the class or the school, for example the number of pets per child in their class, or the number of children in each class. They can use their data to work out the mode, mean and median.

Be aware

- Children need to be aware that many people say 'average' when they actually mean the mean. This is not the only way to compare data.

Outcomes

- I can find the mode, mean, median and range of sets of numbers.
- I can use the mode, mean, median and range to interpret results and find solutions.

Summary

Y5 ☆ C1.4

Imperial or metric?

Individuals, pairs or groups working independently

Year 5 Challenge Textbook page 16

Containers with weights shown; bottles with capacities shown; the internet (optional)

Abacus Evolve objectives

- Suggest suitable units and measuring equipment to estimate or measure length
- Record estimates and readings from weighing scales
- Suggest suitable units and measuring equipment to estimate or measure weight

Framework objectives

- Interpret a reading that lies between two unnumbered divisions on a scale

Teacher notes

Activity
Children work from Textbook page 16. They read about why we use both metric and imperial units of measurement, and about the origins of some imperial units. They are then encouraged to think about the units we use to measure everyday items.

If you have time
Children could research who originally calculated how long a metre was, and how this was calculated.
Children could discuss why we fill our cars up with litres of petrol but measure the distance we drive in miles.

Information
One metre is supposed to be one ten-millionth of the distance from the north pole to the equator. It was calculated by two French astronomers in the eighteenth century, Jean-Baptiste-Joseph Delambre and Pierre-François-André Méchain.
The metre is now officially $\frac{1}{299\,792\,458}$ the distance travelled by light in a vacuum in one second.

Be aware

- We cannot mix different units of measurement. This can cause confusion when children are taught metric units of measurement but are surrounded by adults who use the imperial system.

Outcomes

- I can understand that there are two different systems of measurement: imperial and metric.
- I can suggest suitable units for measuring.

Challenge Plan: Year 5

C1: frequency tables, pictograms and bar graphs; bar line graphs; units of length; units of weight

Summary

Y5 ⭐ **C1.5**

Rectangles and rhombuses

Individuals, pairs or groups working independently

Year 5 Challenge Textbook page 17

 Squared paper; rulers

Abacus Evolve objectives

- Measure and draw lines to the nearest millimetre
- Explain a generalised relationship (formula) in words

Framework objectives

- *Draw and measure lines to the nearest millimetre; measure and calculate the perimeter of regular and irregular polygons; use the formula for the area of a rectangle to calculate the rectangle's area*

Teacher notes

Getting started
Ensure that children are accurate at drawing lines to 1 mm and are confident in working out the areas of rectangles and the areas of regular polygons using rectangles.

Activity
Children work from Textbook page 17. They explore drawing a rectangle, and then creating a sequence of rhombuses and rectangles within it. Children investigate how the area of a rhombus is calculated by using the lengths of diagonals and propose a basic general formula for this.

Children may also be able to show that the area of the first rhombus is half the area of the first rectangle by cutting off the corners of the rectangle and placing them over the rhombus. They are exactly equal.

Information
Pythagoras' theorem can be used to calculate the length of the sides of a rhombus accurately. This is advanced, but if a child has discovered this link then it may be suitable for them to explore by using calculation rather than by drawing.

Be aware

- We use the formula length × width to find the area of a rectangle. Children sometimes think that all plane shapes follow the same rule, but this does not work for a rhombus.

Outcomes

- I can draw shapes carefully.
- I can investigate the areas of rectangles and rhombuses.
- I can find a pattern and explain it.

Summary

Y5 **C1.6**

The best buy

A small group working with an adult

Year 5 Challenge PCM 9

Four food tins; sticky labels; calculators; the internet (optional)

Abacus Evolve objectives

- Convert from one larger metric unit of length to another smaller unit
- Use, read and write standard metric units of weight: kg, g
- Convert from one larger metric unit of weight to another smaller unit
- Know the equivalent of $\frac{1}{2}$, $\frac{1}{4}$, $\frac{3}{4}$, $\frac{1}{10}$, $\frac{1}{100}$ of 1 kg in g
- Solve simple problems involving proportion

Framework objectives

- Read, choose, use and record standard metric units to estimate and measure length, weight and capacity to a suitable degree of accuracy, e.g. the nearest centimetre; convert larger to smaller units using decimals to one place, e.g. change 2·6 kg to 2600 g
- Use sequences to scale numbers up or down; solve problems involving proportions of quantities, e.g. decrease quantities in a recipe designed to feed six people
- Understand the process of decision making

Teacher notes

Preparation

Write the following weights and prices on labels, and stick them onto four food tins (these match the tins of beans on PCM 9).

- 420 g   52 p   (This is 12·38 p per 100 g)
- 415 g   50 p   (This is 12·05 p per 100 g)
- 220 g   26 p   (This is 11·82 p per 100 g)
- 400 g   40 p   (This is 10 p per 100 g)

Activity

- Show the four tins. *Which is the best value?*
- Agree that it is not easy to compare. *It would be easier to work out the cost if the weights were the same.*
- *In the supermarket have you ever looked closely at the labels on the shelves? They often show two prices: the price of one item, and the price per 100 g or 100 ml or per 1 kg or 1 l. This makes it easier to compare.*
- Demonstrate finding the cost of 1 g of beans by dividing the cost of a tin by the number of grams.
  52 ÷ 420 = 0·1238095 pence
- *This is a very small number so we multiply by 100 to find the cost per 100 g.*
  0.1238095 × 100 = 12.38095 pence. This is 12.38 pence to two decimal places.
- *So beans which cost 52 p for 420 g, cost 12·38 p per 100 g.*
- Ask children to work out the cost per 100 g for the other three tins of beans. *Which is cheapest?* (Price 4)
- Children work from PCM 9, and circle the best price for each product.

Extra help

You may need to point out to some children that they need to treat two products differently from the others:

- The tea bags are priced individually, rather than by weight.
- The milk is measured in metric and imperial units. Children should find the cost of 100 ml of milk in each case.

You could write out the following for children to refer to:
1 pint = 568 ml.

If you have time

Children could write a short shopping list and use a supermarket website to look at prices and decide what to buy to get the best value for money.

As a home activity, children could look at shelf tags in the supermarket and bring in information that they have collected about pricing and comparisons.

Be aware

- Children may not realise at first that the product that is the cheapest is not necessarily the best value.

Outcomes

- I can find the cheapest product by comparing prices.
- I can solve problems involving proportion.

Challenge Plan: Year 5

D1: reflective symmetry and axis of symmetry; 3D shapes; number pairs that total 100; differences through next multiple of 10, 100, or 1000

Summary

Y5 ⭐ D1.1

In the mirror

A small group working with an adult

Year 5 Challenge Textbook page 18

Year 5 Challenge PCM 10

Mirrors

Abacus Evolve objectives

- **Y6** Rehearse the concept of reflection
- **Y6** Recognise where a shape will be after reflection in a mirror line touching the shape at a point
- **Y6** Recognise where a shape will be after reflection in two mirror lines at right angles

Framework objectives

- **Y6** *Visualise and draw on grids of different types where a shape will be after reflection, after translations, or after rotation through 90° or 180° about its centre or one of its vertices*
- **Y6** Make and draw shapes with increasing accuracy and apply knowledge of their properties

Teacher notes

Preparation

Photocopy PCM 10, one for each child. Cut out all the shapes so that children have a set of shapes each. Make a copy of PCM 10 on A3 if you would like to use it to demonstrate. Provide mirrors and encourage children to use them to check for lines of symmetry throughout the activity.

Activity

Children work from Textbook page 18. They use the questions to discuss the properties of the 2D shapes.

Give each child a set of shapes from PCM 10.
- *Find a shape which has:*
  one line of symmetry   two lines of symmetry
  more than two lines of symmetry   no lines of symmetry
- *The line of symmetry is called an axis of symmetry.*
Encourage children to name each shape correctly. Confirm the properties of each shape (for example a square has four equal sides and four right angles).
- With four copies of shape E, ask children to make a shape which has two lines of symmetry. Then four lines of symmetry. Then one line of symmetry. Then no lines of symmetry.
- Draw the following shape and ask children to make it using shape E.
- *Can we add one square to this shape to make a shape with two lines of symmetry? Can we add one square to make a shape with one line of symmetry? Can we add one square to make a shape with more than two lines of symmetry? Can we add one square to make a shape with no lines of symmetry?*
- *What is the same about shapes B and C? What is different about them?*
- *Make a symmetrical shape using four of shape E, one of shape B and one of shape C. Can we move one piece and keep the shape symmetrical? How?*
- *What is the same about shapes A, B and C? What is different about them?*
- *Can we use shape A and shape D to make symmetrical shapes which have two lines of symmetry?*
- Draw two mirror lines which cross at right angles (bisect each line in the middle). Arrange any four pieces on one quadrant and ask children to make the full reflections along the mirror lines with their shapes.

If you have time

Make more shapes for children to work with, for example other quadrilaterals such as a parallelogram, a trapezium, a rhombus or a kite.

Be aware

- Children should be aware that a square has four lines of symmetry. A rectangle only has two lines of symmetry.

Outcomes

- I can say how many lines of symmetry a shape has.
- I can make symmetrical and non-symmetrical shapes.

D1: reflective symmetry and axis of symmetry; 3D shapes; number pairs that total 100; differences through next multiple of 10, 100, or 1000

Summary

Y5 ⬡ D1.2

Polyominoes

Individuals, pairs or groups working independently

Year 5 Challenge Textbook page 19

Squared paper; rulers; scissors

Abacus Evolve objectives

- Visualise 3D shapes from 2D drawings and identify different nets of 3D shapes
- Understand, measure and calculate perimeters of rectangles

Framework objectives

- Identify, visualise and describe properties of rectangles, triangles, regular polygons and 3D solids; use knowledge of properties to draw 2D shapes, and to identify and draw nets of 3D shapes
- *Draw and measure lines to the nearest millimetre; measure and calculate the perimeter of regular and irregular polygons; use the formula for the area of a rectangle to calculate the rectangle's area*
- Understand the process of decision making

Teacher notes

Getting started
Make sure children are familiar with nets, in particular the net of an open cube. Also ensure children know how to calculate the perimeter of regular shapes.

Activity
Children work from Textbook page 19. The activity explores the 12 pentominoes. Children decide which ones will fold into an open cube by drawing, cutting out and folding the shapes. Children calculate the perimeter of each shape and consider which have the longest and shortest perimeters. Children try to find a rule for this.

Be aware

- Not all pentominoes make an open cube. Children should be encouraged to practise folding each pentomino to prove this.

Outcomes

- I can solve a problem involving pentominoes.
- I can make a rule for the longest and shortest perimeters of pentominoes.

Supporting resources

Children can find out all about polyominoes here:
- http://math.rice.edu/~lanius/Lessons/Polys/poly1.html

Challenge Plan: Year 5

D1: reflective symmetry and axis of symmetry; 3D shapes; number pairs that total 100; differences through next multiple of 10, 100, or 1000

Summary

Y5 ⊙ D1.3

Platonic solids

Individuals, pairs or groups working independently

Year 5 Challenge Textbook page 20

 3D shapes (cube, tetrahedron, octahedron, icosahedron, dodecahedron); protractors

Abacus Evolve objectives

- Rehearse the names and properties of common 3D shapes
- Rehearse the terms 'polyhedron', 'tetrahedron' and begin to use 'octahedron'

Framework objectives

- Identify, visualise and describe properties of rectangles, triangles, regular polygons and 3D solids; use knowledge of properties to draw 2D shapes, and to identify and draw nets of 3D shapes
- Plan and manage a group task over time by using different levels of planning

Teacher notes

Getting started

Give children real examples of the Platonic solids: a cube, a tetrahedron, an octahedron, an icosahedron and a dodecahedron. Ensure that children are familiar with using vocabulary associated with solid shapes, for example *edge*, *face*, *vertex*.

Activity

Children work from Textbook page 20. They read about Plato and his five regular polyhedra, the Platonic solids. They consider why Plato found that these shapes would make fair dice. Children explore the properties of the Platonic solids, by counting faces and measuring angles.

Further extension

Plato associated the five Platonic solids with five elements (earth, fire, air, water and the universe). Children could use the internet to explore this connection.

Information

It is possible to make other solids with regular sides, for example a six-sided solid with identical triangular faces, but there are no other 3D shapes with regular properties.

Be aware

- Children should not confuse terminology that is used for 2D shapes with terminology for 3D shapes. For instance the sides on a 2D shape are referred to as edges on a 3D shape.

Outcomes

- I can recognise the five Platonic solids.
- I can explore the Platonic solids and understand why they would make a fair dice.

Supporting resources

Children can research Euclid here:
- http://www.mcs.surrey.ac.uk/Personal/R.Knott/Fibonacci/phi3DGeom.html#Plato

If children want to know more about the use of Platonic solids as dice, they can look here:
- http://www.mcs.surrey.ac.uk/Personal/R.Knott/Fibonacci/phi3DGeom.html#fivereg

Find the properties of polyhedra here:
- http://www.coolmath4kids.com/polyhedra/index.html

Challenge Plan: Year 5

D1: reflective symmetry and axis of symmetry; 3D shapes; number pairs that total 100; differences through next multiple of 10, 100, or 1000

Summary

Y5 ⬡ D1.4

Find the rule

A small group working with an adult

Year 5 Challenge Textbook page 21

Abacus Evolve objectives

- Continue to derive quickly pairs of numbers that total 100
- Explain a generalised relationship (formula) in words

Framework objectives

- Use knowledge of rounding, place value, number facts and inverse operations to estimate and check calculations
- Explore patterns, properties and relationships and propose a general statement involving numbers or shapes; identify examples for which the statement is true or false

Teacher notes

Getting started

Ensure children are confident in adding two 2-digit numbers.

Activity

Children work from Textbook page 21. This activity looks at reversing digits and patterns that arise when using them in calculations. Counter-examples (ones that do not work) are also included.

- Read the first part of Textbook page 21 together.
- *What do you notice about the numbers 45 and 54?*
- Confirm they are reverses of each other, that the digit total is 9, and that they are multiples of 9.
- Ask children to add these two numbers together and take the total from 100. Confirm that 1 remains.
- *Can you suggest another pair of numbers with the same properties as 45 and 54?* (Reverses that total 9, for example 18 and 81.)
- *Work out the total of this pair of numbers and subtract it from 100.* Again confirm that 1 remains.
- *Can you find a rule for these numbers?*
- *Can you find more number pairs which follow this rule?*

- Read the second part of Textbook page 21 together. Children begin to find the rule for 26 and 62.
- *Add these two numbers together and take the total from 100. What remains?*

- Ask children to work through the rest of the Textbook page as a group.

Further extension

Children can explore this pattern with multiples of 10p totalling £10, for example £5·40 and £4·50. The same pattern can be observed. Children can explore if this pattern can be used with reversed number pairs that total 999, 888, 777, and so on. (Children will discover that reversed number pairs can be found for even numbers such as 888 and 666 but it is impossible to find any for odd numbers such as 999 and 777.)

Information

The rule is that number pairs total 99, 88, 77, and so on when the digits are reversed. The subsequent remainders from 100 increase by 11 each time, i.e. 1, 12, 23, and so on. The exception is when the digits total 10 or more, for example 28 and 82. Also the total of the two numbers is always a multiple of the digit sum of each of the two numbers.

Be aware

- When finding number pairs to 100, children may make one number 10 too big, for example 54 and 56 rather than 54 and 46.

Outcomes

- I can identify patterns and properties of numbers.
- I can use these to predict other numbers.

Challenge Plan: Year 5

D1: reflective symmetry and axis of symmetry; 3D shapes; number pairs that total 100; differences through next multiple of 10, 100, or 1000

Summary

Y5 ⭐ **D1.5**

Will it divide?

Individual, pairs or groups working independently

Year 5 Challenge PCM 11

Internet (optional)

Abacus Evolve objectives

- **Y6** Consolidate knowledge of tests of divisibility by 2, 4, 5, 10 and 100
- **Y6** Know and apply tests of divisibility by 3, 6 and 9
- **Y6** Know and apply tests of divisibility by 8 and 25
- **Y6** Use tests of divisibility to estimate and check results of calculations

Framework objectives

- **Y6** Use approximations, inverse operations and tests of divisibility to estimate and check results
- **Y6** Use a range of oral techniques to present persuasive argument

Teacher notes

Preparation
Photocopy PCM 11, one for each child, pair or group. Cut out the number cards so that each child has a set.

Getting started
Familiarise children with the tests of divisibility. These are summarised in the **Information** section.

Activity
Children work from PCM 11. They use the rules of divisibility to complete the grid by placing their number cards in the appropriate spaces, making sure that each number fits the horizontal and the vertical description. Some of the numbers may fit in more than one place on the grid and some will not fit at all. Each card can only be used once. There will be four numbers left over.

If you have time
Ask children to use the internet to explore methods for testing divisibility by 7. They exist but they are not as straightforward as the other tests of divisibility.

Information
Tests of divisibility:
- Divisibility by 2: is the number even?
- Divisibility by 3: add the digits – do they total 3, 6 or 9?
- Divisibility by 4: is the number even? Can it be halved to give another even number?
- Divisibility by 5: does the number end in 0 or 5?
- Divisibility by 6: is the number even? Add the digits – do they total 3, 6 or 9?
- Divisibility by 8: is the number even? Can it be halved twice to give another even number?
- Divisibility by 9: add the digits – do they total 9?
- Divisibility by 10: does the number end in 0?
- Divisibility by 25: does the number end in 00, 25, 50 or 75?
- Divisibility by 50: does the number end in 00 or 50?
- Divisibility by 100: does the number end in 00?

Be aware

- Children should be able to recognise all the prime numbers up to 19 and know that prime numbers are only divisible by themselves and 1. The number 1 is not a prime number and the number 2 is the only even prime number.

Outcomes

- I can use tests of divisibility to solve a problem.
- I understand that 6 is a multiple of 2 and a multiple of 3 as well.

Challenge Plan: Year 5

D1: reflective symmetry and axis of symmetry; 3D shapes; number pairs that total 100; differences through next multiple of 10, 100, or 1000

Summary

Y5 D1.6

Cross-numbers

Individuals, pairs or groups working independently

Year 5 Challenge Textbook page 22

Year 5 Challenge PCM 12

Abacus Evolve objectives

- Find differences by counting on through the next multiple of 10, 100 or 1000
- Find what to add to a 3-digit number to make the next higher multiple of 100

Framework objectives

- Use knowledge of rounding, place value, number facts and inverse operations to estimate and check calculations
- Understand the process of decision making

Teacher notes

Preparation
Photocopy PCM 12, one for each child, pair or group.

Getting started
Familiarise children with the concept of a 'cross-number' as being similar to a crossword but using numbers instead of words.

Activity
Children work from Textbook page 22 and fill in their answers on PCM 12. This activity practises rounding to nearest numbers. Children are shown a set of 15 numbers and 12 clues. They read each clue and find the number that matches it. Some simple subtraction calculations are involved. Some clues will lead to more than one possible number. There will be some numbers left over which are not the answers to any of the clues. Once children have found possible answers for all the clues, they try to fit the answers into the cross-number grid.
Where they have more than one possibility for a clue, they will have to work out which number fits in with the other numbers in the grid.

Be aware

- Children may be confused when rounding numbers such as 699 to the nearest 10. This will give the same answer as rounding to the nearest 100. Make sure children understand why this is.

Outcomes

- I can use clues to identify numbers with particular properties.
- I understand that 459 to the nearest 100 is 500.

Supporting resources

Use these websites to generate more number puzzles:
- http://puzzlemaker.discoveryeducation.com/
- http://users.tpg.com.au/users/puzzles/index.html

E1: doubles and halves of integers; doubles of multiples of 10 and 100; improper fractions and mixed numbers; equivalent fractions

Summary

Y5 E1.1

Doubling numbers

A small group working with an adult

Year 5 Challenge Textbook page 23

Place-value cards (Th, H, T, U); decimal place-value cards (t, h)

Abacus Evolve objectives

- **Y6** Consolidate the derivation of doubles of multiples of 10 to 1000, and the corresponding halves
- **Y6** Consolidate the derivation of doubles of multiples of 100 to 10 000, and the corresponding halves
- **Y6** Derive doubles of 2-digit numbers, e.g. 3·8 × 2, 0·76 × 2, and the corresponding halves

Framework objectives

- **Y6** *Use knowledge of place value and multiplication facts to 10 × 10 to derive related multiplication and division facts involving decimals (e.g. 0·8 × 7, 4·8 ÷ 6)*

Teacher notes

Getting started

Ask children to double some 2-digit numbers, for example 23, 47, 52. Discuss strategies for doing this, encouraging children to focus on partitioning numbers into tens and units, doubling each part and then recombining.

Make the number 423 with place-value cards. How can we partition this number to find its double?

(double 400 + 20 + 3 = 800 + 40 + 6 = 846)

Repeat with 368. *What is different about this number?* (6 and 8 are greater than 5 so doubling the 60 and the 8 affects the value of the next place along.)

Demonstrate how recording each number systematically helps to double numbers like 368.

(double 300 + 60 + 8 = 600 + 120 + 16 = 736)

Refer children to the example on Textbook page 23. Try doubling a few more 4-digit numbers by partitioning, until you feel children are confident in using this method.

Activity

Children work from Textbook page 23. They use partitioning to double numbers, including 4-digit numbers and numbers with two decimal places. Children are then asked to check their answers using a suitable method. Children should recognise that they can use the inverse operation (halving) to check their answers.

If you have time

Which numbers did you find the hardest to double? Which were the easiest? Why?

Be aware

- Some children will find the decimal examples harder to double, particularly when the tenths digit is larger than 5. Support them in partitioning, recording each number systematically and adding them up carefully.

Outcomes

- I can double 3- and 4-digit whole numbers.
- I can double decimal numbers.

Challenge Plan: Year 5

E1: doubles and halves of integers; doubles of multiples of 10 and 100; improper fractions and mixed numbers; equivalent fractions

Summary

Y5 ☆ E1.2

Find my double

Individuals, pairs or groups working independently

Year 5 Challenge PCM 13

Abacus Evolve objectives

- Use known number facts and place value to multiply or divide mentally
- Derive doubles of integers up to 100 and 2-digit decimals and their corresponding halves
- Identify near doubles using known doubles, including decimals
- Derive doubles of multiples of 10 to 1000, and the corresponding halves

Framework objectives

- *Use knowledge of place value and addition and subtraction of two-digit numbers to derive sums and differences and doubles and halves of decimals (e.g. 6·5 ± 2·7, half of 5·6, double 0·34)*

Teacher notes

Preparation
Photocopy PCM 13, one for each child.

Getting started
All of the numbers on PCM 13, except for two, can be paired up so that one number is double the other number. Who can be the fastest to find all the matching pairs and say which two numbers are the odd ones out?

Activity
Children record the pairs of numbers as they find them, for example 380 and 760. They mark them off on their grid. Children race to be the first to find the two odd numbers out.

Further extension
Give children a blank grid and ask them to create their own version of this activity, using numbers of their choice. They can swap their grids with other children in the class and try to solve each other's puzzles.

Be aware

- Children should look for pairs with similar numbers of digits. However when the largest place value digit is 5 or more, its double will have an extra digit, for example double 660 is 1320. This may be confusing. Encourage children to use partitioning to understand why this happens.

Outcomes

- I can double and halve numbers.

Challenge Plan: Year 5

E1: doubles and halves of integers; doubles of multiples of 10 and 100; improper fractions and mixed numbers; equivalent fractions

Summary

Y5 ⭐ E1.3

Half price sale

Individuals, pairs or groups working independently

Year 5 Challenge Textbook page 24

Squared paper

Abacus Evolve objectives

- Derive doubles of integers up to 100 and 2-digit decimals and their corresponding halves

Framework objectives

- *Use knowledge of place value and addition and subtraction of two-digit numbers to derive sums and differences and doubles and halves of decimals (e.g. 6·5 ± 2·7, half of 5·6, double 0·34)*
- *Represent a puzzle or problem by identifying and recording the information or calculations needed to solve it; find possible solutions and confirm them in the context of the problem*

Teacher notes

Getting started
Discuss strategies for halving. Children should be encouraged to use different mental strategies rather than formally dividing the amounts by 2. For example, halving the significant digits first:
£3·54 = £3 + 50p + 4p
$\quad$ £1·50 + 25p + 2p = £1·77

Activity
Children work from Textbook page 24. They draw up a table showing the original price and the half price sale price of each item. They use this table to help them find out if £50 is enough to buy all the items in the sale.

If you have time
Children can halve more prices using a receipt or a price list from a local shop, or by finding prices on the internet.

Further extension
Children can make up similar problems for other children in the class.

Be aware

- Children may not be sure what to do when a problem has an odd number of pence. Help children to see that in these cases they should round up by adding 1p to the original price before they halve it.

Outcomes

- I can find half of decimal numbers.
- I can solve a money problem.

Challenge Plan: Year 5

E1: doubles and halves of integers; doubles of multiples of 10 and 100; improper fractions and mixed numbers; equivalent fractions

Summary

Y5 ⭐ E1.4

Improper fractions game

Individuals, pairs or groups working independently

Year 5 Challenge Textbook page 25

Year 5 Challenge PCM 14

Number cards 5–25; 6-sided dice

Abacus Evolve objectives

- Use fraction notation, including mixed numbers, and the vocabulary 'numerator' and 'denominator'
- Change an improper fraction to a mixed number, and vice versa

Framework objectives

- Express a smaller whole number as a fraction of a larger one (e.g. recognise that 5 out of 8 is $\frac{5}{8}$); find equivalent fractions (e.g. $\frac{7}{10} = \frac{14}{20}$, or $\frac{19}{10} = 1\frac{9}{10}$); relate fractions to their decimal representations
- Plan and manage a group task over time by using different levels of planning

Teacher notes

Preparation
Photocopy PCM 14, one for each child. Provide each child, pair or group with a set of number cards and a 6-sided dice.

Getting started
Run through the rules of the game with children and, if necessary, play an example round together to check that they understand.

Activity
Children work from Textbook page 25. They play a game by randomly generating improper fractions using number cards and a dice. They must then convert the fraction to a mixed number to work out where to place it on a 1–10 number line. They have 10 minutes to try and fill as many boxes as possible on the number line. Children then answer questions to investigate the properties of the improper fractions that they have generated.

Further extension
Children can play the game again but this time using number cards with a wider range (for example 10–50) and a 1–8 or a 1–12 dice.

Information
Children should find that there are more ways to generate improper fractions that go in the central positions on the number line.

Be aware

- Children may be keen to play for more than 10 minutes and try to fill all the boxes on the number line. However some of the boxes are more difficult to fill than others so it is best to play to a time limit.

Outcomes

- I can make an improper fraction by finding a numerator and a denominator.
- I can change an improper fraction to a mixed number.

Challenge Plan: Year 5

E1: doubles and halves of integers; doubles of multiples of 10 and 100; improper fractions and mixed numbers; equivalent fractions

Summary

Y5 ⭐ **E1.5**

Fractions

A small group working with an adult

Year 5 Challenge Textbook page 26

Abacus Evolve objectives

- **Y6** Consolidate recognition of equivalent fractions
- **Y6** Reduce a fraction to its simplest form by cancelling common factors in the numerator and denominator
- **Y6** Order fractions by converting them to fractions with a common denominator

Framework objectives

- **Y6** Express a larger whole number as a fraction of a smaller one (e.g. recognise that 8 slices of a 5-slice pizza represents $\frac{8}{5}$ or $1\frac{3}{5}$ pizzas); simplify fractions by cancelling common factors; order a set of fractions by converting them to fractions with a common denominator

Teacher notes

Getting started

Rehearse equivalent fractions with children.

How many fractions do you know that are equal to $\frac{1}{3}$? ($\frac{2}{6}$, $\frac{3}{9}$, $\frac{4}{12}$, etc.) Establish that $\frac{1}{3}$ is the fraction in its simplest form. Repeat with $\frac{3}{5}$.

Using the first example box on Textbook page 26, demonstrate how to reduce a fraction to its simplest form. Children should see that this is like finding equivalent fractions, but 'in reverse'.

How can we reduce an improper fraction to its simplest form? Demonstrate with $\frac{20}{16}$.

- We can divide the numerator and the denominator by 2. $\frac{20}{16} = \frac{10}{8}$
- Now we can divide the numerator and the denominator by 2 again. $\frac{10}{8} = \frac{5}{4}$
- Now we can write it as a mixed number. $\frac{5}{4} = 1\frac{1}{4}$

Then use the second example box on the Textbook page to demonstrate how to compare fractions by finding a common denominator.

Activity

Children work from Textbook page 26. They use the techniques that they have just learned to reduce fractions to their simplest form, and to compare fractions by finding a common denominator.

Extra help

If children find it hard to find a common multiple of the denominators then ask them to write down all the multiples of each denominator and then find one in common. Avoid telling them to simply multiply the two denominators. This does give a common multiple, but it may not be the simplest.

Be aware

- Make sure that children are confident in understanding and using the terms common denominator, common factor, common multiple and simplest form.

Outcomes

- I can recognise equivalent fractions.
- I can reduce fractions to their simplest form.
- I can compare the size of fractions by finding a common denominator.

Supporting resources

For more information on teaching fractions, look at this site:
- http://www.ncetm.org.uk/mathemapedia/Preparing%20to%20teach%20fractions

This Fractions ITP is useful for modelling fractions:
- http://nationalstrategies.standards.dcsf.gov.uk/node/47750?uc=force_uj

Challenge Plan: Year 5

E1: doubles and halves of integers; doubles of multiples of 10 and 100; improper fractions and mixed numbers; equivalent fractions

Summary

Y5 ☆ E1.6

Finding proportions

Individuals, pairs or groups working independently

Year 5 Challenge Textbook page 27

Abacus Evolve objectives

- Estimate simple proportions such as one third, seven tenths
- Solve simple problems involving proportion

Framework objectives

- Use sequences to scale numbers up or down; solve problems involving proportions of quantities (e.g. decrease quantities in a recipe designed to feed six people)

Teacher notes

Getting started
Check that children understand the concept of changing the amount of ingredients proportionally.

Activity
Children work from Textbook page 27. They are given an original recipe for eight people and must adjust it proportionally for other amounts of people.

Further extension
Children can choose their own number of people to cater for. They look at which numbers of people are easier to calculate for and which are more difficult.

Be aware

- Children can often confuse proportion with ratio. Proportion is in fact another way of expressing a fraction. Proportion is a part of a whole, whereas a ratio is the comparison of two parts.
- If children look up their own recipes they may find unfamiliar units such as fluid ounces. Make sure children understand why it will be easier for them to work with metric units.

Outcomes

- I can use proportion to solve a problem with a recipe.

Supporting resources

This is a good source of recipes for children:
- http://www.bbc.co.uk/food/recipes/mostof_cookingwithchildrenhugh.shtml

Challenge Plan: Year 5

A2: rounding; decimal notation for tenths and hundredths; multiplying or dividing by 10 or 100; multiples and common multiples

Summary

Y5 ✧ A2.1

Rounding and converting distances

Individuals, pairs or groups working independently

Year 5 Challenge Textbook page 28

Calculators

Abacus Evolve objectives

- Make and justify estimates of large numbers
- Round any integer up to 10 000 to the nearest 10, 100 or 1000

Framework objectives

- *Explain what each digit represents in whole numbers and decimals with up to two places, and partition, round and order these numbers*
- *Represent a puzzle or problem by identifying and recording the information or calculations needed to solve it; find possible solutions and confirm them in the context of the problem*

Teacher notes

Activity

Children work from Textbook page 28.

- In part 1 children round distances to the nearest 100 and 1000 miles or kilometres.
- In part 2 children round to the nearest 10 and incorporate an element of problem solving, calculating the fuel used and time taken for the journeys. Children should be confident in multiplying and dividing by 50 or 500 for this. They can use a calculator.

Extra help

Some children may need a bit of adult explanation before beginning part 2. This exercise requires children to multiply by 50 and divide by 500, which they can do using place value for × 100 or ÷ 1000 and then halving for × 50 and doubling for ÷ 500. If you have time, you could show children how this works.

Further extension

The activities consider air distances in both km and miles. To extend, children could convert distances to either miles or km and compare them. An online route finder such as Google Maps will give road distances to destinations in Europe for children to compare distances by air with distances by car.

Be aware

- Children must consider when to round. Errors can arise if the calculation is rounded at intermediate stages rather than at the end.
- Children may need to be reminded that an estimate is a calculation using rounded numbers, rather than a guess.

Outcomes

- I can round any number up to 10 000 to the nearest 10, 100 or 1000.

Supporting resources

More distances for children to work with can be found at:
- http://www.trans-arena.com/en/distance-london-europe.php
- http://www.answers.com/topic/distances-world-cities-in-miles

Road distances can be found using Google Maps:
- http://maps.google.co.uk/maps?hl=en&tab=wl

Challenge Plan: Year 5

A2: rounding; decimal notation for tenths and hundredths; multiplying or dividing by 10 or 100; multiples and common multiples

Summary

Y5 ☆ A2.2

Imperial and metric conversions

Individuals, pairs or groups working independently

Year 5 Challenge Textbook page 29

Year 5 Challenge PCM 15

Items to be weighed or measured (optional); bottles of water of various sizes (optional)

Abacus Evolve objectives

- Use decimal notation for tenths and hundredths
- Know what each digit represents in a number with up to two decimal places
- Order a set of decimal numbers
- Know the equivalent of $\frac{1}{2}$, $\frac{1}{4}$, $\frac{3}{4}$, $\frac{1}{10}$, $\frac{1}{100}$ of 1 km in m, 1 kg in g, 1 litre in ml
- Know imperial units of length: miles

Framework objectives

- *Explain what each digit represents in whole numbers and decimals with up to two places, and partition, round and order these numbers*
- Read, choose, use and record standard metric units to estimate and measure length, weight and capacity to a suitable degree of accuracy, e.g. the nearest centimetre; convert larger to smaller units using decimals to one place, e.g. change 2·6 kg to 2600 g

Teacher notes

Preparation
Copy PCM 15 for children to complete.

Getting started
Make sure children are confident with the concept of working with both metric and imperial measurements. For example, it may help to provide 1 lb of cheese and 500 g of cheese for children to compare the relative weights.

Activity
Children work from Textbook page 29 and record the measurements on PCM 15. This exercise requires children to work with mass, length and capacity and:
- convert all measurements into metric equivalents from imperial measures
- convert kg, l or km from g, ml, or m or cm
- decide which of three given items is greatest and which is smallest.

Extra help
Provide evidence of units of measure using groceries that are priced in imperial and metric. Children can see how each is used. To reinforce the importance of using the correct units, you could mention that the Mars Climate Orbiter Spacecraft was lost because one NASA team used imperial units while another used metric units for a key spacecraft operation!

If you have time
- Children could work out their journey to school in both metric and imperial measurements.
- Set up a number of bottles of water, all with differing amounts and ask children to estimate how much is in each bottle. Make this more challenging by using different shaped bottles.
- Provide real items for children to guess the amount, e.g. the weight of a tin of beans, the length of a strip of ribbon. If the amount is marked on the packaging, be sure to cover it with a sticky label.

Be aware

- When using a mixture of imperial (roads in miles) and metric (fruit in kg) it is important that children know the equivalents.
- Children may need to be reminded that we use both imperial and metric units in everyday life.

Outcomes

- I can change an amount in kilograms to an amount in grams, and vice versa.
- I can change a metric measurement to an imperial measurement.
- I know rough equivalents for 1 pint, 1 pound and 1 mile.

Supporting resources

This is a good web-link to help with conversions:
- http://www.initium.demon.co.uk/converts/metimp.htm

A2: rounding; decimal notation for tenths and hundredths; multiplying or dividing by 10 or 100; multiples and common multiples

Summary

Y5 ⬡ A2.3

Rounding and estimating using place value

A small group working with an adult

Year 5 Challenge PCM 16

Calculators

Abacus Evolve objectives

- **Y6** Round any integer to the nearest 10, 100 or 1000
- **Y6** Consolidate rounding a number with two decimal places to the nearest whole number
- **Y6** Round a number with two decimal places to the nearest tenth
- **Y6** Use known number facts and place value to consolidate mental multiplication and division

Framework objectives

- **Y6** Use decimal notation for tenths, hundredths and thousandths; partition, round and order decimals with up to three places, and position them on the number line
- **Y6** Calculate mentally with integers and decimals: U.t ± U.t, TU × U, TU ÷ U, U.t × U, U.t ÷ U
- **Y6** Use a range of oral techniques to present a persuasive argument

Teacher notes

Preparation
Cut up the cards on PCM 16. Remove any you do not want children to tackle yet, e.g. multiplication by 0·2.

Getting started
- *Make these numbers 10 times bigger: 0·6, 8·1, 3.* Demonstrate this using place value, moving all digits to the left. Point out the use of 0 as place holder after each decimal point. Use a calculator to prove the same effect.

	T	U	·	tenths
× 10		0	·	6
	6	·		0

- *Make these numbers 10 times smaller: 3, 50, 2·4.* Demonstrate this using place value, moving all digits to the right.

	T	U	·	tenths
÷ 10		3	·	0
		0	·	3

- Write these two calculations: 6 × 5 and 0·6 × 50. *What is the same about these two calculations and what is different? The digits are the same but the value of the digits is different.* Can children recognise that the products are the same? If necessary show this on a calculator.
- *We can multiply by decimals mentally by adjusting both numbers. We change the decimal into a whole number by multiplying by 10, but we must then divide the other number by 10 (× 10 and ÷ 10 are inverses).*
- *Set children the following calculations to solve mentally: 1·2 × 400; 0·12 × 2000; 0·5 × 200.*

Activity
Children play the game using cards from PCM 16. Encourage them to find quick mental methods, including this adjustment method. The cards can be rounded to 20 × 20, 2 × 200 or 0·2 × 2000 and all have the approximate answer 400.
- Share out the cards equally, face down.
- *Each turn over the top card from your pile.*
- *Estimate who has the biggest product.* (Children estimate by rounding each number to the nearest 0·1, 1, 10, 100, 1000 where appropriate.)
- *Find the answers to your calculations.* (Children must agree to all use either a mental method, a written method or a calculator.)
- The person with the biggest product takes the other players' cards and puts them to the bottom of their pile.
- The winner is the person with the most cards after 15 minutes.

Further extension
- On the cards, can children find the calculations that are the quickest to work out and explain their method? For example, × 20: × 2 then × 10.
- Can children predict which calculation will give the biggest product? The smallest product?

Be aware
- You may need to explain the term *inverse*.
- Children must consider when to round. Errors can arise if the calculation is rounded at intermediate stages rather than at the end.
- Children may need to be reminded that an estimate is a calculation using rounded numbers, rather than a guess.

Outcomes
- I can round whole and decimal numbers to give an estimated answer, and I understand that this answer will not usually be exact.
- I can multiply a 2-digit number by another 2-digit number using my chosen method.

Challenge Plan: Year 5

A2: rounding; decimal notation for tenths and hundredths; mul[ ]
or dividing by 10 or 100; multiples and common multiples

Summary

Y5 ⭐ **A2.4**

Quick calculation without a calculator

Individuals, pairs or groups working independently

Year 5 Challenge Textbook page 30

Calculators; the internet

Abacus Evolve objectives

- Multiply or divide any integer up to 10 000 by 10 or 100 and understand the effect
- Multiply decimals by 10, 100 or 1000
- Recognise and explain patterns and relationships, generalise and predict

Framework objectives

- Use understanding of place value to multiply and divide whole numbers and decimals by 10, 100 or 1000
- Explore patterns, properties and relationships and propose a general statement involving numbers or shapes; identify examples for which the statement is true or false

Teacher notes

Preparation
The Trachtenberg method for multiplying by 11 is very straightforward. If it is new to you, read Textbook page 30 to familiarise yourself with it before the lesson.

Activity
Children work from Textbook page 30. This activity introduces the idea of speed multiplication. Children read about Trachtenberg and then explore his method for multiplying by 11 and then 110.

Further extension
There are also methods of multiplication known as the Egyptian and Russian methods. Children can explore these by searching for information on the Internet. The websites below have details of both these methods

Be aware

- We sometimes consider that there is only one way to multiply correctly. Children need to be exposed to other approaches, and made aware that they can use these methods in their own multiplications.

Outcomes

- I can multiply 1- or 2-digit numbers by other 2-digit numbers.
- I can multiply using non-standard methods.

Supporting resources

Read about Trachtenberg's method here:
- *The Trachtenberg Speed System of Basic Mathematics* (Paperback) by Jakow Trachtenberg
You can find out more about the Trachtenberg, Egyptian and Russian methods of multiplication here:
- http://www.cimt.plymouth.ac.uk/projects/mepres/book7/y7s6act.pdf
- http://www.blss.portsmouth.sch.uk/resources/numericalmeth.shtml
- http://mathforum.org/dr.math/faq/faq.peasant.html

A2: rounding; decimal notation for tenths and hundredths; multiplying or dividing by 10 or 100; multiples and common multiples

Summary

Y5 ⭐ A2.5

Investigating days and dates

Individuals, pairs or groups working independently

Year 5 Challenge Textbook page 31

An online calendar or diary; days of birth of ten children in the class

Abacus Evolve objectives

- Recognise and explain patterns and relationships, generalise and predict

Framework objectives

- Explore patterns, properties and relationships and propose a general statement involving numbers or shapes; identify examples for which the statement is true or false
- Understand different ways to take the lead and support others in a group

Teacher notes

Getting started
It is straightforward to find days and dates with an online calendar or diary. You can enter almost any date and find out what day it fell on. Show children how to find specific days and dates using this tool.

Activity
Children work from Textbook page 31. This activity explores when dates and days fall. Most of the questions are dependent on whether the year a child was born is a leap year and how many leap years have passed since the child was born. Dates of birth before March 1st in a leap year will affect their findings.

Two of the questions ask children to collect data from other children in the class and from other year groups.

The 'Extra' activity asks children to research why we have leap year days on February 29th and the conventions which rule them.

Further extension
What is special about the years 1800, 1900, 2100, 2200 and 2300, but not 2000?
(1800, 1900, 2100, 2200 and 2300 are not leap years but the year 2000 is a leap year. This is because in the Gregorian calendar, leap years occur in years exactly divisible by four, but years ending in 00 are only leap years if they are divisible by 400.)

Be aware

- Children will need to recognise that the days on which their birthdays fall do not always follow in order year to year. One day is skipped every four years because of a leap day.

Outcomes

- I can sometimes predict when certain days will fall.
- I can explain what I've found out in an organised way.

Challenge Plan: Year 5

A2: rounding; decimal notation for tenths and hundredths; multiplying or dividing by 10 or 100; multiples and common multiples

Summary

Y5 ⭐ **A2.6**	**Common multiples and prime factors**
	A small group working with an adult
📖	Year 5 Challenge Textbook page 32

◦◦◦◦▷ **Abacus Evolve objectives**	**Framework objectives**
• **Y6** Recognise multiples of numbers up to the tenth multiple, and beyond • **Y6** Find common multiples of two or three numbers	**Y6** Recognise that prime numbers have only two factors and identify prime numbers less than 100; find the prime factors of two-digit numbers

---

Teacher notes

Getting started
Check that children understand the concepts of **factors**, **multiples** and **prime numbers** to at least 19 by asking:
• *Which of these numbers is the odd one out: 3, 4 or 6? Your answer should include the word 'factor'.*
  (Possible answers: 4 is the odd one out as it is not a factor of 6, 12 and 18; 3 is the odd one out because it is the only factor of 3.)
• *Tell me a **multiple** of 4. Tell me two different **multiples** of 5. Tell me three different **multiples** of 6.*
• *Tell me a **prime number** which is even. ... which is bigger than 10. ... which is bigger than 8 but less than 15.*

Activity
Explain that **common multiples** are numbers which occur in several times tables. For example, 12 and 24 are common multiples of 2, 3 and 4.
• Multiples of 2: 2, 4, 6, 8, 10, <u>12</u>, 14, 16, 18, 20, 22, <u>24</u>, ...
• Multiples of 3: 3, 6, 9, <u>12</u>, 15, 18, 21, <u>24</u>, ...
• Multiples of 4: 4, 8, <u>12</u>, 16, 20, <u>24</u>, ...
What other numbers are common multiples of 2, 3 and 4? Is there a common multiple of 2, 3 and 4 bigger than 60?
Now ask children to complete the first part of Textbook page 32.

Explain how to factorise into **prime factors** using a factor tree.
  30   Divide by smallest possible prime number, in this case 2

2   15   Divide by smallest possible prime number, in this case 3

  3   5
So the prime factors of 30 are 2 × 3 × 5.
Now ask children to complete the second part of Textbook page 32.

Information
Every number can be expressed as prime factors; the number 6 is 2 × 3, 12 is 2 × 2 × 3 and 24 is 2 × 2 × 2 × 3. From this we can see that 2 × 3 is in each of these factor lists so each of these numbers are multiples of 2, 3 and 6. Therefore 6, 12 and 24 are common multiples of 2, 3 and 6.

The definition of a prime number is a number with only two factors: itself <u>and</u> 1. As 1 is the only factor of 1 it cannot be considered prime and cannot be a prime factor.

Be aware	**Outcomes**
• Children will need to be familiar with the concepts of *factors, multiples, prime numbers* and *common multiples*. • There are an infinite number of common multiples; they go beyond 12 × 12. Children often stop at the 12 times table. • Factors of numbers do not have to be prime numbers.	• I can find common multiples of two or more numbers. • I can find prime factors of some numbers.

Challenge Plan: Year 5

B2: multiplication; doubling and halving; coordinates; names and properties of 2D shapes

Summary

Y5 **B2.1**

Multiplication investigation

Individuals, pairs or groups working independently

Year 5 Challenge Textbook page 33

Calculators (optional)

Abacus Evolve objectives

- **Y6** Multiply by partitioning, e.g. $87 \times 6 = (80 \times 6) + (7 \times 6)$, $3 \cdot 4 \times 3 = (3 \times 3) + (0 \cdot 4 \times 3)$
- **Y6** Use known number facts and place value to consolidate mental multiplication and division

Framework objectives

- **Y6** *Use knowledge of place value and multiplication facts to 10×10 to derive related multiplication and division facts involving decimals (e.g. $0 \cdot 8 \times 7$, $4 \cdot 8 \div 6$)*
- **Y6** *Represent and interpret sequences, patterns and relationships involving numbers and shapes; suggest and test hypotheses; construct and use simple expressions and formulae in words then symbols (e.g. the cost of c pens at 15 pence each is 15c pence)*

Teacher notes

Getting started
Make sure children are familiar with using a multiplication grid for 1-digit × 2-digit and 2-digit × 2-digit calculations.

Look together at the grid on Textbook page 33. *What two numbers are multiplied to get an answer for each of the six blank squares?* (30×200, 30×70, 30×6, 2×200, 2×70 and 2×6) *Let's think about how to multiply 200 by 30. What 1-digit multiplication sum does this relate to?* ($2 \times 3 = 6$) *So what is 2×30?* (60) 20×30? (600) 200×30? (6000) *Why is it important to get the number of zeros right?*

Discuss children's predictions for question 3 on Textbook page 33. Encourage understanding of place value to say which answer is largest and which is smallest.

Activity
Children work from Textbook page 33. This activity builds on children's understanding of the grid multiplication method. Children complete a multiplication grid and use it to solve a 3-digit × 3-digit calculation. Children make predictions about the answers to multiplication calculations, then use multiplication grids to solve the calculations, check their predictions and explain their answers using their understanding of place value. Children should solve the calculations individually but can be encouraged to discuss their findings amongst each other and say how drawing grids helped solve the problems.

If you have time
Children may use calculators to check answers.

Information
The activity consolidates the knowledge that if $7 \times 6 = 42$ then $7 \times 60 = 420$ and $7 \times 600 = 4200$.

Be aware

- Children may already be competent at using a standard method of multiplication but should still use the grid method for this activity to encourage problem-solving using understanding of place value.
- Some children will notice that in the grid they must add a zero to the tens and two zeroes to the hundreds, but may not notice the digit shift and the reason for it.

Outcomes

- I can use grid multiplication to solve 3-digit multiplication problems.
- I can make predictions and check answers.

Summary

Y5 ☆ B2.2

Egyptian multiplication

Individuals, pairs or groups working independently

Year 5 Challenge Textbook page 34

Calculators (optional)

◁∘∘▷ Abacus Evolve objectives

- Use doubling and halving to help multiply
- Use doubling or halving to find new facts from known facts
- Multiply using closely related facts

Framework objectives

- Extend mental-methods for whole-number calculations, for example to multiply a two-digit by a one-digit number (e.g. 12 × 9), to multiply by 25 (e.g. 16 × 25), to subtract one near-multiple of 1000 from another (e.g. 6070 − 4097)
- Represent a puzzle or problem by identifying and recording the information or calculations needed to solve it; find possible solutions and confirm them in the context of the problem

📖 Teacher notes

Preparation
Familiarise yourself with the Egyptian multiplication method by looking at Textbook page 34.

Getting started
Children should practise doubling some random numbers before they start the activity.

Activity
Children work from Textbook page 34. They learn about the Egyptian number system and the Egyptian method for multiplication. This method involves doubling and children should be encouraged to choose an appropriate doubling strategy for each number. For 2-digit numbers children should be able to partition and double mentally. Some may also be able to do this for 3-digit numbers, or they may prefer a mixture of mental strategies and jottings. The method works in exactly the same way for 3-digit numbers. Children can use other methods or a calculator to check their answers.

Further extension
Children could use the Egyptian multiplication method to work out the calculations on Textbook page 34.

Be aware

- Doubling 3-digit numbers mentally (particularly when the hundreds digit is more than 5) can be much trickier than doubling 2-digit numbers. Encourage children to make notes to help them with the calculation.

Outcomes

- I can use a new multiplication method.
- I can double to help me multiply.
- I can estimate and check calculations using different methods.

Supporting resources

This site has a PowerPoint demonstration of Egyptian multiplication:
- http://www.numeracysoftware.com/xm.html

Summary

Y5 ⭐ **B2.3**

Double up!

Individuals, pairs or groups working independently

Year 5 Challenge Textbook page 35

Abacus Evolve objectives

- Use doubling and halving to help multiply
- Use doubling or halving to find new facts from known facts
- Multiply using closely related facts

Framework objectives

- Extend mental-methods for whole-number calculations, for example to multiply a two-digit by a one-digit number (e.g. 12 × 9), to multiply by 25 (e.g. 16 × 25), to subtract one near-multiple of 1000 from another (e.g. 6070 − 4097)
- Represent a puzzle or problem by identifying and recording the information or calculations needed to solve it; find possible solutions and confirm them in the context of the problem

Teacher notes

Getting started
Ask children to discuss the first example on Textbook page 35 and familiarise themselves with the concept before doing any calculations themselves.

Activity
Children work from Textbook page 35. They double several numbers a set amount of times and find out how large the total is. This activity will work best if children record their doubling systematically, for example as a table. If you have an opportunity, encourage them to think about their methods, and model an appropriate technique if necessary.

Day 1	£3
Day 2	£6
Day 3	£12
Day 4	£24
Day 5	....
Day 6	....
Day 7	....
Day 8	
Day 9	
Day 10	

Extra help
When the numbers start to get very large, children should be encouraged to record jottings to support their mental calculations.

Further extension
Children comfortable using a spreadsheet should be able to set up a simple program to successively double numbers.

If you have time
Children may be interested in exploring the chessboard and rice or wheat problem which involves doubling one grain of rice or wheat 63 times. (See below.)

Be aware

- Children may be surprised by how quickly the numbers become very large in these problems. Help children to understand that this is the nature of successively multiplying by a factor, compared to simply adding the same amount each time.

Outcomes

- I can make a prediction and solve a problem by working systematically.
- I can use doubling to help find new facts.

Supporting resources

Children can find out more about the chessboard and rice or wheat problem here:
- http://mathforum.org/~sanders/geometry/GP11Fable.html
- http://en.wikipedia.org/wiki/Wheat_and_chessboard_problem

Summary

Y5 ☆ B2.4   **Coordinates**

A small group working with an adult

Year 5 Challenge Textbook page 36

Year 5 Challenge PCM 17 and 18 (optional)

Rulers

Abacus Evolve objectives

- **Y6** Read and plot coordinates in all quadrants
- **Y6** Draw the position of shapes on a coordinate grid after rotations and translations

Framework objectives

- **Y6** *Visualise and draw on grids of different types where a shape will be after reflection, after translations, or after rotation through 90° or 180° about its centre or one of its vertices*
- **Y6** Use a range of oral techniques to present persuasive argument

Teacher notes

Preparation
Photocopy PCM 17 and PCM 18, one copy of each per child.

Getting started
Discuss coordinates together and check that children know how to read coordinate points correctly (horizontal, vertical). *On a grid the x-axis can be extended to the left into negative numbers and the y-axis can be extended down into negative numbers. This gives a grid with four different areas called quadrants.*

Activity
Children work from Textbook page 36. Together agree the coordinates of Points A–H on the grid. Ensure that children are reading the negative coordinates correctly and maintaining the (horizontal, vertical) order. For example point H is (⁻4, 4).

Give out PCM 17 and go around the group asking children to give the coordinates of the corner points of each shape. In each case start at the top left-hand corner of the shape and go around clockwise. Ensure children are comfortable reading the negative coordinates for shapes C and D. Children follow the instructions on Textbook page 36 and carefully translate each shape using a ruler. Children note the new coordinates of each shape's corners; again they should start at the top left-hand corner and go clockwise around the shape.

Children will need PCM 17 if they have time to work on the Extra activity.

Be aware

- Some children may need reminding that, although translation, reflection and rotation are all types of transformation, each one is different.
- Some able children may still be untidy or inaccurate with spatial drawing, so stress the need to use a ruler and a sharp pencil to draw shapes carefully.

Outcomes

- I can read coordinates in two quadrants.
- I can draw the position of a shape after a translation.

B2: multiplication; doubling and halving; coordinates; names and properties of 2D shapes

Summary

Y5 ⬡ B2.5

Reflecting with coordinates

Individuals, pairs or groups working independently

Year 5 Challenge PCM 19

Rulers; mirrors

Abacus Evolve objectives

- Read and plot coordinates in the first quadrant
- Recognise where a shape will be after a translation
- Recognise where a shape will be after reflection in a mirror line parallel to one side

Framework objectives

- *Read and plot coordinates in the first quadrant; recognise parallel and perpendicular lines in grids and shapes; use a set-square and ruler to draw shapes with perpendicular or parallel sides*
- Complete patterns with up to two lines of symmetry; draw the position of a shape after a reflection or translation

Teacher notes

Preparation
Photocopy PCM 19, one copy for each child.

Getting started
Check that children can locate the x-axis and the y-axis on a grid.

Activity
Children work from PCM 19. They draw shapes using sets of coordinates then draw the reflections of these shapes in the y-axis. Children use mirrors to check the positions of the reflections.

Be aware

- Make sure that children are confident in referring to the x- and y-axis of a coordinate grid and do not confuse the two.

Outcomes

- I can read coordinates in two quadrants.
- I can draw the position of a shape after a reflection.

Summary

Y5 B2.6

Investigating diagonals

Individuals, pairs or groups working independently

Year 5 Challenge Textbook page 37

Year 5 Challenge PCM 20

Rulers

Abacus Evolve objectives

- Rehearse the names and properties of common 2D shapes
- Rehearse regular and irregular polygons
- Know the meaning of 'diagonal' of a polygon

Framework objectives

- Identify, visualise and describe properties of rectangles, triangles, regular polygons and 3D solids; use knowledge of properties to draw 2D shapes, and to identify and draw nets of 3D shapes

Teacher notes

Getting started
Photocopy PCM 20, one copy for each child.

Activity
Children work from Textbook page 37. They investigate what shapes are made by the diagonals in three different pentagons. They then do the same with hexagons, including an irregular hexagon that they have drawn themselves.

Information
Children will find that the diagonals of the regular shapes produce multiple versions of the same pairs of shapes; with a regular pentagon this is an isosceles triangle and an isosceles trapezium, for example

A hexagon will make either two isosceles trapezia, for example

or an isosceles triangle and an irregular pentagon, for example

The more irregular the initial shape is, the greater variety of shapes that can be formed by its various diagonals.

Be aware

- Children may not be confident describing the features of a trapezium. (A trapezium has one pair of parallel sides of different lengths.) The two trapezia formed by the diagonal that is a line of symmetry across a regular hexagon are good examples of isosceles trapezia.

Outcomes

- I can identify and name regular and irregular 2D shapes.
- I can find diagonals of different polygons.

Supporting resources

This is a useful reference list of 2D shapes and their properties:
- http://www.cimt.plymouth.ac.uk/projects/mepres/book8/bk8i6/bk8_6i1.htm

Summary

Y5 ☆ C2.1

Stamp sizes

Individuals, pairs or groups working independently

Year 5 Challenge Textbook page 38

Calculators

Abacus Evolve objectives

- Understand area measured in square centimetres
- Understand and use the formula in words 'length × breadth' for the area of a rectangle

Framework objectives

- *Draw and measure lines to the nearest millimetre; measure and calculate the perimeter of regular and irregular polygons; use the formula for the area of a rectangle to calculate the rectangle's area*
- Use a calculator to solve problems, including those involving decimals or fractions, e.g. to find $\frac{3}{4}$ of 150 g; interpret the display correctly in the context of measurement
- Plan and manage a group task over time by using different levels of planning

Teacher notes

Getting started

Make sure children are aware of these standard paper sizes:
- A4 (210 mm × 297 mm)
- A3 (297 mm × 420 mm)
- A2 (420 mm × 594 mm)
- A1 (594 mm × 841 mm)
- A0 (841 mm × 1189 mm).

If possible prepare samples of each size of paper for children to look at.

Activity

Children work from Textbook page 38. The activity looks at the area of postage stamps and sheets of paper in mm. Children investigate how many stamps can be cut from different-sized sheets of paper with the least waste. They should try both portrait and landscape orientation of the stamps to explore this. Children should be encouraged to reach a conclusion about the most efficient layout.

If you have time

Have a competition for children in the class to design their own stamp.

Information

The Queen's head on a stamp is the only indication that the stamp is from Britain.

Be aware

- Children may not often use mm. Ensure they understand that there are 10 mm in 1 cm.
- Make sure that children only count the whole stamps that fit on the sheet of paper.

Outcomes

- I can calculate area in mm².
- I can investigate how many stamps will fit on different sheets of paper.
- I can explain which layout is best and why.
- I can use a calculator to help me.

Supporting resources

Visit the Royal Mail website to find out more about printing stamps, and their prices and sizes:
- http://www.royalmail.com/portal/rm

Summary

Y5 ⬠ C2.2

Surface area

A small group working with an adult

Year 5 Challenge PCM 21

A large number of 1 cm linking cubes (at least 216); 6 × 6 cm squares of paper; sticky tape; calculators; card (optional); scissors (optional); ribbon (optional)

Abacus Evolve objectives

- **Y6** Calculate the area of a rectangle
- **Y6** Calculate the surface area of a box, where the faces are rectangles
- **Y6** Consolidate the calculation of perimeters of rectangles
- **Y6** Calculate the perimeters of compound shapes

Framework objectives

- **Y6** Calculate the perimeter and area of rectilinear shapes; estimate the area of an irregular shape by counting squares

Teacher notes

Preparation
Photocopy PCM 21, one for each child. With 1 cm linking cubes, make a solid cube 6 × 6 × 6 cm.

Activity
- Show the 6 × 6 × 6 cm cube. *What is the volume?*
- Establish that volume is height × length × depth. Show that the volume is 6 × 6 × 6 = 216 cm³.
- *How much card would we need to make an empty box the same size as the cube?* Children can explore with pieces of paper. *We would need 6 squares of 6 × 6 cm.*
- Explain that this is the surface area.
- *For this cube the volume and the surface area are the same. This does not happen for every cube.*
- Ask children to make solid cuboids from linking cubes. They should use the same number of linking cubes that was used for the 6 × 6 × 6 cm cube.
  Examples: 6 × 9 × 4 cm; 2 × 18 × 6 cm; 3 × 9 × 8 cm; 9 × 12 × 2 cm; 3 × 12 × 6 cm; 3 × 24 × 3 cm.
- *What if the cuboid was only 1 cm high? What if the cuboid was only 1 cm high and 1 cm long? The volume of each cuboid is still 216 cm³.*
- Children look at PCM 21 and discuss the properties of the first two cuboids. *Can you see how the surface area is calculated? (It is double the total area of the three different-sized faces.)* Children complete PCM 21.
- Children find the surface area of the solid cuboid they made.

If you have time
Children could make their own cuboids using stiff card and fill them with rice to compare the volumes.

Further extension
Children could explore how much ribbon would be needed to gift wrap their cuboid.

Be aware

- Ensure that children realise that the volume is not always equal to the surface area. The example 6 × 6 × 6 cm cube is a special case.

Outcomes

- I can calculate the surface area of a cuboid.
- I can understand and use the formula to find the area of a rectangle.
- I can answer questions about area, volume and surface area.

C2: formula for area of rectangle; perimeters of rectangles; units of time; 24-hour digital clock times

Summary

Y5 ☆ C2.3

Area and perimeter

Individuals, pairs or groups working independently

Year 5 Challenge Textbook page 39

Abacus Evolve objectives

- Explain a generalised relationship (formula) in words

Framework objectives

- Explore patterns, properties and relationships and propose a general statement involving numbers or shapes; identify examples for which the statement is true or false

Teacher notes

Activity

Children work from Textbook page 39. They look at five shapes and read statements relating to the area and perimeter of the shapes. Children match each statement to the corresponding shape. Where a statement does not correspond to a shape, children explain why the statement is incorrect.

Children should recognise that the area of some more complex-looking shapes can be found by dividing them into simpler regular shapes and finding the total area.

Further extension

Children can use the internet to find formulas for calculating the areas of more complex shapes such as trapezia and regular octagons.

Be aware

- Draw children's attention to the fact that formulas are written as efficiently as possible. For example, Area = length × width can also be written $A = lw$.
- Make sure that children understand that the terms 'width' and 'breadth' mean the same thing.

Outcomes

- I can understand how to find the perimeter of a rectangle, a triangle, a hexagon and some irregular shapes.
- I can find the perimeter and the area of an 'L' shape.

Challenge Plan: Year 5

C2: formula for area of rectangle; perimeters of rectangles; units of time; 24-hour digital clock times

Summary

Y5 C2.4 — **Calendars**

Individuals, pairs or groups working independently

Year 5 Challenge Textbook page 40

The internet; calculators (optional)

Abacus Evolve objectives

- Use, read and write units of time (including decade, millennium, leap year)
- Convert from one unit of time to another
- Know the number of days in each month
- Read the time on a 24-hour digital clock and use 24-hour clock notation
- Use timetables

Framework objectives

- Read timetables and time using 24-hour clock notation; use a calendar to calculate time intervals
- Present a spoken argument, sequencing points logically, defending views with evidence and making use of persuasive language

Teacher notes

Activity

Children work from Textbook page 40. They read an article about the origins of the Gregorian calendar and the Julian calendar.

Children use the internet to explore facts about these calendars, and compare and discuss their accuracy. They also answer some questions about the relationship between years, months, weeks, days, hours, minutes and seconds. Children consider the possibility of changing to decimal time (100 minutes in an hour, 100 hours in a day).

Be aware

- Times are sometimes given in decimal seconds, particularly in sport. Make sure that children understand that these cannot be translated directly into normal time.
- Encourage children to not use a calculator when working with time, because calculators use units that are not equivalent to time. For example 0·5 of a day is 12 hours not 5 hours.

Outcomes

- I can explore different calendars and think about how accurate they are.
- I can discuss why we should or should not use decimal time.

Supporting resources

Children can research the Atomic Clock using these websites:
- http://www.atomic-clock.org.uk/atomuhr.html
- http://news.bbc.co.uk/1/hi/sci/tech/4587919.stm
Children can find out about decimal time here:
- http://www.lab6.com/old/time.html
- http://www-groups.dcs.st-and.ac.uk/~history/HistTopics/Decimal_time.html

C2: formula for area of rectangle; perimeters of rectangles; units of time; 24-hour digital clock times

Summary

Y5 C2.5

Number patterns

A small group working with an adult

Year 5 Challenge Textbook page 41

Abacus Evolve objectives

- **Y6** Make and investigate a general statement about familiar numbers or shapes by finding examples that satisfy it
- **Y6** Recognise and explain patterns and relationships, generalise and predict
- **Y6** Develop from explaining a generalised relationship in words to express it in a formula using letters as symbols

Framework objectives

- **Y6** Represent and interpret sequences, patterns and relationships involving numbers and shapes; suggest and test hypotheses; construct and use simple expressions and formulae in words then symbols, e.g. the cost of c pens at 15 pence each is 15c pence

Teacher notes

Getting started

Ensure that children are comfortably able to give lists of multiples of 2, 3, 5, 6, 10 and 15.

Activity

- *Joey, Kaila and Ling eat school dinners, but not every day. Joey eats a school dinner every two days, Kaila eats a school dinner every three days and Ling eats a school dinner every five days.*
- *Over six weeks, how many times do the three children eat school dinners together? Are there any days when none of them eats a school dinner?*
- Ask children to make suggestions of ways to solve this problem, and encourage them to propose solutions.
- Show children how the information can be represented in a table:

1	2	3	4	5	6	7	8	9	10	11	12	13	14	15
Mon	Tue	Wed	Thu	Fri	Mon	Tue	Wed	Thu	Fri	Mon	Tue	Wed	Thu	Fri
	J		J		J		J		J		J		J	
		K			K			K			K			K
				L					L					L

16	17	3	4	20	21	22	23	24	25	26	27	28	29	30
Mon	Tue	Wed	Thu	Fri	Mon	Tue	Wed	Thu	Fri	Mon	Tue	Wed	Thu	Fri
J		J		J		J		J		J		J		J
		K			K			K			K			K
				L					L					L

- *When do two of the children eat together? Is it always the same two children?*
- *Predict the next time all three children will have lunch together.*
- Explain how this table shows that 30 is a multiple of 2, 3 and 5; that 6, 12, 18, 24 and 30 are common multiples of 2 and 3; and that 7 could be a prime number. Emphasise the use of tables to help with visualising patterns, such as multiples.

- *Roshan, Sara and Tomas all play basketball, but not every day. Roshan plays every two days, Sara plays every five days and Tomas plays every seven days. Predict when all three will play on the same day. When do two children play on the same day? Are there any days when none of them play basketball?*
- Ask children to draw a table to solve this problem.
- Encourage them to use words such as factors, common factors, multiples, common multiples and prime number to explain their thinking.

- Children work from Textbook page 41. They investigate a problem involving getting six children to school.

Be aware

- You may need to remind children that some questions have many answers.

Outcomes

- I can find a method to predict events.
- I can clearly present my workings and my findings.

Summary

Y5 ⭐ C2.6

Schedules

Individuals, pairs or groups working independently

Year 5 Challenge Textbook page 42

Year 5 Challenge PCM 22

Television guides (optional)

Abacus Evolve objectives

- Use, read and write units of time (including decade, millennium, leap year)
- Convert from one unit of time to another
- Read the time on a 24-hour digital clock and use 24-hour clock notation
- Use timetables

Framework objectives

- Read timetables and time using 24-hour clock notation; use a calendar to calculate time intervals
- Understand the process of decision making

Teacher notes

Preparation
Photocopy PCM 22, one for each child.

Getting started
Ensure that children are comfortable in working with 24-hour clock notation.

Activity
Children work from Textbook page 42 and write their answers on PCM 22. The activity explores the scheduling of television programmes. Children work out on what day and at what time each programme should be shown to make the best use of the time available. They give all times using 24-hour clock notation.

If you have time
Supply children with real television guides. Discuss how each channel's programming has been put together and why this is not an easy job. Can children see any patterns? Children can try to make up a schedule for a channel for 24 hours using real programmes and times from these television guides.

Be aware

- Make sure that children are able to work with time intervals even when the hour is crossed.
- Encourage children to not use a calculator when working with time, because calculators use units that are not equivalent to time. For example 0·5 of a day is 12 hours not 5 hours.

Outcomes

- I can use 24-hour time.
- I can try out ideas to find an answer and explain it.

D2: add 1-digit numbers and multiples of 10; mental addition/subtraction strategies; add near multiples of 10; add/subtract decimal numbers

Summary

Y5 **D2.1**

Perfect numbers

Individuals, pairs or groups working independently

Year 5 Challenge Textbook page 43

Calculators (optional)

Abacus Evolve objectives

- **Y6** Add several numbers
- **Y6** Consolidate knowledge of tests of divisibility by 2, 4, 5, 10 and 100
- **Y6** Know and apply tests of divisibility by 3, 6 and 9
- **Y6** Know and apply tests of divisibility by 8 and 25
- **Y6** Use tests of divisibility to estimate and check results of calculations

Framework objectives

- **Y6** Calculate mentally with integers and decimals: U·t + U·t, U·t − U·t, TU × U, TU ÷ U, U·t × U, U·t ÷ U
- **Y6** Use approximations, inverse operations and tests of divisibility to estimate and check results

Teacher notes

Getting started
Children should be confident in finding the factors of numbers up to 30.

Activity
Children work from Textbook page 43. They read a short article about perfect numbers. A perfect number is a number where the sum of its factors (not including itself) is the same as the number. Children complete a table of factor sums to find the first perfect number (6). Children then continue the table themselves to find the next perfect number (28). Encourage children to discuss what they find as they go along. There is only one other perfect number less than 500, which is 496. It would be unreasonable for children to search long enough to find this.

If you have time
Children could explore other numbers with special properties, such as friendly or amicable numbers.

Information
The first seven perfect numbers are: 6, 28, 496, 8128, 33 550 336, 8 589 869 056, 137 438 691 328.
Pythagoras also explored 'friendly numbers' (also called 'amicable numbers'). Friendly numbers come in pairs, such as 220 and 284. Their special property is that each is equal to the sum of the other's factors.
The factors of 220 are: 1, 2, 4, 5, 10, 11, 20, 22, 44, 55, 110. The sum of these is 284.
The factors of 284 are: 1, 2, 4, 71, 142. The sum of these is 220.

Be aware

- Children should understand that numbers with properties such as these are still being discovered. There is no definitive list of all the possible perfect numbers.

Outcomes

- I can find factors of numbers up to 30.
- I can add the factors together to find perfect numbers.

Supporting resources

There is more information about perfect numbers here:
- http://djm.cc/amicable.html#perfect

Challenge Plan: Year 5

D2: add 1-digit numbers and multiples of 10; mental addition/subtraction strategies; add near multiples of 10; add/subtract decimal numbers

Summary

Y5 **D2.2**   **Adding with a difference**

    A small group working with an adult

    Year 5 Challenge Textbook page 44

Abacus Evolve objectives

- Use known number facts and place value for mental addition and subtraction
- Check the sum of several numbers by adding in reverse order

Framework objectives

- *Use efficient written methods to add and subtract whole numbers and decimals with up to two places*
- Use knowledge of rounding, place value, number facts and inverse operations to estimate and check calculations
- Understand the process of decision making

Teacher notes

Activity

This activity explores the properties of number squares.

- Look together at the first number square on Textbook page 44.
- *What numbers are in this square?*
- *Add together the two numbers in diagonally opposite corners, then add together the two numbers in the other diagonally opposite corners. What do you notice?* (They both total 17.)
- *What rule can you see?* (Pairs of diagonals add to make the same total.)
- *Show me another pair of numbers which total 17. And another. And another.* (5 + 12, 3 + 14) *What do these four numbers make if we add them together?* (34) *Look at the positions of these numbers.*
- *Using this rule, show me another set of four numbers which total 34. And another. And another. Do you think there are any more?*
- *I know the total of four numbers is 34. One of the numbers is 15. What are the other three numbers?* (15 + 2, 14 + 3) *Look at where these numbers are on the grid.*
- Now look together at the second number square on Textbook page 44. *What is the same as the first number square?* (The numbers increase in value.) *What is different?* (In the first square each row increases by 4, in the second square each row increases by 8.)
- *Add together the two numbers in diagonally opposite corners. (7 + 52 = 59, 12 + 47 = 59) Then find the total of all four corner numbers.* (118)
- *What other pairs of numbers can you find that have this total?* (For example 8 + 51 and 11 + 48, 9 + 50 and 10 + 49, 15 + 44 and 20 + 39, 16 + 43 and 19 + 40, 17 + 42 and 18 + 41, 23 + 36 and 28 + 31, 24 + 35 and 27 + 32, 25 + 34 and 26 + 33.) *What have you noticed about where these numbers are on the grid?*
- Now look together at the third number square on Textbook page 44. *Can we do the same with this square?*
- Children use the properties that they have noted to complete the fourth number square on Textbook page 44.

Extra help

This pattern is based on symmetry. The sets of numbers which total the same as the four corner numbers, share the same line of symmetry.

Be aware

- Ensure children can see that these number squares are based on consecutive numbers, but not necessarily the counting numbers. They would also work with multiples.
- Children may have encountered a Magic Square before. Be sure they understand that this is not the same thing.

Outcomes

- I can work out sums and differences.
- I can find two numbers which total a set number.

D2: add 1-digit numbers and multiples of 10; mental addition/subtraction strategies; add near multiples of 10; add/subtract decimal numbers

Summary

Y5 ☆ D2.3

Make the calculation

A small group working with an adult

Year 5 Challenge PCM 23

Counters (two different colours); calculators (optional)

Abacus Evolve objectives

- Develop further the relationship between addition and subtraction
- Recognise that from one addition or subtraction fact, three other related facts can be found

Framework objectives

- *Use efficient written methods to add and subtract whole numbers and decimals with up to two places*
- Understand the process of decision making

Teacher notes

Getting started
Photocopy PCM 23, one for each child or team.

Activity
- Write *70 − 23 =*. *What do we know about the answer to this calculation?* (It will be odd; it will be less than 70; it will be more than 23; it will be around 50.)
- Confirm that the answer is 47. Encourage children to say the calculation out loud using different words such as *subtract*, *is less than*, *is more than*.
- *Can we write this subtraction as an addition using the same numbers?* (Every set of three numbers in a subtraction can make one other subtraction and two additions, for example 70 − 23 = 47, 70 − 47 = 23, 23 + 47 = 70, 47 + 23 = 70.)

- Write *89 + ? = 135*. *What do we know about the missing number?* (It is even; it is smaller than 135.) *How do we know that?* (O + E = O; it totals 135 when added to 89, so it cannot be greater than 135.)
- Confirm that the missing number is 46. *Find all the addition and subtraction calculations for these three numbers.* (89 + 46 = 135, 46 + 89 = 135, 135 − 89 = 46, 135 − 46 = 89)
- *Tell me three more numbers we can use to make correct additions and subtractions.*
- Children use what they have learned to play the game on PCM 23 in pairs or two teams. The object of the game is to identify as many sets as possible of three numbers which make a correct addition or subtraction. Children may use calculators if they wish.

Be aware

- Children will need to remember that:
  - odd + odd = even
  - odd + even = odd
  - even + even = even
  - odd − odd = even
  - odd − even = odd
  - even − even = even
  - even − odd = odd

Outcomes

- I know that four different calculations can be made from one addition or subtraction.

Challenge Plan: Year 5

D2: add 1-digit numbers and multiples of 10; mental addition/subtraction strategies; add near multiples of 10; add/subtract decimal numbers

Summary

Y5 ✩ D2.4

Fair share

Individuals, pairs or groups working independently

Year 5 Challenge Textbook page 45

Interlocking cubes

Abacus Evolve objectives

- Use known number facts and place value for mental addition and subtraction
- Make general statements about odd or even numbers, including their sums and differences
- Make and investigate a general statement about familiar numbers or shapes by finding examples that satisfy it
- Explain a generalised relationship (formula) in words
- Recognise and explain patterns and relationships, generalise and predict

Framework objectives

- *Use efficient written methods to add and subtract whole numbers and decimals with up to two places*
- Explore patterns, properties and relationships and propose a general statement involving numbers or shapes; identify examples for which the statement is true or false
- Understand different ways to take the lead and support others in a group

Teacher notes

Activity
Children work from Textbook page 45. This activity requires recognition of consecutive numbers and the addition of sets of numbers. Children use the context of sharing chocolates to explore how to combine consecutive numbers up to 20. (Children work out which sets of consecutive boxes you can share out equally between two people if each set must include box 1.) Children can use interlocking cubes to support their investigation.

Information
This investigation is based on triangular numbers. The total of trays 1–4 is 10; this will share evenly between two boxes. The total of trays 1–5 is 15; this will not share evenly between two boxes.
The first 20 triangular numbers are:
1, 3, 6, 10, 15, 21, 28, 36, 45, 55, 66, 78, 91, 105, 120, 136, 153, 171, 190, 210.
The rule is that the chocolates can be divided equally if the total number of chocolates is an even triangular number.

Further extension
Children could explore sharing the triangular numbers into sets of 4 or 5.

Sets of 4:

Trays	Total chocolates	Set 1	Set 2	Set 3	Set 4
Trays 1–7	28	7	1 6	2 5	3 4
Trays 1–8	36	1 8	2 7	3 6	4 5
Trays 1–15	120	1 14 15	2 3 12 13	4 5 10 11	6 7 8 9
Trays 1–16	136	1 2 15 16	3 4 13 14	5 6 11 12	7 8 9 10

Sets of 5:

Trays	Total chocolates	Set 1	Set 2	Set 3	Set 4	Set 5
Trays 1–9	45	9	1 8	2 7	3 6	4 5
Trays 1–11	55	1 10	2 9	3 8	4 7	5 6

Be aware

- Children may need reminding of the rule that only consecutive boxes must be used and box 1 must be included.

Outcomes

- I can investigate a rule and find examples which fit it.

Challenge Plan: Year 5

D2: add 1-digit numbers and multiples of 10; mental addition/subtraction strategies; add near multiples of 10; add/subtract decimal numbers

Summary

Y5 ⬠ **D2.5**

Odd one out

Individuals or pairs working independently

Year 5 Challenge Textbook page 46

Calculators

Abacus Evolve objectives

- Check with the inverse operation when using a calculator

Framework objectives

- Use knowledge of rounding, place value, number facts and inverse operations to estimate and check calculations

Teacher notes

Getting started
Discuss with children that + and − are inverses of each other and × and ÷ are inverses of each other.

Activity
Children work from Textbook page 46. They are shown statements with three possible answers, one of which is incorrect. Children must reverse the calculations in each statement in order to find out which answers are correct. They must then explain how they know that the remaining answer is incorrect.

Further extension
Children could make up their own odd-one-out questions for the rest of the group to try.

Be aware

- When solving problems such as these it is possible that children may come up with solutions that you have not considered. Be prepared to discuss a range of explanations with them.

Outcomes

- I can use the inverse calculations to solve a problem.

Challenge Plan: Year 5

D2: add 1-digit numbers and multiples of 10; mental addition/subtraction strategies; add near multiples of 10; add/subtract decimal numbers

Summary

Y5 ☆ D2.6

Money steps

Individuals, pairs or groups working independently

Year 5 Challenge Textbook page 47

Abacus Evolve objectives

- **Y6** Consolidate adding two decimal numbers, with one or two decimal places, using standard column addition
- **Y6** Continue to subtract one integer from another, each less than 10 000, using standard written methods
- **Y6** Continue to subtract one decimal number from another, both with one or two decimal places, using standard written methods

Framework objectives

- **Y6** *Use efficient written methods to add and subtract integers and decimals, to multiply and divide integers and decimals by a one-digit integer, and to multiply two-digit and three-digit integers by a two-digit integer*
- **Y6** *Understand and use a variety of ways to criticise constructively and respond to criticism*

Teacher notes

Getting started
This activity requires confidence in the addition and subtraction of money.

Activity
Children work from Textbook page 47. They play the game to find a path across the swamp, collecting and losing money on the way. The aim is to get to the other side with the most money possible. Children will be adding and subtracting decimals in the form of money. Some values are given in pounds and some are in pence so children will need to convert to like units before performing each calculation. Children then explore the largest amount of money it is possible to collect in six steps and the smallest amount that can be collected, without losing all their money at any point.

Be aware

- Make sure children are aware of the importance of converting to like units before performing each calculation.

Outcomes

- I can add and subtract decimals in the form of money.

Challenge Plan: Year 5

E2: multiplying HTU × U using informal and standard written methods; relate fractions to division; tests of divisibility

Summary

Y5 ⬡ E2.1

Multiplication challenge

Pairs or groups working independently

Year 5 Challenge PCMs 24, 25 and 31 (optional)

A 1–6 dice; calculators (optional); a 1–8 dice (optional)

Abacus Evolve objectives

- Multiply HTU × U using standard written methods

Framework objectives

- Refine and use efficient written methods to multiply and divide HTU × U, TU × TU, U·t × U and HTU ÷ U
- Understand different ways to take the lead and support others in a group

Teacher notes

Preparation
Photocopy PCM 24 and PCM 25, one copy of each per child.

Getting started
Children work from PCM 24. They play a game, taking it in turns to use four dice throws to make and solve a multiplication problem. They use the rules to determine who gets a point for that round. The winner has the most points after six rounds.

Children then work from PCM 25. They play a similar game, but first they make up their own rules to determine who gets a point each round.

Children can use a variety of informal and standard methods to solve the multiplication problems. If necessary children may use a calculator to check answers.

If you have time
Try these variations of the game:
- Use a 1–8 dice or the 0–9 spinner on PCM 31, rather than a standard 1–6 dice.
- Each child can choose to pass on one throw per round, and throw again.
- Each child is allowed to make one 'joker' throw for their opponent.

Extra help
Children can arrange their four numbers in any order, so they should be encouraged to discuss the strategies they are using to try and win each round, thinking in particular about the most significant digit in the calculation (tens or hundreds). For example if the target is 2000 then 4 and 5 would be good numbers to have in the tens places in a 2-digit by 2-digit calculation.

Further extension
Children can play the game again, this time making 3-digit × 3-digit multiplications to solve.

Be aware

- Ensure children understand that the 'closest to' can be a number above or below the target number, for example 928 is closer to 1000 than 1078 is.

Outcomes

- I can choose a good method to multiply 2-digit or 3-digit numbers.

Challenge Plan: Year 5

E2: multiplying HTU × U using informal and standard written methods; relate fractions to division; tests of divisibility

Summary

Y5 ☆ E2.2

Multiplication problems with time

Individuals, pairs or groups working independently

Year 5 Challenge Textbook page 48

Abacus Evolve objectives

- Multiply HTU × U using standard written methods

Framework objectives

- Solve one- and two-step problems involving whole numbers and decimals and all four operations, choosing and using appropriate calculation strategies, including calculator use

Teacher notes

Getting started
Run through the example on Textbook page 48 to make sure that children understand how to compare different units of time.

Activity
Children work from Textbook page 48. This is an activity about the relationships between different units of time. In each case the larger time unit must be multiplied by the number of the smaller unit that make it up, to solve the problem. Children are encouraged to make estimates before they find the answers.

Extra help
Remind children how to convert from days to minutes: multiply by 24 to find the number of hours, then multiply by 60 to find the number of minutes.

Further extension
Children can think of their own two-step questions, like question 10 on the Textbook page. They can then solve their own questions, or give them to another child to solve.

Be aware

- Children are encouraged to estimate and so may think they can solve all the problems using informal methods. However because of the large numbers and the variety of units, they should record each calculation formally.
- Children may notice that they could solve these problems using division, for example 1250 hours ÷ 24 = 52·083 days. However, as most of the divisions will produce a remainder it would be difficult to say how much longer a time period was. You may need to explain to children why division is not a suitable method to use with these calculations.

Outcomes

- I can choose a good method to multiply 2-digit or 3-digit numbers.
- I can solve problems with measures of time.

Challenge Plan: Year 5

E2: multiplying HTU × U using informal and standard written methods; relate fractions to division; tests of divisibility

Summary

Y5 ⭐ E2.3

Decimal multiplication

A small group working with an adult

Year 5 Challenge Textbook page 49

Abacus Evolve objectives

- **Y6** Rehearse multiplying U·t × U using standard written methods
- **Y6** Multiply U·th × U using standard written methods

Framework objectives

- **Y6** *Use efficient written methods to add and subtract integers and decimals, to multiply and divide integers and decimals by a 1-digit integer, and to multiply 2- and 3-digit integers by a 2-digit integer*

Teacher notes

Getting started
What is an approximate answer to 15·3 × 6? (Around 90, as 15 × 6 = 90.)
What is an approximate answer to 4·72 × 7? (Around 30, as 4 × 7 = 28.)
In which question does the decimal make more difference to the estimate? Why? (4·72 × 7, because the decimal amount is greater.)
Demonstrate how to set the questions out formally, stressing the importance of setting them out carefully and paying attention to place value. Solve the multiplications together and then encourage children to compare the answers to their estimates, to check that they are right and that the decimal point is in the correct place.

Activity
Children work from Textbook page 49. They use the method they have learned to work through the first half of the page. Then they apply this method to multiplication problems in the context of money, on the second half of the page.

Further extension
Children can use a shop catalogue to extend the money context questions to four digit problems, i.e. TU·th × U.
For example if an item costs £24·63, how much would six of this item cost?

Be aware

- Some children will find the questions with zeros trickier (such as q6 and q7). Ensure that children know what happens when you multiply by zero and can apply this knowledge.

Outcomes

- I can use a suitable written method to multiply decimal numbers.

Challenge Plan: Year 5

E2: multiplying HTU × U using informal and standard written methods; relate fractions to division; tests of divisibility

Summary

Y5 E2.4

Fractional amounts

A small group working with an adult

Year 5 Challenge Textbook page 50

Counters in different colours

Abacus Evolve objectives

- Relate fractions to division
- Use division to find fractions, including tenths and hundredths of numbers and quantities

Framework objectives

- Find fractions using division (e.g. $\frac{1}{100}$ of 5 kg), and percentages of numbers and quantities (e.g. 10%, 5% and 15% of £80)
- Understand the process of decision making

Teacher notes

Getting started
Check that children understand how to find a fractional amount of a number. For example $\frac{3}{4}$ of 56: divide 56 by 4 then multiply by 3. (56 ÷ 4 = 14, 14 × 3 = 42) Run through Hassan's problem on Textbook page 50. He has solved a fraction problem and the answer is 24. *What could the original fraction question have been?* Children work in pairs to find as many examples as they can. They may suggest unit fractions based on the 24 times table: $\frac{1}{3}$ of 72, $\frac{1}{4}$ of 96, $\frac{1}{5}$ of 120, etc. Ask children to list this sequence. Encourage them to also find other examples, such as $\frac{4}{5}$ of 30, $\frac{3}{4}$ of 32, $\frac{4}{7}$ of 42. *What do you notice about these fractions?* (The numerator is a factor of 24.)

Activity
Children work from Textbook page 50. They use what they have learned to work through the second question. They then move on to play the fractions game. Each child has 12 counters in one colour. Children take turns to find a fractional amount that gives one of the numbers on the grid. They cover that number with one of their counters. Where a number is on the grid more than once, a different fraction must be used each time. Equivalent fractions could also be used, for example $\frac{1}{2}$ of 48 = 24, $\frac{2}{4}$ of 48 = 24, $\frac{4}{8}$ of 48 = 24. Children can discuss this and decide if they are allowed to be used in the game. The winner is the first person to get a line of four counters horizontally, vertically or diagonally.

If you have time
Review the different ways that children have found for reaching each target number. Children can think about whether there is a finite number of answers, or if they could keep on generating more and more examples.

Be aware

- Throughout the activity, make sure that children understand the difference between unit fractions (fractions with a numerator of 1) and non-unit fractions (fractions with a numerator greater than 1).

Outcomes

- I can relate fractions to division.
- I can find fractional amounts of different numbers.

Challenge Plan: Year 5

E2: multiplying HTU × U using informal and standard written methods; relate fractions to division; tests of divisibility

Summary

Y5 E2.5

Fractions problems

Individuals, pairs or groups working independently

Year 5 Challenge Textbook page 51

Calculators

Abacus Evolve objectives

- Relate fractions to division
- Use division to find fractions, including tenths and hundredths of numbers and quantities

Framework objectives

- Find fractions using division (e.g. $\frac{1}{100}$ of 5 kg), and percentages of numbers and quantities (e.g. 10%, 5% and 15% of £80)

Teacher notes

Preparation
Familiarise yourself with the paradox of Achilles and the tortoise and the reasons why the logic is incorrect. It is a paradox because although the explanation seems correct theoretically, the faster speed of Achilles means that he will of course overtake the tortoise at some point.

Getting started
Read through the story. Allow children some time to discuss the paradox.

Activity
Children work from Textbook page 51. After having read the paradox of Achilles and the tortoise, children work through a set of fraction questions in the context of distance and speed around a racetrack. Children find fractional amounts of the length of the track to determine which of two fractions is the larger. They then work out the time it will take for Achilles and the tortoise to travel around given fractions of the track.

Further extension
Children can try to answer the questions again, but this time imagining that the race track is longer. They can choose the length themselves. *What new length would be easy to calculate with? What length would be more difficult?*

Information
To solve the second set of questions (the length of time taken to travel around fractions of the track), the fractional amount travelled needs to be found first. Children can then use what they know about the speed of Achilles and the tortoise to calculate how long it will take them to complete a portion of the race. For example $\frac{9}{20}$ of 1000 m is 450 m. Achilles runs at 200 m per minute so it will take him 5 minutes (300 seconds) to run 1000 m. It will take him 0·3 seconds to run 1 m, so it will take him 135 seconds to run 450 m.

Be aware

- Children may already be confident in other methods of comparing fractions (for example using a common denominator). However, in this context they should find fractional amounts of the length of the track, for example $\frac{3}{4}$ of 1000 m is 750 m, whereas $\frac{7}{10}$ of 1000 m is 700 m. This shows that $\frac{3}{4}$ is larger than $\frac{7}{10}$.

Outcomes

- I can find fractions using division.
- I can use fractions to solve problems.

Supporting resources

Children can read more about the paradox of Achilles and the tortoise, and Zeno's other paradoxes, here:
- http://en.wikipedia.org/wiki/Zeno's_paradoxes#Achilles_and_the_tortoise
- http://www.archim.org.uk/eureka/27/metamathematics.html

Challenge Plan: Year 5

E2: multiplying HTU × U using informal and standard written methods; relate fractions to division; tests of divisibility

Summary

Y5 ⭐ E2.6

Divisibility

Individuals, pairs or groups working independently

Year 5 Challenge Textbook page 52

Calculators (optional)

Abacus Evolve objectives

- **Y6** Consolidate knowledge of tests of divisibility by 2, 4, 5, 10 and 100
- **Y6** Know and apply tests of divisibility by 3, 6 and 9
- **Y6** Use tests of divisibility to estimate and check results of calculations

Framework objectives

- **Y6** Use approximations, inverse operations and tests of divisibility to estimate and check results

Teacher notes

Preparation
Read Textbook page 52 and familiarise yourself with two methods of finding out if a 3-digit number is divisible by 7.

Getting started
Using the example on Textbook page 52, go over the two methods for finding out if a 3-digit number is divisible by 7.

Activity
Children work from Textbook page 52. They choose a method for finding out if a 3-digit number is divisible by 7 and apply it. They then work with a method for finding out if a 4-digit number is divisible by 7.

Further extension
Children can investigate methods for testing for divisibility by 11 and 13.

Be aware

- Make sure that children are confident in using the vocabulary of division; divisible, divisibility, factor, multiple.
- The method for checking the divisibility of 4-digit numbers by 7 may result in a 3-digit number. If children are not immediately sure if this number is divisible by 7 they should be encouraged to use one of the methods to find out, rather than checking with a calculator.

Outcomes

- I can test numbers for divisibility by 7.
- I can follow a set of instructions for testing divisibility.

Supporting resources

Here are some methods for checking divisibility by numbers up to 10:
- http://www.easymaths.com/Curious_Maths_division.htm

Information about divisibility by 11 and 13 can be found here:
- http://www.bbc.co.uk/dna/h2g2/A23502863

Challenge Plan: Year 5

A3: ordering positive and negative numbers; rounding decimal numbers; multiplying larger numbers; multiplying U.t × T

Summary

Y5 ⭐ A3.1

Extreme temperatures

Individuals, pairs or groups working independently

Year 5 Challenge Textbook page 53

200 ml warm coloured water; a clear 250 ml bottle; modelling clay; a clear plastic straw; a thin strip of card; sticky tape; a marker pen; a thermometer; a large saucepan; 200 ml hot water (all optional)

Abacus Evolve objectives

- Order a given set of positive and negative numbers
- Calculate a temperature rise or fall across 0 degrees

Framework objectives

- Count from any given number in whole number and decimal steps, extending beyond zero when counting backwards; relate the numbers to their position on a number line
- Understand the process of decision making

Teacher notes

Activity

Children work from Textbook page 53. The activity requires them to order temperatures and calculate differences between positive and negative temperatures where the difference is over 100. For this exercise the Fahrenheit scale is used.

Extra help

A number line marked in 10s from ⁻100 to ⁺100 will help with ordering temperatures, particularly negative numbers.

If you have time

Children could make their own thermometer:
1. Half fill a small bottle with 200 ml of lukewarm coloured water. Use modelling clay to seal a drinking straw into the neck of the bottle so that 5 cm of the straw is in the water and the rest is sticking out. Make sure that no air can get into the bottle.
2. Stick a strip of white card to the section of straw which is sticking out of the bottle, on which to mark temperatures.
3. Leave the bottle until the water has cooled to room temperature. The water level in the straw should drop slightly. Mark the water level on the card. Take the temperature of the room with a real thermometer and write that number next to your mark.
4. Now put the bottle into a pan filled with 200 ml of hot water. This will warm up the water in the bottle and make the water rise up the straw. Once the water level has stopped rising, mark the new level on the straw. Take the temperature of the water in the pan and write that number next to your mark.
5. To complete your thermometer, mark equally-spaced lines between your two numbers and write in the missing temperatures.

Be aware

- Degrees centigrade and degrees Celsius are essentially the same measurement. However children should be discouraged from using the term centigrade as this has fallen from common use and Celsius is the preferred term.

Outcomes

- I can understand that there are different ways of saying temperatures.
- I can put positive and negative temperatures in order.
- I can find differences between positive and negative temperatures.

Supporting resources

If you would like to continue the work from the Textbook page, you can find more statistics here:
- http://www.factmonster.com/ipka/A0762380.html

Challenge Plan: Year 5

A3: ordering positive and negative numbers; rounding decimal numbers; multiplying larger numbers; multiplying U.t × T

Summary

Y5 ⭐ A3.2

Using your calculator

A small group working with an adult

Year 5 Challenge Textbook page 54

Calculators; number line ⁻10–⁺10; strips of card (optional)

Abacus Evolve objectives

- Recognise a negative number on a calculator
- Check with the inverse operation when using a calculator

Framework objectives

- Use a calculator to solve problems, including those involving decimals or fractions, e.g. to find $\frac{3}{4}$ of 150 g; interpret the display correctly in the context of measurement
- Understand different ways to take the lead and support others in a group

Teacher notes

Preparation
If you like you can write the questions below on strips of card for children to pass around and consider.

Activity
When we use a calculator we must be very careful to interpret the display in a way that helps us answer the question correctly.

1. Write the following problems on the board:
   - *£16 is shared equally between 5 friends. How much does each person receive?*
   - *5 volunteers take equal turns in a sponsored silence for 16 hours. How long must each person stay quiet?*

Ask children to note the numbers and operations they would enter on a calculator to solve these problems. Children should identify the calculation as 16 ÷ 5 = 3·2. Discuss with children what the units are in each question. *How can we give our answers in the same units as the questions?* (3·2 = £3·20, 3·2 = 3 hours 12 minutes. Make sure children understand how to translate a decimal into hours and minutes.). *Our calculators gave the answer 3·2 and then we interpreted the display to find the actual answer to the question.*

2. Write the following scenarios on the board and ask children what they notice. (Each time, the person ends up with a negative amount of money.)
   - *I have £2 but have to give my friend £3.*
   - *I owe my friend £3 but only have £2 to give her.*
   - *I owe my friend £2 and she then lends me another £3*

What calculations might we use to solve these problems?
2 − 3 = ⁻1, ⁻2 + −3 = ⁻5, ⁻3 + 2 = ⁻1). Note suggestions on the board. Encourage children to discuss the fact that we always get a negative result if we try to take more than we have. Use a number line marked in ones from ⁻10 to +10 to demonstrate why this happens. Ask children to enter the calculations on their calculator. Show them how to use the +/− key. Confirm with children that we could do these calculations in our head but the calculator helps us to see negative numbers, which shows how much is owed.

Children work from Textbook page 54. This activity explores using a calculator to work with both positive and negative integers. Children experiment with calculations using only selected numbers and functions to make all the integers from ⁻10 to ⁺20. Children then use more complex functions to make larger numbers.

Be aware

- Look out for children misunderstanding the answer they see on their calculator. Children must understand calculator displays before they are able to use one accurately.
- Avoid using calculators for time problems as the calculator answer can be misinterpreted.

Outcomes

- I can use the +/− key on a calculator and I know what a − sign means.
- I can use a calculator efficiently.

Supporting resources

If you would like to project a large calculator onto a whiteboard, here is one option:
- http://www.metacalc.com/

Challenge Plan: Year 5

A3: ordering positive and negative numbers; rounding decimal numbers; multiplying larger numbers; multiplying U.t × T

Summary

Y5 ⭐ A3.3

Working with seconds

Individuals, pairs or groups working independently

Year 5 Challenge Textbook page 55

Year 5 Challenge PCM 26

The internet; a blank number line in hundredths (optional); a stopwatch (optional)

Abacus Evolve objectives

- **Y6** Consolidate rounding a number with two decimal places to the nearest whole number
- **Y6** Round a number with two decimal places to the nearest tenth
- **Y6** Use decimal notation for tenths, hundredths and thousandths
- **Y6** Know what each digit represents in a number with up to three decimal places
- **Y6** Order a mixed set of decimal numbers with up to three decimal places

Framework objectives

- **Y6** Use decimal notation for tenths, hundredths and thousandths; partition, round and order decimals with up to three places, and position them on the number line

Teacher notes

Getting started
Children should be confident with times in seconds to at least one decimal place.

Activity
Children work from Textbook page 55. This activity involves comparing, rounding and finding the difference between speeds, in the contexts of swimming, running and cycling. Children use PCM 26 to interpret results from tables. In the first section times are rounded to the nearest half second. In the second section children work with rounding to the nearest hundredth of a second and subtracting decimals to one decimal place. In the third section children round and order results to the nearest tenth of a second.

Extra help
You could provide a blank number line marked in hundredths to help with ordering times from fastest to slowest.

If you have time
Children could time their own running or swimming events with a stopwatch and compare them with the times in the Textbook. Children could explore why some times from the 2008 Olympic cycling events are given to the nearest hundredth of a second and some to the nearest thousandth of a second.

Be aware

- Children often look at the number of digits in a number to order them without considering the place value, for example thinking that 0·123 is bigger than 0·22.
- Children sometimes read a decimal as a whole number, e.g. 0·81 as nought point eighty one.

Outcomes

- I can order decimal numbers.
- I can round decimals to three places.
- I can calculate with numbers to one or two decimal places.
- I know that in races the lowest time wins.

Supporting resources

The Official Website of the 2008 Olympics in Beijing:
- http://en.beijing2008.cn/

Challenge Plan: Year 5

A3: ordering positive and negative numbers; rounding decimal numbers; multiplying larger numbers; multiplying U.t × T

Summary

Y5 **A3.4**

A different way to multiply

A small group working with an adult

Year 5 Challenge Textbook page 56

Calculators (optional); the internet (optional)

Abacus Evolve objectives

- Use known number facts and place value to multiply or divide mentally
- Multiply using closely related facts
- Multiply by 19, 21, … by multiplying by 20, … and adjusting
- Develop higher multiplication tables, e.g. the ×12 table from the ×10 and ×2 tables

Framework objectives

- Extend mental methods for whole-number calculations, for example to multiply a 2-digit by 1-digit number (e.g. 12 × 9), to multiply by 25 (e.g. 16 × 25), to subtract one near multiple of 1000 from another (e.g. 6070 − 4097)

Teacher notes

Preparation

It may help to familiarise yourself with the Vedic multiplication method before starting this activity.

Activity

The Vedic method is based on the principal of **vertically and crosswise**. Demonstrate this process to children with 21 × 23.

- Multiply **vertically** the two numbers on the left:
  2 × 2 = **4**.
  This gives the first figure of the answer.
- Multiply **crosswise** 2 × 3 and 1 × 2, add these together:
  6 + 2 = **8**
  This gives the middle figure.
- Multiply **the two numbers on the right, vertically**:
  1 × 3 = **3**
  This gives the last figure of the answer: **483**

Work through 21 × 43 with children, asking them what the answer will be at each stage.

If you end up with a 2-digit number, carry the ten to the left. Demonstrate this to children with these examples.

 becomes 378   becomes 375

Children work from Textbook page 56 to see if this method can be used with any 2-digit number multiplications. Calculators can be used for checking.

If you have time

Children explore Vedic Squares on the internet. Multiplication squares give interesting geometric patterns.

Be aware

- Children may need to be reminded that there is more than one method for most calculations. Our standard written methods are not universal.

Outcomes

- I can use the Vedic method to multiply 2-digit numbers.
- I am confident at using a different approach to multiplying.

Supporting resources

Find out more about Vedic maths and Vedic Squares here:
- http://vedicmaths.org/Introduction/Tutorial/Tutorial.asp
- http://www.blss.portsmouth.sch.uk/resources/nmfax_bk.shtml

Summary

Y5 A3.5 — **Cross the river**

Pairs or groups working independently

Year 5 Challenge PCMs 27, 28 and 29

Calculators (optional); coloured paper

Abacus Evolve objectives

- Multiply U·t × U using informal written methods
- Multiply U·t × U using standard written methods

Framework objectives

- Refine and use efficient written methods to multiply and divide HTU × U, TU × TU, U·t × U, and HTU ÷ U
- Plan and manage a group task over time by using different levels of planning

Teacher notes

Preparation
Photocopy the two sets of cards and the game board on PCMs 27, 28 and 29 onto different coloured paper. Cut out the playing cards.

Getting started
Explain the rules of the game.

Activity
This game rehearses multiplying a whole number by a decimal.
- Two children or two teams each have a set of cards, shuffled and face down.
- Each child takes it in turn to turn over a card from their pile and complete the calculation (either verbally or in writing).
- The child then places their card on top of the answer on the game board.
- If a child calculates incorrectly they miss a go and do not place a card on the board.
- The winner is the first person or team to make a line of their cards across or down from one side of the board to the other.

If you have time
Encourage children to find a range of calculations which have the same product, e.g.
$80 \times 0·6 = 48$
$40 \times 1·2 = 48$
$12 \times 4 = 48$
$6 \times 8 = 48$
$60 \times 0·8 = 48.$

Be aware

- Children should recognise that different calculations can give the same answers as easier ones. They should be able to use this to help with problems that seem tricky.
- Calculators should not be needed as children should be encouraged to recall their knowledge of tables. However, calculators can be used for checking.

Outcomes

- I can multiply numbers with one decimal place by 1- and 2-digit numbers.

Challenge Plan: Year 5

A3: ordering positive and negative numbers; rounding decimal numbers; multiplying larger numbers; multiplying U.t × T

Summary

Y5 ⭐ **A3.6**

Solving money matters

Individuals, pairs or groups working independently

Year 5 Challenge Textbook page 57

Calculators (optional); internet (optional)

Abacus Evolve objectives

- **Y6** Consolidate rounding a number with two decimal places to the nearest whole number
- **Y6** Continue to multiply using closely related facts
- **Y6** Check with the inverse operation when using a calculator
- **Y6** Multiply U.th × U using standard written methods
- **Y6** Divide £.p by a 2-digit number to give £.p

Framework objectives

- **Y6** Solve multi-step problems, and problems involving fractions, decimals and percentages; choose and use appropriate calculation strategies at each stage, including calculator use
- **Y6** Use a range of oral techniques to present persuasive argument

Teacher notes

Activity

Children work from Textbook page 57. Children investigate the most cost effective camp site for a school residential trip. There are different price options for each location and for extra items required. Children need to find the most efficient way to hire coaches and tents, taking into account that adults/children and males/females need separate tents.

Different activities are available at each site and children should also consider these when deciding on a venue.

Children can work individually or in pairs or small groups to calculate the most favourable option. They answer questions about the number of coaches required, the number and size of tents required, and how much each child must pay for the trip. Children then compare their choices as a group and reach a final decision together, taking into account value for money and the activities they consider to be the most appealing.

Extra help

Children could use a calculator for this activity.

If you have time

Children could use the internet to explore prices at real camp sites and plan a fun, cost effective trip.

Children could conduct a survey asking children in their class which of the activities they would prefer to do. They could then choose a suitable method to present their data.

Be aware

- Children may assume that the greater the quantity, the cheaper it will be per person.
- Children may round some numbers down because that is the nearest number, without realising that it is necessary to round up in this context.

Outcomes

- I can find an answer to the problem, and show my workings.

Challenge Plan: Year 5

B3: addition – large numbers and decimals using written methods; subtraction – large numbers and decimals using formal/informal methods

Summary

Y5 ☆ B3.1

Big addition game

Pairs or groups working independently

Year 5 Challenge Textbook page 58

Calculators

Abacus Evolve objectives

- Add more than two integers less than 10 000
- Add two integers less than 10 000 using informal written methods
- Add two integers less than 10 000 using standard written methods

Framework objectives

- *Use efficient written methods to add and subtract whole numbers and decimals with up to two places*
- Respond appropriately to others in the light of alternative viewpoints

Teacher notes

Getting started
Make sure children understand the rules of the game before they start to play.

Activity
Children work from Textbook page 58. They play the game in pairs or two groups. Children work through the questions, taking turns to find one or two possible answers using the numbers in the grid. They calculate and record their answers using their choice of informal or formal written method. Children then swap and check each other's solutions, using a calculator if necessary. They score one point for each correct solution.
There are at least four answers to each question, so each child will be able to get up to two points for each question. Make sure children take turns to be the first to answer each question.

Be aware

- Check that children aren't finding two numbers, and then simply reversing them for their next answer. This does not count as two different solutions.

Outcomes

- I can choose a method to add two or more numbers and show my working.

Challenge Plan: Year 5

**B3: addition – large numbers and decimals using written methods;
subtraction – large numbers and decimals using formal/informal methods**

Summary

Y5 ⭐ B3.2

Decimal spin off

A small group working with an adult

Year 5 Challenge Textbook page 59

Year 5 Challenge PCM number 30

Counters; paper clips; sharp pencils

Abacus Evolve objectives

- **Y6** Consolidate adding two decimal numbers, with one or two decimal places, using standard column addition

Framework objectives

- **Y6** *Use efficient written methods to add and subtract integers and decimals, to multiply and divide integers and decimals by a one-digit integer, and to multiply two-digit and three-digit integers by a two-digit integer*

Teacher notes

Preparation
Photocopy PCM 30, one for each child. Provide each child with a paper clip, a sharp pencil and counters (in a different colour for each child).

Getting started
Let each child spin the spinner a few times. Ask them to read the number that the paper clip lands on and check that they are reading the numbers correctly. Point at 7·206. *What does each of the digits represent*? Repeat this with another number and continue until you are confident that children are comfortable with decimals.

Activity
Children work from Textbook page 59 and use the spinner on PCM 30. Talk through the game rules together. Discuss what happens when numbers come up that have different numbers of digits. Model the need to be careful about how to set out workings. *Remember to line digits up in the right place!*

For example 0·06 + 22·1 should
be set out like this:

```
  0·06
+ 22·1
_____
```

Not like this:

```
  0·06
+ 22·1
   ____
```

Ask children to explain why.
Repeat this demonstration with another example and encourage children to explain it in terms of place value rather than 'putting the decimal points above each other'.

Further extension
Give children a blank spinner (with six or eight segments) and a grid. Ask them to create a similar game board. They must make sure that the grid contains all the possible totals of two numbers from the spinner.

Be aware

- Some children may find it difficult to line digits up accurately. They can be helped significantly by using squared paper.

Outcomes

- I can add two decimal numbers with different numbers of digits, by setting out my calculations in columns.

Challenge Plan: Year 5

B3: addition – large numbers and decimals using written methods; subtraction – large numbers and decimals using formal/informal methods

Summary

Y5 ⬡ B3.3   **Heavy reading**

A small group working with an adult

Year 5 Challenge Textbook page 60

Abacus Evolve objectives

- Add two decimal numbers, with one or two decimal places, using standard written methods

Framework objectives

- *Use efficient written methods to add and subtract whole numbers and decimals with up to two places*

Teacher notes

Activity
Children work from Textbook page 60. They are shown the weights of eight heavy books.
Work through the example together: *What is the total weight of books D (753 g) and H (1 kg 27 g)?*
How can we find out the total weight? Encourage children to point out that it is difficult because the two weights are written in different formats.
First we need to change both weights to kilograms, using decimals.
(0·753 kg and 1·027 kg)
Now that both weights use the same units it is much easier to add them up.

```
    0·753
  + 1·027
    1·780
       1
```

Ask children to use this method to answer question 1 on Textbook page 60. Emphasise the need for children to set out the additions in columns.

Children work individually or in pairs to answer the other questions. Remind them to convert the weights into kilograms in decimal format before trying to find the total weights.

If you have time
Encourage children to go through and use the inverse operation (in this case subtraction) to check their answers.

Be aware

- Children may confuse the relationship between kg and g with the relationship between m and cm. For example they might read 1 kg 27 g as 1·27 kg. Ensure that children understand why this is incorrect.

Outcomes

- I can add decimals by setting out my calculations in columns.

Challenge Plan: Year 5

Summary

Y5 ✪ B3.4

Subtraction game

Pairs or groups working independently

Year 5 Challenge PCMs 31 and 32

Paper clips; sharp pencils; paper

Abacus Evolve objectives

- Subtract one integer from another, each less than 10 000, using standard written methods
- Subtract one integer from another, each less than 10 000, using informal written methods

Framework objectives

- *Use efficient written methods to add and subtract whole numbers and decimals with up to two places*
- Understand different ways to take the lead and support others in a group

Teacher notes

Preparation
Photocopy PCMs 31 and 32, one copy of each per child. Provide each child with a paper clip and a sharp pencil to make a spinner.

Getting started
Ensure children understand the rules of the game on PCM 31.

Activity
Children play the game on PCM 31 in pairs or two groups. They record their subtractions on PCM 32. Children take it in turns to spin the spinner and write the digit anywhere they choose in their subtraction sentence. The round ends when each child has completed their number sentence. Then children find the difference between the two numbers they have generated. They should set their subtractions out using a standard written method. They check each other's workings, by using the inverse operation. The child whose pair has the largest difference wins a point.

Further extension
Children can play the game again using these alternative rules. Each child can have one 'joker' turn. In this turn, rather than placing the digit on their grid, they can choose to place it on their opponent's grid.

Be aware

- Make sure children understand why it is not a good idea for the second number to be larger than the first number when creating their subtractions.

Outcomes

- I can show my workings for subtracting large numbers.
- I can check my calculations by using the inverse operation.

Challenge Plan: Year 5

**B3: addition – large numbers and decimals using written methods;
subtraction – large numbers and decimals using formal/informal methods**

Summary

Y5 ⬠ B3.5

Football stadiums

Individuals, pairs or groups working independently

Year 5 Challenge Textbook page 61

Football match attendance figures (optional)

Abacus Evolve objectives

- **Y6** Continue to subtract one integer from another, each less than 10 000, using standard written methods

Framework objectives

- **Y6** *Use efficient written methods to add and subtract integers and decimals, to multiply and divide integers and decimals by a one-digit integer, and to multiply two-digit and three-digit integers by a two-digit integer*
- **Y6** Use approximations, inverse operations and tests of divisibility to estimate and check results

Teacher notes

Preparation
It may be useful to find recent football match attendance figures from newspapers or on the internet.

Activity
Children work from Textbook page 61. They find the differences in capacity between 12 football stadiums. Children can choose which method they use, but they should be encouraged to record their workings, and then check their answers using inverse operations.

If you have time
Children could find out the capacity of other league club stadiums, or stadiums in Scotland or other countries, and make up their own questions about them.

Be aware

- Check that children are reading large numbers properly. For example the capacity of Anfield is *forty-five thousand, three hundred and sixty-two,* rather than *four-five-three-six-two.*

Outcomes

- I can show my workings for subtracting large numbers.
- I can check my calculations by using the inverse operation.

Supporting resources

This website has the ground capacity of all the English football league clubs:
- http://www.footballgroundguide.com/index.html

This website has the ground capacity of all the Scottish football league clubs:
- http://www.scotlandfootballyears.com/stadiums/

This website has a list of the capacities of the ten largest sports stadiums in the world:
- http://www.top10land.com/top-ten-biggest-sports-stadiums-in-the-world.html

Challenge Plan: Year 5

B3: addition – large numbers and decimals using written methods; subtraction – large numbers and decimals using formal/informal methods

Summary

Y5 ⬡ **B3.6**

Basketball throws

Individuals, pairs or groups working independently

Year 5 Challenge Textbook page 62

Abacus Evolve objectives

- Subtract one decimal number from another, both with one or both with two decimal places, using informal and standard written methods

Framework objectives

- Use efficient written methods to add and subtract whole numbers and decimals with up to two places

Teacher notes

Getting started
Check that children understand the relationship between m and cm, and are clear about how to write all the children's throws as decimals.

Activity
Children work from Textbook page 62. They are shown the distances that eight children threw a basketball. They convert the distances into metres in a decimal format and find the difference between the eight children's throws. Emphasise the need for children to set their subtractions out appropriately in columns and encourage them to check their answers using the inverse operation (in this case, addition).

Be aware

- Some children can find column subtraction more difficult than column addition. Make sure they are using standard written methods correctly.
- Some children may prefer to use informal mental methods. This is fine but they should be encouraged to use the standard written method to check their answers.

Outcomes

- I can subtract decimals and show my workings.

Challenge Plan: Year 5

C3: classifying events by likelihood; drawing and interpreting line graphs; units of capacity; estimating, measuring and drawing angles in degrees

Summary

Y5 ☆ C3.1

Probability

Individuals, pairs or groups working independently

Year 5 Challenge Textbook page 63

Year 5 Challenge PCM 33

Dice; coins; blue counters, red counters, yellow counters, green counters; cloth bags

Abacus Evolve objectives

- Classify events based on degrees of likelihood
- Recognise the distinction between 'impossible', 'unlikely', 'likely' and 'certain'
- Draw and interpret frequency tables, pictograms and bar graphs

Framework objectives

- Describe the occurrence of familiar events using the language of chance or likelihood
- *Construct frequency tables, pictograms and bar and line graphs to represent the frequencies of events and changes over time*
- Plan and manage a group task over time by using different levels of planning

Teacher notes

Preparation
Photocopy PCM 33, one for each child.

Getting started
Give each child/pair/group one coin, two dice, a cloth bag, one blue counter, two red counters, three yellow counters and four green counters.

Activity
Children work from Textbook page 63. They carry out three experiments: throwing a coin three times; throwing two dice; and taking coloured counters from a bag. They use PCM 33 to complete tally charts of their results and then draw bar graphs to represent the data. They use their bar graphs to investigate the statements in the Textbook and draw accurate probability lines that reflect their own results.

If you have time
Discuss with children that experiments do not always prove theoretical probability. Ask children to consider why this might be.

Be aware

- Make sure that children realise that if they throw a coin three times and get the result HTH, this is different from the result HHT. Although they appear to be the same, the heads and tails occurred in a different order, which is significant.
- Children should be aware that theoretical probability and experimental probability do not always match.

Outcomes

- I can carry out probability experiments.
- I can use my findings to solve a problem.
- I can use probability words such as 'more likely', 'equally likely', 'certain', 'impossible'.
- I can draw frequency tables and bar graphs.

Challenge Plan: Year 5

C3: classifying events by likelihood; drawing and interpreting line graphs; units of capacity; estimating, measuring and drawing angles in degrees

Summary

Y5 C3.2

Weather

Individuals, pairs or groups working independently

Year 5 Challenge Textbook page 64

Abacus Evolve objectives

- **Y6** Recognise events that are equally likely
- **Y6** Predict the outcome of equally likely events
- **Y6** Introduce the probability scale of 0 to 1 on the number line
- **Y6** Understand percentage as the number of parts in every 100
- **Y6** Express simple fractions as percentages, and express one quantity as a percentage of another.

Framework objectives

- **Y6** Solve multi-step problems, and problems involving fractions, decimals and percentages; choose and use appropriate calculation strategies at each stage, including calculator use
- **Y6** Describe and predict outcomes from data using the language of chance or likelihood

Teacher notes

Activity
Children work from Textbook page 64. They read about traditional ways of predicting weather using patterns described in sayings and rhymes. They then read about how present-day weather forecasters use technology and statistics to prepare weather reports.

Children work with weather data and use probability vocabulary to interpret the information and write a weather forecast.

Further extension
Children could record a weather log over time and write their own weather report.

If you have time
Film the children presenting their weather forecasts.

Be aware

- Confirm with children that weather reports can never be completely certain, because they are based on predictions.

Outcomes

- I can use probability words to write a weather forecast.

Supporting resources

There are more traditional weather rhymes for children to explore, here:
- http://www.dgsgardening.btinternet.co.uk/folklore.htm
- http://www.metoffice.gov.uk/education/primary/index.html

If children would like to find data from their local weather station, they can do so here:
- http://www.metoffice.gov.uk/climate/uk/stationdata/index.html

More school resources from the Met Office can be found here:
- http://www.metoffice.gov.uk/education/primary/index.html

Challenge Plan: Year 5

Summary

Y5 ⬡ C3.3

The best deal

Individuals, pairs or groups working independently

Year 5 Challenge Textbook page 65

Year 5 Challenge PCM 34

Abacus Evolve objectives

- Draw and interpret a line graph

Framework objectives

- *Construct frequency tables, pictograms and bar and line graphs to represent the frequencies of events and changes over time*

Teacher notes

Preparation
Photocopy PCM 34, one for each child.

Getting started
Make sure that children are familiar with line graphs, and understand how to interpret them.

Activity
Children work from Textbook page 65. They interpret the line graph on PCM 34 to work out which of two mobile phone contracts gives the better deal. Children answer questions about the graph and write a report advising which option offers better value.

Extra help
Using different coloured pencils to mark certain points on the graph can help children highlight key information.

Further extension
Children could collect information about a range of mobile phone contract rates and compare them.

Be aware

- Children may not immediately think of plotting costs on a line graph, but straight line graphs are a good way of comparing value for money.

Outcomes

- I can interpret line graphs to solve a problem.

Challenge Plan: Year 5

C3: classifying events by likelihood; drawing and interpreting line graphs; units of capacity; estimating, measuring and drawing angles in degrees

Summary

Y5 ✦ **C3.4** **Luggage sizes**

Pairs or groups working independently

Year 5 Challenge Textbook page 66

Empty cosmetics/toiletry bottles of various sizes (optional)

Abacus Evolve objectives

- Use, read and write standard metric units of capacity: l, ml
- Know the equivalent of $\frac{1}{2}$, $\frac{1}{4}$, $\frac{3}{4}$, $\frac{1}{10}$, $\frac{1}{100}$ of 1 litre in ml
- Use, read and write standard metric units of weight: kg, g
- Know the equivalent of $\frac{1}{2}$, $\frac{1}{4}$, $\frac{3}{4}$, $\frac{1}{10}$, $\frac{1}{100}$ of 1 kg in g

Framework objectives

- Read, choose, use and record standard metric units to estimate and measure length, weight and capacity to a suitable degree of accuracy, e.g. the nearest centimetre; convert larger to smaller units using decimals to one place, e.g. change 2·6 kg to 2600 g
- Interpret a reading that lies between two unnumbered divisions on a scale

Teacher notes

Activity

Children work from Textbook page 66. They read about the luggage size and capacity limits of five airlines and decide which person is flying with which airline based on the dimensions and weight of their luggage. To do this, they will need to convert from mm to cm, and from g to kg. Children also consider restrictions on the amount of liquid that can be taken on board in hand luggage and, by converting from l and cl to ml, decide who will have to take some products out of their hand luggage before they can fly.

Extra help

Remind children that there are 10 ml in 1 cl and 100 cl in 1 l.
Children might find it helpful to compare a drinks can marked 33 cl with one marked 330 ml.

Further extension

Children could collect empty cosmetics/toiletry bottles and decide which combinations of products they would be able to take on a plane. They could also compare the different ways that the manufacturers choose to give the capacity and discuss any similarities and differences.

Information

1 l of water weighs 1 kg.

Be aware

- The word 'centilitres' is in common use and although children will not use it regularly, they should be able to use it confidently and not confuse it with millilitres or litres.

Outcomes

- I can solve problems using length and weight.
- I can choose and use the right units of measurement.

Challenge Plan: Year 5

C3: classifying events by likelihood; drawing and interpreting line graphs; units of capacity; estimating, measuring and drawing angles in degrees

Summary

Y5 ⬡ C3.5

New ways of measuring

A small group working with an adult

Year 5 Challenge PCMs 35 and 36

15 cm strips of card; sticky notes; kg weights (optional); balance (optional)

Abacus Evolve objectives

- **Y6** Record estimates and readings from capacity scales
- **Y6** Suggest suitable units and measuring equipment to estimate or measure capacity
- **Y6** Make and investigate a general statement about familiar numbers or shapes by finding examples that satisfy it

Framework objectives

- **Y6** Read and interpret scales on a range of measuring instruments, recognising that the measurement made is approximate and recording results to a required degree of accuracy; compare readings on different scales, e.g. when using different instruments
- **Y6** Represent and interpret sequences, patterns and relationships involving numbers and shapes; suggest and test hypotheses; construct and use simple expressions and formulae in words then symbols, e.g. the cost of c pens at 15 pence each is 15c pence

Teacher notes

Preparation
Photocopy and cut out the strips on PCM 35. Give a blank strip to each child and keep the numbered strips for yourself.

Getting started
The Golomb Ruler is a set of positive integers where no two pairs of numbers have the same difference. The integers used are called marks and the largest integer is the length of the ruler. Familiarise yourself with this.

Activity
- Give each child a strip of card with 1 cm intervals marked.
- *If we want to make a ruler and measure up to 6 cm, do we need to write all the numbers to 6 on it?*
- *Try making a ruler that goes up to 6 cm with only four numbers marked. No two pairs of numbers can have the same difference. You can use zero.*
- Children explore this by writing numbers on sticky notes to add to their 'ruler'.
- Discuss the suggestions and show the solution on your 0, 1, 4, 6 ruler. *This ruler shows us how long 1, 2, 3, 4, 5 and 6 cm are, even though we haven't written on all the numbers. 0 cm to 1 cm is 1 cm, 4 cm to 6 cm is 2 cm, 1 cm to 4 cm is 3 cm, 0 cm to 4 cm is 4 cm, 1 cm to 6 cm is 5 cm and 0 cm to 6 cm is 6 cm.*
- *Try again, but this time try to make a ruler that can measure as many distances up to 11 cm as possible.*
- Children experiment and discuss what they have found. Show the solutions on your 0, 1, 4, 9, 11 ruler (*but this one doesn't show us 6 cm*) and 0, 2, 7, 8, 11 ruler (*but this one doesn't show us 10 cm*). Ask children to demonstrate how they can show some of the lengths from 0 to 11 cm.
- Children then work from PCM 36. They explore a problem with weighing scales and missing weights. Children complete the table to show how to weigh objects from 1 kg to 13 kg using only one 1 kg weight, one 3 kg weight, and one other. Children can experiment with a real balance and weights if they find this helpful.

Be aware

- Ensure that children remember to include 0 when they are exploring numbers for their Golomb rulers.
- Children may assume that rulers must be fully graduated in order to measure lines.

Outcomes

- I can explore different ways of finding lengths and weights.
- I can look for a solution by trying out my ideas.

Supporting resources

Find out more about Golomb rulers here:
http://www.inference.phy.cam.ac.uk/cds/part16.htm

Challenge Plan: Year 5

C3: classifying events by likelihood; drawing and interpreting line graphs; units of capacity; estimating, measuring and drawing angles in degrees

Summary

Y5 ⬡ C3.6

Angles and degrees

 A small group working with an adult

📖 Year 5 Challenge Textbook page 67

✎ 30 cm pieces of string; rulers; A4 paper; 1 cm × 20 cm strips of paper

Abacus Evolve objectives

- Use a protractor to measure and draw acute and obtuse angles to the nearest 5 degrees
- Understand and use angle measure in degrees
- Estimate an angle in degrees

Framework objectives

- Estimate, draw and measure acute and obtuse angles using an angle measurer or protractor to a suitable degree of accuracy; calculate angles in a straight line
- Understand different ways to take the lead and support others in a group

Teacher notes

Getting started
Familarise yourself with the practical steps on Textbook page 67.

Activity
In this activity children explore angles and find ways to construct regular shapes without using a protractor.
- *Are there any angles around us that we know without measuring them with a protractor?* For example, the corners on books and boards are right angles.
- Refer children to Textbook page 67 and demonstrate how to make a right-angled triangle using a knotted piece of string. With a protractor prove that the angle is 90°. Children try this themselves.
- *We know that the angle in the corner of a piece of A4 paper is 90°. Can we use this piece of paper to measure another angle?* Fold the right angle in half. *This angle is 45°.* Unfold the paper and then fold the angle into thirds. *This angle is 30°.* Prove this with a protractor.
- Refer children to Textbook page 67. Children follow the instructions to use knotted string to make a right-angled triangle and knot a strip of paper to make a regular pentagon. They check the internal angles with a protractor to prove that it is a regular pentagon.
- Children then make an equilateral triangle by folding and cutting a piece of A4 paper. They predict what the internal angles of the triangle will be and check them with a protractor.

If you have time
Children could look on the internet at the web links below and try making other shapes and angles.

Be aware

- By knowing what a right angle looks like, children should be able to estimate any angle to within 10°.

Outcomes

- I can make and check angles and use them to measure other angles.
- I can measure and draw angles.

Related activities and resources

Children can explore other novel ways to make angles here:
- http://www.cyffredin.co.uk/Magic%20A%20PaPER/Folding%20Shapes%20from%20A%20Paper.htm
- http://www.ics.uci.edu/~eppstein/junkyard/knot.html

Challenge Plan: Year 5

D3: degrees and right angles; acute, obtuse and reflex angles; HTU ÷ U using informal written methods; HTU ÷ U using standard written methods

Summary

Y5 ☆ D3.1

The Shipping Forecast

Individuals, pairs or groups working independently

Year 5 Challenge Textbook page 68

Year 5 Challenge PCMs 37 and 38

Recording of the Shipping Forecast (optional)

Abacus Evolve objectives

- Rehearse the relationship between degrees and right angles
- Make and investigate a general statement about familiar numbers or shapes by finding examples that satisfy it

Framework objectives

- Estimate, draw and measure acute and obtuse angles using an angle measurer or protractor to a suitable degree of accuracy; calculate angles in a straight line
- Plan and pursue an enquiry; present evidence by collecting, organising and interpreting information; suggest extensions to the enquiry

Teacher notes

Preparation
If possible prepare a recording of the Shipping Forecast for children to listen to before starting the activity. Photocopy PCMs 37 and 38, one of each for each child.

Getting started
Make sure children are happy using eight points of the compass and clockwise and anticlockwise directions.

Activity
Children work from Textbook page 68. This activity explores the Shipping Forecast, wind direction and wind speed. Children use the Shipping Forecast to calculate angles of movement and changes in wind direction based on the eight points of the compass. They also interpret whether the movement is clockwise or anticlockwise.

Be aware

- Check that children are aware that angles of movement can be anticlockwise as well as clockwise.

Outcomes

- I can calculate how many degrees there are between points of a compass.

Supporting resources

Children can read the day's Shipping Forecast here:
- http://www.bbc.co.uk/weather/coast/shipping/
- http://www.metoffice.gov.uk/weather/marine/shipping_forecast.html

Children can use this site to find out more about the Beaufort scale of wind speed:
- http://www.bbc.co.uk/weather/features/understanding/beaufort_scale.shtml

Challenge Plan: Year 5

D3: degrees and right angles; acute, obtuse and reflex angles; HTU ÷ U using informal written methods; HTU ÷ U using standard written methods

Summary

Y5 ◇ D3.2

Interior angles

Individuals, pairs or groups working independently

Year 5 Challenge Textbook page 69

Protractors (optional); mats (optional)

Abacus Evolve objectives

- Identify, estimate and order acute, obtuse and reflex angles
- Recognise acute and obtuse angles in polygons

Framework objectives

- Estimate, draw and measure acute and obtuse angles using an angle measurer or protractor to a suitable degree of accuracy; calculate angles in a straight line

Teacher notes

Getting started
Remind children of the properties of an equilateral triangle – all sides and angles are equal and each internal angle is 60°.

Activity
Children work from Textbook page 69. They are shown seven different polygons, each made up of equilateral triangles. All of the interior angles of these shapes are multiples of 60°.

Children identify the acute, obtuse and reflex angles, then calculate the total interior angles of each shape.

Extra help
A protractor will help confirm actual size of angles if children are unsure, but they should be encouraged to calculate the answers mentally using their knowledge of the properties of equilateral triangles.

Further extension
The exterior angles of any regular polygon always total 360°. Lay out mats on the floor in polygon shapes and ask children to walk around them to prove this.

Information
Exterior angles are found by extending each side of a polygon and measuring the angle made, for example

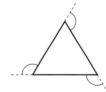

Be aware

- Check that children understand the correct way to measure an external angle.

Outcomes

- I can recognise acute, obtuse and reflex angles.
- I can calculate the total of the internal angles of a polygon.

Challenge Plan: Year 5

D3: degrees and right angles; acute, obtuse and reflex angles; HTU ÷ U using informal written methods; HTU ÷ U using standard written methods

Summary

Y5 ⭐ D3.3

Looking at triangles

A small group working with an adult

Year 5 Challenge Textbook page 70

Year 5 Challenge PCM 39

Protractors; rulers

Abacus Evolve objectives

- **Y6** Consolidate the estimation of an angle in degrees
- **Y6** Recognise that the sum of the angles of a triangle is 180 degrees
- **Y6** Calculate angles in a triangle

Framework objectives

- **Y6** Estimate angles, and use a protractor to measure and draw them, on their own and in shapes; calculate angles in a triangle or around a point

Teacher notes

Preparation
Photocopy PCM 39, three copies for each child, pair or group, and three for yourself. Cut out the triangles so that children have 18 triangles each.

Activity
Children work from Textbook page 70. Ask children to describe the properties of each shape, comparing sides and angles, and thinking about the total of the internal angles. (Children should use their knowledge of the properties of triangles, rather than measuring with rulers and protractors.) *Do you know the size of any of the angles without measuring? How do you know you are correct?* Ask children to estimate the size of the angles in each triangle and write them down. *What is the total of the three angles in each triangle?*

Discuss with children how many degrees there are along a straight line (180°). Demonstrate this using a protractor. Lay the three copies of triangle P along a ruler with the three different corners together. Confirm with children that when angles a, b and c are together it makes a straight line. *What will happen when we do this with the other triangles? How close were your estimates?* Discuss that for each triangle the angles make a straight line of 180°, showing that the internal angles of the triangle total 180°.

What shapes do you make by fitting the triangles together? What are the names of the shapes? What is different about each shape? What is the size of the other internal angles in each shape?

Further extension
Children can match the sides of two identical triangles to make these quadrilaterals:
parallelogram rhombus rectangle square kite arrowhead
How do you know these shapes are correct?
Children then use three identical triangles to make trapezia with different properties and discuss why each one is different.

If you have time
Discuss the interior angles of quadrilaterals (they total 360°).

Information
Trapezia have one set of parallel sides and can look very different, for example

Be aware

- Ensure that children do not confuse the names and properties of different quadrilaterals.

Outcomes

- I know that the interior angles of any triangle total 180°.
- I can describe the properties of quadrilaterals such as a rhombus and a trapezium.

Challenge Plan: Year 5

D3: degrees and right angles; acute, obtuse and reflex angles; HTU ÷ U using informal written methods; HTU ÷ U using standard written methods

Summary

Y5 ⭐ D3.4

How many are there?

Individuals, pairs or groups working independently

Year 5 Challenge Textbook page 71

Abacus Evolve objectives

- Rehearse dividing TU ÷ U using informal written methods
- Divide HTU ÷ U using informal written methods (with integer remainder)
- Know by heart all multiplication facts up to 10 × 10

Framework objectives

- Refine and use efficient written methods to multiply and divide HTU × U, TU × TU, U·t × U and HTU ÷ U
- Recall quickly multiplication facts up to 10 × 10 and use them to multiply pairs of multiples of 10 and 100; derive quickly corresponding division facts
- Solve one-step and two-step problems involving whole numbers and decimals and all four operations, choosing and using appropriate calculation strategies, including calculator use
- Understand the process of decision making

Teacher notes

Getting started
Check that children are confident in writing out extended multiplication tables and patterns before they begin the activity.

Activity
Children work from Textbook page 71. They are given a word problem and an example of how to use multiplication facts to solve it. Children then solve five similar problems themselves.

These problems can all be solved by recalling multiplication facts and adding remainders to them. Some questions have more than one possible answer.

If you have time
Give children this Chinese puzzle:
An old lady breaks her eggs on the way to market. Her insurance company wants to know how many she had. She doesn't know the number but she knows that if she put them in groups of 2, 3, 4, 5 or 6 there was always one left over but there were none left over if they were in groups of 7. What is the smallest number of eggs she could have had?

Information
The answers to these problems are all based on common multiples.

Be aware

- Make sure children are aware that there could be more than one answer and do not stop as soon as they have reached the first solution.

Outcomes

- I can use my knowledge of multiples to solve word problems.

Challenge Plan: Year 5

D3: degrees and right angles; acute, obtuse and reflex angles; HTU ÷ U using informal written methods; HTU ÷ U using standard written methods

Summary

Y5 ⭐ D3.5

Using digit roots

A small group working with an adult

Year 5 Challenge PCMs 40 and 41

Calculators

Abacus Evolve objectives

- Understand the effect of and relationships between the four operations (multiplication and division)
- Rehearse dividing TU ÷ U using informal written methods
- Divide HTU ÷ U using informal written methods (with integer remainder)

Framework objectives

- Use knowledge of rounding, place value, number facts and inverse operations to estimate and check calculations

Teacher notes

Preparation
Copy PCM 40 and PCM 41, one copy for each child. Do not hand out PCM 41 until children have completed PCM 40.

Activity
The activity explores using digit roots to make a Vedic square. This arrangement of digital roots has interesting properties and will produce symmetrical patterns.

Show children PCM 40. *Do you know what number will go into the first blank white square? How do you know?* Encourage children to use multiplication to fill in as many blank white squares as they can.

What number goes here? (Point to the grey square below 19.) *How do you know?* Encourage children to use division to fill in the grey squares. *Has this helped us fill in any more squares?* Children complete the grid.

Children then work out the digital roots of each answer and complete the second blank grid. Children join up each 7 on the grid to make a Vedic square.

Children then join other numbers to complete six more Vedic squares on PCM 41.

Extra help
A digital root is found by adding the digits in a number until you reach a single digit from 1 to 9.
For example 1234
$1 + 2 + 3 + 4 = 10$
$1 + 0 = 1$
The digital root of 1234 is 1.

Further extension
Children could explore the patterns used in Moorish tiling.

Be aware

- This activity may need to be extended over more than one lesson so that children have the opportunity to complete it.

Outcomes

- I can use multiplication and division to complete a multiplication square.
- I can work out digital roots and use them to create patterns.

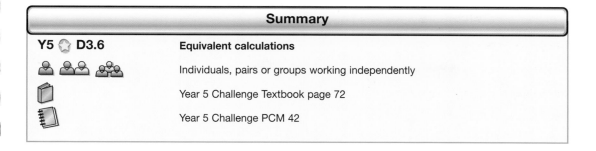

Challenge Plan: Year 5

D3: degrees and right angles; acute, obtuse and reflex angles; HTU ÷ U using informal written methods; HTU ÷ U using standard written methods

Summary

Y5 ⬠ D3.6

Equivalent calculations

Individuals, pairs or groups working independently

Year 5 Challenge Textbook page 72

Year 5 Challenge PCM 42

Abacus Evolve objectives

- **Y6** Rehearse dividing HTU ÷ U using standard written methods (mixed number answer)
- **Y6** Divide HTU ÷ TU using standard written methods (whole number answer)
- **Y6** Divide TU·t ÷ U using standard written methods
- **Y6** Divide TU·th ÷ U using standard written methods

Framework objectives

- **Y6** *Use efficient written methods to add and subtract integers and decimals, to multiply and divide integers and decimals by a one-digit integer, and to multiply two-digit and three-digit integers by a two-digit integer*

Teacher notes

Preparation
Photocopy PCM 42, one for each child. Cut out the cards.

Getting started
Make sure children are confident in doubling and halving, multiplying and dividing by 10 and dividing by numbers less than 6.

Activity
Children work from Textbook page 72. They follow the instructions to play the matching game using the cards on PCM 42. Children work together to solve the calculations and sort them into groups with equivalent answers.

Further extension
Children can write multiplication calculations based on the division calculations on PCM 42.
For example 67 ÷ 0·2 = 335 can be rewritten as 335 × 0·2 = 67.

Be aware

- Ensure that children are adjusting numbers to solve the calculations and understanding why this makes them easier to answer.

Outcomes

- I know that calculations can be adjusted to make them easier.

Challenge Plan: Year 5

E3: fractions and decimals; percentages of whole numbers; square numbers to at least 10 × 10; pairs of factors of numbers up to 100

Summary

Y5 ✦ E3.1

Fractions to decimals

Individuals, pairs or groups working independently

Year 5 Challenge Textbook page 73

Year 5 Challenge PCM 43 (optional)

Calculators

Abacus Evolve objectives

- Recognise equivalence between fractions and decimals

Framework objectives

- Express a smaller whole number as a fraction of a larger one, (e.g. recognise that 5 out of 8 is $\frac{5}{8}$); find equivalent fractions, (e.g. $\frac{7}{10} = \frac{14}{20}$, or $\frac{19}{10} = 1\frac{9}{10}$); relate fractions to their decimal representations

Teacher notes

Getting started
Show Textbook page 73. Check that children are comfortable using the method of finding decimal equivalents of fractions (divide the numerator by the denominator, using a calculator where necessary). Ask them to give the decimal equivalents of a few simple fractions such as $\frac{1}{2}$ (0·5) and $\frac{3}{4}$ (0·75). Also ensure that children understand how and why to round long decimal numbers to three decimal places.

Activity
Children work from Textbook page 73. They find the decimal equivalents of fractions by dividing the numerator by the denominator. Children should use a calculator for this activity. They then use this method to compare pairs of fractions, and then to arrange sets of three fractions from smallest to largest.

Extra help
If children find it hard to make comparisons between the decimals, they can arrange them on the 0–1 number line marked in tenths and hundredths, on PCM 43.

Information
Changing fractions to decimals to compare is a useful way of dealing with fractions that have awkward denominators; to compare ninths and sevenths using the idea of lowest common denominator would require changing fractions to sixty thirds.

Be aware

- Children may not be sure how to work with fractions that produce recurring decimals, such as sixths and ninths. Reassure children that these can also be rounded to three decimal places.

Outcomes

- I can use a calculator to find decimal equivalents of fractions.
- I can compare different fractions by changing them to decimals.

Supporting resources

Children can find more information about fractions and decimals here:
- http://www.bbc.co.uk/skillswise/numbers/fractiondecimalpercentage/comparing/fractionsdecimals/factsheet.shtml

Challenge Plan: Year 5

E3: fractions and decimals; percentages of whole numbers; square numbers to at least 10 × 10; pairs of factors of numbers up to 100

Summary

Y5 ☆ E3.2

Fruity percentages

Individuals, pairs or groups working independently

Year 5 Challenge Textbook page 74

Fruit juice bottles and cartons (optional)

Abacus Evolve objectives

- Begin to understand percentage as the number of parts in every 100
- Begin to express simple fractions as percentages
- Begin to find simple percentages of small whole-number quantities

Framework objectives

- Understand percentage as the number of parts in every 100 and express tenths and hundredths as percentages
- Find fractions using division (e.g. $\frac{1}{100}$ of 5 kg), and percentages of numbers and quantities (e.g. 10%, 5% and 15% of £80)

Teacher notes

Preparation
If possible, provide some fruit juice bottles and cartons to set the context of the activity.

Getting started
Run through the method of finding trickier percentages by using known percentages. For example 12% can be found by finding 10% and 1% of the amount and adding to find 12%. Encourage children to use this method for the activity.

Activity
Children work from Textbook page 74. Children find the percentage of real fruit in different sized bottles and containers of four products.

Information
Some children may also be familiar with using decimals to find percentage amounts, for example to find 12% of 700 ml multiply 700 by 0·12. Suggest that they use known percentages to find the answer and then check it using the decimal method.

Be aware

- Some capacities are given in millilitres and some in litres. Remind children that it will be easiest to convert all the capacities to millilitres in order to find each percentage. Make sure children know how many millilitres are in a litre.

Outcomes

- I can understand percentages.
- I can use known percentages to find percentages of whole number quantities.

Supporting resources

Children can read more about the misleading labelling of food here:
- http://news.bbc.co.uk/1/hi/health/7258826.stm

Challenge Plan: Year 5

E3: fractions and decimals; percentages of whole numbers; square numbers to at least 10 × 10; pairs of factors of numbers up to 100

Summary

Y5 ⭐ E3.3

Ratio and proportion

A small group working with an adult

Year 5 Challenge Textbook page 75

Interlocking cubes, red and blue

Abacus Evolve objectives

- **Y6** Understand the meaning of ratio and relate this to proportion
- **Y6** Solve simple problems involving ratio and proportion

Framework objectives

- **Y6** Solve simple problems involving direct proportion by scaling quantities up or down

Teacher notes

Preparation
Provide each child with 20 interlocking cubes (ten red, ten blue).

Getting started
Throughout the activity ask children to make the cube models that you are making.
Show a stick of five interlocking cubes: three red cubes and two blue cubes.
Ratio and proportion are both used for comparison, but they are different.
***Proportion** is comparison with a whole amount. Here the proportion of cubes that are red is 3 out of 5. This is very similar to saying what fraction of the cubes is red. What proportion of cubes is blue?* (2 out of 5)
***Ratio** is comparing the amounts that make up a whole. Here the ratio of red cubes to blue cubes is 3 : 2. What is the ratio of blue cubes to red cubes?* (2 : 3) *Draw attention to the colon that is always used with a ratio.*

Imagine that there are ten cubes: six are red, four are blue. What is the proportion of each colour? (red: 6 out of 10; blue: 4 out of 10)
Now imagine that there are ten cubes with the same ratio of red cubes to blue cubes. How many red cubes would you have? (five) *How many blue cubes?* (five) *What if there were 20 cubes?* (ten red cubes, ten blue cubes) *100 cubes?* (50 red cubes, 50 blue cubes)

Proportions and ratios can be simplified like fractions, by dividing the numerator and denominator by a common factor. So a ratio of 6 : 4 can be written as 3 : 2 and a proportion of 8 out of 10 can be simplified to 4 out of 5.

Look at the first pattern of squares on Textbook page 75. *How many squares are there altogether? How many squares are shaded?* (six) *How many are unshaded?* (six) *What proportion of the squares is shaded?* (6 out of 12) *Unshaded?* (6 out of 12) *What is the ratio of shaded to unshaded squares?* (6 : 6) *Can these be simplified?* (1 out of 2 and 1 : 1) *What would happen to the proportion and ratio of shaded and unshaded squares if the total number of squares was doubled?* (It would stay the same.)

Activity
Children work from Textbook page 75. They continue to find the proportion and ratio of shaded and unshaded squares in patterns. Encourage children to work together on questions 7–12, finding different amounts of squares with various ratios. Ask children to explain their answers to the group.

Information
Proportions and ratios are used when the whole quantity may change but relative amounts stay the same. A good example is changing quantities in a recipe for more or less people by scaling up or down accordingly.

Be aware

- The phrase 'in every' can be used with proportion and 'for every' with ratio. However they can seem very abstract so it is important that children use cubes to demonstrate what is meant.

Outcomes

- I understand the difference between ratio and proportion.
- I can solve problems with ratios and proportions.

Challenge Plan: Year 5

E3: fractions and decimals; percentages of whole numbers; square numbers to at least 10 × 10; pairs of factors of numbers up to 100

Summary

Y5 ✪ E3.4

Square numbers

Individuals, pairs or groups working independently

Year 5 Challenge Textbook page 76

Squared paper (optional)

Abacus Evolve objectives

- Know squares of numbers to at least 10 × 10
- Recognise and explain patterns and relationships, generalise and predict

Framework objectives

- Identify pairs of factors of two-digit whole numbers and find common multiples (e.g. for 6 and 9)
- Explore patterns, properties and relationships and propose a general statement involving numbers or shapes; identify examples for which the statement is true or false

Teacher notes

Getting started

Make sure children understand and know how to use the terms 'difference', 'consecutive' and 'successive'.

Activity

Children work from Textbook page 76. They investigate patterns in the differences between successive square numbers. Children can draw the squares on squared paper if this will help with their investigation. Children should notice that the difference between successive square numbers is the sequence of odd numbers, 3, 5, 7, … 19. This pattern continues beyond 10 × 10 and can be used to generate further square numbers.

Extra help

If children are struggling to explain the pattern, ask them to look at the diagram.
Children should be able to see clearly how many squares are added on to create each new square number. *Count the number of squares that are added on each time, and tell me what you notice.* (To make the next square number, two more squares must be added, than were added the time before.)

Further extension

Explain why square numbers are always alternately odd and even. (An odd number is always added to a square number to create the next square number. Odd + Odd = Even and Even + Odd = Odd.)

Be aware

- Not all children will be familiar with the use of ^{2} to indicate a squared number. Make sure that they understand it and are using it correctly.

Outcomes

- I know the square numbers up to at least 10 × 10.
- I can find a pattern and explain it.

Challenge Plan: Year 5

E3: fractions and decimals; percentages of whole numbers; square numbers to at least 10 × 10; pairs of factors of numbers up to 100

Summary

Y5 ⬡ E3.5

Find the factor

Pairs working independently

Year 5 Challenge PCMs 44 and 45

Counters in two colours; sharp pencils; paper clips; calculators (optional)

Abacus Evolve objectives

- Find all the pairs of factors of any number up to 100

Framework objectives

- Identify pairs of factors of two-digit whole numbers and find common multiples (e.g. for 6 and 9)
- Plan and manage a group task over time by using different levels of planning

Teacher notes

Preparation
Photocopy PCM 44 and PCM 45, one copy of each per pair.

Getting started
Run through the rules of the game with the children.

Activity
Children play the game on PCM 44. They make a spinner using PCM 45, a pencil and a paper clip. Players take turns to use the spinner to generate a random number. They identify a number on the game board with that number as a factor and cover it with a counter. The winner is the first person to get a continuous line of four counters horizontally, vertically or diagonally.

After playing the game children should discuss which were the best numbers to get with the spinner and why these were better. (Smaller numbers are better as they are factors of more numbers.) Children can also discuss if there were any numbers on the game board that it was impossible to cover and why that might have been. (Some are prime numbers that only have themselves and 1 as factors.)

Extra help
Children may have a calculator to check, using division, if a number is a factor of another number.

Further extension
Extend the game by letting each child spin the spinner twice and find a number that has both of the numbers as factors.

Be aware

- Ensure that children are familiar with the definition of a prime number. They will encounter some on the game board.

Outcomes

- I can find the factors of 2-digit numbers.

Supporting resources

Children can find more information about factors here:
- http://www.bbc.co.uk/skillswise/numbers/wholenumbers/whatarenumbers/multiplesandfactors/index.shtml

Challenge Plan: Year 5

E3: fractions and decimals; percentages of whole numbers; square numbers to at least 10 × 10; pairs of factors of numbers up to 100

Summary

Y5 ⭐ **E3.6**   **Factors and prime numbers**

A small group working with an adult

Year 5 Challenge Textbook page 77

Year 5 Challenge PCM 46

Abacus Evolve objectives

- **Y6** Recognise prime numbers up to at least 20
- **Y6** Understand a prime number as one that has exactly two factors

Framework objectives

- **Y6** Recognise that prime numbers have only two factors and identify prime numbers less than 100; find the prime factors of two-digit numbers

Teacher notes

Preparation
Photocopy PCM 46, one copy per child.

Getting started
Ensure that children are familiar with the vocabulary of number patterns, such as factor and prime number.
What numbers are factors of 15? (1, 3, 5, 15)
What numbers are factors of 30? (1, 2, 3, 5, 6, 10, 15, 30)
How can we check?
Look together at the example on Textbook page 77. *Factors come in pairs. We can check the factors by multiplying pairs of factors together.* Read Melanie's statement and discuss it with the children. *We can try out some more examples to see if Melanie is right.*

Activity
Children work from Textbook page 77. They explore Melanie's statement that if you double any number then that number will always have twice as many factors as the original number. Children check this by working on three further examples. (Children will find that Melanie is incorrect and her statement only applies to 25 and 50.)

A prime number is a number that has only one pair of factors (itself and 1). Tell me some numbers that are prime numbers. Children then return to Textbook page 77 and use what they have just discussed to explain why 2 is the only even prime number and why 1 is not a prime number.

Children can then explore Bernie's statement that all numbers ending in 7 are prime numbers. (27, 57, 77 and 87 are not prime numbers, so Bernie's statement is not true.)

Children then use the 1–100 square on PCM 46 to find all the prime numbers between 1 and 100. Start by discussing numbers which are definitely not prime (for example all even numbers except 2, all multiples of 5). Children cross these off. They then work together to cross off all multiples of 3, 4, 6 and so on. Children will be left with 25 prime numbers. (2, 3, 5, 7, 11, 13, 17, 19, 23, 29, 31, 37, 41, 43, 47, 53, 59, 61, 67, 71, 73, 79, 83, 89, 97)

Be aware

- Many children may think that 1 is a prime number. Help them to disregard this idea by reminding them that factors come in pairs and letting them identify pairs of factors of prime numbers.

Outcomes

- I can find pairs of factors for any number up to 100.
- I can find all the prime numbers between 1 and 100.

Supporting resources

Read more about this method of finding prime numbers here:
- http://www.teachingideas.co.uk/maths/prime.htm
There are some great prime number games here:
- http://www.murderousmaths.co.uk/games/primcal.htm

Factors and prime numbers

Assessment Foci: L4/5 Using and applying mathematics (Problem solving; Communicating; Reasoning); L5 Number (Numbers and the number system)

Resources: PCMs A–D; coloured pencils

Lesson 1 – preparation – 1 hour

Part 1 – introduction – 20 minutes

As a group or in pairs, children list the factors of 12, 18, 29, 25, 31, 36 and 51. They discuss the number of factors for each. If needed, prompt children's discussion using questions such as:

- *Why do factors of a number occur in pairs?* (Factors can always be multiplied by another factor.)
- *Which ones have an odd/even number of factors?* (Square numbers have an odd number of factors because one factor is repeated.)
- *Which ones have the smallest number of factors?* (Prime numbers have just two factors.)

Part 2 – development – 30 minutes

Bring the group back together for a five-minute discussion comparing their work so far. Make sure the discussion includes the numbers with only two factors. Explain to children that these are called *prime numbers*.

Children work individually from PCM A. They learn about 'factor record-breakers', and find all the record-breakers up to 45.

Children work individually from PCM B. They colour the numbers on the grid in different colours according to the number of factors. Encourage them to discuss any patterns that they notice.

Part 3 – plenary – 10 minutes

At the end of the lesson, bring the group back together for a short plenary. Look at PCM B. Point out that the prime numbers are predominantly in the first and fifth column. *Why is this?*

If you want to give children work to continue at home, they could continue searching for factor record-breakers beyond 45, or they could extend the 'unusual number grid' up to 200.

You could also give children PCM C to give them a head-start on choosing which of the two options they would like to investigate.

Lesson 2 – investigation – 1 hour

Part 1 – introduction – 10 minutes

Give each child a copy of PCM C. They each choose an investigation. (Option A is harder than option B.) They write down their reasons for choosing that option, and brief initial ideas and conjectures about the investigation. Encourage them to plan how they will record their work.

Part 2 – investigation – 30 minutes

Children work individually to develop their lines of investigation, recording their journey and any findings.

If some children need prompting, you could ask questions such as this:

A) Abundant and deficient numbers
- *Can you see any links to the factor record-breakers?*
- *What do you notice about the deficient numbers you have found so far?*
- *Are all multiples of 10 from 20 onwards abundant? Can you say why?*

B) Goldbach's theories
- *Which prime numbers were used more than others in the sums?*
- *Which was the least used? Are any prime numbers never used?*
- *Why doesn't the rule work for numbers less than 6?*

Children who successfully exhaust their chosen option before the end of the session can move on to attempt option C.

C) Coprimes are pairs of numbers that do not have any common factors other than 1. 15 and 28 are coprime because the factors of 15 (1, 3, 5, 15) and the factors of 28 (1, 2, 4, 7, 14, 28) do not have a common factor except for 1. Are 45 and 28 coprime? Investigate how many other pairs you can find and if any patterns occur.

Part 3 – conclusions – 20 minutes

Children write a final report of their investigation, showing their journey and findings along the way, with any conclusions or fresh ideas.

Ask children to complete the self-assessment sheet on PCM D.

Factors and prime numbers

Objectives

These are the objectives that could be met by children doing this Assessment Activity.

Strand	Abacus Evolve objectives	Framework objectives
Using and applying mathematics	**Y5** Make and investigate a general statement about familiar numbers or shapes by finding examples that satisfy it **Y5** Explain a generalised relationship (formula) in words **Y5** Recognise and explain patterns and relationships, generalise and predict	**Y5** Represent a problem by identifying and recording the calculations needed to solve it; find possible solutions and confirm them in the context of the problem **Y5** Plan and pursue an enquiry; present evidence by collecting, organising and interpreting information; suggest extensions to the enquiry **Y5** Explore patterns, properties and relationships and propose a general statement involving numbers or shapes; identify examples for which the statement is true or false **Y5** Explain reasoning using diagrams, graphs and text; refine ways of recording using images and symbols
Knowing and using number facts	**Y5** Know and apply tests of divisibility by 2, 4, 5, 10 and 100 **Y5** Know squares of numbers to at least 10 × 10 **Y5** Find all the pairs of factors of any number up to 100 **Y6** Consolidate finding all the pairs of factors of any number up to 100 **Y6** Recognise that a number with an odd number of factors is a square number **Y6** Recognise prime numbers up to at least 20 **Y6** Understand a prime number as one that has exactly two factors **Y6** Factorise numbers up to 100 into prime factors **Y6** Know and apply tests of divisibility by 3, 6 and 9 **Y6** Know and apply tests of divisibility by 8 and 25	**Y5** Identify pairs of factors of 2-digit whole numbers and find common multiples, e.g. for 6 and 9 **Y6** Recognise that prime numbers have only two factors and identify prime numbers less than 100; find the prime factors of 2-digit numbers **Y6** Use approximations, inverse operations and tests of divisibility to estimate and check results

Factors and prime numbers

Note: these answers are not exhaustive.

Preparation

Part 1 – introduction

- 12 has six factors
- 18 has six factors
- 29 has two factors (prime number)
- 25 has three factors (square number)
- 31 has two factors (prime number)
- 36 has nine factors (square number)
- 51 has four factors

Part 2 – development

PCM A: the 'factor record-breakers' up to 100 are:

- 2 (two factors)
- 4 (three factors)
- 6 (four factors)
- 12 (six factors)
- 16 (five factors)
- 24 (eight factors)
- 36 (nine factors)
- 48 (10 factors)
- 60 (12 factors)

Apart from 2 and 4, all the record-breakers are either multiples of 6 or square numbers.

Part 3 – plenary

PCM B: the prime numbers appear in columns 1 and 5 because prime numbers are odd – except for 2 – so they won't appear in columns 2, 4 or 6; the numbers in column 3 are all multiples of 3, so they can't be prime.

Investigations

A) Abundant and deficient numbers

The first 22 **abundant** numbers are: 12, 18, 20, 24, 30, 36, 40, 42, 48, 54, 56, 60, 66, 70, 72, 78, 80, 84, 88, 90, 96, 100.

- Abundant numbers are nearly always even. The first odd abundant number is 945.
- All multiples of perfect numbers are abundant. This means that multiples of 6 are abundant. Children might spot a link between this and the factor record-breakers, most of which are multiples of 6.
- All multiples of abundant numbers are abundant. This means that all multiples of 12 are abundant, all multiples of 18, all multiples of 20, etc.

The first 20 **deficient** numbers are: 1, 2, 3, 4, 5, 7, 8, 9, 10, 11, 13, 14, 15, 16, 17, 19, 21, 22, 23, 25.

- All prime numbers are deficient.
- All prime powers are deficient. A prime power is a positive integer power of a prime number. For example: 4, 8, 9, 16, 25, 27 and 32. $(4 = 2^2, 8 = 2^3, 9 = 3^2, 16 = 2^4, 25 = 5^2, 27 = 3^3, 32 = 2^5)$
- All divisors of deficient or perfect numbers are deficient. For example, 28 is a perfect number. Its divisors are 2, 4, 7 and 14. These four numbers are all deficient.

The first three **perfect** numbers are: 6, 28 and 496.

B) Goldbach's conjectures

Goldbach's conjecture about even numbers greater than 4 has never been formally proven. The difficulty comes because primes are defined in terms of divisibility, and the conjecture is about addition. So far, the has been shown to be true for even numbers up to 300 000 000 000 000 000.

Children should be able to show that the conjecture is true for a significant quantity of even numbers.

One conclusion they may draw is that If a number divided by 2 gives a prime number, then the number can be made by adding that prime number to itself.

Year 5 Spring Assessment Activity

Magic squares

Assessment Foci: L4/5 Using and applying mathematics (Problem solving; Communicating; Reasoning)

Resources: PCMs E–H and D; sheets of 3 by 3 squares; digit cards 0–8

Lesson 1 – preparation – 1 hour

Part 1 – introduction – 30 minutes

As a group, children look at the semi-magic square on PCM E. They discuss its properties and describe them in the notes box.

In pairs, children try to make another square that uses the same nine numbers and has the same properties. They could use digit cards 0–8 to make it easy to try different options.

Bring the group back together for a 5-minute discussion of what they have done so far. They should look at the different semi-magic squares they have found. *Are any the same but rotated, or the same but reflected?*

Children then work individually from PCM F. They choose one of their semi-magic squares and explore its rotations and reflections.

Part 2 – development – 20 minutes

Look at PCM G with the group. Give children time to think about what the rule might be for transforming the semi-magic square. (The rule is '× 2 then + 1'.) The new square is still semi-magic, but the total is 27 instead of 12.

Children then work individually to transform one of their own semi-magic squares using their own rule. They make a copy of their transformed square, leaving out five of the nine numbers, but in such a way that the missing numbers can be deduced. They pass this copy to another child in the group. Children then try to find the missing numbers in each other's squares, and find the rule used to transform the original squares.

Part 3 – plenary – 10 minutes

Bring the group back together. Ask children to look at all the semi-magic squares that have been produced in the lesson, focusing on the diagonal totals. xplain that these squares are semi-magic because the two main diagonals do total the same as the rows and columns. In a truly magic square, each row, column, and the two main diagonals add up to the same number.

Lesson 2 – investigation – 1 hour

Part 1 – introduction – 10 minutes

Remind the group about the rules for magic and semi-magic squares. Give each child a copy of PCM H. They each choose either option A or option B. They write down their reasons for choosing that option, and brief initial ideas and conjectures about the investigation. Encourage them to plan how they will record their work.

Part 2 – investigation – 35 minutes

Children work individually to develop their lines of investigation, recording their journey and any findings.

Children who successfully exhaust their chosen option before the end of the session can move on to option C on PCM H.

Highly gifted children could investigate option D:

D) Children try to create 3 by 3 semi-magic or magic squares using only prime numbers. You may wish to give children a list of the first 15 prime numbers: 2, 3, 5, 7, 11, 13, 17, 19, 23, 29, 31, 37, 41, 43, 47.

Part 3 – conclusions – 15 minutes

Children write a final report of their investigation, showing their journey and findings along the way, with any conclusions or fresh ideas.

Ask children to complete the self-assessment sheet on PCM D.

Magic squares

ese are the objectives that could be met by children doing this Assessment Activity.

Strand	Abacus Evolve objectives	Framework objectives
Using and applying mathematics	**Y5** Recognise and explain patterns and relationships, generalise and predict	**Y5** Solve one- and two-step problems involving whole numbers and decimals and all four operations, choosing and using appropriate calculation strategies, including calculator use
		Y5 Represent a problem by identifying and recording the calculations needed to solve it; find possible solutions and confirm them in the context of the problem
		Y5 Plan and pursue an enquiry; present evidence by collecting, organising and interpreting information; suggest extensions to the enquiry
		Y5 Explore patterns, properties and relationships and propose a general statement involving numbers or shapes; identify examples for which the statement is true or false
		Y5 Explain reasoning using diagrams, graphs and text; refine ways of recording using images and symbols
Knowing and using number facts	**Y5** Check the sum of several numbers by adding in reverse order	**Y5** Use knowledge of rounding, place value, number facts and inverse operations to estimate and check calculations
Calculating	**Y5** Continue to add several 1-digit numbers **Y5** Use known number facts and place value for mental addition and subtraction	**Y5** Use efficient written methods to add and subtract whole numbers and decimals with up to two places

Year 5 Spring Assessment Activity

Magic squares

Answers – investigations

Note: these answers are not exhaustive.

A) Creating magic squares

Consecutive numbers

2	7	6
9	5	1
4	3	8

Magic total: 15

Three sets of numbers

3	14	10
16	9	2
8	4	15

Magic total: 27

Consecutive multiples

12	32	28
40	24	8
20	16	36

Magic total: 72

Evenly spaced numbers

9	29	25
37	21	5
17	13	33

Magic total: 63

General rule

$n-3$	$n+2$	$n+1$
$n+4$	n	$n-4$
$n-1$	$n-2$	$n+3$

Magic total: $n \times 3$

Positive and negative

-3	2	1
4	0	-4
-1	-2	3

Magic total: 0

Conclusions:

- These sets of numbers will always make a magic square:
  - Nine consecutive numbers
  - Nine consecutive multiples of a given number
  - Nine evenly spaced odd or nine evenly spaced even numbers
  - Nine evenly spaced numbers, positive or negative.
- Three sets of three consecutive numbers will only make a magic square if the gap between each set is the same.
- The middle number in the sequence, *n*, must always go in the centre cell.
- The magic total is the centre number multiplied by 3.

B) Transforming magic squares

Start square:

2	7	6
9	5	1
4	3	8

Magic total: $n \times 3$

Rule: × 4

8	28	24
36	20	4
16	12	32

Magic total: $(n \times 4) \times 3$

Rule: + 6

8	13	12
15	11	7
10	9	14

Magic total: $(n + 6) \times 3$

Rule: + 5 then × 2

14	24	22
28	20	12
18	16	26

Magic total: $((n + 5) \times 2) \times 3$

Rule: − 7

−5	0	−1
2	−2	−6
−3	−4	1

Magic total: $(n - 7) \times 3$

Rule: ÷ 5

0·4	1·4	1·2
1·8	1	0·2
0·8	0·6	1·6

Magic total: $(n \div 5) \times 3$

Conclusions:

- If the numbers in the initial magic square are consistently transformed using addition, subtraction, multiplication, division or a combination of these, the resulting square will still be magic.
- The magic total is always the centre number multiplied by 3. Therefore it is possible to predict what the magic total of a new square will be when you know what the rule for transformation is. If the middle number is *n*, the magic total is $n \times 3$. This formula can be expanded to include the rule for transformation, as shown to the right.

C) 4 by 4 magic squares

Solutions:

1	2	15	16
13	14	3	4
12	7	10	5
8	11	6	9

3	14	8	9
15	2	12	5
10	7	13	4
6	11	1	16

13	2	8	11
3	16	10	5
12	7	1	14
6	9	15	4

14	15	1	4
2	3	13	16
11	10	8	5
7	6	12	9

4 by 4 magic squares are much harder to create than 3 by 3 magic squares, and trial and error cannot always be used. However, children may notice some patterns in the positioning of the numbers 1 to 16 in the examples, so may be able to find other combinations that work.

Just using the numbers 1 to 16, 880 magic squares can be made.

5 Summer Assessment Activity

Areas on a pinboard

Assessment Foci: L4/5 Using and applying mathematics (Problem solving; Communicating; Reasoning); L5 Shape, space and measures (Properties of shape; measures)

Resources: PCMs I–K and D; square dot paper; square-based 25-pin pinboards; triangle dot paper

---

Lesson 1 – preparation – 1 hour

Part 1 – introduction - 30 minutes

As a group, children look at shape 1 on PCM I. They make a collaborative decision about the unit of area they will all work in. They then work together to find the area of shape 1. They write the unit of area plus the area of shape 1 in the notes box, along with any workings.

Children then work individually to calculate the areas of shapes 2–5, and to answer the questions shown in the notes boxes.

The strategies that children are likely to use are:

- *Symmetry:* identifying two identical parts, working out the area of one, then doubling
- *Cut-and-paste:* mentally or actually cutting out part of the shape and moving it to another place to simplify the shape
- *'Inside-out':* breaking up the inside area of a shape into simpler shapes and then adding the areas of these
- *'Outside-in':* surrounding the shape with a simpler shape such as a rectangle, then subtracting the excess area.

Children should work on shape 6 as a group, as this one is useful for comparing methods.

Part 2 – development – 30 minutes

Bring the group back together for a 5-minute discussion of what they have done so far. They should compare their answers, sharing their strategies.

Give each child PCM J. They work individually to find the areas of the shapes, recording their workings.

If children complete PCM J before the end of the lesson, they can create their own shapes on pinboards or on square dot paper, and challenge other children to find the areas.

At the end of the lesson, bring the group back together for a short plenary in which children can discuss the lesson as a whole.

Lesson 2 – investigation – 1 hour

Part 1 – introduction – 10 minutes

Make sure each child has PCM K. They each choose whether they want to investigate option A or B. They write down their reasons for choosing that option, and brief initial ideas and conjectures about the investigation.

Part 2 – investigation – 35 minutes

Children work individually to develop their lines of investigation, recording their journey and any findings.

Children who successfully exhaust their chosen option before the end of the session can move on to either option C or option D on PCM K.

Highly gifted children could investigate option E or option F:

E) Consider the number of points or dots on the outside perimeter of each shape, and the number of internal points or dots. Work from these to finding the areas of triangles, quadrilaterals and other polygons.

F) Consider the effect of the overlaps of two polygons on the pinboard. The polygons created by these overlaps may not have vertices at the points of the board. Can you find strategies for determining their areas?

Part 3 – conclusions – 15 minutes

Children write a final report of their investigation, showing their journey and findings along the way, with any conclusions or fresh ideas.

Ask children to complete the self-assessment sheet on PCM D.

Year 5 Summer Assessment Activity

Areas on a pinboard

Objectives
These are the objectives that could be met by children doing this Assessment Activity.

Strand	Abacus Evolve objectives	Framework objectives
Using and applying mathematics	**Y5** Make and investigate a general statement about familiar numbers or shapes by finding examples that satisfy it **Y5** Explain a generalised relationship (formula) in words **Y5** Recognise and explain patterns and relationships, generalise and predict	**Y5** Plan and pursue an enquiry; present evidence by collecting, organising and interpreting information; suggest extensions to the enquiry **Y5** Explore patterns, properties and relationships and propose a general statement involving numbers or shapes; identify examples for which the statement is true or false **Y5** Explain reasoning using diagrams, graphs and text; refine ways of recording using images and symbols
Measuring	**Y5** Understand area measured in square centimetres **Y5** Understand and use the formula in words 'length × breadth' for the area of a rectangle **Y6** Calculate the area of a rectangle **Y6** Calculate the area of compound shapes that can be split into rectangles **Y6** Estimate the area of an irregular shape by counting squares **Y6** Calculate the area of a right-angled triangle by considering it as half a rectangle	**Y5** Identify, visualise and describe properties of rectangles, triangles, regular polygons and 3D solids; use knowledge of properties to draw 2D shapes and identify and draw nets of 3D shapes **Y6** Calculate the perimeter and area of rectilinear shapes; estimate the area of an irregular shape by counting squares
Understanding shape	**Y5** Recognise properties of rectangles **Y6** Rehearse the concept of reflection **Y6** Begin to understand the concept of rotation	**Y5** *Draw and measure lines to the nearest millimetre; measure and calculate the perimeter of regular and irregular polygons; use the formula for the area of a rectangle to calculate its area* **Y6** *Visualise and draw on grids of different types where a shape will be after reflection, after translations or after rotation through 90 degrees or 180 degrees about its centre or one of its vertices*

Areas on a pinboard

swers – preparation activity

Note: these answers are not exhaustive.

1	**Area: 5** The group should realise that the area is 5, perhaps by drawing in the lines shown. This establishes a group agreement as to the unit of area to be used.
2	**Area: 10** Children should realise that although this shape can be split into five squares, these squares are larger than the unit of area agreed on in question 1. 'Inside-out': this shape can be split into five identical squares, each with area 2.
3	**Area: 12** 'Cut-and-paste': the two triangles on the right can be removed and replaced on the left, to create a 4 by 3 rectangle.
4	**Area: 6** 'Inside-out': the shape can be divided into a 2 by 2 square and two triangles of area 1. 'Symmetry': two trapeziums, each with area 3. 'Outside-in': draw a 2 by 4 rectangle around the shape, then remove four triangles of area 0·5.
5	**Area: 3** 'Symmetry': this shape has rotational symmetry, and can be divided into two triangles, each with area 1·5.
6	**Area: 5** 'Symmetry': the shape can be divided into two identical quadrilaterals. The 'outside-in' strategy can be used to find the area of one quadrilateral: enclose it in a 2 by 3 rectangle, then remove a square of area 2, two triangles of area 1 and a triangle of area 0·5.

7	**Area: 12** 'Symmetry': this hexagon has four identical quarters. The area of one quarter can be found by using the 'outside-in' strategy: the quarter can be enclosed in a 2 by 2 square, then a triangle of area 1 can be removed.
8	**Area: 5·5** 'Inside-out': this shape can be divided into two identical triangles and a pentagon. The area of each of the triangles is 1. The area of the pentagon can be found using the 'outside-in' strategy: enclose it in a 2 by 2 square, then remove the triangle with area 0·5.
9	**Area: 8** 'Symmetry': this parallelogram has rotational symmetry, so it can be split into two identical triangles. To find the area of one triangle, the 'inside-out' strategy can be used to divide it into two smaller triangles, one with area 1 and one with area 3.
10	**Area: 6** 'Symmetry': this kite has reflectional symmetry, so it can be split into two identical triangles. To find the area of one triangle, the 'inside-out' strategy can be used to split it into two smaller triangles, one with area 1 and one with area 2.
11	**Area: 10** 'Outside-in': a 4 by 4 square can be drawn around the shape, then four triangles of area 1·5 can be removed. 'Inside-out': divide the shape into a central 2 by 2 square and four triangles of area 1·5.
12	**Area: 6** 'Outside-in': enclose the shape in a 4 by 4 square. Remove three triangles with areas 1, 1·5 and 3. Then split the quadrilateral in the corner into a 1 by 2 rectangle and two triangles of area 1.

Areas on a pinboard

Answers – investigations

Note: these answers are not exhaustive.

A) Dotty triangles

Conclusion: triangles with the same base and height have the same area.
For example: these three triangles have base 4 and height 4, and area 8.

Conclusion: the area of a triangle can be found using the formula
(base × height) ÷ 2. For example:

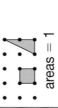

$(5 \times 2) \div 2 = 5$ $(2 \times 3) \div 2 = 3$

$(4 \times 2) \div 2 = 4$

B) Areas of shapes

Conclusion: all the shapes with an area of 0·5 are triangles, with base 1 and height 1. For example:

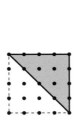

Conclusion: for area 1, one square can be made, then all the rest are triangles. The triangles have either base 1, height 2; or base 2, height 1. For example:

Conclusion: to make shapes of area 1, two shapes with area 0·5 can be placed together. For example:

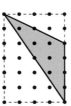

C) Areas on a triangle grid

Conclusion: no shapes with area 0·5 can be made.

Conclusion: shapes with area 1 are all triangles with base 1 and height 1.

Conclusion: in comparison with making shapes on square dot paper, the shapes on the triangle dot paper seem 'pushed over', and the area is doubled.

areas = 1

areas = 2

D) Dotty fraction shapes

Conclusion: when each small square has an area of $\frac{1}{16}$, the total areas of shapes are 16 times smaller than when each small square has an area of 1. Children may recognise that they can simply transform their previous area results to find the new areas.

Children may also work directly with the new unit of area and solve new shapes on that basis. This will involve them working with the special set of fractions: sixteenths, eighths, quarters and halves. They may need to add and subtract these, and will find dividing by 16 from previous results leads to the use of equivalent fractions, e.g. a previous area of 12 (on a grid of 16 squares) becomes $\frac{3}{4}$.

PCM Contents

Abacus Evolve Year 5 Challenge PCM © Pearson Education Ltd 2009

Triangular and square numbers

Position	Triangular number	Made by adding
1st	1	1
2nd	3	1 + 2
3rd	6	1 + 2 + 3
4th	10	
5th	15	
6th	21	
7th	28	
8th	36	
9th	45	
10th	55	

Position	Square number	Made by multiplying	Made by adding triangular numbers	Positions of triangular numbers
1st	1	1 × 1	1	1st
2nd	4	2 × 2	1 + 3	1st and 2nd
3rd	9	3 × 3	3 + 6	2nd and 3rd
4th	16			
5th	25			
6th	36			
7th	49			
8th	64			
9th	81			
10th	100			

Multiplying and dividing decimals I

0·2	0·3	0·4	2	5	10
100	100	125	125	250	250
25	25	50	50	50	50
10	10	12·5	12·5	20	20
5	5	7·5	7·5	10	10
4	4	5	5	5	5
2	2	2	2	3	3
0·5	0·5	0·75	0·75	1	1
0·2	0·2	0·3	0·3	0·4	0·4

Abacus Evolve Year 5 Challenge PCM © Pearson Education Ltd 2009

Multiplying and dividing decimals 2

Position the number cards in the correct places on the grid.

Be careful, some of the cards may not be correct and some may be missing!

Do this → / to this ↓	× 2	× 0·2	× 5	× 0·5	÷ 2	÷ 0·2	÷ 5	÷ 0·5
1								
25								
50								
10								
2								
1·5								

Discuss what you have found out with other children in the class.

Abacus Evolve Year 5 Challenge PCM © Pearson Education Ltd 2009

Equivalent fractions

Dividend	Divisor	Quotient	Decimal
28	3	$9\frac{1}{3}$	$9.\dot{3}$
56		$9\frac{2}{6}$	$9.\dot{3}$
	9	$9\frac{3}{}$	$9.\dot{3}$
	12	$9\frac{}{12}$	$9.\dot{3}$
140		$9\frac{5}{}$	$9.\dot{3}$
	18	$9\frac{}{}$	$9.\dot{3}$
196		$9\frac{}{}$	$9.\dot{3}$
	24	$9\frac{}{}$	$9.\dot{3}$

Abacus Evolve Year 5 Challenge PCM © Pearson Education Ltd 2009

Making quadrilaterals I

Abacus Evolve Year 5 Challenge PCM © Pearson Education Ltd 2009

Making quadrilaterals 2

	Parallel sides	No parallel sides
Perpendicular sides		
No perpendicular sides		

Abacus Evolve Year 5 Challenge PCM © Pearson Education Ltd 2009

Abacus Evolve Year 5 Challenge PCM © Pearson Education Ltd 2009

Tables and graphs

Graph I

Bar graph showing the average temperature for 28 days in October

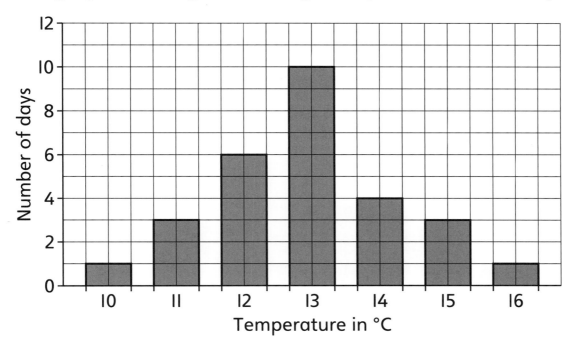

Graph 2

Line graph showing temperature change over a day in October

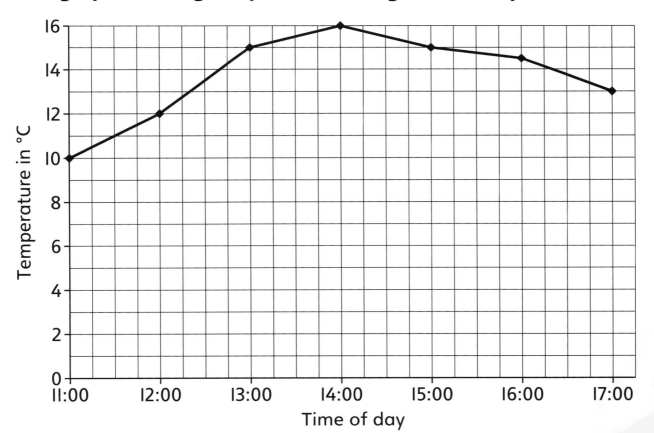

Line graphs and conversion graphs

Using the information in Table I on Textbook page 14, draw a line graph of the population of London since 1801 (not all years have data).

Plot the points for which you have the data and predict where the line would be for missing data.

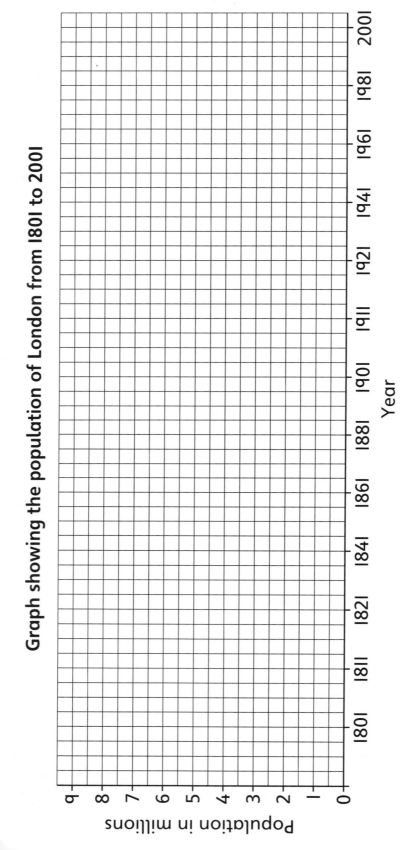

Graph showing the population of London from 1801 to 2001

Year

Population in millions

Abacus Evolve Year 5 Challenge PCM © Pearson Education Ltd 2009

Year 5 Block C1 • Challenge PCM 9

The best buy

Look at this list of items and help with the shopping by choosing the best value offer for each product.

Circle your choices.

	Price 1	Price 2	Price 3	Price 4
Potatoes	2·5 kg for £2·38	1 kg for £1·19	2 kg for £1·99	300 g for 41p
Baked beans	420 g for 52p	415 g for 50p	220 g for 26p	400 g for 40p
Soap	4 × 125 g for £1·58	2 × 200 g for £1·05	125 g for 39p	2 × 125 g for £1·02
Crackers	12 × 25 g for £1·99	10 × 17 g for £1·23	7 × 25 g for £1·25	150 g for £1·12
Fruit squash	$\frac{1}{2}$ litre, 2 for £1·50	150 ml for 24p	$\frac{1}{3}$ l for 43p	8 × 25 cl for £2·95
Detergent	2·47 kg for £6·47	950 g for £2·38	$\frac{1}{2}$ kg for £1·57	780 g for £1·98
Cabbage	1·5 kg for 68p	1 kg for 50p	730 g for 43p	160 g for 7p
Butter	500 g for £1·70	$\frac{1}{4}$ kg for 94p	1000 g for £2·98	125 g for 50p
Tea bags	160 for £2·35	240 for £3·29	80 for £1·29	120 for £1·49
Milk	4 pints for £1·44	2 l for £1·19	2 pints for 80p	568 ml for 42p

Abacus Evolve Year 5 Challenge PCM © Pearson Education Ltd 2009

In the mirror

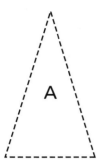 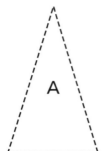 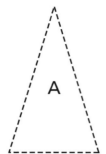 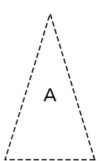

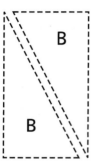 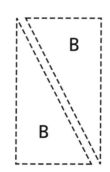 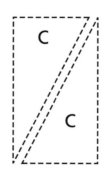 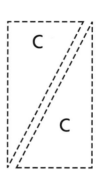

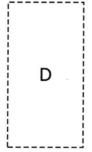 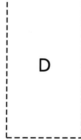

Will it divide?

	Multiple of 2	Multiple of 4	Multiple of 25	Multiple of 9
Multiple of 3				
Multiple of 10				
Multiple of 8				
Multiple of 6				

Cut out these number cards. Using the tests of divisibility, arrange the cards on the grid. Make sure each number fits the horizontal and the vertical description. Some numbers will not go on the grid at all.

68 210	2325	8250	7290	36 160
7146	4567	2625	2916	1104
5704	28 416	5600	4032	10 001
19 284	7777	9900	4257	5472

Abacus Evolve Year 5 Challenge PCM © Pearson Education Ltd 2009

Cross-numbers

Complete the cross-number using the clues on Textbook page 22.

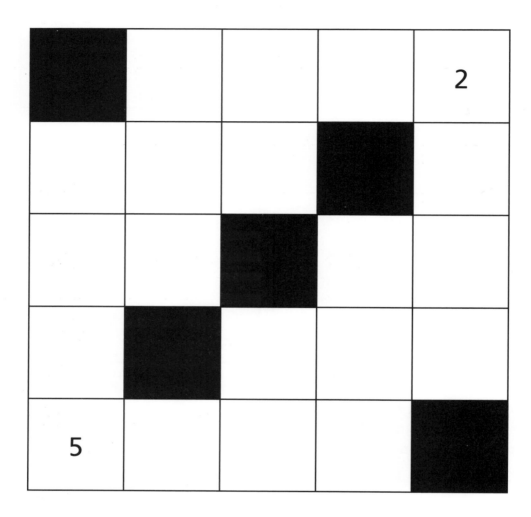

Abacus Evolve Year 5 Challenge PCM © Pearson Education Ltd 2009

Find my double

660	1466	3452	3202
6904	1474	135·6	737
490	774	96·1	1320
1551	3102	1601	380
733	391	4·87	9·74
387	367	67·8	6·16
3·08	760	2345	90·74
34·7	203	15·48	904
69·4	7·74	734	452
4690	980	45·37	782

Improper fractions game

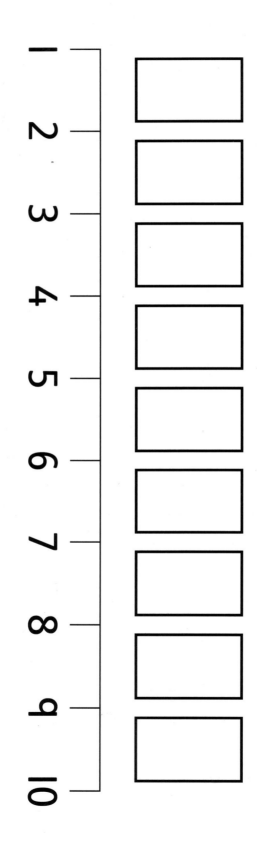

Imperial and metric conversions

Copy out the amounts that you are given for each item.
Convert the amounts for each item into the same unit of measurement.
Suggested units of measurement are given for you.
Circle the greatest amount and underline the smallest amount each time.
The first one has been done for you.

Item	Amount	Conversion
I Cheese	0·5 kg	(0·500) kg
	I lb	0·454 kg
	450 g	_0·450_ kg
2 Milk		l
		l
		l
3 Roads		km
		km
		km
4 Glasses of juice		l
		l
		l
5 Apples		kg
		kg
		kg
6 Lengths of rope		km
		km
		km
7 Rabbits		kg
		kg
		kg

Abacus Evolve Year 5 Challenge PCM © Pearson Education Ltd 2009

Rounding and estimating using place value

18 × 21	17 × 23	16 × 24	15 × 22	19 × 22
1·8 × 210	170 × 2·3	1·6 × 240	150 × 2·2	1·9 × 220
1800 × 0·21	1·7 × 230	0·16 × 2400	1·5 × 220	1900 × 0·22
17 × 24	16 × 23	15 × 23	19 × 23	18 × 23
1·7 × 240	1·6 × 230	150 × 2·3	190 × 2·3	1·8 × 230
1700 × 0·24	0·16 × 2300	1·5 × 230	1·9 × 230	0·18 × 2300
15 × 21	17 × 22	16 × 21	18 × 24	19 × 24
1·5 × 210	170 × 2·2	1·6 × 210	180 × 2·4	190 × 2·4
0·15 × 2100	1700 × 0·22	0·16 × 2100	1800 × 0·24	1900 × 0·24
19 × 21	15 × 24	18 × 22	16 × 22	17 × 21
190 × 2·1	150 × 2·4	1·8 × 220	1·6 × 220	1·7 × 210
1900 × 0·21	0·15 × 2400	1800 × 0·22	0·16 × 2200	1700 × 0·21

Abacus Evolve Year 5 Challenge PCM © Pearson Education Ltd 2009

Coordinates

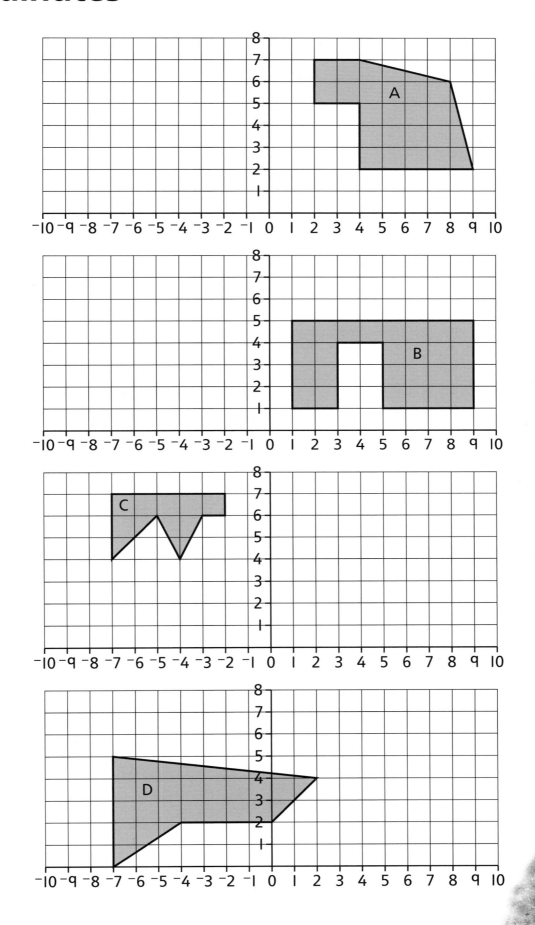

Abacus Evolve Year 5 Challenge PCM © Pearson Education Ltd 2009

Coordinates grids

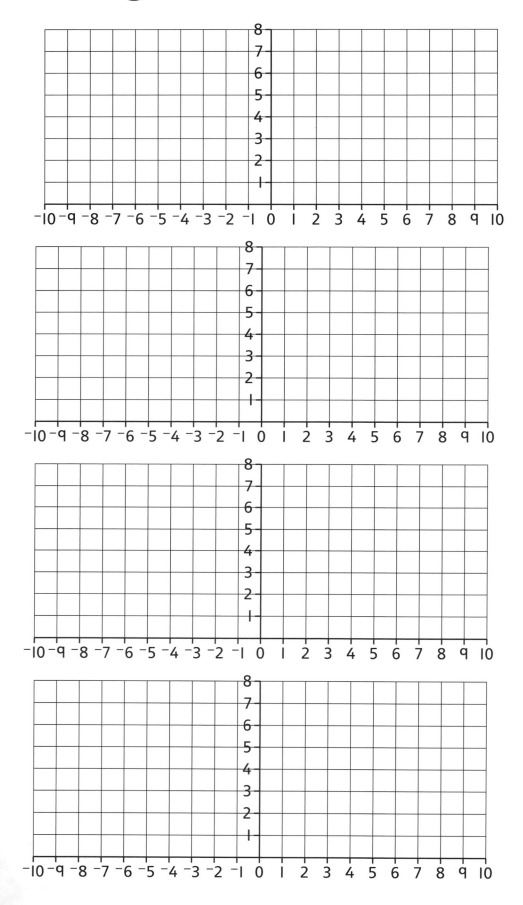

Abacus Evolve Year 5 Challenge PCM © Pearson Education Ltd 2009

Abacus Evolve Year 5 Challenge PCM © Pearson Education Ltd 2009

Reflecting with coordinates

Plot each set of coordinates and join up the corners of the shapes.
Reflect each shape in the *y*-axis. Draw the reflection and check with a mirror.
What are the coordinates of the corners of each reflected shape?

1 (1, 2) (1, 5) (2, 7) (7, 7) (7, 4) (4, 5) (3, 2)

New shape: _____

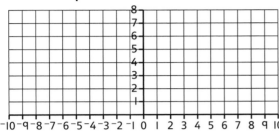

2 (⁻8, 7) (⁻2, 8) (⁻1, 2) (⁻4, 2) (⁻4, 6) (⁻8, 6)

New shape: _____

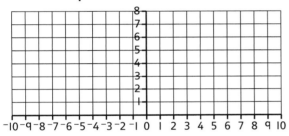

3 (0, 3) (3, 6) (7, 5) (7, 2) (3, 0)

New shape: _____

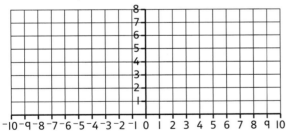

4 (⁻8, 6) (⁻4, 4) (⁻2, 6) (0, 0) (⁻4, 2) (⁻6, 0)

New shape: _____

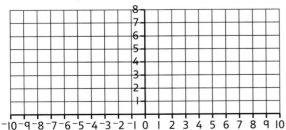

Is there an easy way to work out the coordinates of the reflected shapes?

Investigating diagonals

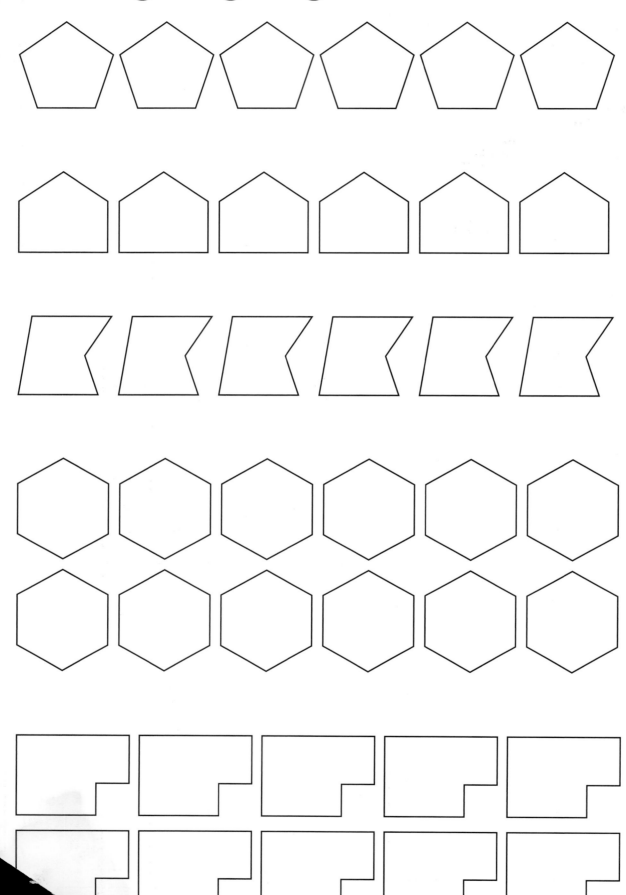

Abacus Evolve Year 5 Challenge PCM © Pearson Education Ltd 2009

Surface area

Abacus Evolve Year 5 Challenge PCM © Pearson Education Ltd 2009

Cuboid	Height	Depth	Length	Volume	Area of face 1	Area of face 2	Area of face 3	Face 1 + face 2 + face 3	Surface area
A	2 cm	2 cm	54 cm	216 cm^3	4 cm^2	108 cm^2	108 cm^2	220 cm^2	440 cm^2
B	2 cm	3 cm	36 cm	216 cm^3	6 cm^2	108 cm^2	72 cm^2		
C	2 cm	4 cm	27 cm	216 cm^3					
D	2 cm	6 cm	18 cm	216 cm^3					
E	2 cm	9 cm	12 cm	216 cm^3					
F	3 cm	2 cm	36 cm	216 cm^3					
G	3 cm	3 cm	24 cm	216 cm^3					
H	3 cm	4 cm	18 cm	216 cm^3					
I	3 cm	6 cm	12 cm	216 cm^3					
J	3 cm	8 cm	9 cm	216 cm^3					

Schedules

Complete the week's television schedule using the information on Textbook page 42.

Monday

Start and end time	Length	Programme
16:00–16:30	30 mins	Race The Clock
	29 mins	Pop News
	12 mins	
17:14–17:59		

Tuesday

Start and end time	Length	Programme
	75 mins	Football Highlights
	4 mins	
17:21– 17:30	9 mins	
	28 mins	Snakes!

Wednesday

Start and end time	Length	Programme
16:00–16:10		Local News
	48 mins	
17:00– 17:30		Can You Spell?
	28 mins	

Thursday

Start and end time	Length	Programme
16:00–	45 mins	Swimming for Gold
		Film News
17:16–17:45		

Friday

Start and end time	Length	Programme
	45 mins	
16:46–17:39		Amazing Animals
17:40–17:49		
	9 mins	Guess the Celebrity

Make the calculation

- Player I uses counters to cover three numbers which make an addition or subtraction calculation and answer.
- Player I keeps going until they can find no more sets of three numbers which make a calculation.
- Player I counts how many squares are left uncovered. This is their score.
- Player 2 does the same.
- The winner is the player with the lowest total. They get I point.
- Continue until one player reaches 10 points and wins the game.

63	88	122	34	40
117	58	27	109	98
82	24	69	51	61
151	137	66	59	29

Abacus Evolve Year 5 Challenge PCM © Pearson Education Ltd 2009

Multiplication challenge I

Rules

- Take turns to throw a dice four times and write the numbers in the blank squares. You can write the numbers in any order.
- Check the list below to see who wins a point each round.
- The person with most points after all six rounds is the winner!

Round 1 The largest product wins 1 point.

Round 2 The smallest product wins 1 point.

Round 3 The product closest to 1000 wins 1 point.

Round 4 The product closest to 2000 wins 1 point.

Round 5 The product closest to 3000 wins 1 point.

Round 6 The product closest to 500 wins 1 point.

Round 1 ☐☐ × ☐☐ =

Round 2 ☐☐ × ☐☐ =

Round 3 ☐☐ × ☐☐ =

Round 4 ☐☐ × ☐☐ =

Round 5 ☐☐ × ☐☐ =

Round 6 ☐☐ × ☐☐ =

Abacus Evolve Year 5 Challenge PCM © Pearson Education Ltd 2009

Abacus Evolve Year 5 Challenge PCM © Pearson Education Ltd 2009

Multiplication challenge 2

Rules

- Before you start to play, think of six rules to decide who will win a point in each round. (Look at the list on PCM 24 for ideas.)

Round 1 _____ wins 1 point.

Round 2 _____ wins 1 point.

Round 3 _____ wins 1 point.

Round 4 _____ wins 1 point.

Round 5 _____ wins 1 point.

Round 6 _____ wins 1 point.

- Take turns to throw a dice four times and write the numbers in the squares. You can write the numbers in any order.
- Check your list to see who wins a point each round.
- The person with the most points after all six rounds is the winner!

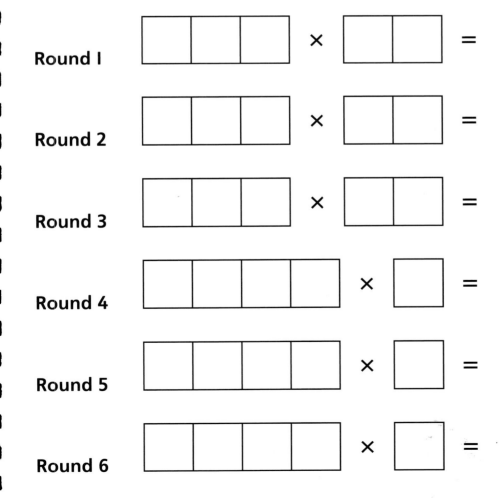

Working with seconds

Race	Name	Boy or Girl	Age	Fastest time (seconds)	Did they qualify? How much by?
Freestyle	Jesse	B	9	34·92	**Qualified by 4·08 seconds**
Freestyle	Emeka	B	9	39·59	
Freestyle	Krishna	G	9	36·99	
Freestyle	Sally	G	10	36·09	
Freestyle	Molly	G	11	33·12	
Freestyle	Cameron	B	12	32·07	
Freestyle	Jasveer	B	10	35·41	
Freestyle	Becky	G	12	31·89	
Backstroke	Max	B	10	42·99	
Backstroke	Conor	B	11	39·30	
Backstroke	Ellie	G	9	44·94	
Backstroke	Neela	G	9	45·05	
Backstroke	Sasha	G	12	37·69	
Backstroke	Tyler	B	9	44·96	
Backstroke	Guang	B	12	37·99	
Backstroke	Amy	G	11	35·86	

Name	Time (seconds)	Time to the nearest tenth of a second	Finishing position
HOY Chris (GB)	10·636		
SIREAU Kevin (FR)	10·570		
KENNY Jason (GB)	10·531		
AWANG Mohd Azizulhasni (MA)	11·010		
MULDER Teun (NE)	10·888		
BOS Theo (NE)	10·777		
BOURGAIN Mickael (FR)	10·734		
LEVY Maximilian (DE)	10·763		

Abacus Evolve Year 5 Challenge PCM © Pearson Education Ltd 2009

Cross the river playing cards 1

Photocopy this PCM onto coloured paper and cut out the cards.
Photocopy PCM 28 (Cross the river playing cards 2) onto different coloured paper.

1·2 × 8	66 × 0·5	41 × 0·7
2·5 × 3	22 × 0·5	1·4 × 5
41 × 0·4	80 × 0·6	2·5 × 8
6 × 0·9	1·2 × 80	55 × 1·4
30 × 0·8	6·1 × 6	6·5 × 4
24 × 0·7	70 × 0·8	1·5 × 4

Abacus Evolve Year 5 Challenge PCM © Pearson Education Ltd 2009

Cross the river playing cards 2

Photocopy this PCM onto coloured paper and cut out the cards.
Photocopy PCM 27 (Cross the river playing cards I) onto different coloured paper.

2·2 × 5	12 × 0·8	4·1 × 7
4·1 × 4	25 × 0·3	52 × 0·5
9 × 0·6	12 × 8	25 × 0·8
80 × 0·3	61 × 0·6	5·5 × 14
84 × 0·2	40 × 1·2	14 × 0·5
5·6 × 10	6·6 × 5	5 × 1·2

Abacus Evolve Year 5 Challenge PCM © Pearson Education Ltd 2009

Abacus Evolve Year 5 Challenge PCM © Pearson Education Ltd 2009

Cross the river game board

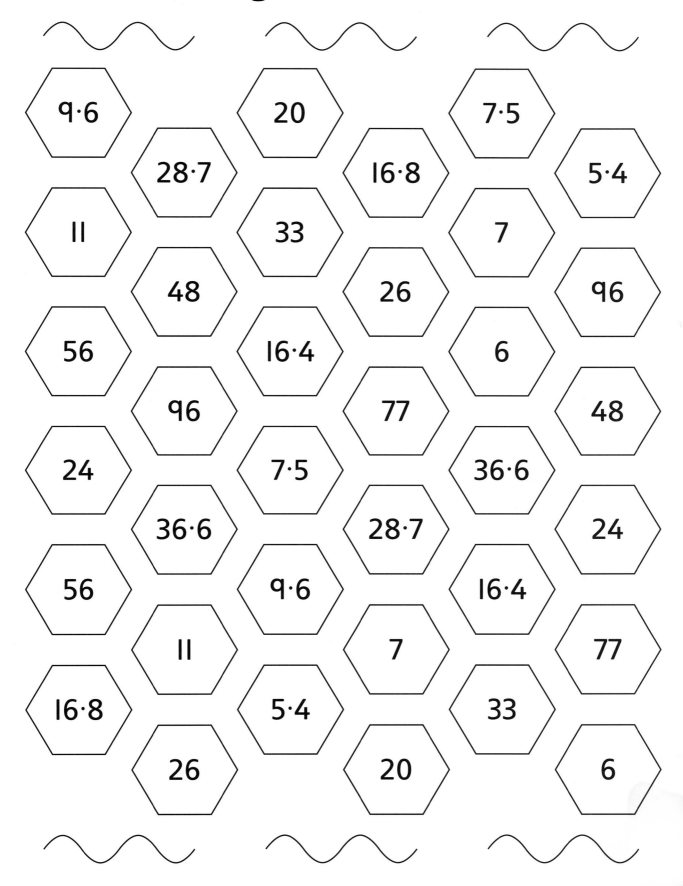

Abacus Evolve Year 5 Challenge PCM © Pearson Education Ltd 2009

Decimal spinner

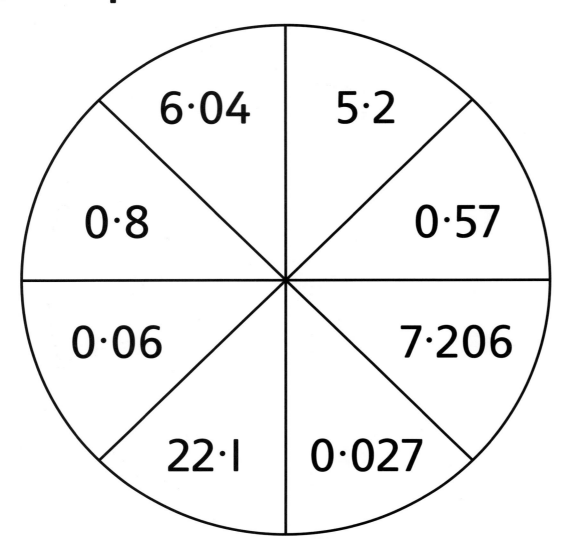

To make your spinner:

- Place a paper clip in the centre of the circle.
- Put the point of a pencil through the wider end of the paper clip.
- Flick the paper clip with your fingernail and watch it spin!

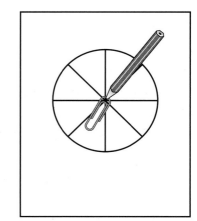

Abacus Evolve Year 5 Challenge PCM © Pearson Education Ltd 2009

Subtraction game spinner

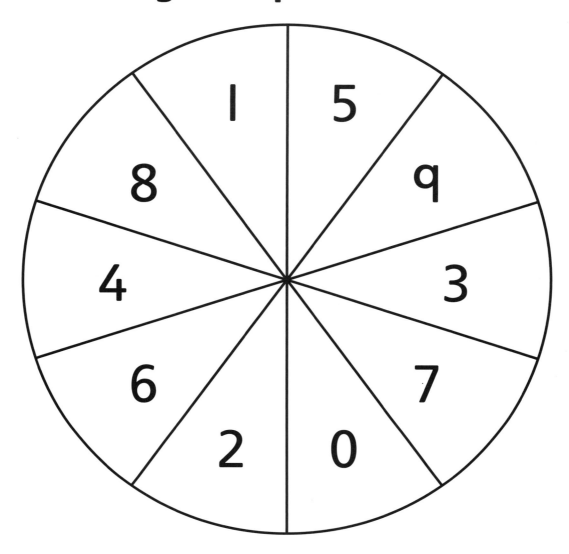

Rules

- Take turns to spin the spinner.
- Write the digit anywhere on your blank number sentence on PCM 32.
- Do this eight times until you have each made a subtraction sentence.
- Solve your subtractions and show your workings.
- Check each other's answers using addition.
- The player whose pair of numbers have the largest difference wins a point.

Think carefully about where to place the numbers in your number sentence. If the second number is larger than the first then you will miss a go and your opponent will get the point.

Subtraction game sheet

Game 1

Round 1

Round 2

Round 3

Round 4

Round 5

- -

Game 2

Round 1

Round 2

Round 3

Round 4

Round 5

Abacus Evolve Year 5 Challenge PCM © Pearson Education Ltd 2009

Probability

Record your results from the experiments on Textbook page 63.

Coins

Coin throw	Tally	Total
HHH		
HHT		
HTH		
THH		
TTT		
TTH		
THT		
HTT		
		50

Dice

Dice total	Tally	Total
I		
2		
3		
4		
5		
6		
7		
8		
q		
I0		
II		
I2		
		50

Counters

Counter colour	Tally	Total
Blue		
Red		
Yellow		
Green		
		50

Abacus Evolve Year 5 Challenge PCM © Pearson Education Ltd 2009

The best deal

Graph to show Jasmine's and Dominic's phone deals

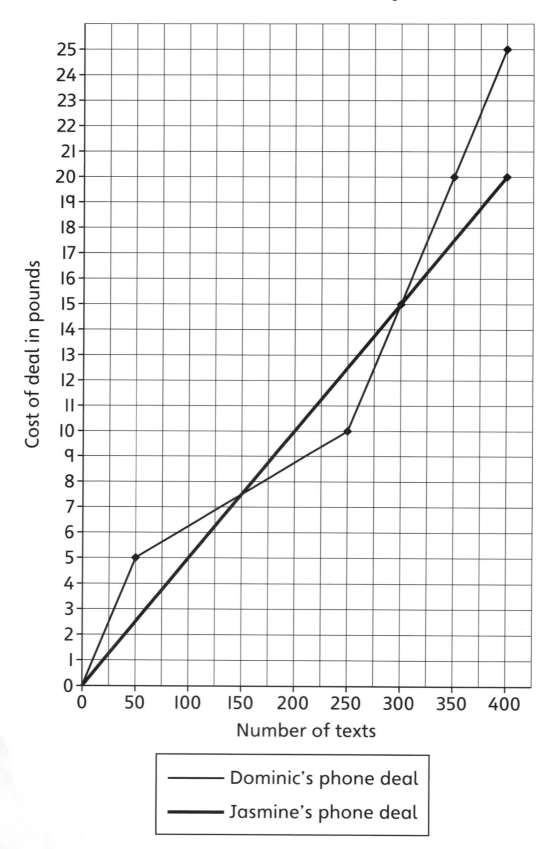

New ways of measuring I

Abacus Evolve Year 5 Challenge PCM © Pearson Education Ltd 2009

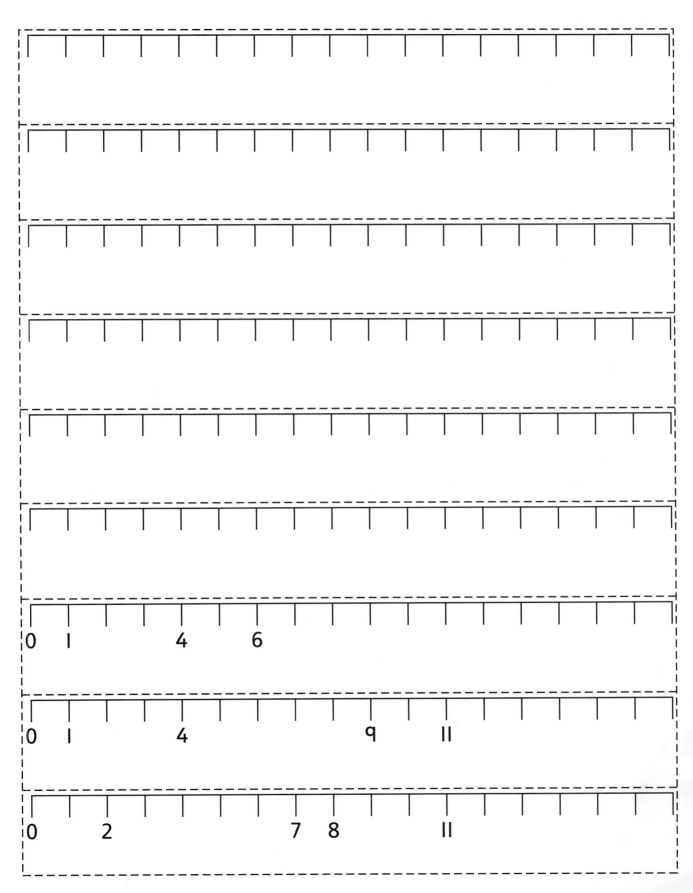

New ways of measuring 2

I have a balance and some kilogram weights.
I have lost some of the weights, including the 2 kg weight.
I have one 1 kg weight, one 3 kg weight and one other weight.
I can use my three weights to balance objects up to 13 kg.

I can put weights on both sides of the balance.

1 How heavy must my third weight be? _____

2 How can I use the 1 kg weight and the 3 kg weight to balance a 4 kg object?

_____

_____

3 Complete this table.

Weight of object	Left balance pan	Right balance pan
1 kg	Object	1 kg weight
2 kg	Object and 1 kg weight	3 kg weight
3 kg	Object	3 kg weight
4 kg		
5 kg		
6 kg		
7 kg		
8 kg		
9 kg		
10 kg		
11 kg		
12 kg		
13 kg		

Abacus Evolve Year 5 Challenge PCM © Pearson Education Ltd 2009

Map of shipping areas around the British Isles

This is a map of the shipping areas around the British Isles.

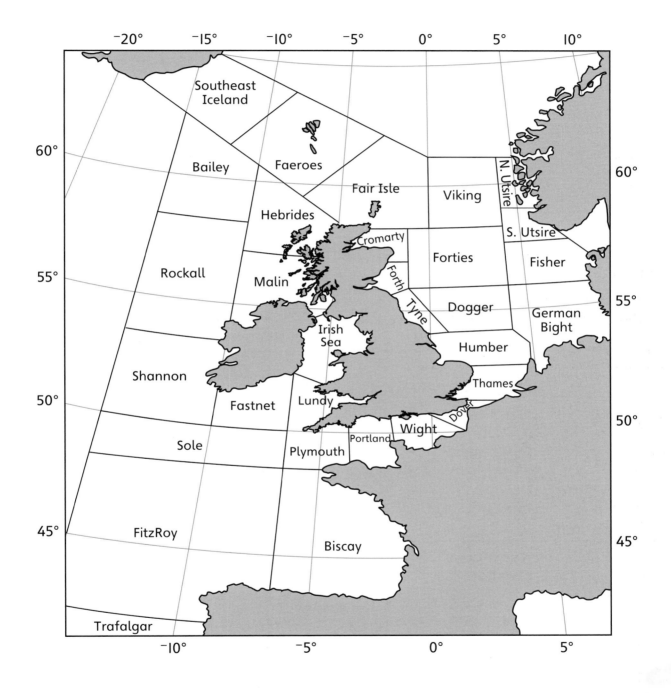

Abacus Evolve Year 5 Challenge PCM © Pearson Education Ltd 2009

The Shipping Forecast

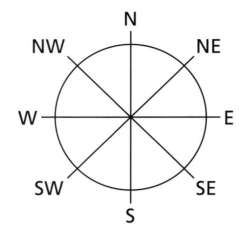

Area	Wind direction	Changes	Movement in degrees
Viking	South-west	None	None
North Utsire	South-west	None	None
South Utsire	West	Backing south-east	Anticlockwise 135°
Forties Cromarty Forth	West	Veering north-west	
Tyne	West	None	
Dogger Fisher German Bight	North-west	Backing south-west	
Humber Thames Dover Wight Portland Plymouth	West	Veering north	
Biscay FitzRoy	North-west	None	
Sole Lundy Fastnet Irish Sea Shannon Rockall	North	Backing west	
Malin	North-west	Backing south	
Hebrides	North-west	Backing south-east	
Bailey	North-west	None	
Fair Isle Faeroes	North-west	Veering north	
Southeast Iceland	North-west	Backing north-east	

Abacus Evolve Year 5 Challenge PCM © Pearson Education Ltd 2009

Looking at triangles

Photocopy this PCM three times for each child, pair or group and cut out the triangles.

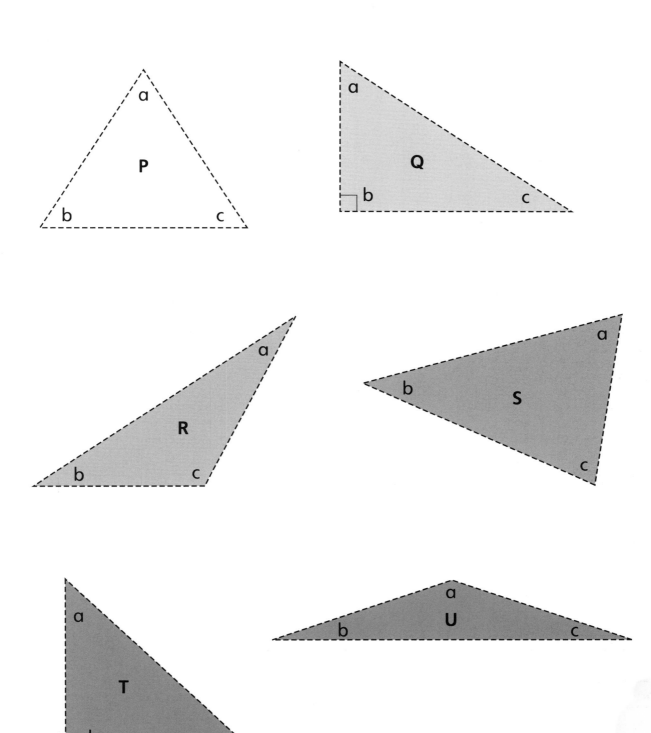

Using digit roots I

I Use your knowledge of division and multiplication tables to fill in the missing numbers on this multiplication grid.

×	28		30	4	23	15		26
19		209	570	76	437	285	133	494
	5·6	2·2	6	0·8	4·6	3	1·4	5·2
1·2	33·6		36	4·8	27·6	18		31·2
	616	242	660		506		154	572
14		154	420	56		210	98	364
0·6	16·8	6·6		2·4	13·8	9	4·2	15·6
	700	275		100	575	375	175	
17	476	187	510		391	255	119	442

2 Fill in this grid by finding the digit total of each number in the grid above. Some numbers have been written in already.

(grid with: 1, 4, 9, 7, 7, 9, 4, 1 along a diagonal)

3 On the second grid, make a Vedic square by joining up the 7s.

4 Fill in the blank grid with the digit totals and make a Vedic square by joining up the 2s.

Abacus Evolve Year 5 Challenge PCM © Pearson Education Ltd 2009

Abacus Evolve Year 5 Challenge PCM © Pearson Education Ltd 2009

Using digit roots 2

1 Join all the 5s.

1	2	3	4	5	6	7	8
2	4	6	8	1	3	5	7
3	6	9	3	6	9	3	6
4	8	3	7	2	6	1	5
5	1	6	2	7	3	8	4
6	3	9	6	3	9	6	3
7	5	3	1	8	6	4	2
8	7	6	5	4	3	2	1

2 Join all the 4s.

1	2	3	4	5	6	7	8
2	4	6	8	1	3	5	7
3	6	9	3	6	9	3	6
4	8	3	7	2	6	1	5
5	1	6	2	7	3	8	4
6	3	9	6	3	9	6	3
7	5	3	1	8	6	4	2
8	7	6	5	4	3	2	1

3 Join all the 8s.

1	2	3	4	5	6	7	8
2	4	6	8	1	3	5	7
3	6	9	3	6	9	3	6
4	8	3	7	2	6	1	5
5	1	6	2	7	3	8	4
6	3	9	6	3	9	6	3
7	5	3	1	8	6	4	2
8	7	6	5	4	3	2	1

4 Join all the 1s.

1	2	3	4	5	6	7	8
2	4	6	8	1	3	5	7
3	6	9	3	6	9	3	6
4	8	3	7	2	6	1	5
5	1	6	2	7	3	8	4
6	3	9	6	3	9	6	3
7	5	3	1	8	6	4	2
8	7	6	5	4	3	2	1

5 Join all the 3s.

1	2	3	4	5	6	7	8
2	4	6	8	1	3	5	7
3	6	9	3	6	9	3	6
4	8	3	7	2	6	1	5
5	1	6	2	7	3	8	4
6	3	9	6	3	9	6	3
7	5	3	1	8	6	4	2
8	7	6	5	4	3	2	1

6 Join all the 6s.

1	2	3	4	5	6	7	8
2	4	6	8	1	3	5	7
3	6	9	3	6	9	3	6
4	8	3	7	2	6	1	5
5	1	6	2	7	3	8	4
6	3	9	6	3	9	6	3
7	5	3	1	8	6	4	2
8	7	6	5	4	3	2	1

Equivalent calculations

$26{\cdot}23 \div 5 =$	$18{\cdot}4 \div 4 =$	$53{\cdot}2 \div 50 =$	$23{\cdot}41 \div 0{\cdot}5 =$	$13{\cdot}6 \div 20 =$
$52{\cdot}46 \div 10 =$	$9{\cdot}2 \div 2 =$	$106{\cdot}4 \div 100 =$	$46{\cdot}82 \div 1 =$	$6{\cdot}8 \div 10 =$
$2{\cdot}623 \div 0{\cdot}5 =$	$184 \div 40 =$	$532 \div 500 =$	$234{\cdot}1 \div 5 =$	$1{\cdot}36 \div 2 =$
$5{\cdot}246 \div 1 =$	$4{\cdot}6 \div 1 =$	$1064 \div 1000 =$	$468{\cdot}2 \div 10 =$	$0{\cdot}68 \div 1 =$
$1928 \div 500 =$	$67 \div 0{\cdot}2 =$	$45{\cdot}9 \div 30 =$	$146 \div 2{\cdot}5 =$	$72{\cdot}12 \div 60 =$
$3856 \div 1000 =$	$33{\cdot}5 \div 0{\cdot}1 =$	$15{\cdot}3 \div 10 =$	$584 \div 10 =$	$12{\cdot}02 \div 10 =$
$3{\cdot}856 \div 1 =$	$670 \div 2 =$	$459 \div 300 =$	$58{\cdot}4 \div 1 =$	$1{\cdot}202 \div 1 =$
$192{\cdot}8 \div 50 =$	$335 \div 1 =$	$153 \div 100 =$	$29{\cdot}2 \div 0{\cdot}5 =$	$7{\cdot}212 \div 6 =$

Abacus Evolve Year 5 Challenge PCM © Pearson Education Ltd 2009

0–1 number line with tenths and hundredths

Abacus Evolve Year 5 Challenge PCM © Pearson Education Ltd 2009

Find the factor game board

Rules
- Take turns to select a number using the spinner on PCM 45.
- Find a number on the game board that your number is a factor of.
- Cover it with a counter.
- The winner is the first person to get a line of four counters horizontally, vertically or diagonally.

21	63	23	66	25	59	45	28
77	30	78	55	33	44	58	70
37	81	54	73	80	42	38	56
64	62	90	48	49	75	51	22
53	39	32	52	57	60	27	35
50	46	26	34	65	24	88	68
69	36	85	72	40	74	61	76

Which were the best numbers to get with the spinner? Why?
Are any numbers on the game board impossible to cover? Why?

Abacus Evolve Year 5 Challenge PCM © Pearson Education Ltd 2009

Abacus Evolve Year 5 Challenge PCM © Pearson Education Ltd 2009

Find the factor spinner

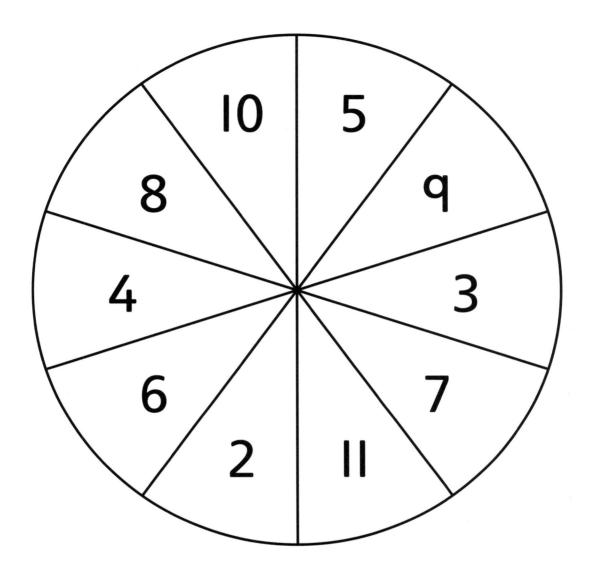

To make your spinner:

- Place a paper clip in the centre of the circle.
- Put the point of a pencil through the wider end of the paper clip.
- Flick the paper clip with your fingernail and watch it spin!

1–100 number square

1	2	3	4	5	6	7	8	9	10
11	12	13	14	15	16	17	18	19	20
21	22	23	24	25	26	27	28	29	30
31	32	33	34	35	36	37	38	39	40
41	42	43	44	45	46	47	48	49	50
51	52	53	54	55	56	57	58	59	60
61	62	63	64	65	66	67	68	69	70
71	72	73	74	75	76	77	78	79	80
81	82	83	84	85	86	87	88	89	90
91	92	93	94	95	96	97	98	99	100

Abacus Evolve Year 5 Challenge PCM © Pearson Education Ltd 2009

Factor record-breakers

I, 2, 4 and 6 are factor record-breakers. Why?

I has just **one** factor	I
2 has **two** factors	I, 2
4 has **three** factors	I, 2, 4
6 has **four** factors	I, 2, 3, 6

In each case they are the smallest number with that number of factors. What is the smallest number that has five factors? ... six factors? ... and so on?

Complete this table, then colour in all the record-breakers.

Number	How many factors?	Number	How many factors?	Number	How many factors?
I		16		31	
2		17		32	
3		18		33	
4		19		34	
5		20		35	
6		21		36	
7		22		37	
8		23		38	
9		24		39	
10		25		40	
II		26		41	
12		27		42	
13		28		43	
14		29		44	
15		30		45	

Abacus Evolve Year 5 Challenge PCM © Pearson Education Ltd 2009

The unusual number grid

Colour numbers with one factor blue, numbers with two factors red, numbers with three factors yellow, and so on.

1	2	3	4	5	6
7	8	9	10	11	12
13	14	15	16	17	18
19	20	21	22	23	24
25	26	27	28	29	30
31	32	33	34	35	36
37	38	39	40	41	42
43	44	45	46	47	48
49	50	51	52	53	54
55	56	57	58	59	60
61	62	63	64	65	66
67	68	69	70	71	72
73	74	75	76	77	78
79	80	81	82	83	84
85	86	87	88	89	90
91	92	93	94	95	96
97	98	99	100	101	102
103	104	105	106	107	108
109	110	111	112	113	114
115	116	117	118	119	120

Abacus Evolve Year 5 Challenge PCM © Pearson Education Ltd 2009

Factors and prime numbers: investigations

Choose option A or option B to investigate.

A Abundant and deficient numbers

An **abundant number** is a whole number that is less than the sum of its factors, excluding the number itself.
12 is an abundant number. Its factors, excluding 12, are 1, 2, 3, 4, 6. The sum of these is 16, which is greater than 12.

A **deficient number** is a whole number that is greater than the sum of its factors, excluding the number itself.
15 is a deficient number. Its factors, excluding 15, are 1, 3, 5. The sum of these is 9, which is less than 15.

A **perfect number** is a whole number that is equal to the sum of its factors, excluding the number itself.
6 is a perfect number. Its factors, excluding 6, are 1, 2, 3. The sum of these is 6.

How many abundant numbers can you find? How many deficient numbers? How many perfect numbers? Write about any patterns you see in your results.

B) Goldbach's conjectures

Christian Goldbach (1690 – 1764) was a Professor of Mathematics at the Russian Imperial Academy. These are two of his ideas:

- Every even number greater than 4 can be written as the sum of two odd prime numbers.
  For example: $24 = 11 + 13$.

- Odd numbers can always be made from the sum of three odd primes.
  For example: $13 = 3 + 5 + 5$.

Investigate Goldbach's ideas. Do you think he was right? Are there any patterns in your search?

Self-assessment sheet

	What I did to show this
I planned and completed my work in an organised way.	
I described patterns that I found.	
I made and tested predictions.	
I explained some of my findings, giving reasons.	
I wrote my conclusions looking back at my working.	
Other things I learned in this work.	

Abacus Evolve Year 5 Challenge PCM © Pearson Education Ltd 2009

Abacus Evolve Year 5 Challenge PCM © Pearson Education Ltd 2009

Semi-magic squares

As a group, discuss the properties of the number square below.
These questions might help you.

- Which numbers are used?
- Are there any patterns?
  - Look at each row of three.
  - Look at each column of three.
- What do you notice?

Describe the properties of the number square in the notes box.

3	2	7
1	6	5
8	4	0

Notes box

Work with a partner. Make your own square using the same nine numbers.
Try to make it have the same kind of patterns you found in the square above.
All nine numbers must be used, so a number cannot be used more than once in a square.

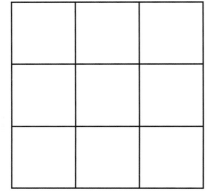
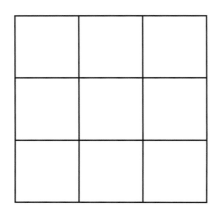

A pattern of semi-magic squares

Work on your own. Choose one of your semi-magic squares. Make different versions of it by rotating it and reflecting it. (Do not rotate or reflect the actual numerals, just their positions!)

Rotate 90° down this column   Mirror   Reflect in this column

Abacus Evolve Year 5 Challenge PCM © Pearson Education Ltd 2009

Abacus Evolve Year 5 Challenge PCM © Pearson Education Ltd 2009

Transforming a semi-magic square

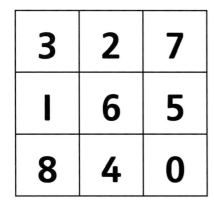

3	2	7
1	6	5
8	4	0

→

7	5	15
3	13	11
17	9	1

What rule has been used to transform the numbers in the left-hand square into the numbers in the right-hand square? Write the rule below the arrow.

The rule transforms the square, but is it still a semi-magic square? _____
The special number was 12 for the original square.
What is the special number for the new square? _____

Use one of your own semi-magic squares, and make up a rule for transforming it. Do not tell anyone else what your rule is. Your rule must include multiplying by a number, and adding or subtracting a number.

Your square		Your rule	Your new square	

→

Copy out your new square, but only fill in four of its numbers. Think about which four you are going to show.
Swap with a partner and try to complete each other's squares.
Remember: keep your own rule secret. Can you work out your partner's rule?

Magic squares: investigations

Choose option A or option B to investigate.
If you finish early you can move on to option C.

A) Creating magic squares

Try creating magic squares using some of these numbers:
- nine consecutive numbers, e.g. 16 to 24
- three sets of three consecutive numbers, e.g. 2, 3, 4, 8, 9, 10, 14, 15, 16
- nine consecutive multiples of a chosen number
- all odd numbers, or all even numbers
- positive and negative numbers
- other sets of numbers of your own devising.

Explain any patterns you discover.

B Transforming magic squares

Try to create new magic squares from your existing set. You could try one of these ideas:
- use addition, subtraction and multiplication rules
- use division to make a square with fractions, mixed numbers or decimals.

What is the magic total for each of your squares?
Explain any patterns you discover.

C) 4 by 4 magic squares

These magic squares use the numbers 1 to 16. Their magic totals are all 34.
Copy and complete the squares.

	2	15	16
13		3	4
	7		
8	11	6	

	14	8	
15			5
10			4
	11	1	16

13		8	
	16		5
12		1	
	9		4

14		1	4
2			
			5
7	6		9

Now try to make your own 4 by 4 magic squares using the numbers 1 to 16.
Are there any patterns to be discovered and explained?

Abacus Evolve Year 5 Challenge PCM © Pearson Education Ltd 2009

Abacus *Evolve* Year 5 Challenge PCM © Pearson Education Ltd 2009

Areas on a pinboard: preparation I

Make these shapes on your pinboard. Work out the area of each shape.
In the workings box show your workings and answer the question.

I	What units of area are you using? Area:
2	Why is the area not 5 squares? Area:
3	Can you turn this shape into a rectangle with the same area? Area:
4	What methods could you use to find the area of this shape? Area:
5	How could you use symmetry to find the area of this shape? Area:
6	Work with your group. Try out some different methods. Area:

Areas on a pinboard: preparation 2

Find the area of the shapes. Record your workings and answers.

7	
8	
9	
10	
11	
12	

Create your own shapes on a pinboard or on square dot paper, then challenge a partner to find the areas.

Abacus Evolve Year 5 Challenge PCM © Pearson Education Ltd 2009

Abacus Evolve Year 5 Challenge PCM © Pearson Education Ltd 2009

Areas on a pinboard: investigations

Choose option A or option B to investigate.
If you finish early you can move on to option C or D.

A) Dotty triangles

You will need: a square-based 25-pin pinboard or square dot paper.
Investigate the area of triangles with the same base and height by constructing them inside rectangles.
Extend to triangles with different bases and heights.
Can you find any patterns in your results and diagrams? Explain any patterns you discover.

B) Areas of shapes

You will need: a square-based 25-pin pinboard or square dot paper.
Find all the shapes you can make with an area of 0·5. Then find all the shapes with an area of 1, 1·5, and so on.
What relationships can you see between shapes with the same area?
Explain any patterns you discover.

C) Areas on a triangle grid

You will need: a triangle-based 25-pin pinboard or triangle dot paper.
Make shapes with different areas on a grid of triangles. The unit of area is one of the equilateral triangles. Find all the shapes you can make with an area of 0·5. Then find all the shapes with an area of 1, 1·5, and so on.
What relationships can you see between shapes with the same area?
Compare your findings with shapes on a grid of squares.
Explain any patterns you discover.

D) Dotty fraction shapes

You will need: a 25-pin pinboard or square dot paper.
Make shapes with different areas on your 25-pin pinboard, or on square dot paper using squares of 25 dots. The unit of area is the 4 by 4 square. So each small square has an area of $\frac{1}{16}$. Investigate what shapes you can make within the 4 by 4 square, finding the areas as fractions.
Compare your findings with shapes in which each small square has an area of 1.
Explain what you discover.

Answers

AI

AI.1

1. At one number per second it would take 11 days, 13 hours, 46 minutes and 40 seconds.
2. Answers will vary.
3. Approximately four 10p coins in 10 cm so approximately £4000. 1 km of £1 coins would be worth around £45 000.

AI.2

1. $a =$ or $\leqslant$; $b <$ or $\leqslant$; $c >$ or $\geqslant$ or $\approx$; $d =$; $e >$ or $\geqslant$
2. Incorrect; $3.4 < 4.3$
3. Correct
4. Incorrect; $170 < 171 < 175 <$
5. Correct
6. Incorrect; $4.05 < 4.1$

Extra

7. Any number greater than 25
8. Any number greater than 52
9. 6 or any correct fractional or decimal answer between 5 and 7
10. Any fractional or decimal number between 1 and 2
11. Any fractional number between $\frac{1}{4}$ and $\frac{1}{2}$

AI.3

PCM I

1.

Position	Triangular number	Made by adding
1st	1	1
2nd	3	1 + 2
3rd	6	1 + 2 + 3
4th	10	1 + 2 + 3 + 4
5th	15	1 + 2 + 3 + 4 + 5
6th	21	1 + 2 + 3 + 4 + 5 + 6
7th	28	1 + 2 + 3 + 4 + 5 + 6 + 7
8th	36	1 + 2 + 3 + 4 + 5 + 6 + 7 + 8
9th	45	1 + 2 + 3 + 4 + 5 + 6 + 7 + 8 + 9
10th	55	1 + 2 + 3 + 4 + 5 + 6 + 7 + 8 + 9 + 10

2.
PCM I

Position	Square number	Made by multiplying	Made by adding triangular numbers	Positions of triangular numbers
1st	1	1 × 1	1	1st
2nd	4	2 × 2	1 + 3	1st and 2nd
3rd	9	3 × 3	3 + 6	2nd and 3rd
4th	16	4 × 4	6 + 10	3rd and 4th
5th	25	5 × 5	10 + 15	4th and 5th
6th	36	6 × 6	15 + 21	5th and 6th
7th	49	7 × 7	21 + 28	6th and 7th
8th	64	8 × 8	28 + 36	7th and 8th
	81	9 × 9	36 + 45	8th and 9th
		10 × 10	45 + 55	9th and 10th

3. The nth square number is n^2 and is made by adding the $(n - 1)$th and the nth triangular number.
4. Yes the sequence continues.

AI.4

PCM 3

Do this → to this ↓	× 2	× 0·2	× 5	× 0·5	÷ 2	÷ 0·2	÷ 5	÷ 0·5
1	2	0·2	5	0·5	0·5	5	0·2	2
25	50	5	125	12·5	12·5	125	5	50
50	100	10	250	25	25	250	10	100
10	20	2	50	5	5	50	2	20
2	4	0·4	10	1	1	10	0·4	4
1·5	3	0·3	7·5	0·75	0·75	7·5	0·3	3

AI.5

1. 0·2222 .... or 0·$\dot{2}$
2. 0·3333 .... or 0·3$\dot{3}$
3. 0·4444 .... or 0·$\dot{4}$
4. 0·5555 .... or 0·$\dot{5}$
5. 0·6666 .... or 0·$\dot{6}$
6. 0·7777 .... or 0·$\dot{7}$
7. 0·8888 .... or 0·$\dot{8}$
8. 1
9. 0·090909 .... or 0·$\dot{0}\dot{9}$
10. 0·181818 .... or 0·$\dot{1}\dot{8}$
11. 0·272727 .... or 0·$\dot{2}\dot{7}$
12. 0·363636 .... or 0·$\dot{3}\dot{6}$
13. 0·454545 .... or 0·$\dot{4}\dot{5}$
14. 0·636363 .... or 0·$\dot{6}\dot{3}$
15. 0·727272 .... or 0·$\dot{7}\dot{2}$
16. 0·909090 .... or 0·$\dot{9}\dot{0}$

Extra

$\frac{2}{7} = 0.285714285714....$

$\frac{3}{7} = 0.428571428571....$

All sevenths give cyclic numbers.

AI.6

1. Answers will vary but will always be two numbers in ratio 20 : 3
2. They will always be two numbers in ratio 20 : 3
3. $5\frac{1}{3}$: any two numbers in ratio 16 : 3

   $4\frac{3}{5}$: any two numbers in ratio 23 : 5

   $1\frac{4}{9}$: any two numbers in ratio 13 : 9

   $8\frac{5}{6}$: any two numbers in ratio 53 : 6

   $4\frac{3}{4}$: any two numbers in ratio 19 : 4

   $3\frac{1}{4}$: any two numbers in ratio 13 : 4

   $7\frac{1}{8}$: any two numbers in ratio 57 : 8

   $2\frac{5}{7}$: any two numbers in ratio 19 : 7

   $13\frac{2}{5}$: any two numbers in ratio 67 : 5
4. Answers will vary, but should note that each ratio is the same.
5. $\frac{20}{30}$, $\frac{6}{9}$, $\frac{8}{12}$, $\frac{10}{15}$, $\frac{30}{45}$
6. No as the denominator would have to be 4·5.

Extra
PCM 4

Dividend	Divisor	Quotient	Decimal
28	3	$9\frac{1}{3}$	$9\cdot\dot{3}$
56	6	$9\frac{2}{6}$	$9\cdot\dot{3}$
84	9	$9\frac{3}{9}$	$9\cdot\dot{3}$
112	12	$9\frac{4}{12}$	$9\cdot\dot{3}$
140	15	$9\frac{5}{15}$	$9\cdot\dot{3}$
168	18	$9\frac{6}{18}$	$9\cdot\dot{3}$
196	21	$9\frac{7}{21}$	$9\cdot\dot{3}$
224	24	$9\frac{8}{24}$	$9\cdot\dot{3}$

BI.I

1. e.g. 48 × 24 = 1152; 48 × 30 = 1440;
   48 × 12 = 576; even × even = even
2. e.g. 45 × 3 = 135; 45 × 5 = 225;
   45 × 27 = 1215; odd × odd = odd
3. e.g. 48 × 3 = 144; 48 × 5 = 240;
   48 × 27 = 1296; even × odd = even
4. even ÷ even = even (48 ÷ 12 = 4)
   or odd fractional (36 ÷ 24= 1·5);
   odd ÷ odd = odd (25 ÷ 5 = 5)
   or even fractional (81 ÷ 5 = 16·2)
   even ÷ odd = even
5. e.g. 25 ÷ 3 = 8·33333 (a recurring odd digit)

Extra

even × even × even × ..... = even

odd × odd × odd × ...... = odd

A product of numbers will always give an <u>even</u> answer if there is any <u>even</u> number in the string.

BI.2

1. Yes as the sequence goes '+ 2 – 4 + 2'.
2. As the sequence starts on an odd number and only moves in multiples of 2 the sequence will stay odd.
3. 30, 50, 70, 90, ...
4. The sequence is made by the steps +9; −2; +4; +9; −2; ...
5. The 10th number is over 1000. ... 669; 639; 840; 810; 1011
6. The 22nd number will be over 2000 (= 2037)
7. 2·36; 2·39; 2·42; 2·45; 2·48; 2·51; 2·54; 2·57; 2·60; 2·63; 2·66; 2·69; 2·72; 2·75
8. ⁻5·9; ⁻5·4; ⁻4·9; ⁻4·4; ⁻3·9; ⁻3·4; ⁻2·9; ⁻2·4; ⁻1·9; ⁻1·4; ⁻0·9; ⁻0·4; 0·1
9. $-3\frac{1}{2}$; $-2\frac{3}{4}$; ⁻2; $-1\frac{1}{4}$; $-\frac{1}{2}$; $\frac{1}{4}$; 1; $1\frac{3}{4}$; $2\frac{1}{2}$; $3\frac{1}{4}$; 4; $4\frac{3}{4}$; $5\frac{1}{2}$
10. 13; $11\frac{3}{5}$; $10\frac{1}{5}$; $8\frac{4}{5}$; $7\frac{2}{5}$; 6; $4\frac{3}{5}$; $3\frac{1}{5}$; $1\frac{4}{5}$; $\frac{2}{5}$; ⁻1; $-2\frac{2}{5}$; $-3\frac{4}{5}$

BI.3

1. 20; 10; 5; 6; 3; 4; 2; 1
2. 7 steps
3. e.g. 23; 24; 12; 6; 3; 4; 2; 1 (7 steps)
4. 66 takes 12 steps.
5. 513 is the number below 1000 which takes the most steps to reach 1. It takes 19 steps.

Extra

Answers will vary.

BI.4
PCM 6

	Parallel sides	No parallel sides
Perpendicular sides	(shapes)	(shapes)
No perpendicular sides	(shapes)	(shapes)

BI.5

1. Shape b (the cross) has the most parallel faces.
2. Shape b (the cross) has the most perpendicular faces.
3. Answers will vary.

B1.6

PCM 5

C1

C1.1

1.

Frequency table

Sunflower height (cm)	Frequency
56	3
57	1
58	2
59	6
60	1
61	3
62	5
63	2
64	4
65	3

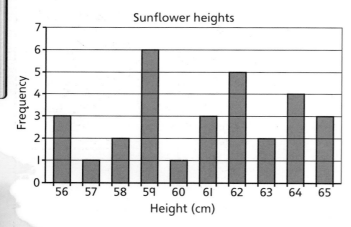

2.

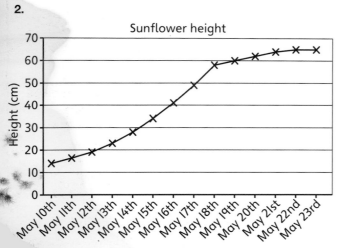

C1.2

1. The population has grown but not always quickly – the rate varied and for some intervals the population decreased.

PCM 8

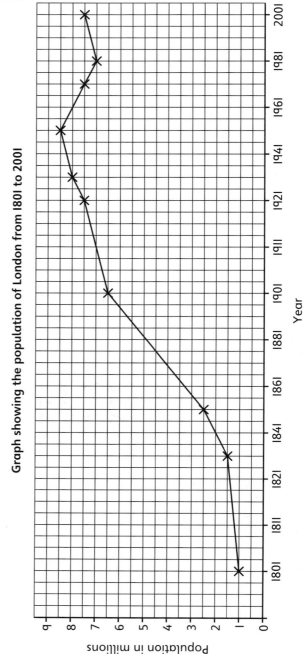

2. Population growth was quickest from 1851 to 1901.
3. Answers will vary. Children may use the graph to extrapolate that population will continue to grow, or may comment, with reasons, that population may again go down.
4. 48 km/h
5. Yes. 60 mph = 96 km/h
6. 69 mph

7.

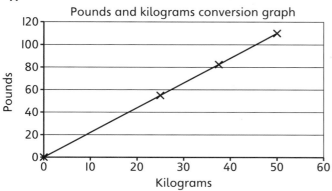

Pounds and kilograms conversion graph

(graph: y-axis labelled "Pounds" from 0 to 120, x-axis labelled "Kilograms" from 0 to 60, with a straight line through plotted points)

8. 14 kg

9. 66 kg

Cl.3

1. Salma
2. 5
3. 6
4. Joe
5. 5·2
6. 4·7
7. Joe
8. 5
9. 5
10. Salma
11. 4
12. 5
13. Mark   mode 5; mean 5·1; median 5; range 6
    Freya   mode 9; mean 6·4; median 6·5; range 6
    Sol   mode 8; mean 6·6; median 7·5; range 6
14. Sol; he has the highest median and mean score.

Extra

Greentown   mode 0; mean 5·3; median 3·5; range 18
Bluebrooke   mode 4; mean 5·3; median 4·5; range 7
Answers will vary, but children should consider the total runs scored which is 53 for both teams.

Cl.4

1. Answers will vary. Children should comment that it is difficult to work in both metric and imperial units at the same time. They may notice that supermarkets often quote prices per unit weight, e.g. 34p for 100g, to help comparisons.

Cl.5

1.

	Rectangle 1	Rhombus 1	Rectangle 2	Rhombus 2
Longest side (cm)	16	10	8	5
Shortest side (cm)	12	10	6	5
Area (cm²)	192	96	48	24
Diagonal 1 (cm)	20	16	10	8
Diagonal 2 (cm)	20	12	10	6

2. Answers will vary but will include: Rectangle 2 has sides $\frac{1}{2}$ those in rectangle 1. Its area is $\frac{1}{4}$ of rectangle 1. Rhombus 2 has sides $\frac{1}{2}$ those in rhombus 1. Its area is $\frac{1}{4}$ of rhombus 1.

3.

	Rectangle 3	Rhombus 3
Longest side (cm)	4	2·5
Shortest side (cm)	3	2·5
Area (cm²)	12	6
Diagonal 1 (cm)	5	4
Diagonal 2 (cm)	5	3

4. Answers will vary.

5. Answers will vary, but should be a variation of $\frac{1}{2}$ × diagonal 1 × diagonal 2

Extra

Starting with a square gives a similar sequence but all the shapes are square. The same relationships exist between squares 1, 3, 5 and 2, 4, 6 as in the rectangle investigation.

Cl.6

PCM 9

	Price 1	Price 2
Potatoes	2·5 kg for £2·38 95·2p/kg	1 kg for £1·19 119p/kg
Baked beans	420 g for 52p 12·4p/100g	415 g for 50p 12·0p/100g
Soap	4 × 125 g for £1·58 31·6p/100g	2 × 200 g for £1·05 26·3p/100g
Crackers	12 × 25 g for £1·99 66·3/100g	10 × 17 g for £1·23 72·4p/100g
Fruit squash	$\frac{1}{2}$ litre, 2 for £1·50 150p/litre	150 ml for 24p 160p/litre
Detergent	2·47 kg for £6·47 261·9p/kg	950 g for £2·38 250·5p/kg
Cabbage	1·5 kg for 68p 45·3p/kg	1k g for 50p 50p/kg
Butter	500 g for £1·70 340p/kg	$\frac{1}{4}$ kg for 94p 376p/kg
Tea bags	160 for £2·35 14·7p/10 tea bags	240 for £3·29 13·7p/10 tea bags
Milk	4 pints for £1·44 63·4p/litre	2 l for £1·19 59·5p/litre

	Price 3	Price 4
Potatoes	2 kg for £1·99 99·5p/kg	300 g for 41p 136·7p/kg
Baked beans	220 g for 26p 11·8p/100g	400 g for 40p 10p/100g
Soap	125 g for 39p 31·2p/100g	2 × 125 g for £1·02 40·8p/100g
Crackers	7 × 25 g for £1·25 71·4p/100g	150 g for £1·12 74·7p/100g
Fruit squash	$\frac{1}{3}$ l for 43p 129p/litre	8 × 25 cl for £2·95 147·5p/litre
Detergent	$\frac{1}{2}$ kg for £1·57 314p/kg	780 g for £1·98 253·8p/kg
Cabbage	730 g for 43p 58·9p/kg	160 g for 7p 43·8p/kg
Butter	1000 g for £2·98 298p/kg	125 g for 50p 400p/kg
Tea bags	80 for £1·29 16·1p/10 tea bags	120 for £1·49 12·4p/10 tea bags
Milk	2 pints for 80p 70·4p/litre	568 ml for 4? 7? 9p/litr?

DI

DI.1

1. a isosceles triangle
   b right-angled scalene triangle
   c right-angled scalene triangle
   d rectangle
   e square
2. a 2 sides and 2 base angles equal, 1 line of symmetry
   b right-angle, no sides or angles equal, no symmetry
   c right-angle, no sides or angles equal, no symmetry
   d 2 opposite pairs of equal sides, 4 right angles, 2 lines of symmetry, rotational symmetry order 2
   e 4 equal sides, 4 right angles, 4 lines of symmetry, rotational symmetry order 4
3. a 1 line of symmetry
   b no symmetry
   c no symmetry
   d 2 lines of symmetry
   e 4 lines of symmetry
4. b and c

DI.2

2. F, L, N, W, Y, Z
3. F 12 cm; I 12 cm; N 12 cm; P 10 cm; U 12 cm; V 12 cm; W 12 cm; Y 12 cm; Z 12 cm
4. They all have perimeter 12 cm except P. The perimeter depends on how the squares are joined. The number of touching pairs of sides is 4 for all the 12 cm perimeter shapes, but 5 for the 10 cm shape.

Extra

There are 35 hexominoes. The shortest perimeter for hexominoes is 10 cm (3 cubes × 2 cubes) with 7 pairs of touching sides. The longest perimeter is 14 cm (6 cubes × 1 cube) with 5 pairs of touching sides.

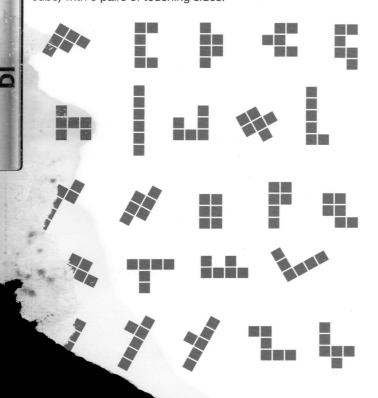

Closed cube nets

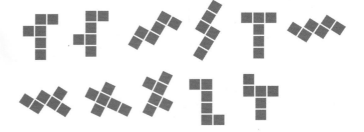

DI.3

Shape	Number and shape of faces	Number of vertices	Number of edges	Size of each angle on each face
cube	6 square	8	12	90°
tetrahedron	4 triangle	4	6	60°
octahedron	8 triangle	6	12	60°
icosahedron	20 triangle	12	30	60°
dodecahedron	12 pentagon	20	30	108°

Extra

Platonic solids make fair dice.

DI.4

1. The digits add to 9 and the digits of one number are the reverse of the other.
2. 18 and 81; 27 and 72; (and 09 and 90)
3. There will be 1p left over from £1 if the digits sum to 9.
4. 35 and 53; 44 and 44; (and 08 and 80)
5. 15 and 51; 24 and 42; 33 and 33 (and 06 and 60)
6. 14 and 41; 23 and 32 (and 05 and 50)
7. 13 and 31, 22 and 22 (and 04 and 40)
8. 67, 78, 89 can be left over
9. 82p + 28 p = £1·10 not £1
10. Pairs that do not work include any with digits that sum to more than 9, e.g. 56 and 65.

Extra

Digit total 11: 56 and 65; 47 and 74; 29 and 92; 38 and 83
Digit total 14: 59 and 95; 68 and 86; 77 and 77
Digit total 12: 39 and 93; 48 and 84; 57 and 75; 66 and 66
Digit total 13: 49 and 94; 58 and 85; 67 and 76
Digit total 15: 69 and 96; 78 and 87
Other answers will vary.

All possible positions are shown. Highlighted figures are those with a fixed position.

	Multiple of 2	Multiple of 4	Multiple of 25	Multiple of 9
Multiple of 3	7146, 2916, 28416, 4032, 19284, 990	2916, 28416, 4032, 19284, 9900	2325, 2625, 9900	7290, 7146, 4032, 9900, 4257
Multiple of 10	68210, 5600, 9900	36160, 5600, 9900	8250, 9900	7290, 9900
Multiple of 8	36160, 1104, 5704, 28416, 5600, 4032, 5472	36160, 1104, 5704, 28416, 5600, 4032, 5472	5600	4032
Multiple of 6	7146, 2916, 1104, 28416, 4032, 19284, 9900	2916, 1104, 28416, 19284, 9900	8250, 9900	7290, 7146, 4032, 19284, 9900

DI.6

PCM 12

	6	4	4	2
8	6	4		8 or 9
7	4		1	9
2		3	6	6
5	4	9	9	

1. 366
2. 6442
3. 19
4. 8725
5. 2896
6. 74
7. 664, 864
8. 864
9. 169
10. 29, 44, 39, 19
11. 5499
12. 2996

EI

EI.1

1. 648
2. 542
3. 952
4. 1124
5. 1552
6. 7740
7. 8414
8. 10 472
9. 15 652
10. 12 934
11. 8·46
12. 12·54
13. 9·66
14. 11·52
15. 12·14

16. Answers will vary, but may include inverse operations or estimation.

Extra

$426 + 427 = 852 + 1 = 853$
$362 + 372 = 724 + 10 = 734$
$4671 + 4571 = 9142 + 100 = 9242$
$7·28 + 7·38 = 14·56 + 0·1 = 14·66$

EI.2

PCM 13

Number	Double
660	1320
733	1466
3452	6904
1601	3202
737	1474
67·8	135·6
490	980
387	774
1551	3102
380	760
391	782
4·87	9·74
367	734
3·08	6·16
2345	4690
45·37	90·74
34·7	69·4
7·74	15·48
452	904
203	No double
96·1	No double

DI

EI.3

1.

	Original price	Sale price
pencil case	£4·86	£2·43
pens	£3·54	£1·77
stationery set	£6·38	£3·19
teddy	£11·26	£5·63
birthday card	£2·72	£1·36
DVD	£12·39	£6·195 (£6·20)
board game	£19·79	£9·895 (£9·90)
toy robot	£25·76	£12·88
computer game	£23·55	£11·775 (£11·78)

2. To buy 1 of each item costs £55·14 so you cannot buy all the items with £50.

Extra

£2·43 + £3·19 + £5·63 + £6·20 + £11·78 = £29·23
so there would be 77p left.

EI.4

1. There are fewer possible combinations for the larger numbers.

2. Many combinations produce whole numbers,
e.g. $\frac{5}{5}, \frac{6}{1}, \frac{6}{2}, \frac{6}{3}, \frac{6}{6}, \frac{7}{1}, \frac{8}{4}, \frac{8}{2}, \frac{9}{1}, \frac{9}{3}, \frac{9}{1}, \frac{10}{5}, \frac{10}{2}, \frac{10}{1}, \ldots$

3. $\frac{5}{3}, \frac{5}{4}$ or $\frac{6}{4}$ or $\frac{7}{4}, \frac{6}{5}$ or $\frac{7}{5}$ or $\frac{8}{5}$ or $\frac{9}{5}, \frac{7}{6}$ or $\frac{8}{6}$ or $\frac{9}{6}$ or $\frac{10}{6}$ or $\frac{11}{6}$

4. $\frac{11}{2}, \frac{17}{3}, \frac{21}{4}$ or $\frac{22}{4}$ or $\frac{23}{4}$

5. $\frac{15}{2}, \frac{22}{3}$ or $\frac{23}{3}$

Extra

$\frac{13}{4}$ is incorrect, could be $\frac{5}{2}, \frac{7}{3}$ or $\frac{8}{3}, \frac{9}{4}$ or $\frac{10}{4}$ or $\frac{11}{4}, \frac{11}{5}$ or $\frac{12}{5}$ or $\frac{13}{5}$
or $\frac{14}{5}, \frac{13}{6}$ or $\frac{14}{6}$ or $\frac{15}{6}$ or $\frac{16}{6}$ or $\frac{17}{6}$

$\frac{18}{4}$ is incorrect, could be any combination listed in question 3

$\frac{16}{3}$ is incorrect, could be $\frac{17}{2}; \frac{25}{3}$

$\frac{21}{2}$ is incorrect, must be $\frac{19}{2}$

EI.5

1. $\frac{5}{8}$

2. $\frac{2}{3}$

3. $\frac{3}{5}$

4. $\frac{3}{5}$

5. $\frac{4}{5}$

6. $\frac{10}{9} = 1\frac{1}{9}$

7. $\frac{5}{3} = 1\frac{2}{3}$

8. $\frac{10}{3} = 3\frac{1}{3}$

9. $\frac{12}{5} = 2\frac{2}{5}$

10. $\frac{13}{4} = 3\frac{1}{4}$

11. $\frac{4}{5}$

12. $\frac{2}{3}$

13. $\frac{5}{2}$

Extra

$\frac{3}{4} = \frac{15}{20}$ and $\frac{4}{5} = \frac{16}{20}$ so $\frac{4}{5}$ is larger

$\frac{5}{6} = \frac{35}{42}$ and $\frac{6}{7} = \frac{36}{42}$ so $\frac{6}{7}$ is larger

$\frac{6}{7} = \frac{48}{56}$ and $\frac{7}{8} = \frac{49}{56}$ so $\frac{7}{8}$ is larger

When the numerator is one less than the denominator the following is true
$\frac{1}{2} < \frac{2}{3} < \frac{3}{4} < \frac{4}{5} < \frac{5}{6}$ etc.

EI.6

1. 100 grams of beans
10 grams of tomato paste
1 onions
0·5 pepper
2 grams of chilli powder
4 tomatoes
80 grams of minced beef

2. 1000 grams of beans
100 grams of tomato paste
10 onions
5 peppers
20 grams of chilli powder
40 tomatoes
800 grams of minced beef

3. 250 grams of beans
25 grams of tomato paste
2·5 onions
1·25 peppers
5 grams of chilli powder
10 tomatoes
200 grams of minced beef

4. 900 grams of beans
90 grams of tomato paste
9 onions
4·5 peppers
18 grams of chilli powder
36 tomatoes
720 grams of minced beef

A2

A2.I

1. Barcelona; Bern; Copenhagen; Düsseldorf; Frankfurt; Hamburg; Marseilles; Milan; Munich; Prague; Zurich

2. Stockholm

3. Belgrade; Budapest; Helsinki; Lisbon; Oslo; Stockholm; Venice; Vienna; Warsaw

4. Nearest Amsterdam, 400 km; furthest Istanbul, 3200 km

5. and 6.

	5.		6.
	miles	gallons	hours
Athens	1490	7450	3
Beijing	5070	25 350	10
Berlin	560	2800	1
Mumbai	4480	22 400	9
Brussels	200	1000	0
Cairo	2190	10 950	4
Jerusalem	2250	11 250	4
Madrid	780	3900	2
Manila	6680	33 400	13
Moscow	1560	7800	3
Nairobi	4230	21 150	8
Sydney	10 560	52 800	21

Extra

Answers will vary

A2.2

PCM 15

Item	Amount	Conversion
1 Cheese	0·5 kg	(0·500 kg) largest
	1 lb	0·454 kg
	450 g	0·450 kg smallest
2 Milk	330 ml	0·330 l
	$\frac{1}{2}$ pint	0·284 l
	$\frac{1}{2}$ litre	(0·500 l)
3 Roads	5 miles	(8·045 km)
	7·5 km	7·500 km
	750 m	0·750 km
4 Glasses of juice	500 ml	0·500 l
	1 pint	0·568 l
	$\frac{3}{4}$ litre	(0·750 l)
5 Apples	$\frac{1}{2}$ lb	0·227 kg
	0·2 kg	0·200 kg
	260 g	(0·260 kg)
6 Lengths of rope	150 cm	0·00150 km
	$\frac{1}{100}$ mile	0·01609 km
	$\frac{1}{4}$ km	(0·25 km)
7 Rabbits	5 kg	(5·000 kg)
	10 lb	4·540 kg
	4950 g	4·950 kg

A2.3

PCM 16

18 × 21 20 × 20 = 400 378	17 × 23 20 × 20 = 400 391	16 × 24 20 × 20 = 400 384	15 × 22 20 × 20 = 400 330	19 × 22 20 × 20 = 400 418
1·8 × 210 2 × 200 = 400 378	170 × 2·3 200 × 2 = 400 391	1·6 × 240 2 × 200 = 400 384	150 × 2·2 200 × 2 = 400 330	1·9 × 220 2 × 200 = 400 418
1800 × 0·21 2000 × 0·2 = 400 378	1·7 × 230 2 × 200 = 400 391	0·16 × 2400 0·2 × 2000 = 400 384	1·5 × 220 2 × 200 = 400 330	1900 × 0·22 2000 × 0·2 = 400 418
17 × 24 20 × 20 = 400 408	16 × 23 20 × 20 = 400 368	15 × 23 20 × 20 = 400 345	19 × 23 20 × 20 = 400 437	18 × 23 20 × 20 = 400 414
1·7 × 240 2 × 200 = 400 408	1·6 × 230 2 × 200 = 400 368	150 × 2·3 200 × 2 = 400 345	190 × 2·3 200 × 2 = 400 437	1·8 × 230 2 × 200 = 400 414
1700 × 0·24 2000 × 0·2 = 400 408	0·16 × 2300 0·2 × 2000 = 400 368	1·5 × 230 2 × 200 = 400 345	1·9 × 230 2 × 200 = 400 437	0·18 × 2300 0·2 × 2000 = 400 414
15 × 21 20 × 20 = 400 315	17 × 22 20 × 20 = 400 374	16 × 21 20 × 20 = 400 336	18 × 24 20 × 20 = 400 432	19 × 24 20 × 20 = 400 456
1·5 × 210 2 × 200 = 400 315	170 × 2·2 200 × 2 = 400 374	1·6 × 210 2 × 200 = 400 336	180 × 2·4 200 × 2 = 400 432	190 × 2·4 200 × 2 = 400 456
0·15 × 2100 0·2 × 2000 = 400 315	1700 × 0·22 2000 × 0·2 = 400 374	0·16 × 2100 0·2 × 2000 = 400 336	1800 × 0·24 2000 × 0·2 = 400 432	1900 × 0·24 2000 × 0·2 = 400 456
19 × 21 20 × 20 = 400 399	15 × 24 20 × 20 = 400 360	18 × 22 20 × 20 = 400 396	16 × 22 20 × 20 = 400 352	17 × 21 20 × 20 = 400 357
190 × 2·1 200 × 2 = 400 399	150 × 2·4 200 × 2 = 400 360	1·8 × 220 2 × 200 = 400 396	1·6 × 220 2 × 200 = 400 352	1·7 × 210 2 × 200 = 400 357
1900 × 0·21 2000 × 0·2 = 400 399	0·15 × 2400 0·2 × 2000 = 400 360	1800 × 0·22 2000 × 0·2 = 400 396	0·16 × 2200 0·2 × 2000 = 400 352	1700 × 0·21 2000 × 0·2 = 400 357

A2.4

1. 1353
2. 5192
3. 6490
4. 101 233
5. 85 547
6. 31 185
7. 135 531
8. 444 444
9. 888 888
10. 26 730
11. 619 850
12. 3 126 200

A2.5

7th, 14th, 21st or 28th June 1987
Tuesday
Answers will vary.
Answers will vary.

5. Answers will vary.
6. Sometimes true
7. Sometimes true
8. Sometimes true
9. 7672 or 7671
10. Not necessarily – they will have been alive for either 7672 or 7671 days.

Extra

It actually takes the earth $365\frac{1}{4}$ days to go round the sun. We have an extra day every four years in order to 'use up' these extra quarter days and keep our calendar in line with the turning of the Earth.

A2.6

1. Answers will vary, for example 60, 24 and 84 are common multiples of 2, 3, 4, 6, 12
2. Answers will vary
3. Answers will vary, for example 60, 24, 84, 36
4. Answers will vary, for example 60, 24, 84, 36, 12

5. Answers will vary, for example 60, 24, 84, 36, 12, 30.

6.
$60 = 2 \times 2 \times 3 \times 5$
$24 = 2 \times 2 \times 2 \times 3$
$25 = 5 \times 5$
$84 = 2 \times 2 \times 3 \times 7$
$36 = 2 \times 2 \times 3 \times 3$
$15 = 3 \times 5$
$9 = 3 \times 3$
$30 = 2 \times 3 \times 5$
$12 = 2 \times 2 \times 3$
$21 = 3 \times 7$
$40 = 2 \times 2 \times 2 \times 5$
$42 = 2 \times 3 \times 7$
$20 = 2 \times 2 \times 5$
$18 = 2 \times 3 \times 3$
$14 = 2 \times 7$
$35 = 5 \times 7$

7. They are all prime numbers.

Extra

All common multiples have the same prime factors.

B2

B2.1

1.

×	200	70	6
30	6000	2100	180
2	400	140	12

2. Total the values in the cells to give the answer = 8832

3. Largest **e** smallest **c**

4. **a**

×	400	30	8
20	8000	600	160
7	2800	210	56

$438 \times 27 = 11\,826$

b

×	400	50	2
30	12 000	1500	60
5	2000	250	10

$452 \times 35 = 15\,820$

c

×	200	90	1
30	6000	2700	30
6	1200	540	6

$36 \times 291 = 10\,476$

d

×	300	80	3
40	12 000	3200	120
5	1500	400	15

$45 \times 383 = 17\,235$

e

×	300	00	6
60	18 000	0	360
7	2100	0	42

$306 \times 67 = 20\,502$

5. Same value (24 420)

6. Same value (25 641)

7. Same value (21 978)

8. The grids shows that partitioning numbers in these cases give the same set of products

Extra

$272 \times 727 = 197\,744 > 772 \times 227 = 175\,244$
$722 \times 277 = 199\,994 > 777 \times 222 = 172\,494$

B2.2

1. Children may do the calculation starting their table with either of the two given numbers.

1	36
2	72
4	144
8	288
16	576
32	1152

$16 + 4 + 1 = 21$; $21 \times 36 = 576 + 144 + 36 = 756$

2.

1	27
2	54
4	108
8	216
16	432
32	864

$16 + 8 + 4 + 2 + 1 = 31$;
$31 \times 27 = 432 + 216 + 108 + 54 + 27 = 837$

3.

1	52
2	104
4	208
8	416
16	832
32	1664
64	3328

$32 + 4 + 2 + 1 = 39$;
$39 \times 52 = 1664 + 208 + 104 + 52 = 2028$

4.

1	28
2	56
4	112
8	224
16	448
32	896
64	1792

$32 + 16 + 4 + 1 = 53$;
$53 \times 28 = 896 + 448 + 112 + 28 = 1484$

5.

1	43
2	86
4	172
8	344
16	688
32	1376
64	2752
128	5504

$64 + 8 + 4 + 1 = 77$;
$77 \times 43 = 2752 + 344 + 172 + 43 = 3311$

Extra

Yes, the method works for all numbers

B2.3

1. £3 doubled for 10 days gives £1536 so £2000 is better.
2. £7 doubled for 15 days gives £114 688 so that is the better option.
3. £5 doubled for 20 days gives £2 621440 so that is the better option.
4. Doubling 10 times gives 1024.
5. Doubling 14 times gives 16 384.
6. Doubling 17 times gives 131 072.
7. Doubling 20 times gives 1 048 576.

Extra

Tripling 7 times gives 2187
Tripling 9 times gives 19 683
Tripling 11 times gives 177 147
Tripling 13 times gives 1 594 323

B2.4

1. A (9,6); B (6,1); C (2,5); D (⁻3, 6); E (0, 2); F (⁻8, 8); G (⁻8, 0); H (⁻4, 4)
2. (⁻6,7)(⁻4,7)(0,6)(1,2)(⁻4,2)(⁻4,5)(⁻6,5)
3. (⁻9,7)(⁻1,7)(⁻1,3)(⁻5,3)(⁻5,6)(⁻7,6)(⁻7,3)(⁻9,3)
4. (⁻1,3)(4,3)(4,2)(3,2)(2,0)(1,2)(⁻1,0)
5. (1,8)(10,7)(8,5)(4,5)(1,3)
6. (⁻7,⁻5)(⁻5,⁻2)(⁻2,⁻3)

Extra

Answers will vary.

PCM 17

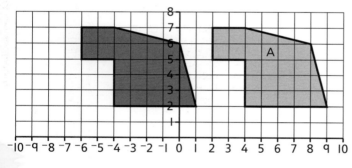

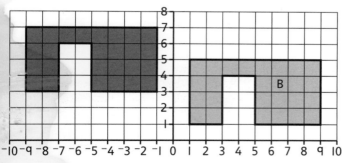

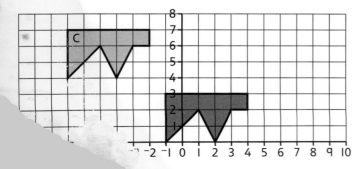

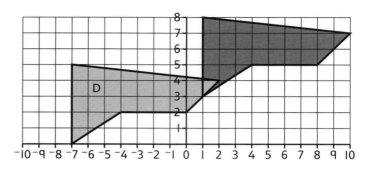

B2.5

PCM 19

1. New shape: (⁻1,2)(⁻1,5)(⁻2,7)(⁻7,7)(⁻7,4)(⁻4,5)(⁻3,2)

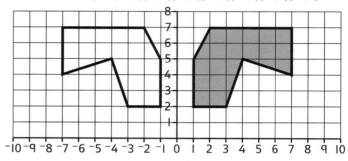

2. New shape: (8,7)(2,8)(1,2)(4,2)(4,6)(8,6)

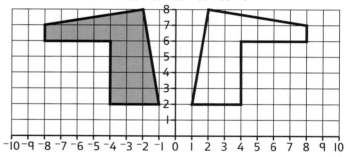

3. New shape: (0,3)(⁻3,6)(⁻7,5)(⁻7,2)(⁻3,0)

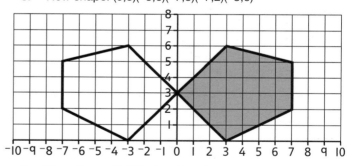

4. New shape: (8,6)(4,4)(2,6)(0,0)(4,2)(6,0)

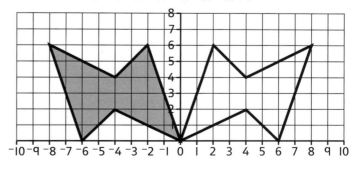

The x coordinates of the reflected shapes have the same value but opposite sign to the original shape. The y coordinates do not change.

B2.6

2. All pentagons have 5 diagonals. (With a concave pentagon some of the diagonals may be outside the shape.)
3. Each diagonal produces a triangle and a quadrilateral. The precise shape of each polygon depends on the dimensions of the original pentagon.
4. All hexagons have 9 diagonals. A diagonal makes either a triangle and a pentagon or 2 quadrilaterals. (With a concave hexagon some of the diagonals may be outside the shape)

Extra

Octagons have 20 diagonals. A diagonal makes either a triangle and a heptagon or a quadrilateral and a hexagon or 2 pentagons.

PCM 20

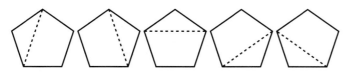

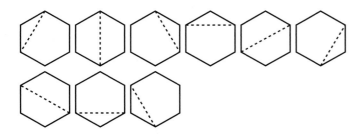

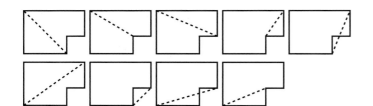

C2

C2.I

1.

	Width	Height	Area
a	34·7 mm	36·5 mm	1266·55 mm²
b	20·3 mm	24·1 mm	489·23 mm²
c	41 mm	26 mm	1066 mm²
d	40·6 mm	29·8 mm	1209·88 mm²

2.

	Width	Height	Area
A4	210 mm	297 mm	62 370 mm²
A3	297 mm	420 mm	124 740 mm²
A2	420 mm	594 mm	249 480 mm²
A1	594 mm	841 mm	499 554 mm²
A0	841 mm	1189 mm	999 949 mm²

3.

	Number of stamps	Total stamp area (mm²)	Wasted area per sheet (mm²)	Wasted area per stamp (mm²)
A3 landscape	20 × 12 = 240	117 415·2	7324·8	30·5
A3 portrait	14 × 17 = 238	116 436·7	8303·3	34·9
A2 landscape	17 × 29 = 493	241 190·4	8289·6	16·8
A2 portrait	20 × 24 = 480	234 830·4	14 649·6	30·5
A1 landscape	24 × 41 = 984	481 402·3	18 151·7	18·4
A1 portrait	29 × 34 = 986	482 380·8	17 173·2	17·4
A0 landscape	34 × 58 = 1972	964 761·6	35 187·4	17·8
A0 portrait	41 × 49 = 2009	982 863·1	17 085·9	8·5

4. Most efficient use of paper is A0 portrait because there is least wasted paper per stamp.

Extra

	Number of stamps	Value 27p	Value 36p	Value 50p	Value 56p
A4 portrait	6 × 8 = 48	£12·96	£17·28	£24·00	£26·88
A4 landscape	8 × 5 = 40	£10·80	£14·40	£20·00	£22·40

C2.2

Cuboid	Height	Depth	Length	Volume	Area of face 1	Area of face 2	Area of face 3	Face 1 + face 2 + face 3	Surface area
A	2 cm	2 cm	54 cm	216 cm³	4 cm²	108 cm²	108 cm²	220 cm²	440 cm²
B	2 cm	3 cm	36 cm	216 cm³	6 cm²	108 cm²	72 cm²	186 cm²	372 cm²
C	2 cm	4 cm	27 cm	216 cm³	8 cm²	108 cm²	54 cm²	170 cm²	340 cm²
D	2 cm	6 cm	18 cm	216 cm³	12 cm²	108 cm²	36 cm²	156 cm²	312 cm²
E	2 cm	9 cm	12 cm	216 cm³	18 cm²	108 cm²	24 cm²	150 cm²	300 cm²
F	3 cm	2 cm	36 cm	216 cm³	6 cm²	72 cm²	108 cm²	186 cm²	372 cm²
G	3 cm	3 cm	24 cm	216 cm³	9 cm²	72 cm²	72 cm²	153 cm²	306 cm²
H	3 cm	4 cm	18 cm	216 cm³	12 cm²	72 cm²	54 cm²	138 cm²	276 cm²
I	3 cm	6 cm	12 cm	216 cm³	18 cm²	72 cm²	36 cm²	126 cm²	252 cm²
J	3 cm	8 cm	9 cm	216 cm³	24 cm²	72 cm²	27 cm²	123 cm²	246 cm²

C2.3

1. Shape c
2. No match. Shape a has perimeter of $4 \times 7 = 28$ cm.
3. Shape e
4. Shape a
5. Shape b
6. No match. Shape c has perimeter $14 \times 6 = 84$ cm.
7. Shape d
8. All areas may be calculated.
   Shape b has area $(6 \times 4) \div 2 = 12$ cm².
   Shape c has area $(12 \times 14) \div 2 \times 6 = 504$ cm².
   Shape d has area 238 cm².
   Shape e has area $3x^2$.

Extra

shape	area	perimeter
a	49 cm²	28 cm
b	12 cm²	16 cm
c	504 cm²	84 cm
d	238 mm²	60 mm
e	192 mm²	64 mm

C2.4

1. The Gregorian and Julian calendars have the same 12 months and the same 365 days with a leap year of 366 every 4th year.
   The Gregorian calendar modifies the Julian calendar's cycle of leap years as follows: Every year that is exactly divisible by 4 is a leap year, EXCEPT for years that are exactly divisible by 100; UNLESS they are also exactly divisible by 400, in which case they are still leap years. For example, the year 1900 is not a leap year; the year 2000 is a leap year.
2. 1 year is 52 weeks (52·1775).
3. 1 year is 8765·82 hours.
4. 1 year is 525 949·2 minutes.
5. 1 year is 31 556 952 seconds.
6. 86 400 seconds (1 day).
7. Answers will vary.
   For: It would be easier to calculate than the existing units, and would bring measuring time in line with the metric system.
   Against: It would be complicated and expensive to get the world to change their system.

8. Atomic clocks use the vibration of atoms to define the second. Originally Caesium atoms were used, but now Strontium is the standard and such atomic clocks lose or gain less than one second in 200 million years.

Extra

Omar Khayyam amended the Persian calendar in 1079. This calendar was then in use across Iran from the 11th to the 20th centuries and is more accurate than the Gregorian calendar. The lengths of the months can vary between 29 and 32 days depending on the moment when the sun crosses into a new area of the zodiac.

C2.5

1. and 2.
Answers will vary.

Monday	Tuesday	Wednesday	Thursday	Friday
E	A	B	A	C
A or B	D	A	B	A
E	A or B	D	A	B
A	F	A or B	D	A
B	A		A or B	D
A	B	A		A or B

No it is not possible. A and B are fixed, D, E and F may start in any place but it is not possible to fit in the others as C, E and F are all multiples of 5. Children should try and arrange all lifts doing about 6 trips each.

Extra

Answers will vary. Changing C to every 6 days starting at day 5 will allow complete cover.

Monday	Tuesday	Wednesday	Thursday	Friday
F	A	B	E	C
B	D	A	B	A
F	B	D	E	B
A	C	B	D	A
F	A	C	E	D
A	B	A	C	A

C2.6

PCM 22

<table>
<tr><th colspan="3">Monday</th></tr>
<tr><th>Start and end time</th><th>Length</th><th>Programme</th></tr>
<tr><td>16:00–16:30</td><td>30 mins</td><td>Race the Clock</td></tr>
<tr><td>1631–17:00</td><td>29 mins</td><td>Pop News</td></tr>
<tr><td>17:01–17:13</td><td>12 mins</td><td>Looking after Dogs</td></tr>
<tr><td>17:14–17:59</td><td>45 mins</td><td>Cycling</td></tr>
</table>

<table>
<tr><th colspan="3">Tuesday</th></tr>
<tr><th>Start and end time</th><th>Length</th><th>Programme</th></tr>
<tr><td>16:00–17:15</td><td>75 mins</td><td>Football Highlights</td></tr>
<tr><td>17:16–17:20</td><td>4 mins</td><td>Painting Contest</td></tr>
<tr><td>17:21–17:30</td><td>9 mins</td><td>World News</td></tr>
<tr><td>17:31–17:59</td><td>28 mins</td><td>Snakes!</td></tr>
</table>

<table>
<tr><th colspan="3">Wednesday</th></tr>
<tr><th>Start and end time</th><th>Length</th><th>Programme</th></tr>
<tr><td>16:00–16:10</td><td>10 mins</td><td>Local News</td></tr>
<tr><td>16:11–16:59</td><td>48 mins</td><td>Ladies' Triathlon</td></tr>
<tr><td>17:00–17:30</td><td>30 mins</td><td>Can You Spell?</td></tr>
<tr><td>17:31–17:59</td><td>28 mins</td><td>Our Clever Pets</td></tr>
</table>

<table>
<tr><th colspan="3">Thursday</th></tr>
<tr><th>Start and end time</th><th>Length</th><th>Programme</th></tr>
<tr><td>16:00–16:45</td><td>45 mins</td><td>Swimming for Gold</td></tr>
<tr><td>16:46–17:15</td><td>29 mins</td><td>Film News</td></tr>
<tr><td>17:16–17:45</td><td>29 mins</td><td>African Safari</td></tr>
<tr><td>17:46–17:59</td><td>13 mins</td><td>The Music Quiz</td></tr>
</table>

<table>
<tr><th colspan="3">Friday</th></tr>
<tr><th>Start and end time</th><th>Length</th><th>Programme</th></tr>
<tr><td>16:00–16:45</td><td>45 mins</td><td>Hockey Tips</td></tr>
<tr><td>16:46–17:39</td><td>53 mins</td><td>Amazing Animals</td></tr>
<tr><td>17:40–17:49</td><td>9 mins</td><td>News Round-up</td></tr>
<tr><td>17:50–17:59</td><td>9 mins</td><td>Guess the Celebrity</td></tr>
</table>

Extra

Animal programmes total 150 mins
News programmes total 86 mins
Competitions total 86 mins
Sports programmes total 258 mins

Answers will vary, but children may consider there is too much time allocated for either Sports or Animal programmes. They may then choose to allocate the extra time to redress any imbalance.

D2

D2.1

1. and 2.

Number	Factors	Sum of factors
1	1	0
2	1, 2	1
3	1, 3	1
4	1, 2, 4	3
5	1, 5	1
6	1, 2, 3, 6	6 perfect
7	1, 7	1
8	1, 2, 4, 8	7
9	1, 3, 9	4
10	1, 2, 5, 10	8
11	1, 11	1
12	1, 2, 3, 4, 6, 12	16
13	1, 13	1
14	1, 2, 7, 14	10
15	1, 3, 5, 15	9
16	1, 2, 4, 8, 16	15
17	1, 17	1
18	1, 2, 3, 6, 9, 18	21
19	1, 19	1
20	1, 2, 4, 5, 10, 20	22
21	1, 3, 7, 21	11
22	1, 2, 11, 22	14
23	1, 23	1
24	1, 2, 3, 4, 6, 8, 12, 24	36
25	1, 5, 25	6
26	1, 2, 13, 26	16
27	1, 3, 9, 27	13
28	1, 2, 4, 7, 14, 28	28 perfect

D2.2

1. They both add to 17.
2. Each number is on a diagonal line.
3. Answers will vary e.g. 6 + 11 and 7 + 10.
4. Diagonal pairs sum to 59, all four total 118.
5. Answers will vary e.g. 16 + 43 and 19 + 40
6. The patterns are exactly the same on any number grid.
7. 31
8. Total of diagonal pairs is 32, sum of all four numbers is 64.

9.

	3	5	
9	11	13	15
17	19	21	23
	27	29	

Extra

Answers will vary.

D2.4

1. It is not possible to have 4 chocolates each. 8 cannot be made by adding 2 consecutive numbers.

2.

Numbers	Total	Shares between 2
1–5	15	
1–6	21	
1–7	28	Y
1–8	36	Y
1–9	45	
1–10	55	
1–11	66	Y
1–12	78	Y
1–13	91	
1–14	105	
1–15	120	Y
1–16	136	Y
1–17	153	
1–18	171	
1–19	190	Y
1–20	210	Y

Extra

Numbers	Total	Shares between 3
1–5	15	Y
1–6	21	Y
1–7	28	
1–8	36	Y
1–9	45	Y
1–10	55	
1–11	66	Y
1–12	78	Y
1–13	91	
1–14	105	Y
1–15	120	Y
1–16	136	
1–17	153	Y
1–18	171	Y
1–19	190	
1–20	210	Y

D2.5

1. b
2. c
3. c
4. a
5. b
6. b

Extra

a $80 \times 1000 \div 400 = 200$ mm
b $80 \times 1000 \div 500 = 160$ mm
c $80 \times 1000 \div 300 = 267$ mm
a $6 \times 400 = 2400$ mm = 2.4 m
b $6 \times 500 = 3000$ mm = 3 m
c $6 \times 300 = 1800$ mm = 1.8 m

D2.6

1. Largest amount: £5·15 + £3·00 + £1·05 + £0·92 + £60 = £70·12
2. Smallest amount: £5·15 + £3·00 − £4·40 + £1·01 − 174p = £3·02

Extra

There are 32 ways across the swamp in exactly 6 steps.

E2

E2.2

1. 40 days = 960 hours. 40 days is longer by 60 hours.
2. 84 days = 2016 hours. 84 days is longer by 16 hours.
3. 100 days = 2400 hours. 2500 hours is longer by 100 hours.
4. 123 days = 2952 hours. 3000 hours is longer by 48 hours.
5. 154 weeks = 1078 days. 1078 days is longer by 78 days.
6. 262 weeks = 1834 days. 2000 days is longer by 166 days.
7. 678 weeks = 4746 days. 5000 days is longer by 254 days.
8. 24 hours = 1440 minutes. 1500 minutes is longer by 60 minutes.
9. 86 hours = 5160 minutes. 5160 minutes is longer by 160 minutes.
10. 7 days = 10 080 minutes. 10 080 minutes is longer by 80 minutes.

E2.3

1. 92·8
2. 348·8
3. 16·08
4. 46·02
5. 164
6. 496·3
7. 27·63
8. 391·8
9. £44·45
10. £48·30
11. £15·84
12. £16·11

Extra

Largest 76·3 × 9 = 686·7
Smallest 67·9 × 3 = 203·7
Largest 73·1 × 9 = 657·9
Smallest 37·9 × 1 = 37·9

E2.4

1. Many possible answers including $\frac{1}{2}$ of 48; $\frac{1}{10}$ of 240
2. Many possible answers including $\frac{1}{2}$ of 40; $\frac{1}{3}$ of 60

E2.5

1. $\frac{3}{4}$ = 750m which is longer than $\frac{7}{10}$ = 700 m
2. $\frac{5}{8}$ = 625 m which is longer than $\frac{3}{5}$ = 600 m
3. $\frac{7}{20}$ = 350 m which is shorter than $\frac{9}{25}$ = 360 m
4. $\frac{33}{40}$ = 825 m which is shorter than $\frac{7}{8}$ = 875 m
5. $\frac{13}{50}$ = 260 m which is longer than $\frac{1}{4}$ = 250 m
6. 4 minutes
7. 1·5 minutes (1 minute 30 seconds)
8. 3·2 minutes (3 minutes 12 seconds)
9. 45 minutes
10. 75 minutes (1 hour 15 minutes)

11. 67·5 minutes (67 minutes 30 seconds or 1 hour 7 minutes 30 seconds)
    Achilles will win the race, because he can overtake the tortoise, even though the paradox seems to show that he cannot.

Extra

$\frac{4}{5}$ of 1600 m = 1280 m.
It will take 6·4 minutes (6 minutes 24 seconds)
$\frac{3}{10}$ of 1600 m = 480 m.
It will take 2·4 minutes (2 minutes 24 seconds)
$\frac{16}{25}$ of 1600 m = 1024 m.
It will take 5·12 minutes (5 minutes 7.2 seconds)
$\frac{9}{20}$ of 1600 m = 720 m.
It will take 72 minutes (1 hour 12 minutes)
$\frac{3}{4}$ of 1600 m = 1200 m.
It will take 120 minutes (2 hours)
$\frac{27}{40}$ of 1600 m = 1080 m.
It will take 108 minutes (1 hour 48 minutes)

E2.6

1. 2 + 75 = 77 or 17 − 10 = 7; yes
2. 4 + 76 = 80 or 27 − 12 = 15; no
3. 6 + 22 = 28 or 32 − 4 = 28; yes
4. 18 + 87 = 105 or 98 − 14 = 84; yes
5. 8 + 55 = 63 or 45 − 10 = 35; yes
6. 10 + 31 = 41 or 53 − 2 = 51; no
7. 6 + 68 = 74 or 36 − 16 = 20; no
8. 16 + 15 = 31 or 81 − 10 = 71; no
9. 18 + 06 = 24 or 90 − 12 = 78; no
10. 12 + 44 = 56 or 64 − 8 = 56; yes
11. Answers will vary.

Extra

Answers will vary but will all be multiples of 21 because they are multiples of both 3 and 7.

A3

A3.1

1. Vostok; Plateau Station; Snag; Verkhoyansk; Fort Selkirk; Eismitte; Oymyakon; Prospect Creek; Northice; Rogers Pass
2. Madras and Tirunelveli; Omdurman and Khartoum; Niamey and Madurai; Aden; Tiruchirapalli; Ouagadougou and Timbuktu
3. Answers will vary.

Extra

To convert from Fahrenheit to Celsius: Subtract 32 from the Fahrenheit temperature then divide the answer by 9 and multiply by 5.

A3.2

1. Answers will vary but may include:

Number	Calculation	Number	Calculation	Number	Calculation
⁻10	5 − 5 − 5 − 5 =	1	5 + 5 − 9 =	11	9 + 9 + 9 + 9 − 5 − 5 − 5 − 5 − 5 =
⁻9	5 − 5 − 9 =	2	9 + 9 + 9 − 5 − 5 − 5 − 5 − 5 =	12	9 + 9 + 9 − 5 − 5 − 5 =
⁻8	5 + 5 − 9 − 9 =	3	9 + 9 − 5 − 5 − 5 =	13	9 + 9 − 5 =
⁻7	5 + 5 + 5 + 5 − 9 − 9 − 9 =	4	9 − 5 =	14	9 + 5 =
⁻6	5 + 5 + 5 + 5 + 5 + 5 − 9 − 9 − 9 − 9 =	5	5 + 9 − 9 =	15	5 + 5 + 5 =
⁻5	9 − 9 − 5 =	6	9 + 9 + 9 + 9 − 5 − 5 − 5 − 5 − 5 − 5 =	16	9 + 9 + 9 + 9 − 5 − 5 − 5 − 5 =
⁻4	5 − 9 =	7	9 + 9 + 9 − 5 − 5 − 5 − 5 =	17	9 + 9 + 9 − 5 − 5 =
⁻3	5 + 5 + 5 − 9 − 9 =	8	9 + 9 − 5 − 5 =	18	9 + 9 =
⁻2	5 + 5 + 5 + 5 + 5 − 9 − 9 − 9 =	9	9 + 5 − 5 =	19	5 + 5 + 9 =
⁻1	9 − 5 − 5 =	10	5 + 5 =	20	5 + 5 + 5 + 5 =

2. Answers will vary but may include:

Number	Calculation
60	7 × 3 × 3 − 3 =
59	7 × 3 + 7 × 3 + 7 + 7 + 3 =
63	7 × 3 × 3 =
80	7 × 3 × 3 + 7 + 7 + 3
1480	3 × 3 × 3 × 7 × 7 + 3 × 7 × 7 + 3 + 7 =

Extra

Answers will vary but may include:
9 × 9 + 5 × 4 = 101
5 × 6 × 7 = 210
200 × 26 − 39 = 5161

A3.3

1.
PCM 26

Race	Name	Boy or Girl	Age	Fastest time	Did they qualify? How much by?
Freestyle	Jesse	B	9	34·92	Qualified by 4·08 seconds
Freestyle	Emeka	B	9	39·59	Did not qualify
Freestyle	Krishna	G	9	36·99	Qualified by 2·01 seconds
Freestyle	Sally	G	10	36·09	Did not qualify
Freestyle	Molly	G	11	33·12	Did not qualify
Freestyle	Cameron	B	12	32·07	Did not qualify
Freestyle	Jasveer	B	10	35·41	Qualified by 0·09 seconds
Freestyle	Becky	G	12	31·89	Qualified by 0·11 seconds
Backstroke	Max	B	10	42·99	Did not qualify
Backstroke	Conor	B	11	39·30	Qualified by 0·20 seconds
Backstroke	Ellie	G	9	44·94	Qualified by 0·06 seconds
Backstroke	Neela	G	9	45·05	Did not qualify
Backstroke	Sasha	G	12	37·69	Qualified by 0·31 seconds
Backstroke	Tyler	B	9	44·96	Qualified by 0·04 seconds
Backstroke	Guang	B	12	37·99	Qualified by 0·01 seconds
	Amy	G	11	35·86	Qualified by 4·14 seconds

2. Any time between 24·88 and 25·88 seconds inclusive.
3. 1.02 seconds
4. Kadi 23·97 s; Zahra 24·99 s
5. 23·98 seconds
6.

Name	Time	Time to the nearest tenth of a second	Finishing position
HOY Chris (GB)	10·636	10·6	3rd
SIREAU Kevin (FR)	10·570	10·6	2nd
KENNY Jason (GB)	10·531	10·5	1st
AWANG Mohd Azizulhasni (MA)	11·010	11·0	8th
MULDER Teun (NE)	10·888	10·9	7th
BOS Theo (NE)	10·777	10·8	6th
BOURGAIN Mickael (FR)	10·734	10·7	4th
LEVY Maximilian (DE)	10·763	10·8	5th

Extra

Chris Hoy (GB) won the Cycling Men's Sprint finals. His time in Race 1 was 10·228 s. His time in Race 2 was 10·216 s. He was 0·012 s faster in Race 2.

A3.4

1. 288p = £2.88
2. 504p = £5.04
3. 567p = £5.67
4. 1008p = £10.08
5. 1260p = £12.60

Extra

Answers will vary.

A3.5

PCM 27

$1·2 \times 8 = 9.6$	$66 \times 0·5 = 33$	$41 \times 0·7 = 28·7$
$2·5 \times 3 = 7.5$	$22 \times 0·5 = 11$	$1·4 \times 5 = 7$
$41 \times 0·4 = 16.4$	$80 \times 0·6 = 48$	$2·5 \times 8 = 20$
$6 \times 0·9 = 5.4$	$1·2 \times 80 = 96$	$55 \times 1·4 = 77$
$30 \times 0·8 = 24$	$6·1 \times 6 = 36·6$	$6·5 \times 4 = 26$
$24 \times 0·7 = 16·8$	$70 \times 0·8 = 56$	$1·5 \times 4 = 6$

PCM 28

$2·2 \times 5 = 11$	$12 \times 0·8 = 9·6$	$4·1 \times 7 = 28·7$
$4·1 \times 4 = 16·4$	$25 \times 0·3 = 7·5$	$52 \times 0·5 = 26$
$9 \times 0·6 = 5·4$	$12 \times 8 = 96$	$25 \times 0·8 = 20$
$80 \times 0·3 = 24$	$61 \times 0·6 = 36·6$	$5·5 \times 14 = 77$
$84 \times 0·2 = 16·8$	$40 \times 1·2 = 48$	$14 \times 0·5 = 7$
$5·6 \times 10 = 56$	$6·6 \times 5 = 33$	$5 \times 1·2 = 6$

A3.6

	Total cost of transport	Total cost tents	Cost per person per night	Total cost for meals	Total campsite cost
Sunny Vale Camp Site	1 × 40-seat and 2 × 45-seat £1900	Children: 20 × 6-man and 2 × 4-man Teachers 2 × 4-man £912	£1638	£3120	£5670
Happy Days Camp Site	3 × 50-seat £2100	Children 14 × 8-man and 6 ×2-man Teachers 3 × 2-man £780	£1690	£ 3380	£5850
Wonder Hills Camp Site	4 × 35-seat £1600	Children 12 × 10-man and 2 × 2-man Teachers 3 × 2-man £1450	£0	£2448	£3898

1. See table
2. See table
3. Wonder Hills is cheapest.
4. (Campsite cost + transport cost) ÷ 124: Sunny Valley £61; Happy Days £64 ; Wonder Hills £44 (to the nearest £)
5. Children's conclusions should consider the activities available as well as the cost.

B3

B3.I

1. Answers will vary, e.g. 5209 + 7201 = 12 410
2. Answers will vary, e.g. 7810 + 6291 = 14 101
3. Answers will vary, e.g. 8007 + 4039 = 12 046
4. Answers will vary, e.g. 8007 + 6291 = 14 298
5. Answers will vary, e.g. 4039 + 1073 = 5112
6. Answers will vary, e.g. 5209 + 1073 = 6282
7. Answers will vary, e.g. 6291 + 5209 = 11 500
8. Answers will vary, e.g. 5411 + 5209 + 5623 = 16 243
9. Answers will vary, e.g. 2288 + 2198 + 1073 = 5559

B3.3

1. 1·56 + 1·452 = 3·012 kg
2. 0·753 + 1·7 = 2·453 kg
3. 1·1 + 1·027 = 2·127 kg
4. 2·043 + 1·7 = 3·743 kg
5. 0·786 + 0·753 = 1·539 kg
   1·56 + 0·786 + 0·753 = 3·099 kg
   43 + 1·7 + 1·1 = 4·843 kg
   1·452 + 1·027 = 3·265 kg

B3.5

1. 36 288
2. 17 983
3. 4793
4. 4387
5. 6426
6. 8796
7.

Old Trafford	74 600
Emirates Stadium	58 932
St James' Park	50 887
Stadium of Light	47 500
City of Manchester	46 500
Anfield	43 862
Villa Park	41 140
Stamford Bridge	40 949
Goodison Park	39 069
Elland Road	38 704
Hillsborough	38 312
White Hart Lane	34 714

B3.6

1. $12·3 - 8·56 = 3·74$ m
2. $13·2 - 6·89 = 6·31$ m
3. $11·06 - 6·89 = 1·8$ m
4. $10·26 - 7·09 = 3·17$ m
5. $11·06 - 6·89 = 4·17$ m
6. $10·26 - 9·26 = 1·0$ m
7. $12·3 - 7·09 = 5·21$ m
8. $13·2 - 8·56 = 4·64$ m

Extra

Gabby 13·2 m
Anwen 12·3 m
Dominic 11·06 m
Faisal 10·26 m
Barney 9·26 m
Esha 8·56 m
Chandra 7·09 m
Hassan 6·89 m
The smallest difference is between Chandra and Hassan
(0·2 m = 20 cm)

C3

C3.1

1. Answers will vary.
2. Children should display <u>their</u> answers to question 1 on a correctly drawn and labelled bar graph.
3. Answers will vary according to children's experimental results. Theoretically the marker for probability of HHT, HTH or THH is correct ($\frac{3}{8}$) and the marker for probability of HHH or TTT is incorrect, it should be $\frac{1}{4}$.
4. Answers will vary.
5. Children should display <u>their</u> answers to question 4 on a correctly drawn and labelled bar graph.
6. Answers will vary according to children's experimental results but the marker for probability of a total of 1 is

correct. Theoretically the markers for probability of a prime number and 2 or more are incorrect. They should be just below evens ($\frac{15}{36}$) and certain, respectively.
7. Answers will vary.
8. Children should display <u>their</u> answers to question 7 on a correctly drawn and labelled bar graph.
9. Answers will vary according to children's experimental results. Theoretically the marker for "I will get a green counter" should be below evens (at $\frac{4}{10}$) and the marker for "I will not get a green counter" should be at $\frac{6}{10}$.

Extra

Answers will vary.

C3.2

Friday 14th November	Partly cloudy with a slight chance of rain.
Saturday 15th November	Partly cloudy with an even chance of rain.
Sunday 16th November	Mostly clear with a slight chance of rain.
Monday 17th November	Clear with rain unlikely.
Tuesday 18th November	Partly cloudy with a slight chance of rain.
Wednesday 19th November	Cloudy with rain certain.
Thursday 20th November	Cloudy with rain likely.

C3.3

1. Jasmine's is cheaper.
2. Both schemes cost the same amount at 150 texts (£7·50) and 300 texts (£15).
3. For 200 texts: Jasmine's scheme £10; Dominic's scheme £8·75.
4. For 300 texts both schemes charge the same amount (£15).
5. 400 texts cost Dominic £25
6. If Saj only wants to spend £10 a month Dominic's deal is better for him.
7. Saj would not save money if he only sent 300 texts a month as the offer is only for over 350 texts.
8. Dominic's deal
9. Jasmine's deal
10. Answers will vary.

C3.4

1.

Airline	
Flyair	No-one
Dashjet	Syed
Gobye	Jake
BIA	Farah
British Jets	Millie

2.

	Shampoo	Deodorant	Toothpaste	Cologne	Sun-cream	Water	Total liquid
Syed	33 cl – too much	10 ml	200 ml – too much	150 ml – too much	$\frac{1}{5}$ l – too much	$\frac{1}{2}$ l – too much	1390 ml
Millie	200 ml – too much	20 ml	150 ml – too much	$\frac{1}{10}$ l	100 ml	200 ml – too much	770 ml
Jake	$\frac{1}{5}$ l – too much	5 cl	10 cl	200 ml – too much	50 ml	100 ml	610 ml
Farah	150 ml – too much	15 ml	$\frac{1}{3}$ l – too much	0·75 l – too much	0·2 l – too much	$\frac{1}{4}$ l – too much	1698 ml

3. Answers will vary.

C3.5

PCM 36

1. As objects to 13 kg can be weighed, the other weight must be 9 kg.
2. Put 1 kg and 3 kg weights in one pan and 4 kg object in the other.
3.

Weight of object	Left balance pan	Right balance pan
1 kg	Object	1 kg
2 kg	Object + 1 kg	3 kg
3 kg	Object	3 kg
4 kg	Object	3 kg + 1 kg
5 kg	Object + 3 kg + 1 kg	9 kg
6 kg	Object + 3 kg	9 kg
7 kg	Object + 3 kg	9 kg + 1 kg
8 kg	Object + 1 kg	9 kg
9 kg	Object	9 kg
10 kg	Object	9 kg + 1 kg
11 kg	Object + 1 kg	9 kg + 3 kg
12 kg	Object	9 kg + 3 kg
13 kg	Object	9 kg + 3 kg + 1 kg

C3.6

Angles in a regular pentagon are 108°.
Angles in an equilateral triangle are all 60°.

Extra

Children may find radians and gradians as alternative units for measuring angles.
⋯ation of radians is too complicated for Year 5 but they could find out that 1 radian ≈ 57.3°.
⋯ also find the gradian (as on scientific calculator) which divides one revolution into 400 units.

D3.1

PCM 38

Area	Wind direction	Changes	Movement in degrees
Viking	South-west	None	None
North Utsire	South-west	None	None
South Utsire	West	Backing south-east	Anticlockwise 135°
Forties Cromarty Forth	West	Veering north-west	Clockwise 45°
Tyne	West	None	None
Dogger Fisher German Bight	North-west	Backing south-west	Anticlockwise 90°
Humber Thames Dover Wight Portland Plymouth	West	Veering north	Clockwise 90°
Biscay FitzRoy	North-west	None	None
Sole Lundy Fastnet Irish Sea Shannon Rockall	North	Backing west	Anticlockwise 90°
Malin	North-west	Backing south	Anticlockwise 135°
Hebrides	North-west	Backing south-east	Anticlockwise 180°
Bailey	North-west	None	None
Fair Isle Faeroes	North-west	Veering north	Clockwise 45°
Southeast Iceland	North-west	Backing north-east	Anticlockwise 270°

D3.2

B

Type of angle	Number of angles	Size of angle	Total of angles
Acute	4	60°	240°
Obtuse	2	120°	240°
Reflex	2	240°	480°
Reflex	1	300°	300°
		Total of interior angles	1260°

C

Type of angle	Number of angles	Size of angle	Total of angles
Acute	2	60°	120°
Obtuse	5	120°	600°
Reflex	3	240°	720°
		Total of interior angles	1440°

D

Type of angle	Number of angles	Size of angle	Total of angles
Acute	5	60°	300°
Obtuse	4	120°	480°
Reflex	4	300°	1200°
		Total of interior angles	1980°

E

Type of angle	Number of angles	Size of angle	Total of angles
Acute	3	60°	180°
Obtuse	4	120°	480°
Reflex	2	300°	600°
		Total of interior angles	1260°

F

Type of angle	Number of angles	Size of angle	Total of angles
Acute	8	60°	480°
Obtuse	2	120°	240°
Reflex	8	240°	1920°
Reflex	2	300°	600°
		Total of interior angles	3240°

G

Type of angle	Number of angles	Size of angle	Total of angles
Acute	7	60°	420°
Obtuse	4	120°	480°
Reflex	4	240°	960°
Reflex	4	300°	1200°
		Total of interior angles	3060°

Extra

Answers will vary.

D3.3

1. P three sides and three angles equal
   Q one right angle, no equal sides or angles
   R no equal sides or angles, one obtuse angle
   S no equal sides or angles
   T one right angle, two sides and two angles equal
   U one obtuse angle, two sides and two angles equal
2. P equilateral triangle
   Q right-angled scalene triangle
   R obtuse-angled scalene triangle
   S acute-angled scalene triangle
   T right-angled isosceles triangle
   U obtuse isosceles triangle
3. Answers will vary, but should include an acute-angled
   ...les triangle.

   ...angled triangles can be out together to make

D3.4

1. 23 cakes: 23 ÷ 3 = 7 r2; 23 ÷ 4 = 5 r3
2. 508 eggs: 508 ÷ 6 = 84 r4; 508 ÷ 10 = 50 r8
   Or 538 eggs: 538 ÷ 6 = 89 r4; 538 ÷ 10 = 53 r8
3. 13 windows: 13 ÷ 2 = 6 r1; 13 ÷ 3 = 4 r1; 13 ÷ 4 = 3 r1
4. 61 flowers: 61 ÷ 5 = 12 r1; 61 ÷ 4 = 15 r1;
   61 ÷ 6 = 10 r1

Extra

71 biscuits: 71 ÷ 2 = 35 r1; 71 ÷ 5 = 14 r1; 71 ÷ 7 = 10 r1

D3.5

PCM 40

1.

×	28	**11**	30	4	23	15	**7**	26
19	**532**	209	570	76	437	285	133	494
0·2	5·6	2·2	6	0·8	4·6	3	1·4	5·2
1·2	33·6	**13·2**	36	4·8	27·6	18	**8·4**	31·2
22	616	242	660	**88**	506	**330**	154	572
14	**392**	154	420	56	**322**	210	98	364
0·6	16·8	6·6	**18**	2·4	13·8	9	4·2	15·6
25	700	275	**750**	100	575	375	175	**650**
17	476	187	510	**68**	391	255	119	442

2.

1	2	3	4	5	6	7	8
2	4	6	8	1	3	5	7
3	6	9	3	6	9	3	6
4	8	3	7	2	6	1	5
5	1	6	2	7	3	8	4
6	3	9	6	3	9	6	3
7	5	3	1	8	6	4	2
8	7	6	5	4	3	2	1

3.

4.

PCM 41

1.

2.

3.

D3

4.

1	2	3	4	5	6	7	8
2	4	6	8	1	3	5	7
3	6	9	3	6	9	3	6
4	8	3	7	2	6	1	5
5	1	6	2	7	3	8	4
6	3	9	6	3	9	6	3
7	5	3	1	8	6	4	2
8	7	6	5	4	3	2	1

5.

1	2	3	4	5	6	7	8
2	4	6	8	1	3	5	7
3	6	9	3	6	9	3	6
4	8	3	7	2	6	1	5
5	1	6	2	7	3	8	4
6	3	9	6	3	9	6	3
7	5	3	1	8	6	4	2
8	7	6	5	4	3	2	1

6.

1	2	3	4	5	6	7	8
2	4	6	8	1	3	5	7
3	6	9	3	6	9	3	6
4	8	3	7	2	6	1	5
5	1	6	2	7	3	8	4
6	3	9	6	3	9	6	3
7	5	3	1	8	6	4	2
8	7	6	5	4	3	2	1

D3.6

PCM 42

1. and 2.

$26 \cdot 23 \div 5 = 5 \cdot 246$	$18 \cdot 4 \div 4 = 4 \cdot 6$	$53 \cdot 2 \div 50 = 1.064$	$23 \cdot 41 \div 0.5 = 46 \cdot 82$	$13 \cdot 6 \div 20 = 0.68$
$52 \cdot 46 \div 10 = 5 \cdot 246$	$9 \cdot 2 \div 2 = 4 \cdot 6$	$106 \cdot 4 \div 100 = 1 \cdot 064$	$46 \cdot 82 \div 1 = 46 \cdot 82$	$6 \cdot 8 \div 10 = 0 \cdot 68$
$2 \cdot 623 \div 0.5 = 5 \cdot 246$	$184 \div 40 = 4 \cdot 6$	$532 \div 500 = 1 \cdot 064$	$234 \cdot 1 \div 5 = 46 \cdot 82$	$1 \cdot 36 \div 2 = 0 \cdot 68$
$5 \cdot 246 \div 1 = 5 \cdot 246$	$4 \cdot 6 \div 1 = 4 \cdot 6$	$1064 \div 1000 = 1 \cdot 064$	$468 \cdot 2 \div 10 = 46 \cdot 82$	$0 \cdot 68 \div 1 = 0 \cdot 68$
$1928 \div 500 = 3 \cdot 856$	$67 \div 0.2 = 335$	$45 \cdot 9 \div 30 = 1 \cdot 53$	$146 \div 2 \cdot 5 = 58 \cdot 4$	$72 \cdot 12 \div 60 = 1 \cdot 202$
$3856 \div 1000 = 3 \cdot 856$	$33 \cdot 5 \div 0 \cdot 1 = 335$	$15 \cdot 3 \div 10 = 1 \cdot 53$	$584 \div 10 = 58 \cdot 4$	$12 \cdot 02 \div 10 = 1 \cdot 202$
$3 \cdot 856 \div 1 = 3 \cdot 856$	$670 \div 2 = 335$	$459 \div 300 = 1 \cdot 53$	$58 \cdot 4 \div 1 = 58 \cdot 4$	$1 \cdot 202 \div 1 = 1 \cdot 202$
$192 \cdot 8 \div 50 = 3 \cdot 856$	$335 \div 1 = 335$	$153 \div 100 = 1 \cdot 53$	$29 \cdot 2 \div 0.5 = 58 \cdot 4$	$7 \cdot 212 \div 6 = 1 \cdot 202$

3. and 4. Answers will vary.

E3

E3.1

1. $0 \cdot 167$
2. $0 \cdot 667$
3. $0 \cdot 429$
4. $0 \cdot 625$
5. $0 \cdot 222$
6. $0 \cdot 833$
7. $0 \cdot 571$
8. $0 \cdot 556$
9. $\frac{4}{9} = 0 \cdot 444$ and $\frac{3}{7} = 0 \cdot 429$; $\frac{4}{9}$ is larger
10. $\frac{2}{5} = 0 \cdot 4$ and $\frac{3}{8} = 0 \cdot 375$ so $\frac{2}{5}$ is larger
11. $\frac{7}{8} = 0 \cdot 875$ and $\frac{9}{11} = 0 \cdot 818$ so $\frac{7}{8}$ is larger
12. $\frac{7}{12} = 0 \cdot 583$ and $\frac{6}{11} = 0 \cdot 545$ so $\frac{7}{12}$ is larger
13. $\frac{15}{17} = 0 \cdot 882$ and $\frac{6}{7} = 0 \cdot 857$ so $\frac{15}{17}$ is larger
14. $\frac{8}{9} = 0 \cdot 889$ and $\frac{18}{19} = 0 \cdot 947$ so $\frac{18}{19}$ is larger
15. $\frac{2}{3} = 0 \cdot 667$, $\frac{5}{8} = 0 \cdot 625$, $\frac{4}{7} = 0 \cdot 571$ so $\frac{4}{7}, \frac{5}{8}, \frac{2}{3}$
16. $\frac{2}{9} = 0 \cdot 222$, $\frac{3}{13} = 0 \cdot 231$, $\frac{1}{6} = 0 \cdot 167$ so $\frac{1}{6}, \frac{2}{9}, \frac{3}{13}$
17. $\frac{14}{17} = 0 \cdot 824$, $\frac{9}{11} = 0 \cdot 818$, $\frac{11}{13} = 0 \cdot 846$ so $\frac{9}{11}, \frac{14}{17}, \frac{11}{13}$
18. $\frac{5}{11} = 0 \cdot 455$, $\frac{3}{7} = 0 \cdot 429$, $\frac{4}{9} = 0 \cdot 444$ so $\frac{3}{7}, \frac{4}{9}, \frac{5}{11}$

Extra

$\frac{1}{9}$	$0 \cdot 111$
$\frac{1}{7}$	$0 \cdot 143$
$\frac{2}{9}$	$0 \cdot 222$
$\frac{2}{7}$	$0 \cdot 286$
$\frac{3}{9}$	$0 \cdot 333$
$\frac{3}{7}$	$0 \cdot 429$
$\frac{4}{9}$	$0 \cdot 444$
$\frac{5}{9}$	$0 \cdot 556$
$\frac{4}{7}$	$0 \cdot 571$
$\frac{6}{9}$	$0 \cdot 667$
$\frac{5}{7}$	$0 \cdot 714$
$\frac{7}{9}$	$0 \cdot 778$
$\frac{6}{7}$	$0 \cdot 857$
$\frac{8}{9}$	$0 \cdot 889$

E3.2

1. 84 ml
2. 30 ml
3. 180 ml
4. 13·5 g
5. 36 g
6. 63 g
7. 70 ml
8. 262·5 ml
9. 420 ml
10. 568 ml
11. 213 ml
12. 994 ml

E3.3

1. a $\frac{1}{2}$ b $\frac{2}{3}$ c $\frac{1}{4}$ d $\frac{3}{5}$ e $\frac{5}{9}$ f $\frac{3}{4}$
2. a $\frac{1}{2}$ b $\frac{1}{3}$ c $\frac{3}{4}$ d $\frac{2}{5}$ e $\frac{4}{9}$ f $\frac{1}{4}$
3. a 1:1 b 2:1 c 1:3 d 3:2 e 5:4 f 3:1
4. a 12, 12 b 16, 8 c 6, 18
   d 12, 8 e 10, 8 f 12, 4
5. a $\frac{1}{2}$ b $\frac{1}{3}$ c $\frac{3}{4}$ d $\frac{2}{5}$ e $\frac{4}{9}$ f $\frac{1}{4}$
6. a 1:1 b 2:1 c 1:3 d 3:2 e 5:4 f 3:1
7. 15 shaded, 25 unshaded
8. 35 shaded, 15 unshaded
9. 16 shaded, 24 unshaded
10. 32 shaded, 8 unshaded
11. 16 shaded, 24 unshaded
12. 32 shaded, 8 unshaded

E3.4

1.

Number	1	2	3	4	5	6	7	8	9	10
Square	1	4	9	16	25	36	49	64	81	100

2. 25 and 36
3. 81 and 100
4. 49 and 64
5. The difference is increasing by 2 each time.
6.

Number	10	11	12	13	14	15	16	17	18	19	20
Square	100	121	144	169	196	225	256	289	324	361	400

21 23 25 27 29 31 33 35 37 39

7. 121 and 144
8. 324 and 361
9. 196 and 225
10. Yes. The difference is still increasing by 2 each time.

Extra

Square numbers	$1^2 + 2^2$	$2^2 + 3^2$	$3^2 + 4^2$	$4^2 + 5^2$	$5^2 + 6^2$	$6^2 + 7^2$	$7^2 + 8^2$	$8^2 + 9^2$	$9^2 + 10^2$
Sum	5	13	25	41	61	85	113	145	181

The sum sequence increases by 8, 12, 16, 20, … (multiples of 4).

E3.6

1. 25 has 3 factors and 50 has 6
2. 20 has 6 factors and 40 has 8
3. 12 has 6 factors and 24 has 8
4. Melanie is wrong.
5. 2 is a prime number because it has only two factors – 1 and 2; all other even numbers have at least three factors – 1, 2 and the number itself.
6. 1 has only one factor and prime numbers have only two factors.
7. 27 is divisble by 3, 57 is divisible by 3, 77 is divisible by 7 and 87 is divisible by 3
8. Bernie is wrong.
9. Prime numbers from 1 to 100 are: 2, 3, 5, 7, 11, 13, 17, 19, 23, 29, 31, 37, 41, 43, 47, 53, 59, 61, 67, 71, 73, 79, 83, 89, 97.

Extra

The double of any prime number has four factors; 1, 2, the number, 2 × the number.

PCM 46

1	2	3	4	5	6	7	8	9	10
11	12	13	14	15	16	17	18	19	20
21	22	23	24	25	26	27	28	29	30
31	32	33	34	35	36	37	38	39	40
41	42	43	44	45	46	47	48	49	50
51	52	53	54	55	56	57	58	59	60
61	62	63	64	65	66	67	68	69	70
71	72	73	74	75	76	77	78	79	80
81	82	83	84	85	86	87	88	89	90
91	92	93	94	95	96	97	98	99	100

Part of Pearson

Ginn is an imprint of Pearson Education Limited, a company incorporated in England and Wales, having its registered office at Edinburgh Gate, Harlow, Essex, CM20 2JE. Registered company number: 872828

www.pearsonschools.co.uk

Ginn is a registered trademark of Pearson Education Limited

Text © Pearson Education Limited 2009

First published 2009

13 12
10 9 8 7 6 5

British Library Cataloguing in Publication Data
A catalogue record for this book is available from the British Library

ISBN 978 0 602 57775 9

Typeset by Tech-Set Ltd, Gateshead
Cover photo/illustration © Per José Karlén
Printed in Britain by Ashford Colour Press

Acknowledgements
Every effort has been made to contact copyright holders of material reproduced in this book. Any omissions will be rectified in subsequent printings if notice is given to the publishers.

Authors

Jon Kurta is currently Primary Strategy Manager in Camden. He has previously worked as a primary teacher and maths subject leader, a numeracy consultant and a lecturer in Initial Teacher Education.

Carol Richardson is a freelance consultant in primary mathematics. She has worked as a class teacher and subject leader across Key Stages 1 to 4. She has also been a Numeracy Consultant in Somerset, where her role included working with the Gifted and Talented Adviser to support teachers in this area.